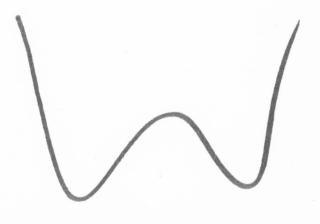

THE FIGHTING
PANKHURSTS

DAVID MITCHELL

THE FIGHTING PANKHURSTS

A Study in Tenacity

JONATHAN CAPE

THIRTY BEDFORD SQUARE LONDON

First Published 1967
© by David Mitchell 1967

PRINTED IN GREAT BRITAIN
BY EBENEZER BAYLIS AND SON, LTD
THE TRINITY PRESS, WORCESTER, AND LONDON
ON PAPER MADE BY JOHN DICKINSON AND CO. LTD
BOUND BY A. W. BAIN AND CO. LTD, LONDON

CONTENTS

CONTENTS

ILLUSTRATIONS

ILLUSTRATIONS

ACKNOWLEDGMENTS

I am particularly indebted to Dr R. K. P. Pankhurst, Director of the Institute of Ethiopian Studies, Addis Ababa, for reading and commenting upon the chapters concerning his mother, to the late Sylvia Pankhurst; Miss Vera Douie, o.b.e., Librarian of the Fawcett Society, London; to Mr Herbert Staples of Toronto for research on Mrs Emmeline Pankhurst's work with the Canadian Social Hygiene Council; to the staff of the *Sun* newspaper's library, and to the editorial director, Mr Sydney Jacobson, for permission to use its extensive cuttings files; to Mr H. W. Treherne and the staff of the *Evening News* cuttings library; to Mr F. W. Torrington and Miss Judith Baskin of the Australia House Reference Library, London; to Mr H. L. White, National Librarian, the Australian National Library, Canberra, for unstinted help and the generous provision of photostats; to Mrs Janet Pearson, Head of the Reference Department of the Public Library, Victoria, B.C., for information about Mrs Pankhurst's visits to Victoria, and for background research on the history of Victoria and on women's suffrage in Canada; to the staff of the Mitchell Library, Sydney; to Mr John T. Parkhill, Head of the Central Library Division, Toronto Public Library, and to Mrs Thelma Jackman, of the Social Sciences Department of Los Angeles Public Library, for photostats, useful contacts and general guidance; to the *Montreal Star*, the *Los Angeles Times* and the *New York Herald Tribune* for research suggestions and the provision of photostats or typed copies of articles relating to Mrs Pankhurst's activities in the U.S.A. and Canada.

I wish to thank the *Sunday Times*, the *Guardian*, the *Woodford Times*, the *Los Angeles Times*, the *Sydney Morning Herald*, the *Montreal Star* and the *Catholic Weekly* (Sydney) for publishing appeals for information which produced much valuable material; Miss Grace Roe for permission to quote from Christabel Pankhurst's correspondence; the *London Express and Feature Service* for permission to quote from Christabel Pankhurst's articles published in the *Weekly Dispatch* in 1921; Commander Venn, r.n. (Retired) for permission to quote from Dame Ethel Smyth's

Female Pipings in Eden; Routledge & Kegan Paul for permission to quote from Sylvia Pankhurst's translation of the poems of Mihail Eminescu; Longmans, Green & Co., for permission to quote from *The Suffragette Movement* by Sylvia Pankhurst; Leonard Woolf Esq. for permission to quote from *A Room of One's Own* by Virginia Woolf; Constable & Co. for permission to quote from *The Strange Death of Liberal England* by George Dangerfield; the Society for Constructive Birth Control Ltd and the Hogarth Press for permission to quote from *Married Love* by Dr Marie Stopes.

My deep appreciation is due to the people listed below for material and/or reminiscences about the Pankhursts:

(i) *Mrs Emmeline Pankhurst:* Mrs Nellie Hall-Humpherson; Commander Venn, R.N. (Retired); Dame Marjorie Maxse, D.B.E.; Miss Dorothy Spencer, C.B.E.; Mr Geoffrey Block of the Conservative Party's Research Department; Lady Katherine Japp; Miss Elsie Bowerman, M.A. (who lent her files of the Women's Guild of Empire *Bulletin*); Mrs Terry Tucker, of Hamilton, Bermuda, for information about Mrs Pankhurst's stay in Bermuda; and to Dr Gordon Bates, General Director of the Health League of Canada.

(ii) *Dame Christabel Pankhurst,* D.B.E.: Henry Devenish Harben, J.P. (for the generous gift of correspondence between him and Dame Christabel); Miss Grace Roe; Dr Gordon Bates; Mr Herbert Van Thal; the late Mrs Teresa Billington-Greig; Mrs Helen Fraser Moyes, of Sydney; the late Miss Theresa Garnett; Miss Jessie Kenney (who gave permission to quote from a letter written by her sister); Mr A. Lindsay Glegg of the Advent Testimony Preparation Movement; Mr Harold Gordon of the Bible Testimony Fellowship; Mrs Gudrun Allen, Los Angeles; Dr and Mrs Rudolf Szekely, Santa Barbara; Mr Douglas Field, Santa Barbara; Miss Jaime Palmer, Los Angeles; Dr Marjorie Greenbie, Washington, D.C.; and others who prefer to be nameless.

(iii) *Sylvia Pankhurst*: Henry Devenish Harben, J.P.; Mrs Norah Walshe; Mrs Charlotte Drake; Miss Gladice L. Arnold (who lent correspondence between her aunt, the late Miss Norah Smyth, and Sylvia Pankhurst); Mrs A. Ashman; Mrs Vera Klein; Princess Rosalie Viazemsky; Lady S. Winstedt; Mr F. Beaufort Palmer; Mr John Lodge; Mr H. D. Molesworth; Mrs Frida Laski; Mrs Elsa Fraenkel; Miss Elsie Bowerman, M.A.; Mr James Klugmann (who provided information about Sylvia Pankhurst's relations with Lenin, the Third International and the Communist Party of Great Britain); Mr Walter E. Spradbery; and the late William Gallacher.

ACKNOWLEDGMENTS

(iv) *Adela Pankhurst Walsh and Tom Walsh:* Mrs Ursula Young, Sydney; Mrs Enid Royes Metcalfe, Adelaide (who gave me her files of the *Empire Gazette*); Mrs Vera Parkinson, Wamberal, New South Wales; Mrs M. Jessop, Artarmon, New South Wales; Mrs G. Merle Christie, Wahroonga, New South Wales; Mrs Helen Fraser Moyes, Sydney; the late Mr Norman Jeffery, Sydney; Councillor Tom Barker, Kentish Town, London; Mr Roger Coates, Arncliffe, New South Wales; Mr J. Normington-Rawling, Gladesville, New South Wales; E. C. Fry and Alastair Davidson, of the Australian National University, Canberra; Mr Edgar Ross, Sydney; and Mrs K. Scarratt, Peakhurst, New South Wales.

I would like to thank Miss Jessie Kenney, Mrs Mary Leigh, Lady Gollancz and the late Miss Theresa Garnett for their suffragette reminiscences.

Last but not least I am grateful to my wife for help with newspaper research and for reading and criticizing the typescript.

DAVID MITCHELL

Benyamina,
Torremolinos,
Spain
April 1967

PREFACE

It was while writing my last book, *Women on the Warpath*, a study of women's emancipation during the first world war, that I became fascinated by the drama and maenadic aggression of the Pankhursts, surely one of the most remarkable families of females in the history of Britain.

What happened to the Pankhursts when the war was over and the vote won, when the dust of the suffragette campaign had settled, when the Women's Social and Political Union had been disbanded, its banners furled and its warriors had melted back into the great humdrum which, for nearly a decade, they had so magnificently disturbed? Did they find other causes to enlist their headlong pugnacity? What did they make of the emancipation for which they had fought so tigerishly and which they had envisioned as the cure for all social ills?

The attempt to answer these questions involved far-flung inquiries: for the four Pankhurst women — Emmeline, Christabel, Sylvia and Adela (the youngest, least known, but extremely formidable daughter) — scattered like grape-shot, to Australia, Canada, the U.S.A. and Ethiopia. They continued to grab headlines and to crackle like an anthological volley of the main socio-political trends of a world which their own original agitation had done so much to alter. Between them, in their ransacking eagerness to set people to rights, they spanned a political gamut from anarchistic communism to High Toryism and even near-Fascism.

Though Christabel was the only conventionally religious one of the four, all were essentially preachers on the grand scale, seeking converts with a rare and unquenchable urgency. Their industry was prodigious, like their disagreements and their puritanism. Mrs Pankhurst exalted the virtue of chastity; Christabel scourged the 'licence' of the flappers; Sylvia (though, in protest against the institution of marriage, she bore her son out of wedlock) objected to the use of cosmetics and to cinematic sex and violence; and Adela lamented the disintegration of the old-fashioned family. Each, in her own way, was powered by the sturdy radicalism which had made Manchester, the Pankhursts' home town, a dynamic force for reform in nineteenth century Britain.

The seething vitality of their later careers, with which this book is concerned, would be unintelligible without an account of the Pankhurst family atmosphere, the influence of Papa Pankhurst on his wife and daughters, and those differences of temperament and interpretation which began to show during the suffrage campaign and were violently accentuated during the first world war. So what follows is, in effect, a first effort to assess the careers and the achievements of the Pankhursts as a whole, from birth to death. While a short survey of the early years is indispensable to an understanding of later developments, these in turn throw back light upon the motivations and tactics of the suffragette war.

For JASON and BIRD

PART ONE

THE MISSIONARIES

Erratum

The Author and Publishers wish to apologize to Professor Edward
Ullendorff, F.B.A., Professor of Ethiopian Studies at the School of
Oriental and African Studies, University of London, for the inaccuracy
of the references to him on pages 290 and 291; these were publicly
withdrawn by Miss Sylvia Pankhurst as reported in The Times of
February 19th, 1954, and in the New Times and Ethiopia News of
February 20th, 1954, to which reports we invite the attention of readers.

CHAPTER ONE

DR PANKHURST'S WOMEN

1890. The last visitor had left the Pankhurst home in Russell Square, London, after yet another meeting of the Women's Franchise League. The two girls, ten-year-old Christabel and eight-year-old Sylvia, who had helped to arrange the flowers and had enjoyed the strawberries, the music, the recitations and the speeches, handed the brocade collection bags to their mother and began to gather the leaflets which were lying around the drawing-room. Servants stacked chairs and cleared away plates and teacups. Dr Pankhurst, who had spoken so eloquently of the cruelty and stupidity of denying political rights to women, of stultifying the energies of half the population, sat down in an armchair and sighed deeply. He had been making very similar speeches for nearly a quarter of a century. His wife Emmeline, sensing his depression, walked over to him. As he often did when he was reading, or abstracted in thought, he reached out to take her hand.

Suddenly he jerked upright. 'Why,' he almost shouted, throwing his hands upwards in a gesture of angry bewilderment, 'Why don't you *force* us to give you the vote? Why don't you *scratch our eyes out?*' Christabel and Sylvia looked up, startled. Even their mother, for all her natural vehemence, was astonished. Dr Pankhurst's gentleness, his infinite capacity for forgiveness, were almost legendary in the family, and in the wider circle of his professional and political activity. Neither wife nor daughters ever forgot this outburst.

At an early age Emmeline Goulden, the eldest of five daughters of a prosperous Manchester cotton manufacturer, had learned that Manchester was a city which took itself and its politics seriously. Her father, a bustling Liberal, was one of the committee which welcomed Henry Ward Beecher when he came to speak in the city, and one of Emmeline's first memories was of taking round a collection purse at a meeting held to raise funds for emancipated American Negro slaves. She heard, too, when she was little more than a child, of the brilliance and public-spiritedness of Richard Marsden Pankhurst, the man who, in a city where reform—

the pushing and prodding of recalcitrant, reactionary London – was a major industry, was known as a Radical of Radicals. His erudition was immense, his activities legion. He was a member of the National Association for the Promotion of Social Science, of the Royal Statistical Society, of the Society for the Reform and Codification of the Law, of the Manchester Chamber of Commerce, and of the Committee of the Union of Lancashire and Cheshire Mechanics' Institutes. Once its academic pride, he was elected a governor of Owen's College, later Manchester University.

But above all, Emmeline's father told her, with the hushed admiration of a successful business man for a reckless idealist, how Pankhurst used his legal ability not to fatten his barrister's fees but to fight for the underprivileged, for a more just society, one in which wealth should be redistributed, land nationalized, the House of Lords ('without doubt the most preposterous institution in Europe') and the monarchy abolished, the Church disestablished, the masses properly educated, the working classes protected by labour laws he himself helped to draft. But his cardinal crime and peculiarity – the one which under the great Gladstone's anti-feminist frown put paid to his prospects of rapid advancement in the Liberal Party – was to insist that women must have the vote and play a full part in public life.

In 1865, when Emmeline was a child of seven, Pankhurst had helped to found a Women's Suffrage Society in Manchester: and for years, until he found himself out of sympathy with her over-cautious approach, was the chief support (and the object of the unrequited passion) of its formidable spinster secretary, Lydia Ernestine Becker. He had challenged the exclusion of women from the Franchise Reform Act of 1867 with a wealth of legal expertise and curious historical precedents. His amendment to the Municipal Corporations Bill of 1869, presented to Parliament by his close friend Jacob Bright, had resulted in the inclusion of women householders on the register of local electors – a notable triumph. He had drafted the Married Women's Property Bill which, in due course, gave wives the right to their earnings and possessions – another foothold in the long climb to equality – and also, in 1870, the first parliamentary bill to give women the vote. This, too, was presented by Jacob Bright (unsuccessfully, though, like other private members' bills with the same object in the next forty-odd years, it had a second reading).

'The Doctor', as he was known, was the best-loved, best-hated public figure of his time in Manchester. His opinions were quoted even in the philistine south. His hair and pointed beard were (symbolically it seemed to some) red, and he cared little, in the whistling rush of his causes, for his personal appearance. His clothes were always bulging with documents and memoranda and pocket editions of his favourite poets, Milton and Shelley. Once a teacher in Sunday School—his father, an auctioneer, was a devout Baptist—he became a thoughtful agnostic, an admirer of the Historical Jesus. To him, integrity in public life, practical compassion for the victims of the chaotic greed of industrialism, was a religion.

He was not a conventionally eligible bachelor. His features, though kindly, were not handsome, and were often set in the protective arrogance of a minor prophet steeling himself to perpetual opposition. His voice was harsh and unusually high-pitched. His ultra-radicalism lost him many a lucrative brief. He had vowed to stay single for the sake of his public crusades. In 1878, when twenty-year-old Emmeline, just back from finishing school in Paris, first met him (she had first heard him speak at a suffrage meeting seven years before), he had turned forty and was still living with his parents. It seemed impossible that the heart of this shy Radical monk—whose main form of relaxation was political discussion with men friends in his club—should ever be disturbed by the physical charms, as opposed to the social and political injustices, of women. Yet at a crowded, noisy reception after a meeting at which he had scathingly denounced Disraeli's jingo imperialism, he fell in love at first sight with the manufacturer's daughter, and she with him. He was pierced by her beauty—her slim, erect, vibrant figure, set off by elegant, carefully-chosen clothes; her plump, firmly-boned cheeks; her jet black hair and arching black eyebrows; her clear, olive skin. There before him was that wonderful, and superlatively photogenic, face, which was to become one of the world's most celebrated symbols, to prove its ability to 'carry' to the outermost person in the largest audience.

The Doctor sensed that her physical vitality was matched by an ardent, reforming Mancunian spirit, a spirit romantically heightened by the fact that her main school friend in Paris, Noémie de Rochefort, was the daughter of the Marquis de Rochefort, one of the most colourful, reckless heroes of the Paris Commune of 1871. His letters, during their short courtship (they married a few months later when Dr Pankhurst's mother died), made it clear that theirs was to be a partnership of stern service as well as a haven of domestic bliss. In all his happiness with Emmeline, he wrote, he felt keenly the responsibilities that were gathering about them ('Every struggling cause shall be ours'). Together they would taste the secret, esoteric joys of social pioneering, 'entering as it were by inspiration into the good time yet far away. Something of its morning glow touches our foreheads, or ever it is by the many even so much as dreamt of ... '

In an impulsive attempt to match his romantic dedication with a gesture of her own, Emmeline suggested that they demonstrate their independenc of convention by dispensing with the odious legal formalities of marriage. Would not a 'free union' express dramatically their contempt for that jungle of outmoded anti-feminism through which the Doctor was hacking a laborious path? He was touched: but unwilling to invite the slanders of respectability which such an action was bound to attract, he dissuaded her from it. Her first great need was to learn to handle the greasy ropes of reform. So he mapped out a reading programme and arranged for her to serve on the Married Women's Property Committee. The birth of three girls – Christabel (1880), Sylvia (1882) and Adela (1885) – and a boy (who died in babyhood) in the next six years dislocated her studies: but just to be with the Doctor was a comprehensive education in the fervours, drudgeries and pitfalls of public service: just to run the growing household was a full-time job – the more so because her husband turned out to be so intensely, if ruefully, unpractical that Emmeline was even expected to carve the family joint. Her part, she decided, was to encourage her awkward Galahad's crusading fervour.

Despite the abandonment of the 'free union' idea, the disapproval of society was borne in upon her. Her father had admired Dr Pankhurst, but he had not thought of him as a son-in-law. He should have remained a bachelor. It was one thing to take risks as a single man, quite another to expose a young, eager wife and innocent children to a life of strain and insecurity. And after all, as people were saying, sometimes solemnly, often with a smirk, the Doctor *was* old enough to be her father. This fact gave freer rein to the facile slander, with which men who supported women's emancipation were commonly smeared, that their 'crusade' was not as pure as they pretended; that it was, really, an excuse to run licentious riot amongst a harem of grateful maidens to whom, otherwise, the iron defences of Victorian middle-class propriety would have denied them access. The mere suggestion that her saintly husband was a sly lecher disgusted and infuriated Emmeline: it also deepened and barbed her loyalty. So did her father's refusal to give her any money or property, with which she had hoped to lessen her husband's dependence on routine legal work and free him to concentrate on higher things.

Britain, she felt (with the intensity of an ardent nature now initiated into the seamy as well as the shining side of public life), *needed* men like her husband. Had he not revealed to her something of the squalid iniquity in high places? Eminent judges, for instance, who viewed sex crimes against children with easy lenience since they themselves frequented brothels where all manner of perverted tastes were catered for. Impatiently she urged the Doctor to stand for Parliament. But the forces of reaction soon blocked this ambition. The open hostility of the local Liberal Association ensured his defeat at a by-election in Manchester in 1883. 'Dr Pankhurst', commented the *Spectator*, 'is substantially a French Red, not an English radical at all' — this of a man whose struggle to make Britain worthy of her power, to give her a true sense of mission, stemmed from a real patriotism of which such dull, complacent oafs had never dreamed! Mrs Pankhurst began the lifelong process of steeping her mind in the sorrows and splendours of a chronic, noble opposition. She began to burn with that inner fire of sacred conviction with which, more than twenty years later, she led her fantastic stage army of women against the barricades of male domination.

When, two years later, Dr Pankhurst stood as a Radical candidate in Rotherhithe, Emmeline — on her first visit to London — braved the missiles and bawdy heckling of a brawling, drunken campaign. Her husband, since he lacked the funds or the inclination to bribe the electors with booze (so *that* was how men used the vote!) had once more to be content with what he called a 'moral victory'. His Tory opponent had alleged, in rushed-out handbills, that the Doctor was an atheistic corrupter of Christian virtue. When Pankhurst brought a libel action, and the judge in effect instructed the jury to find for the defendant, Emmeline courted imprisonment (even then her mind leaped easily, eagerly to extremes) by writing a letter of passionate resentment to the bewigged hypocrite: 'My Lord: Your judgment and summing up are the concluding acts of a conspiracy to crush the public life of an honourable public man. It is to be regretted that there should be found on the English Bench a judge who will lend his aid to a disreputable section of the Tory Party in doing their dirty work. But for what other reason were you ever placed where you are?'

Her taunt was ignored, but her husband listened to her when she insisted that he should rent a house in London, which, like it or not, was the centre of affairs. For seven years, though Dr Pankhurst was often away for long spells on legal business in the north, the Pankhursts lived in London.

Emmeline was convinced that her husband's election to Parliament would be speeded if he displayed his eloquence and ability nearer to Westminster. She also made a disastrous attempt to supplement the family income by opening a fancy goods shop called Emerson's in the West End. But her real joy and focus was her 'salon' in the house in Russell Square. Here she played hostess to socialists, anarchists and progressives of all types—Tom Mann, William Morris, Annie Besant (who had left her clergyman husband and continued to shock the bourgeois with her cropped hair and short skirts as well as her political radicalism), Italian and Russian refugees, Elizabeth Cady Stanton, the veteran American suffragist leader, and her daughter, Harriot Stanton Blatch. Though money was short, the house looked bright—furnished largely with unsold stock from Emerson's, which also provided presents for the children—and she herself was always impeccably groomed and gowned; for in her opinion the representatives of a cause should strive to be a credit to it in raiment as well as in argument.

Though many individual Liberal M.P.s were nominal supporters of women's suffrage, women were not included in the Franchise Reform Act of 1884. In 1889, the year when Mrs Pankhurst's second son, Harry, was born, she and her husband founded the Women's Franchise League, a ginger group determined to be more aggressive than the older suffrage societies, hamstrung by Liberal loyalties and a perennial optimism about a change of Liberal leaders' hearts. The children's education was casual— both parents distrusted conventional schools, with their reactionary ethos and religious clap-trap, and felt that the girls could learn all that a true citizen needed to know at home. Though conventionally enough punished for naughtiness and forced to finish their food, Christabel and Sylvia were encouraged to attend meetings and report them in *Home News*, a little journal which Dr Pankhurst read and discussed with them. The atmosphere was inclined to be tense, rather humourless, and strongly tinged with a sense of duty none the less puritan for being humanist. Dr Pankhurst was widely read, earnestly cultured: but he favoured writers, even poets, for their ideological content, as much as for their aesthetic genius. The Pankhurst children played hard at politics, grew early accustomed to a diet of debate and pamphlets. Years later, when Sylvia told the socialist leader Keir Hardie (himself tautly austere, a teetotaller and deeply suspicious of the theatre) of this exciting but lopsided regime, he remarked: 'So *that* is what is the matter with you! You heard too much serious talk. Children ought not to be brought up like that.'

Dr Pankhurst, weakened by thirty years of reckless overwork, began to wilt, plagued by gastric ulcers. But when the family, to lessen the strain on its head and to reduce expenses, moved back to Manchester, the pace did not slacken. At Manchester High School, Christabel and Sylvia (especially Sylvia, always her father's most uncompromising disciple) were jeered at because the Doctor was 'against' the Queen and refused to let them attend Scripture lessons. In 1894 he broke completely with the Liberals and joined the tiny, newly formed Independent Labour Party (I.L.P.) – one of the first of his class and professional standing to do so. Keir Hardie and Tom Mann were frequent visitors, and the Pankhurst home was open to all visiting socialist speakers. The City Council ceased to retain the 'Red Doctor' for legal business, and he lost yet another gruelling and expensive election campaign, this time at West Gorton as an I.L.P. candidate.

At least, though, he had the pleasure of watching Emmeline begin to blossom as a public figure in her own right, the pretty but formidable creation of his tender, relentless, Pygmalion devotion. He was proud to see her plunge, smart pink bonnet and all, into the thick of a prolonged and successful defiance of an attempt by the City Fathers to ban Boggart Hole Clough, a public park, to I.L.P. speakers. Stoned by Tory roughs when she electioneered for Tom Mann, she was feeling and relishing her own strength just as his was tragically ebbing.

She organized free canteens for the starving unemployed in the crisis winter of 1894. In that bitter winter, too, she had her first personal experience of the pettiness of officialdom when she was elected to the Chorlton Board of Guardians. Scathingly and effectively she raged when she found that the little girls in the workhouse were forced to wear eighteenth-century dresses, low-necked and sleeveless, and were not provided with underclothes or nightdresses: all because the matron and some prissy female guardians, though well aware of the deficiency and of its threat to the children's health, had been too refined to mention such matters to the all-powerful men on the board. This was the kind of canting, slave-minded gentility that Mrs Pankhurst (so fastidious in her own way) could not and would not endure.

What other force, she began to reason, but a phalanx of good, determined, socially conscious women could ever break the nation-wide conspiracy of silence of which this was a small but significant example? And how could they break it unless they forced men to give them the vote, whatever methods they had to use?

CHAPTER TWO

DR PANKHURST'S
LEGACY

So were the seeds of the suffragette campaign, which were to mature in Mrs Pankhurst's mind for another decade, sown. From first to last, though more obviously in its closing stages, it was, under her inspiration, a campaign for honesty and decency, for the truth pure and very simple, as her husband had helped her and her daughters to see it.

In attacking the Establishment of her time she had no intention, any more than Dr Pankhurst, of upsetting the old moral values. She was concerned rather with forcing men of the ruling classes to live up to them, even as they had forced their women folk – even to the point of screaming sex neurosis, as vividly described by Florence Nightingale – to observe them. The double standard had to go, men had to climb out of the mire and on to the dangerous pedestal which they had designed for the immobilization of 'good' women (their wives and daughters). She saw the vote as a kind of pitchfork with which to prod them to make the painful ascent. In this sense alone was she a New Woman. Like feminist leaders in America and Australia, but with a greater intensity, she believed in the moral and spiritual superiority (albeit enforced) of middle- and upper-class women, and in their mission to cleanse and, with a grand swoosh of undammed energy, to revitalize public life. Perhaps it was necessary in England, where the aristocratic tradition had built a subtle system of defence in depth (and was continually gaining *arriviste* converts to its deadly gospel of female gentility), to have such a childlike faith.

But before her fashioning as an instrument of destiny was complete, Mrs Pankhurst had to endure new trials. In 1898 her husband died in great agony with perforated stomach ulcers. To his widow and four children he left little money. His legacy was rather a rich fund of moral uplift, political experience – and, above all, resentment. Bitter resentment for what she considered his public crucifixion was an important factor in his widow's unswerving hostility to the Liberal Party in the struggle that lay ahead. But she, who had seen him crushed by the weight of his many commitments and hurt by those whom he had gone out of his way to help, realized the need to concentrate on *one* objective and to stiffen ideals with ruthlessness. The men who had victimized her husband for his championship of women would be attacked with deeds as well as words, though heaven knows there were plenty of words bursting for utterance. She would make Parliament Square into a battlefield, the Old Bailey itself into a place where spiritually crass judges were themselves judged, and she would give a new meaning to the term 'moral victory', of which the much-defeated Doctor had been so fond.

But first she had to look to her family and finances, to sell books and furniture to pay creditors, to find a smaller house, into which one of her brothers moved to share the expenses. She refused an offer from Robert Blatchford, editor of the socialist *Clarion*, to raise a fund for the education of the children: why, she said, should working people give her money for something which they could not afford for their own children? She did, though, after some demur, accept a testimonial fund from wealthy friends and admirers of Dr Pankhurst: but her main source of income was the salary she received as Registrar of Births and Deaths in the Rusholme district of Manchester, an official post to which her colleagues on the Board of Poor Law Guardians got her appointed. She and her sister Mary were still trying to squeeze some profit out of Emerson's which, with obstinate persistence, she had re-opened in Manchester: and Christabel and Sylvia, when they left school, were expected to help in the shop.

At the same time, Mrs Pankhurst continued her honorary public work, this time as an I.L.P. member of the Manchester School Board. In 1900, acting as she knew her late husband would have wished, she resigned from the Fabian Society (a group dedicated to gradual, 'evolutionary' socialism, in which George Bernard Shaw was prominent) because of its refusal to oppose the imperialist aggression of the Boer War. It was the turn of the two younger Pankhurst children, now at school, to suffer for their parent's convictions. In the violent emotions aroused by the Boer War (Lloyd George was nearly lynched for opposing it), and partly perhaps because it was a woman, their mother, who was double outraging convention by flouting the accepted view, Adela and Harry experienced far rougher treatment than had Christabel (who in fact had been studiously unprovocative and quite popular) and Sylvia. For speaking against the war, Harry was beaten unconscious by his schoolfellows, though he was so gentle that people joked that he was the only girl in the family; and Adela was injured when a book, flung in a classroom, hit her in the face.

Distressed by these incidents, Mrs Pankhurst kept the children at home and protested to the School Board. She was, perhaps, also worried that, in the familiar Pankhurst welter of radicalism, she was in danger of blunting that single cutting edge which alone might slice a pound or two of flesh from a bloated, indifferent society. It was Christabel, her first-born and favourite child, who unexpectedly supplied the discipline and logic needed to harness her mother's outstanding gifts of emotional evangelism. With a marvellously cocksure, clever student's gift of analysis, and an utter refusal to follow the will o' the wisp of sentimental diffusion, she worked out the simple, dynamic programme which Mrs Pankhurst craved, but had not the time, or perhaps the heart, to formulate. Unlike Sylvia, Christabel had fitted easily, even triumphantly, into the pattern of school. She *enjoyed* herself (just as she did later in the school-like hierarchy and atmosphere of the suffragettes). She did not kick against the pricks of convention (if they were pricks to her, which Sylvia darkly suspected they were not). Though obviously intelligent, she did not work very hard, standing almost mockingly apart from the family tradition of shuddering conscientiousness. But she showed an effortless knack for gaining the admiration and allegiance of her fellow-pupils, and was soon marked out by the teachers as good prefect material. Her main talent seemed to be for dancing, a career which appealed to Mrs Pankhurst's love of the theatrically romantic, her longing to escape from the humdrum. Yet her father's reputation for public service edged her—almost it seemed against her will—onto the family treadmill of reform.

Esther Roper, secretary of the North of England Society for Woman Suffrage, and Eva Gore-Booth, secretary of the Manchester Women's Trade Council, recruited her to help in their campaign to interest working women in the suffrage campaign. They also persuaded her to study for a legal degree at the university, a task in which, though she was brilliantly successful, Christabel knew that she was condemning herself to a professional dead end: for women could not practise the law. But she got what she knew she, as a Pankhurst, even though the least typical one, needed—a rigorous training in realism. She used this to diagnose the reasons for the failure of a suffrage agitation which had now lasted for nearly forty years without making any appreciable impact on public opinion.

It was useless, she argued, to rely on private members' bills, ever at the mercy of the Government, which could always plead a press of other priorities, a lack of urgency, an absence of massive support. It was useless, too, to expect serious backing from the Labour movement. It would be years before Labour was a force to be reckoned with in Parliament, and the prospect of a Labour Government seemed infinitely remote. In any case it was clear that, despite Keir Hardie's inclinations, the movement was not willing to make a firm commitment about women's suffrage. How could a working-class movement be expected to show enthusiasm for the enfranchisement of about two million middle- and upper-class women householders (who would presumably vote either Liberal or Tory), which was all that any suffrage agitation could realistically demand?

The Conservative Party, though it was widely predicted that a limited female electorate would be predominantly Tory, was solidly, if illogically, opposed to opening the sluice gates even a crack. The political tide, moreover, was turning for a Liberal victory in the general election of 1906. The obvious strategy was to continue with the attempt to win support from working-class women, pointing out that the 'ladies' would use the vote to improve women's position throughout society; to refuse to commit oneself to *any* political party, and to attract funds and backing from women on a sex-war basis—which would in itself create a fighting, if temporary, democracy of the dispossessed; to use every chance, at general elections, by-elections, and major political meetings of all kinds, and by spectacular individual or mass demonstrations, to force the *Government* either to sponsor a women's suffrage bill or to expose its refusal to do so. Every twist in the struggle which was bound to follow would have a fourfold advantage. The Government would be put on the defensive; newspapers would be forced to give space to the contest; the essential idiocy of anti-suffragism of whatever political nuance would be driven into the open (so proving that this was *not* a political or philosophical but a sex war, and inevitably rousing the latent militancy in women all over the country); and last, but by no means least, when the Pankhursts had organized this militancy it would mean that, however long the fight, women would cease to act like slaves and begin to work out their own salvation. The vote, in this perspective, would serve its purpose as the symbol of a holy crusade—which nevertheless would be planned and waged with every refinement of political sagacity. The Irish Nationalists, the Ulster Unionists, the trade unions, even the preposterous old Lords, were prepared to declare war on the Government in their own interests. Were women alone, numerically the strongest and at least as rich in exploitable injustice, to shrink from the battlefield?

With this daring thesis, expanded step by step and resoundingly endorsed over the next nine remarkable years, Christabel, to the fury of orthodox suffragists, went straight to the top of the feminist class. By

1908, in Bow Street police court, where she appeared on a charge of inciting a Trafalgar Square crowd to 'rush' the House of Commons, she was coolly cross-examining two cabinet ministers (Lloyd George and Herbert Gladstone) in the witness box, and merrily pillorying the inconsistency of a Government whose Liberalism stopped short at the sex barrier. Her mother, in court with her, had the satisfaction of hearing Christabel quote, in extenuation of the militancy of their Women's Social and Political Union (W.S.P.U.), the words of William Ewart Gladstone himself: 'I am sorry to say that if no instructions had ever been addressed in political crises to the people of this country except to remember to hate violence and to love order, the liberties of this people would never have been attained.'

Lloyd George was adroitly manœuvred into admitting that the women's agitation could easily be ended by giving them what they asked for. Mrs Pankhurst paraded the record of her own work as a public servant and constitutional suffragist, and added: 'We are driven to this. We are determined to go on with the agitation. We are in honour bound to do so until we win. Just as it was the duty of our forefathers to do it for you, it is our duty to make this world a better place for women. We believe that if we get the vote it will mean changed conditions for our less fortunate sisters. The average pay of women wage-earners is only seven shillings and sixpence a week. There are women who have been driven to live an immoral life because they cannot earn enough to live decently … '

Here she touched upon her special contribution to the embodiment of the precocious Christabel's blueprint of revolt. Because of her prominence in the agitation she had been obliged to resign from her registrarship, and to be content with a suffragette salary of four guineas a week, travelling expenses, and the use of the W.S.P.U. car. She saw Christabel lionized as a political genius (which she was), housed, fed and holidayed by the wealthy, childless Pethick-Lawrences, who since 1906 had supplied the premises, the administrative acumen and the fund-raising ability which transformed the W.S.P.U. from a provincial foray into a national institution. But she had not forgotten the sordid connection between anti-suffragism and vice, the need to spotlight and abolish the Double Standard. As registrar she (who had never been able to bring herself to talk to her own children about the Facts of Life: 'Father', she would begin vaguely, 'says I ought to talk to you … ', and then lose herself and the subject in a pleasant wilderness of birds, bees and flowers) had been shocked by the number of young girls who came to record the births of illegitimate babies. 'In many cases', she wrote later, 'I found that the child's own father or some near male relative was responsible for her state.' Yet if, as sometimes happened, a desperate unmarried mother exposed her baby so that it died, or if it perished through sheer hunger, she was hanged for murder, while 'the wretch who was the real murderer received no punishment at all'.

Here was the easily grasped, emotive heart of the matter, as far as she was concerned: and increasingly, as the Government procrastinated and intensified its attempt to frighten the suffragettes out of action, it was the heart of the matter as far as tens of thousands, perhaps hundreds of thousands of women, and an increasing number of men were concerned. The Government, willing enough under pressure to come to terms with Irishmen, Ulstermen, and militant male trade unionists, developed a mental block when women urged their claims. Scratched by the suffragettes, Liberal ministers (members of what was described as perhaps the most brilliant, intellectual Cabinet ever thrown up by the processes of British political democracy) revealed the cave man, the old neanderthal Adam, which lurked, stubborn and ludicrous, beneath their frock-coated, stripe-trousered, top-hatted façades. This revelation, at once laughable and sinister, was one of the great achievements of the Pankhursts. Lloyd George talked about 'mewing cats', Churchill, after a roasting heckle from Sylvia Pankhurst, sneered at 'hen-peckers'. Stewards at Liberal meetings chucked out suffragette interrupters with a violence not seen again until the rallies of Mosley's British United Fascists in the 1930s.

This, said the W.S.P.U., was the hysterical rage of the clubman at the female intruder who threatened to spoil his sport: and spoiling his sport meant cleansing public life, abolishing the causes of prostitution, banishing the sleazy, fascinating Edwardian demi-monde where men and women met in the equality of fun and lust—the *only* equality women were likely to know, the Pankhursts hinted, until they (or at least the most responsible of them, who knew what was best for the others) got the vote. Churchill, the chubby epitome of the anti-spoil-sport brigade, was the target of more actual or attempted physical chastisement than any other politician. Life, in his opinion, was the richer for its shadows, a poor thing without its reprehensibilities. He feared the carbolic influence of the public-spirited female. Had he not, some suffragettes may have recalled, while he was still a cadet at Sandhurst in the 1890s, led a gang of young bloods in tearing down the screens put up (to protect the public from the tarts who strolled on the other side) in the promenade of the Empire Theatre, Leicester Square, as a result of a music-hall purity campaign launched by a female member of the London County Council? By 1910, as Home Secretary in charge of the Government campaign of forcible feeding and police scrimmages with suffragette demonstraters, Churchill seemed the very caricature of the Old Chivalry turned nasty in the defence of its own low convictions. His resentment of female meddlers was, of course, shared by many men of the lower orders, to whom there was no better sport than helping the police to manhandle 'she-males', and even, if opportunity offered, dragging them up a side street and indecently assaulting them (a sister of Field Marshal Earl Haig died as the result of such an assault). On visits to the biblically patriarchal Welsh Chapel Belt, Lloyd George let his mask slip right off. 'I remember', he told one audience, when bothered by suffragette hecklers, 'little eisteddfodau at which prizes were given for the best hazel stick. One of those sticks would be rather a good thing to have just now.' Yet the hecklers, though kicked, beaten, and stripped almost naked, braved an even more obscene ordeal a few days later in Lloyd George's native village, Llanstymdwy.

The use of forcible feeding, with its overtones of sexual brutality, screwed the tragi-comic, sado-masochistic spectacle, avidly reported by the press, to a new pitch of intensity. As provocation and counter-provocation mounted, the W.S.P.U. was shaken by internal dissensions. In 1907 Mrs Charlotte Despard, disapproving of the autocratic methods of the Pankhursts, split off with some sympathizers to form the more 'democratic' Women's Freedom League. Then in 1912 Mr and Mrs Pethick-Lawrence, critical of attacks on property, parted company with Emmeline and Christabel. 'The W.S.P.U.', commented Mrs Pankhurst, 'is simply a suffrage army in the field. It is purely a volunteer army, and no one is obliged to remain in it. We declared that we would wage war not only on all anti-suffrage forces, but on all neutral and non-active forces. Every man with a vote was considered to be a foe to woman suffrage unless prepared actively to be a friend.'

It was the classic formula of fanaticism: yet despite the suffering endured by that tiny guerilla band, life in the heart of the Pankhurst whirlwind had, often, a tremendous gaiety, a reckless, joyful abandon. There is a glimpse of this in Mrs Despard's description of Mrs Pankhurst's demeanour during the first suffragette 'raid' on the lobby of the House of Commons in 1906. She was 'lying on the marble floor with two policemen over her. Horrified, I rushed to her assistance, to be met with a brief

glance from a fearless and amused pair of eyes.' Mrs Pankhurst could be
a Merry as well as a Mighty Widow. 'I was to understand that this was
just an episode in the fight, a mere trifle.' The ubiquitous heckling, carried
out with a vaudevillian sense of timing and deflation; the superbly
disruptive interventions at by-elections; the pavement chalking; the
massive parades; the window smashing; the cutting of golf greens,
bowling greens and paintings in public galleries; the firing of pillar boxes,
empty houses, castles, churches, grandstands and cricket pavilions – there
had never been, and there never has been since, such a stinging, hilarious
slap in the face of solemn frivolity and entempled triviality.

The damage was done, said Mrs Pankhurst, 'not at all in a spirit of
wanton mischief, but with the direct and practical object of reminding
the dull and self-satisfied English public that when the liberties of English
women were being stolen from them it was no time to think of sport.'
She thumpingly turned the tables on ecclesiastical critics by asserting that
the W.S.P.U.'s onslaught on the false gods of property was a spiritual
service to the community. 'If we women are wrong in destroying
private property in order that human values may be restored, then I say
in all reverence that it was wrong for the Founder of Christianity to
destroy private property, as He did when he lashed the money changers
out of the Temple and drove the Gadarene swine into the sea ... '

In March 1912 Christabel, leaving her mother and the Pethick-
Lawrences in the hands of the police, escaped in the nick of time to
France, and for the next two years directed the last and most hectic phases of
militancy from Paris. She was aware of the criticisms that would be made.
'Any laurels', she wrote later, 'that might belong to the pioneer prisoner'
(she and Annie Kenney had been the first suffragettes to be jailed, in
October 1905) 'would certainly wither from my brow. But I could not
depend on any of the others to stay abroad through thick and thin.
Least of all could I depend on Mother to do it! I knew her ardent spirit
too well ... Whatever my limitations, I knew that in two respects I was
well equipped – in the capacity to control affairs from a distance, and in
the capacity to read the mind of particular cabinet ministers and of the
Government in general.' In Paris Christabel was known as 'Amy Richards'.
Annie Kenney and other trusted lieutenants, also provided with aliases
(and elaborate disguises) travelled to Paris for orders and to collect
Christabel's copy for the *Suffragette*. The cloak-and-daggerism could
be exhilarating. 'The Saturdays in Paris', wrote Annie Kenney, 'were a
joy. We would walk along the river or go into the Bois ... with stacks of

2

newspapers, pockets stuffed with pencils and a knife to sharpen them.' Christabel, wonderful, infallible Christabel, had influential aristocratic friends. Once Miss Kenney found her in the drawing-room of the Princesse de Polignac's house. 'It was the largest room I ever saw,' thrilled Annie, who had worked in an Oldham cotton mill until she joined the W.S.P.U. 'I felt so tiny! There were beautiful books everywhere. I picked up one and found it was a translation of Sappho's poetry. The colour of the leather binding was the shade of a ripe pink cherry ... '

Despite luxurious interludes, leadership from exile was a psychological strain. The knowledge that intensified militancy, with its acts of arson and use of home-made bombs, exposed young women to new dangers, longer sentences, and the serial ordeal of the 1913 Cat and Mouse Act; the knowledge that, as the supreme executive of her daughter's policy, Mrs Pankhurst, tried and re-tried, hunger, thirst and sleep striking, making speeches as police fought with the audience to rearrest her, was living out a deliberate public martyrdom on the near verges of death; the knowledge, too, that in England there were whispers that Christabel, whose place was surely with her troops, was actually *enjoying* her exile— all this tested her self-confidence and moral stamina to the limit, and perhaps, though she contrived to give no sign of it, a little beyond.

Four times, between imprisonments, Mrs Pankhurst contrived to cross the Channel to be with her beloved Christabel. Her appearance after her hunger strikes was terrifying—weakened as she was by gastric pain, her skin yellow and so tightly stretched that the bones seemed about to pierce through, her eyes feverish and sunk in dark bruises of exhaustion. Yet in a few days this miraculously resilient woman, then in her middle fifties, would recover. The pleasure of being with Christabel and in Paris—her favourite city ever since her schooldays—revived her. More naturally sociable than her daughter, who in any case probably felt honour-bound *not* to have too good a time, she loved to go shopping, to bargain for a new dress, to air her fluent French, to see Sarah Bernhardt in a new play. 'This is more like home than anything I have known for years,' she wrote to Dr Ethel Smyth, the composer, a close friend and fellow militant. 'Paris suits me and Berthe' (Christabel's maid in the flat on the Avenue de la Grande Armée) 'cooks food that agrees with me. I can potter about seeing things, get up and go to bed when I like, see whom I like. And I love to be with C in this way and tidy her up ... I am at peace for a few weeks and I snatch the fearful joy and mean to make the most of it before the fight begins again.'

Sometimes Christabel moved to Boulogne to shorten her visitors' journey. Thither in 1912 came the Pethick-Lawrences (he, poor man, had not only been forcibly fed in prison, but expelled from the Reform Club) to plead for a mitigation of militancy. When, during a walk along the cliffs, Christabel refused to change her tactics, they parted not only from an organization which they had done so much to create, but from one who had become to them almost an adopted daughter. To Boulogne, too, came George Lansbury, fresh from his famous outburst in the Commons against Asquith ('You will go down to history as the man who tortured innocent women! You ought to be driven from public life!') and his resignation from Parliament on the suffrage issue. He consulted Christabel about his re-election campaign which, obedient to her suggestion, he fought—and lost—on a Votes for Women platform.

Emissaries from the Men's Political Union, a group of militant male sympathizers, came to Paris for a conference. Henry Harben, a former Liberal parliamentary candidate, and Harold Laski, then still an undergraduate at Oxford, travelled together. Their reception was chilly, for they, like Lansbury, urged a closer alliance between the W.S.P.U. and socialist militancy as represented by the newly launched *Daily Herald*. Christabel was immediately and stiffly on the defensive. 'Between the W.S.P.U. and the Daily Herald League and Movement', she wrote to Harben, 'there can be no connection. Ours is a Woman's Movement and the Herald League is primarily a Man's Movement, or at any rate a Mixed Movement. Women must grow their own backbone before they are going to be any use to themselves or to humanity as a whole. It is helpful and good *for men themselves* when they try to promote women's emancipation; but they have to do it from the outside, and the really important thing is that women are working out their own salvation— and are able to do it, even if not a living man takes any part in bringing it about.' There were other important considerations. 'The Herald League', Christabel argued, 'tends to be a class movement. Ours is not a class movement at all. We take in everybody—the highest and the lowest, the richest and the poorest. The bond is womanhood! The socialists are fighting against certain evils which they believe to be attributable to the spirit of injustice as between man and man. I am not at all sure that women, if they had had their due influence from the beginning, would not have brought about a totally different state of affairs ... It comes to this. The men must paddle their own canoe, and we must paddle ours.'

In April 1913 Mrs Pankhurst achieved what she had long demanded.

She was tried at the Old Bailey, after accepting responsibility for an attempt to blow up Lloyd George's new house, then under construction at Walton Heath near London. Once more, and in greater detail than before, she expounded her central theme. The judge could, if he wished, send her to prison for up to fourteen years, yet the maximum penalty for offences of the most revolting kind against little girls was only two years. She had learned from her own husband, a barrister, about the corruption of those entrusted with the administration of man-made law — of a judge of assize, for instance, who after passing trivial sentences on the perpetrators of serious crimes against women, was himself found dead in a brothel. 'Only this morning', she declared, 'I have been informed that there is in this very city of London a regulated traffic, not only in women of full age, but in little children: that they are being purchased and trained to minister to the vicious pleasures of persons who ought to know better in their positions in life … Suffragettes believe that the horrible evils which are ravaging our civilization will never be removed until women get the vote. They know that the very fount of life is being poisoned … that because of bad education, of unequal standards of morals, even mothers and children are being destroyed by the vilest diseases … There is only one way to put a stop to this agitation — by doing us justice. I have no sense of guilt. I look upon myself as a prisoner of war. I am under no moral obligation to conform to, or in any way accept, the sentence imposed upon me.'

Despite the jury's recommendation to mercy, she was sentenced to three years' penal servitude. Under the Cat and Mouse Act, a hunger striker could be released on 'ticket of leave' when her health was seriously weakened, and re-arrested as soon as she was considered well enough to resume her sentence. Her body (always carefully gowned: a wardress in Holloway was horrified when, refusing to use the plank bed, she lay down on the stone floor in a beautiful velvet dress) had become a sort of temple of the dashingly masochistic rites of her sect. Only someone fortified by an invulnerable sense of self-righteousness and a veritable ecstasy of self-mortification could have faced the prospect of working off such a sentence by repeated bouts of starvation. Mrs Pankhurst added to the hunger strike a refusal to sleep or drink — a refinement of well-publicized self-torture pioneered by her daughter Sylvia, so that she was only in prison for a very short while before her condition became critical. In the next twelve months she was rearrested twelve times, serving a total of some thirty days.

Christabel, shocked by her mother's terrific ordeal, not only stepped up the tempo of militancy, but stoked up the sex war in the pages of the *Suffragette*. 'I now know', wrote Dr Ethel Smyth in one article, 'that in England more women are brutally ill-treated, more children outraged, than in any other quarter of the globe. The Recorder of Sandwich described the violation of babies as a crime on a different footing to forgery and theft, since any *otherwise* decent man might succumb to this temptation!' The Piccadilly Flat Case, in which 'Queenie' Gerald, a twenty-six-year-old actress, was sent to prison for three months on charges of keeping a brothel which catered for a wide range of sexual perversions, and of procuring very young girls for wealthy, elderly clients, provided a good propaganda chance. Why, commented Christabel, should 'Queenie' Gerald get only three months when Mrs Pankhurst got three years? Was it not the case that many eminent personages, whose names had been carefully hushed up, had been involved? Why should they escape punishment? 'In this case, with its foul revelations and still fouler concealments, is summed up the whole case against Votes for Women. The anti-suffragist believes that women are of value only because of their sex functions. The danger of Votes for Women is, more than all, a revolt against the evil system under which women are regarded as sub-human and the sex slaves of men.' 'Queenie' Gerald's was only one of many such establishments. Thousands of 'respectable' husbands and fathers no doubt went home from such places, told their wives and daughters not to meddle with the suffrage question, and denounced the suffragettes as hooligans. The conclusion was obvious: 'Let all women who want to see humanity no longer degraded by impure thought and physical disease come into the ranks of the W.S.P.U. and help to win the Vote!'

In succeeding numbers of the *Suffragette* (the circulation of which was soaring, as were contributions to the W.S.P.U. in general) Christabel followed this advantage up by a series on venereal disease – the Great Scourge as she called it – and how to cure it. 'The education of men on sexual matters', wrote this personable young spinster, 'is one of the most urgent needs of the day.' Men's impossible ideal, of course, was to persist in immorality and remain free from sexual disease. But many innocent wives and children had paid dearly for this ideal. Regulation of vice was no sure remedy, even if it was morally desirable, nor was the ingenuity of medical science. 'The real cure is a two-fold one – Votes for Women, which give women greater self-reliance and a stronger economic position, and *Chastity for Men*.' Contrary to male superstition, continence was not bad, but good, for the health. In support of this, Christabel cited Clement Dukes, M.D., physician of Rugby School ('it is simply a base invention to cover sin and has no foundation in fact'), and James Foster Scott, M.D. ('the proper subjugation of the sexual impulses and the conservation of the complex seminal fluid, with all its wonderfully invigorating influence, develop all that is best and noblest in man').

The sex instinct of many men, she alleged, was so perverted that intercourse with virtuous women did not satisfy them. 'They crave for intercourse with women whom they feel no obligation to respect. They want to resort to practices which a wife would not tolerate.' (By this time a number of experts, including a certain Dr Marie Carmichael Stopes, were formulating a different theory: the theory that the trouble with many women, especially among the classes from which the maiden or married warriors of the W.S.P.U. were drawn, was that they were secretly longing to tolerate such practices, that there was an urgent need for both sexes to come clean about copulation and usher in a new era of sexual harmony and mutual satisfaction. The Wife-Mistress rather than the Embattled Social Hygienist was to be the symbol of that era). 'Lewdness and obscenity', continued Christabel, 'is what these men ask for and what they get in houses of ill-fame.' Small wonder that decent women were loth to marry: until men accepted the same standards of morality as women, how could it be said that they were fit companions for them? Twenty per cent of the adult male population, she estimated, contracted syphilis, but eighty per cent had gonorrhea at one time or another. The ravages of gonorrhea, in fact, had created a situation in which 'womanhood itself has almost come to be looked upon as a disease'. Christabel quoted a medical specialist's opinion that 'from the husband's latent gonorrhea many women contract conditions which alter life and even character ... causing headache, backache, irregular and painful menstruation, urinary disorders, localized peritonitis, loss of healthful beauty, lassitude, hysteria, sterility, miscarriages and premature death'. (Many of these symptoms could have been due, not only to sexual frustration, but to over-frequent pregnancy: contraceptive techniques, again pioneered in Britain by Dr Stopes, did more than any amount of sermons to liberate women from the 'disease of womanhood'.)

Summarizing this series, which she entitled, rather conservatively, *The Dangers of Marriage*, Christabel ended: 'What a cruel mockery it is that men have alleged the very weakness of which their own behaviour is the cause as a reason why women should be condemned to political inferiority!' This astonishing manifesto from Miss Pankhurst's Parisian ivory tower, this *tour de force* of anguished prejudice, though it stung the Government to sterner measures in its war on the suffragettes, was warmly welcomed by no less a person than Helen Keller as an important contribution to the breaking of a shameful conspiracy of silence. Some men were eager to extend the Pankhurst challenge. George Lansbury's *Daily Herald* suggested the formation of a Guild of Honour for mothers who would vow not to conceive any more children until the vote was won. When Asquith proposed to give more men the vote while still denying it altogether to women, the *Eye-Opener*, journal of the Men's Society for Women's Rights (the secretary of which was a naval officer), blazed with an indignation in which class loyalty mingled curiously, furiously, with old-fashioned chivalry – the Pankhurst net of purity drew in some strange fish. Why should the Government wish to enfranchise 'a million or more half-educated, irresponsible youths, to open the way for any and every wastrel, hooligan and street-corner loafer to have his say in the government of the Empire? Are the most splendid and honoured of our women to stand helplessly by and see the laws which govern them and their young daughters decided by the votes of the sexually depraved degenerates who are spewed out nightly from thousands of tap-rooms and even more evil resorts?'

Emmeline and Christabel were at the height of their power. Each time Mrs Pankhurst was re-arrested, women picketed the prison gates, watching for her release, singing the *March of the Women* and the *Women's Marseillaise*. When one of them was arrested for obstruction, she said proudly: 'When the Queen is in prison, her subjects must wait outside.' Such was the measure of her moral victory, of her romantic grip on the imagination and the loyalty of Britain's Better Half. Well-bred young suffragettes hissed King George V himself when he went to the theatre, and yelled 'You Russian Tsar!' because he refused to receive a deputation headed by *their* Monarch. Mrs Pankhurst, in eight gruelling years of incarnation of Christabel's blueprint, had not won the vote. But she had become the undisputed Queen of a suffragette state-within-the-state, and the idol of women in every corner of the land. W.S.P.U. headquarters in London were the largest, and certainly the most efficient, of any political organization in Britain.

CHAPTER THREE

PROBLEM CHILDREN

Mrs Pankhurst's younger daughters, Sylvia and Adela, could not be counted among her uncritical subjects, and showed themselves increasingly restless under Christabel's leadership.

Perhaps their rebellion was partly motivated by a natural jealousy of their elder sister and of her near-monopoly of Mrs Pankhurst's affection. But there were other reasons. Sylvia especially had been close to her father, and both she and Adela found it hard to separate the fight for women's emancipation from the wider compassion of the socialist movement. Dr Pankhurst had risked so much to join the I.L.P. which, after all, despite its refusal to fight, as a body, for what it called 'Votes for Ladies', was nevertheless fighting for *all* the underprivileged. Furthermore its leader, Keir Hardie, and later, George Lansbury were the only M.P.s who consistently, and with a noble disregard of their personal interests, championed the women's movement. Christabel's separatist logic began to seem fantastic when, as time went on, and Labour increased its parliamentary representation, it involved the hounding and heckling of Keir Hardie himself. It was painful to see their hero classed with such blatant opportunists as Ramsay MacDonald, who did not disguise his exasperation with militant suffragism ('mere tomfoolery' he called it). Painful, too, to know that suffragette activities at by-elections had the effect of increasing the votes cast for Tory reaction, and to listen to humiliating accusations that the W.S.P.U. was largely financed by 'Tory gold'.

In the absence of her mother and Christabel on a holiday in Switzerland, Sylvia had been alone with her father when he died. She felt it a sacred duty to emulate the self-sacrificing intensity of his socialism. She never forgot his words: 'Drudge and drill! Drudge and drill! If you do not work for other people you will not have been worth the upbringing!' Sometimes this pale, over-conscientious young woman wished she could forget them. Her talent as a painter, or even as an imaginative writer, might have ensured her escape into a personal, blessedly non-political world. Yet ironically enough it was Christabel, with her total, artistic absorption in the game of politics, who achieved this escape. Sylvia, with her temperamental hatred of the 'dirtiness' of politics, was doomed to a lifetime of self-denial. The very frenzy of her renunciation told of the inner tension, the fundamental resentment, which this often renewed sacrifice caused. Christabel and she, though close companions in childhood, had always been psychological poles apart. In the small, stunted garden behind the house in Russell Square, Sylvia sat alone lost in romantic imaginings—fancies which neither of her parents, insulated by their own strictly functional idealism, could share, and which she felt ashamed of indulging. She saw in the sooty patch visions of yellow sands, palm trees, barges glowing with exotic fruits, shimmering fabrics, glittering jewels, all the sensuousness of a life in which agitation, pamphlets, speechmaking and public meetings had no part. But always the gloomy clouds of social concern would roll over to obliterate the vision, and she would accept them as in some mysterious sense a Higher Necessity.

She was invited to stay on in Venice, which she chose as her field of study when she won a travelling art scholarship, but felt bound to refuse. Mrs Pankhurst wanted her to help in the shop, and she must go back to release Christabel for full-time attendance at the university. In 1904 she won a much-coveted national scholarship to the Royal College of Art in London. Even there, on a bare subsistence grant of fifty pounds a year, she risked the wrath of the authorities (how could she be quiet, when her mother and Christabel were already striking blows for women?) by protesting against the obvious prejudice shown against the work of girl students. She even persuaded Keir Hardie to ask a parliamentary question about it. When she sold designs for cotton prints, she sent most of the money home for the W.S.P.U. funds. The two rooms she rented in a poor street in Park Walk off the Fulham Road were used as suffragette headquarters in the struggling early days of the W.S.P.U. Mrs Pankhurst stayed with her, expecting her to take days off from the college to lobby M.P.s, fuming and orating about the woes of women until Sylvia feared for her health, even for the balance of her sanity. The next seven years were a strain. Refusing to go on the W.S.P.U. payroll because she wanted to guard her independence, Sylvia nevertheless spent more and more of her time on W.S.P.U. missions, half fascinated, half repelled by the movement. Sometimes the excitement, the sheer impudent bravado, stimulated her. Often she was depressed by the necessity for such stupid, brawling childishness. Her first imprisonment, in 1906 when suffragettes were still being stripped and searched and treated as common criminals, stiffened her loyalties. But when she found herself at a by-election working with an eccentric, acidulated upper-class spinster who barked that married women were contaminated traitors to their sex, her misgivings rose to sharp anger.

While travelling on suffragette business, she interviewed and made drawings of women industrial workers, in the midlands, in Glasgow, in the coalmines of Lancashire. Their degradation and exploitation made her determined to fight for full adult suffrage: yet she put off the day when she challenged Christabel's policy openly. Occasional artistic or journalistic commissions enabled her to eke out a meagre living, and in 1910 she got a contract to write a swift history of militancy, the *Suffragette*. But the chore which gave her most satisfaction was the designing and (with the help of three ex-art student friends) painting of the decorations for the great W.S.P.U. exhibition at Prince's Skating Rink, Knightsbridge, in 1909. Working on the twenty-foot-high panels which surrounded a hall measuring 250 by 150 feet, she felt momentarily that she was what she longed to be — an artist in the service of humanity, a pictorial warrior of progress. This was an ambition first kindled in her at Manchester Art School by her teacher Walter Crane, the great socialist draughtsman, a friend of William Morris.

The beauty-hungering, anti-mechanical, medieval utopianism of Morris, with its quest for a grand wholeness of nature overlaid by the grime and squalor of a greedy industrialism, was the ideal for which she craved. But there was another, more austere influence: one which strengthened the teaching of her father, and drove her to the end of her days. The influence of Keir Hardie, the Scottish miners' leader and first British Socialist M.P. He it was who befriended her in her first loneliness in London, who got her commissions for articles and drawings, who took her to the Lobby of the House of Commons and pointed out the eminent politicians as they strolled past in all their sleek solemnity, who invited her to his rooms in Neville Court, off Fleet Street. There she saw some of the pilgrims, not only from all over Britain, but from as far away as India; social workers, writers, painters, musicians, people with bold and lovely dreams to whom this craggily handsome man of the people was a legend and an inspiration. Living frugally, cooking for himself, blacking his own boots, Hardie was fiercely determined not to be corrupted by the lures of Westminster, nor lose touch with those for whose sake he had become a Member of Parliament. After leaving the House at midnight, he often went to help at a Salvation Army shelter for the relief of the destitute before returning to his rooms to work at his vast correspondence or write an article. Then after a few hours' sleep, he would go breakfastless to the East End to march with unemployed demonstrators to Trafalgar Square—breakfastless because he would not go fed among starving people.

It was this contact with a dogged, ascetic identification which made Sylvia decide, in 1912, to open her campaign among the Cockney working women of the East End. A hectic three-month tour of the U.S.A. and Canada in 1910, during which she spoke often three times a day, travelled almost every night, penetrated as far afield as Tennessee, California and New Brunswick (and addressed a joint convention of the Iowa Senate and House of Representatives, lectured the Michigan Legislative Assembly and harangued the Judiciary Committee of Illinois and of New York State), though exciting and exhausting, did not stifle the feeling that all this, though it might be necessary, was not enough. She must get closer to the people. The men of the East End had shown their mettle. Could she not rouse the women, and in so doing help to prove that the suffrage agitation was a genuine mass movement and not just a storm in a drawing-room teacup? At first wealthy West End branches of the W.S.P.U. helped her to open centres of propaganda in Bow, Bethnal Green, Limehouse and Poplar. Christabel disapproved. Why did Sylvia bother with these women, so debilitated by poverty and squalor, who had no leisure, even if they had the will or the intelligence, for agitation?

Some of the W.S.P.U. helpers were too ladylike for Cockney audiences; their accents and their mannerisms aroused laughter, even anger, rather than zeal for the cause. So Sylvia, while retaining the services of a small number of leisured suffragette friends (among them Lady Sybil Smith, daughter of Lord Antrim; the Hon. Evelina Haverfield, daughter of Lord Abinger; and, loyalest of all, Miss Norah Smyth, daughter of a wealthy Liverpool merchant), began to train speakers and organizers from among the Cockney women themselves. George Lansbury and his teeming family lived in Bow, and Jessie Lansbury, the wife of one of his sons, was made honorary secretary of Sylvia's group. Charlotte Drake, once a barmaid and sewing machinist, now a labourer's wife and mother of five, was not only a forceful speaker but an efficient organizer. Sylvia paid her thirty shillings a week to employ a domestic to free her for the new struggle: a struggle in which her husband, like those of Sylvia's other star recruits, urged her to take part. Melvina Walker, once a lady's maid and now a docker's wife, was full of richly scandalous stories about High Society and such a popular speaker that she also was paid to work full-time. Others gave their services free, and even, like Mrs Pascoe, who by charring and work at home supported a tubercular husband and an adopted orphan child, went to prison despite desperate financial insecurity. Mrs Nellie Cressall, mother of six and wife of a worker in a paint factory, proved such an apt pupil that she became a councillor and, later, Mayor of Poplar.

Now, for the first time, Sylvia was happy. This was her kingdom, her own creation. Sensing the comradeship and touching trust which clustered about her, she abandoned herself to a frenzy of self-immolation which matched, even over-matched, her mother's. This period began in February 1913, when, after leading a window-smashing raid on a local police station, she was sentenced to two months' hard labour. She was forcibly fed (Mrs Pankhurst never was: it was said that the Government feared the retaliation which might ensue) and released after a hunger, thirst and sleep strike during which she paced, crawled and dragged herself about her cell for twenty-eight hours on end. She was the centre of dramatic mêlées between East Enders and plain-clothes policemen. Her devotees passionately defended their odd, saintly leader—'Our Sylvia' as they called her—and even provided her with a personal bodyguard, 'Kosher' Hunt, a well-known local prize-fighter. Norah Smyth, a sturdy woman, formed a People's Army of Defence and drilled recruits in street fighting tactics. Twice Sylvia was smuggled out to Woodford by Willie Lansbury, a timber merchant, concealed by bundles of wood as she lay on the floor of a horse cart. Her identification with her people was complete when she went to live in Bow. She and Norah Smyth lived with Mrs Jessie Payne and her husband, both shoemakers, in a small house at the back of the hall (converted from a disused factory) which was the headquarters of her East London Federation of the Suffragettes.

Somehow Sylvia found time to launch and edit the *Women's Dreadnought*, a news sheet which printed articles of unvarnished vigour written by her pupils. Her socialist allegiance was openly confirmed when she spoke at an Albert Hall meeting on the same platform with George Lansbury and James Connolly, the Irish Marxist, demanding the release from prison of Jim Larkin, the Irish labour leader. 'Every day', commented the *Daily Herald*, 'the industrial rebels and the suffragette rebels march nearer together.' This was too much for Christabel. Sylvia was summoned to Paris and given the alternative of abandoning her socialist alignment or breaking all official connection with the W.S.P.U. Mrs Pankhurst pleaded with Christabel to spare the East Enders, even if independent, a small subsidy from the ample funds of the W.S.P.U.: but Christabel, plump, rosy-cheeked (by contrast with the prison pallor of the other two), and sensibly ruthless, refused. The pretence of family unity was abandoned.

By now Sylvia's international reputation rivalled that of her mother and Christabel. She had lectured in Denmark and Norway, and was much interviewed and even filmed during a visit to Budapest and Vienna in the autumn of 1913. 'Goodbye, dear Sylvia,' said one Hungarian newspaper on the eve of her departure. 'Take your political childishness to other countries, where other earnest, long-bearded men, with the smell of beer and wine in their clothes, will smile at your hysterical programme ... Everywhere there will be some who for *your* childishness would gladly change their political ripeness—that ripeness which has made clubs and public houses out of the Parliaments of Europe.' It was a pleasant tribute, one which she always treasured and whose advice she never ceased to act upon.

In June 1914, released from Holloway prison for the seventh time in a state of physical prostration—her stamina, for one who had never been robust and was often afflicted with what she called nervous neuralgic pains, was amazing—Sylvia staged a last grand theatrical assault on the Government's nerves and the sympathy of the public. She would, she told Prime Minister Asquith, neither eat nor drink again, *in or out of prison*, unless he agreed to receive a deputation of working women and listen to the case for adult suffrage. Driven to the House of Commons direct from Holloway, she was laid, terrifying in her emaciation, on a stretcher on the pavement. Surrounded by weeping, indignant disciples, she awaited Asquith's answer. He, no doubt influenced by the nearness of a general election, agreed to receive a deputation of six women, including Mrs Payne. He declared himself impressed by their evidence and in favour of a democratic measure 'if we are going to give the franchise to women'. That 'if' was overlooked in the excited talk of a breakthrough, even of Asquith's 'conversion', which followed this unique event. Christabel predictably denounced it as a pseudo-event, another example of Asquith's prevarication. The stern fight must go on until the Government drafted and passed a definite measure. But Sylvia grieved that 'the flame of youthful valour should be expended between the fight against the stomach tube in the narrow cell and the stealthy destruction of the incendiary'. There must be an end to such negative courage, an end to the destruction of fine old churches and precious works of art which were the common heritage of all, and in a sense just as valuable as the human lives which the W.S.P.U. so constantly boasted of not taking. There should be no more violence, she felt – only a holy blaze of self-sacrifice to torture the national and official conscience into submission. Why, she asked, wait for imprisonment before hunger striking? Could not women take the initiative by hunger striking in their hundreds, even thousands, publicly and of their own free will, until the vote was granted? Why confine the glory of rebellion within the jealous, monomaniacal limits set by the young tyrant in Paris, with her walks in the Bois, her elegant friends and her Pomeranian lap dog?

As if Sylvia's uncontrollable impracticality was not enough, Adela also showed signs of becoming a problem Pankhurst, though not yet on so spectacular a scale. As a child, she had suffered from a weakness of the legs which prevented her from walking until she was three. Perhaps to compensate for this physical immobility, she created a fantasy world in which she moved freely, improvising fairy tale dramas in which she herself played all the characters. Very small for her age, she had been a favourite with visitors, whom she would pluck at and badger: 'Shall I tell you a tale?' Despite her unfortunate experiences as a schoolgirl, she began her working life as an elementary school teacher in Manchester, but was soon diverted into full-time work for the W.S.P.U. Unlike Sylvia, she became a paid organizer, one of the most efficient and tireless of all. In October 1906, together with such prominent agitators as Annie Kenney, Mrs Pethick-Lawrence, Mrs Dora Montefiore and Teresa Billington, she was imprisoned after a demonstration in Parliament Square. Her duties took her all over the country. She was arrested in Edinburgh, Glasgow and Dundee, and was one of the first suffragette hunger strikers. A forceful speaker, she was recklessly dedicated, arriving in Scotland in midwinter to conduct a by-election campaign while seriously ill with pleurisy. But her outspoken socialism was an increasing cause of concern to Christabel and Mrs Pankhurst. In Yorkshire she mustered local W.S.P.U. members in support of a strike of textile workers, persuading some of them to act as pickets and writing an account of the incident for the *Labour Record*.

When, in 1912, she collapsed under the strain of constant campaigning, her mother was quick to use the opportunity to rid the movement of a family deviationist who had already antagonized those people of wealth and local prestige upon whom the W.S.P.U. increasingly relied for support and funds. A great believer in the recuperative powers of the open-air life, Mrs Pankhurst offered to send Adela for a course at Studley Horticultural College, Worcestershire, on the condition that she entirely abandoned public speaking. Adela agreed, and eventually got a job as a gardener. But finding that, as a woman, she could not break into the horticultural research work in which she was interested, she longed to return to the women's movement. The only way she could do this without breaking her promise to Mrs Pankhurst was to leave England. Vida Goldstein, an Australian feminist leader who had worked for a time with the W.S.P.U., hearing (probably through Mrs Pankhurst) of her predicament, offered her a job as an organizer with the militant Women's Political Association in Melbourne. Jennie Baines, an old W.S.P.U. colleague and fellow socialist, whose health had also broken, had just left for Melbourne with her husband and children. On February 2nd, 1914, Adela, with twenty pounds in her pocket and the memory of a rather frigid leavetaking in Paris from Christabel and Mrs Pankhurst, sailed for Melbourne on the *Geelong*.

Sylvia and Adela were troubled by family tensions: Harry, the only surviving son, was killed by them. His handsome, even sturdy, physique belied a chronic psychological and constitutional weakness. Deceived by this, his mother set herself against any 'pampering'. His eyesight was bad, but she refused to take him to an optician. His schooling was interrupted not only by physical illness, but by the nervous collapses caused by his pathetic determination to stand up for his parents' socialist principles. Craving affection, he saw little of either of his parents. After his father's death he was left, at the age of nine, in a family of women girding themselves to right the wrongs of their sex and bitterly scornful of men's shortcomings. Anxious to be accepted, he developed into a kind of honorary suffragette. His short life was spent in trying, like a sickly knight-errant weighed down by strange, ill-fitting armour, to prove himself worthy of the four ladies of his nightmare devotion.

Only one of them—Sylvia—appreciated his efforts or his sufferings. When, for a short time, he was at West Heath School, Hampstead, and she a student at the Royal College of Art, she took him to see Keir Hardie, an experience which intensified his vague, poetic knight-errantry. In 1907, when he was seventeen, his mother, in sudden despair at his lack of academic progress, apprenticed him to a builder of her acquaintance in Glasgow, a keen I.L.P. man who, by some freak, had been converted to Buddhism. Work on building sites in the raw winter months made Harry ill, and the business soon failed. Since Mrs Pankhurst was seldom at home in Manchester, he came to London to stay with Sylvia. His mother paid for him to take a course in shorthand and typing, Sylvia and Christabel had his eyes tested and bought him some spectacles. Determined to help his sisters, he worked as an office boy at W.S.P.U. headquarters, chalked pavements with announcements of meetings, even tried to do his share of heckling and street-corner speaking.

Embarrassed by his awkward adolescent zeal, Mrs Pankhurst sought a new career for him. When, after reading William Morris, he showed enthusiasm for a 'return to the land', a renascence of rustic values, she arranged for him to become a pupil-labourer on an Essex farm owned by the millionaire American philanthropist Joseph Fels (a friend of Hardie and Lansbury). The open-air life, she was sure, would make a man of him. Again the combination of heavy manual labour and psychological tension caused a breakdown, this time with worse symptoms, including a serious inflammation of the bladder. He spent several weeks at the London nursing home of Sisters Pine and Townsend, which was now almost entirely given over to the resuscitation of casualties of the militant campaign, of which Harry could fairly claim to be one. A further spell of farm work (against medical advice) soon ended with his return to the nursing home, this time paralysed from the waist down with poliomyelitis. His mother, though distraught by his condition, kept an engagement to speak in America – the first of three tours made before 1914 – not only because the exigencies of the cause overshadowed all else, but because she hoped to set aside some of her lecture fees to pay for Harry's expensive treatment.

Sylvia agreed to watch over him, just as she had agreed to watch over the invalid Dr Pankhurst in the last few weeks of his life. The end came early in 1910, when Harry was twenty, just after Mrs Pankhurst's return from America. Heartbroken, and for once heedless of her personal appearance, she accompanied Sylvia in the funeral procession and asked her to choose a headstone and an inscription. 'Blessed are the pure in heart' were the words Sylvia chose: and in the quiet of her room she read, weeping, a poem written by Harry to a girl with whom he had fallen in love, and whom Sylvia had persuaded to be with him in his last weeks:

I saw thee, beloved,
And having seen, shall ever see,
I as a Greek, and thou,
O Helen, within the walls of Troy.
Tell me, is there no weak spot
In this great wall, by which
I could come to thee, beloved?

Melodrama was the breath of life to the Pankhursts, but Mrs Pankhurst and Sylvia never ceased to be moved, and chastened, by the memory of Harry's disjointed life and tragic death. Dr Pankhurst, with that incurable bibliolatry so typical of Victorian agnostics, had often said to his assembled children: 'You are the four pillars of my house!' Now there were only three: and their conceptions of pillardom, of public service, were drawing ever more widely apart.

THE GREAT WAR
OF THE PANKHURSTS

The First World War shattered many illusions. The illusion of international socialist solidarity; the pretence that women, who for nearly a century, and in their hundreds of thousands, had been the heavy drudges of the nation in home and factory, and for half a century had been developing an administrative expertise second to none in the suffrage campaign, could make no significant contribution to the war effort; the *canard* that the suffragettes were anarchistic hooligans willing to accept not only Tory Gold but secret subscriptions from the Kaiser in the blind anti-patriotism of their sex fury.

Mrs Pankhurst and Mrs Fawcett immediately suspended their own hostilities (though reserving the right to resume them after the Great Emergency if that should prove necessary) and called on their followers to serve their country in whatever capacity offered. There was no point, said Mrs Pankhurst, in continuing to fight for the vote when there might no longer be a country to vote in; the Prussian philosophy, said Christabel, with its *hausfrau* vulgarity, was a monstrosity which every militant should strive, with mingled patriotic and feminist zeal, to destroy. Mrs Pankhurst and Christabel, with the inner circle of W.S.P.U. leaders, notably 'General' Flora Drummond, Annie and Jessie Kenney, and Grace Roe, felt free to place their organizational experience and evangelistic drive at the disposal of the Government. No doubt they could teach it a thing or two—since for some years they had been developing the techniques of total war.

If, in the artificial unity of crisis, even socialists could sneak into the Cabinet, surely the Pankhursts could find a place at least on the influential fringes of the Establishment. By October 1914, no doubt with high-level approval, Christabel was beginning a six-month tour of America—a shrewd move, since her notoriety as the suffragette master mind drew huge audiences to hear what amounted to a ringing plea to Americans to enter the war with the Allies. Mrs Pankhurst urged Britain to sterner endeavours—universal compulsory national service for both sexes, and a stringent system of food rationing to emphasize class unity. In 1915, at the request of Lloyd George, then Minister of Munitions, the tiny but dynamic nucleus of the W.S.P.U. organized a mammoth Women's Right to Serve demonstration in London to help overcome the still lively resistance of trade union leaders to the mass introduction of female labour. In 1916 Mrs Pankhurst, now the acknowledged Queen of Hun-hating British Womanhood, again travelled to America (where on her last pre-war visit, she had been detained on Ellis Island and had narrowly escaped deportation), this time to raise funds for 'stricken' Serbia. She and Christabel had launched an energetic campaign for the rights of small or would-be nations, notably Czechoslovakia. Tomas Masaryk and Eduard Benes, the exiled Czech leaders, were close friends. In Paris, which she did not finally quit until 1917, Christabel kept an eye on Euro-pean cross currents and was in direct touch with Lloyd George, soon to supplant Asquith as Britain's wartime Prime Minister.

In 1917 Mrs Pankhurst, with the encouragement of Lloyd George and an invitation from Russian women's organizations, went to Petrograd and Moscow to urge Russian women to do their utmost to keep their wavering menfolk in the war. She even got an interview with Kerensky, the distraught head of the Provisional Government, and told him to take a firm line with the Bolsheviks. Later she denounced Kerensky as a shifty fraud. With all her fundamental conservatism aroused by the spectacle of deliberate sabotage by professional communist revolution-aries, she returned to Britain to demand armed intervention to aid 'loyal' elements in Russia in maintaining order and resurrecting the war effort. In 1918, again with Government backing, she toured America and Canada to speak on women's war service and the evils of Bolshevism.

The mass hysteria, the overheatedly noble, bloodthirsty civilian ethos of wartime Britain—so different from the weary cynicism of the trenches —made the change from one form of militancy to another easy for the elder Pankhursts. Cooler brains than theirs were overthrown, with far less excuse, by the prevailing emotionalism. Their weekly paper, the *Suffragette*, renamed *Britannia* in 1915, was remarkable for the swingeing virulence with which it expressed prejudices common to much of the pop-ular press, and especially the papers controlled by Lord Northcliffe (who now declared his admiration for the Pankhursts and promised to support votes for women). Hun-hatred was fostered by detailed atrocity stories, scurrilous attacks were made on pacifists (including Keir Hardie), conscien-tious objectors, anyone in favour of a negotiated peace, and the Foreign

Office (riddled with pro-Germans, according to Christabel). Asquith was flayed not only for hounding suffragettes instead of spending more time and thought on national rearmament, but for feeble wartime leadership. Only such uncompromising advocates of the 'knock-out blow' as Lloyd George, Sir Edward Carson (the 'Ulster Pirate'), and William Hughes, the bitter little Australian Prime Minister, escaped criticism. Born in London of Welsh parents, Hughes was perhaps the most outspokenly jingo member of the Imperial War Cabinet, and a great favourite with *Britannia*.

Both he and Lloyd George took a keen interest in the W.S.P.U.'s 'industrial peace' campaign. Begun in 1915 with the financial and moral backing of prominent industrialists (some of whose country mansions had been burned down by Pankhurst arsonettes only a year or two previously), this was run by picked, salaried officials, often ex-suffragettes, from centres in England, Scotland and Wales. Speakers, including Christabel, Mrs Pankhurst, Flora Drummond and Annie Kenney, denounced the insidious machinations of 'Bolshevik' shop stewards who were fomenting class war, and appealed especially to the patriotism of women factory workers and the wives of men still left in key industrial jobs. Men, they said, were more easily led astray by the dangerous, immature nonsense of socialism. Women, more practical and proof against foreign theories, must see to it that men understood their duty and their true interests. The campaigners' efforts were concentrated, bravely and quite successfully, in the areas of greatest industrial unrest — in the north of England, around Glasgow, and in the mining districts of south Wales. Progress reports and spot analyses were sent regularly to the Prime Minister, to whom Mrs Pankhurst had gone in person to describe her impressions of the situation in Russia.

In November 1917, with an eye to post-war political action, the W.S.P.U. was reformed as the Women's Party. In February 1918, shortly after the first instalment of women's suffrage had become law, Christabel urged women to rally to the suffragette leaders who had been the true architects of victory — even though women's massive war effort had clinched it and given the Government no alternative but to see reason. The Women's Party programme advocated 'a clean sweep of all officials of enemy blood or connections from Government depart-ments'; the maintenance of national authority as opposed to international control through a League of Nations; the control of essential industries and the transport system in Britain and the British Empire by officials 'of British descent and wholly British connections'; the alteration of the law of naturalization to prevent Germans and their allies 'from acquiring and exploiting British nationality'. Apart from this new (racial) purity drive, Christabel urged the streamlining of industry by the abolition of trade unions and consultative committees: instead, there should be direct legislation by Parliament on hours, wages and conditions of work. Housing (she recommended large blocks of flats with communal services to reduce domestic drudgery), education, and health services (to include maternity benefits) must be radically improved. Women must get equal pay for equal work, equal marriage and divorce laws, the same rights of guardianship of children as their husbands, and equality of opportunity in the professions and in the public service.

In framing this programme and building up a political machine, it was almost as though Christabel had advance information that the Government, to offset their decision not to give women parity of franchise, intended to give them the right to stand as parliamentary candidates. The Act which made this momentous change was, however, rushed through a mere three weeks before the general election of December 1918. Sixteen women candidates entered the lists, but Christabel, in the new industrial constituency of Smethwick, near Birmingham, appeared to have the best chance of success. The Tory candidate withdrew, leaving her, with Lloyd George's official blessing and the backing of the North-cliffe press, a straight fight against J. E. Davison, a trade union representative. Children were persuaded to sing a jingle which (to the tune of an old folk song) went:

As I went through Smethwick, through Smethwick, through
   Smethwick,
As I went through Smethwick I heard the people say,
You vote for Christabel, for Christabel, for Christabel,
You vote for Christabel, for she will win the day.

Mrs Pankhurst, Flora Drummond and Annie Kenney electioneered vehemently, but Christabel had lost (if she had ever possessed) the common touch, and her authoritarian plans for industry did not commend her to a working-class electorate. It was a close contest, but after a recount, she was defeated by 775 votes, coming nearer to victory than any other woman candidate.

Under the partisan pressures of 1914–18, the Pankhurst family split widened. In the East End, close to the human tragedies and moral squalor of war, Sylvia's socialism became more sharply radical. She continued, though with drooping enthusiasm, to advocate adult suffrage for both sexes, but the attempt to influence the antiquated bourgeois machinery of Parliament began to seem to her a mere waste of time. Parliament, after all, was primarily a place where new and vital ideas were done to death or distorted beyond recognition in the interests of the Master Class. What did Parliament know or care about the miseries of the slums? Why did it not use some of its new quasi-dictatorial powers to set up some adequate welfare services? In the *Workers' Dreadnought* (the change from 'Women' to 'Workers' in the title reflected her changed values), which she herself sold in the streets and in public houses, she acted as a Poor People's Advocate. The meanness and tardiness of separation allowances to servicemen's wives, the plight of old-age pensioners, the wages and conditions of women factory workers, the semi-starvation of the poor, the snooping impertinence of officialdom—all came under her raking journalistic fire. She and her lieutenants, Norah Smyth, Charlotte Drake and Melvina Walker, organized and led a series of deputations to Government ministries. With the help of a handful of voluntary workers, she pioneered social services in Bow—maternity and infant clinics staffed by women doctors giving treatment (and milk) free; a nursery school to look after the children of mothers working in local factories; a toy factory to give work to those who preferred not to make the weapons of capitalist murder; a cost price restaurant which fed a hundred and fifty people at a sitting (with free meal tickets for the destitute).

Nor was this all. On the Bow Council she lashed the timidity of other members, including the well-meaning George Lansbury. She fixed up a toy contract with Gordon Selfridge, and persuaded Nancy Astor to contribute to her welfare fund. Yet all the time, with characteristically reckless integrity, she continued, in print and at street corners, to attack the tragedy and futility of mass murder in the interests of capitalism. In south Wales, on Clydeside, in Leeds and Sheffield, she spoke with those revolutionaries of industry whose doctrines were the special target of the wrath of the Women's Party and Christabel's industrial peace campaign. With Mrs Despard and Helen Crawfurd, a Scottish ex-suffragette, she helped to form the Women's Peace Army, which demanded a negotiated peace and openly deplored the 'bloodthirstiness' of Mrs Pankhurst. Sylvia greeted the Russian Revolution with ecstasy—in her opinion Britain's apathetic masses, drugged by the lies of the Northcliffe press, sorely needed a galvanic touch of Bolshevism, which after all was only socialism which meant business. The stand of the conscientious objectors, and especially of the fifteen hundred 'absolutists' (most of them socialists) who, refusing any alternative service, were repeatedly court-martialled and spent more than three years in prison, she held up as an example of truly heroic militancy.

In 1918, after an inflammatory speech to an audience of Derbyshire miners, she was fined fifty pounds with the alternative of three months' imprisonment. The miners paid her fine, but she did not abate her Bolshevism. Of the decision to allow women to stand as M.P.s she observed in the *Dreadnought* that this was yet another contemptible ruse to tame the forces of rebellion. Threatened by genuine revolution, 'the old fogeys of Parliament and the powers behind them are saying: "We must do something to popularize the old institution. Let us bring in the women." ' What was wanted was not so-called 'new blood' in the House of Commons, but the creation of a system of working-class Soviets on the Russian model.

While Sylvia was impatiently conducting her one-woman communist-cum-feminist band in England, Adela emerged with startling suddenness as one of the most formidable leaders of the socialist-feminist movement in Australia. Australian politicians had shown more wisdom than Gladstone and Asquith. Realizing that a limited vote for women of property would strengthen conservative interests, they did not wait to be harried by suffragists. Between 1894 and 1905 five of the six states had granted the vote. Only in Victoria, traditionally ultra-conservative, was the gesture delayed until 1909. Some thought the delay was due to the activities of the Women's Political Association (W.P.A.), formed in 1903 by Vida Goldstein to support her candidacy for the Federal Senate (she was the first woman in the British Empire to become a parliamentary candidate). Taking over a Pankhurst-type separatism (women needed a party of their own) and that note of spiritual and moral superiority common to many of the feminist organizations which sprang up in Australia after the vote had been granted, she had mixed in a strong tinge of socialism. The W.P.A. paper, *The Women's Sphere*, with its criticism of food standards, penal conditions and the exploitation of women workers, and its support for land taxation, generous old-age pensions and militant trade unionism, angered male politicians who had come to regard 'educated' women as innate Tories. The W.P.A. also (like the W.S.P.U.) aroused the hostility of orthodox women voters who, at the first hint of a socialist feminism, hastened to form the Australian Women's National League to 'combat state socialism and to support loyalty to the throne and the purity of family life'.

The W.P.A. welcomed Adela Pankhurst and Jennie Baines as valuable organizers of its fight to rouse women to a progressive use of the vote, and to shape a political organization which would be a real force in the creation of a radical democracy. Vida Goldstein also hoped to break down the common conception of Australia as a 'man's society', a conception which was the legacy of Australia's origin as a convict settlement, and of the masculine ethos of the pioneering days when the struggle with the soil and the elements left no time or energy for the development of feminist ideals. The W.P.A. programme could not have been better calculated to appeal to its two new expatriate officers. In her fifties, Mrs Baines, who had hunger struck in prison five times in England, had lost none of the revivalist ardour which she had first learned in the ranks of the Salvation Army in Stockport. Adela was soon making her presence felt by the authorities, who, though they had given the vote to some women, resisted any attempt to challenge the male structure of society. As in Britain, magistrates ordered women out of court when 'delicate' cases were being heard. Adela, representing the W.P.A., refused to leave, explaining that sexual offences against small girls, and the way in which the magistrate dealt with them, were of special interest to women. To stay put, time after time, in a courtroom crackling with violent disapproval, must have required real courage: yet Adela's motive, according to some newspaper reports, was mere prurience.

With the outbreak of war the Women's Political Association, renamed the Women's Peace Army, played an important part not only in left-wing socialist opposition to the war, but in the memorable struggle against conscription. In March 1915 Adela, who by now had recovered the self-confidence which had dribbled out of her during her last two miserable years in England, was the star speaker at a Sunday night meeting in the Bijou Theatre, Melbourne. Her subject was 'The War and the White Slave Traffic'. She claimed that war not only crippled souls and national economies, but brought a fearful increase in venereal disease. The passionate exaggeration of this rather unworldly young woman of thirty, small, plump and pleasantly featured, made even Christabel's hyperboles seem cautious. 'Women even now are being destroyed body and soul,' the *Socialist* reported her as saying. 'But the aftermath—God! The thought of it is appalling! With a shortage of men and a huge surplus of women, the latter will be called upon to do men's work, but not at men's rate of pay, and the whole standard of living will be impoverished. There will be only one profession—ever the best paid—open to millions of women, and they will not be to blame if they fall victims to White Slavery.' Only the creation of a Co-operative Socialist Commonwealth of Nations could abolish both war and the exploitation of women.

A pacifist booklet—*Put Up The Sword!*—by Adela was issued in November 1915 by the Victorian Socialist Party (inspired by Tom Mann in 1905 during a long sojourn in Australia) and became a best-seller. In 1916 the W.P.A. threw its full energy into the anti-conscription campaign. The decision of Prime Minister Hughes, the nominally socialist head of the wartime coalition Government, to introduce conscription (in response to an appeal from the Imperial General Staff for more men for the Western Front) caused a drastic split in the Labour movement. It was not only a question of socialist principles and individual liberty, but of what might happen behind the conscripts' backs—was this an excuse to strip the country of able-bodied men and flood it with cheap coloured labour? The ideal of White Australia mingled with pacifism, Marxist anti-capitalism, Irish Roman Catholic hatred of Britain, and embattled feminism. This strangely assorted mass of opposition was welded into a temporarily united force by the aggressive anarchism of the Australian branch of the Industrial Workers of the World (I.W.W.), led by Tom Barker, a young English immigrant, and the suffragette tactics of the W.P.A., of which Adela was now secretary. Tom Barker, the son of a Westmorland farm labourer, had worked as a milk roundsman and tram conductor in Liverpool and spent three years in the 8th Hussars before emigrating to New Zealand. Moving to Australia in 1914, he became editor of the I.W.W. paper, *Direct Action*. When Adela met him he had already been twice in jail, and was about to be jailed again for a sarcastic poster:

TO ARMS!   TO ARMS!

Capitalists   Parsons   Politicians   Landlords

And Other Stay-at-Home Patriots

Your Country Needs YOU In The Trenches!

Workers—Follow Your Masters!

To him the anti-war, anti-conscription issue was a grand opportunity for rollicking social sabotage. He spoke with harsh, roughly humorous jibes, Adela with a quivering idealistic sincerity (which he found rather touching and unsophisticated). But, he remembers, she 'was a good, forceful open-air speaker—you had to be in Australia—and gloriously vehement. When she got really worked up her long, fine hair (just like Sylvia's) used to work loose and tumble about her shoulders'. She did not quail before the rowdiest mobs. She was frequently knocked down and hurled about during 'peace' meetings, and was pelted with eggs by enraged farmers. When soldiers tried to remove the W.P.A. flag from the top of the Guildhall in Melbourne she and Cecilia John, the chief organizer (her companion on nation-wide speaking tours), turned a fire hose on them.

It was during this turbulent period that she met Tom Walsh—in the Melbourne home of R. S. Ross, secretary of the Victorian Socialist Party and editor of the *Socialist*. Working on the Australia-New Zealand run as a seaman, Walsh had helped anti-conscriptionists to escape as stow-aways from the severe military repression in New Zealand. Adela spent three months in New Zealand in the summer of 1916, and the meeting with Tom Walsh, a militant socialist, together with the news that Jennie Baines had joined the Victorian Socialist Party, set her thinking of a break with the W.P.A. This, though socialist in outlook, refused to join the Socialist Party because of Vida Goldstein's insistence that it must remain a separate women's organization. Tom Walsh, born in County Cork the son of a shoemaker, had gone to sea as a boy, and had been in Australia since the early 1890s. In Brisbane he had joined the Social Democratic Vanguard, founded by E. H. Lane and R. H. Ross, and had for long been active in the Seamen's Union. By 1909 he was its New-castle agent, and in 1917 was prominent in a left-wing rank-and-file revolt against union leadership. Originally intended for the priesthood, he was a lapsed Roman Catholic. Toughened by the hardships of a pioneer socialist with three children to raise, he had been saddened by the mental breakdown of his wife, who died in a hospital for the insane. He was deeply influenced by I.W.W. syndicalism (imported to Australia from I.W.W. headquarters in Chicago), which urged the workers to ignore 'reformist' Labour politicians and to concentrate on militant industrial action, on building a new society 'within the shell of the old'.

In January 1917 Adela resigned from the W.P.A. and joined the Victorian Socialist Party (V.S.P.) as an organizer. She was considered a notable catch. 'Miss Pankhurst', enthused the *Socialist*, 'has consented to place her splendid talents and energies at the disposal of the party.' In

February she left for a tour of Western Australia with Jack Curtin, who later became leader of the Australian Labour Party and, in 1941, Prime Minister. They attacked the Hughes Administration for its attempts to repress freedom of speech and of the press, and for the imprisonment of I.W.W. leaders in Sydney. Adela's frequent articles for the *Socialist* were much admired for their dramatic, un-Marxist style. Prophesying another, and a worse, war if competitive capitalism was not abolished, she described how 'the mother, rushing to the small-arms factory, will leave her wailing, sickly child to be poisoned by the purveyors of adulterated food; the girls whose sweethearts' bones are bleaching on the battlefields will make the bullets to render some other girls forlorn, and all the while the disinherited men will be drilling'. She wrote a five-act propaganda play—*Betrayed*—which showed Australia as a militarist state after conscription, with workers dragooned by soldiers from Britain (this for the benefit of the Irish), cheap Chinese labour, and white women forced to prostitute their bodies to Asiatics. The play was a remarkable, if barely actable, compendium of anti-conscriptionist fears and prejudices.

As tireless and versatile, though by no means as intellectually able, a journalist as Sylvia, Adela also edited *Dawn*, a monthly socialist newsletter for children ('We have no religious doctrine to preach, only a morality that is big enough to include all religions and that should give offence to none'). The socialist moral to be drawn from Hans Andersen's story of the Ugly Duckling was that 'Labour wanders about the swamps in the frost and snow, wearing his grey coat, seeing the beautiful swans clothed in the plumage of knowledge, art and science. He hangs his head like the Ugly Duckling, but soon when the springtime comes he will look into the clear waters of truth and see his plumage shining glorious.'

By June 1917, such was her fame, the *Socialist* was advertising a 'plaster bust of Miss Pankhurst' for sale at 3s. 6d. In September she and Mrs Baines were arrested for leading processions of the Socialist Women's League to demand equitable rationing of food and clothes, and for inciting the unemployed to break the windows of a big store in Melbourne, and help themselves to clothes and blankets. The last of four suffragette-style marches on Parliament was dispersed by a police charge and Adela was led away, smiling defiantly, between three burly constables. Tom Walsh addressed a meeting of protest, and on September 30th, soon after her release on bail, married her at the Free Religious Fellowship. This was a surprise to many young men in the socialist movement who had ogled her from a distance, but who felt that somehow, as one of the almost fabulous Pankhursts, she was out of reach, 'above' them. The difference in the ages of the bride and bridegroom – eighteen years – was emphasized by the presence of his teenage daughters, one of whom, Hannah, acted as bridesmaid.

Tried for offensive behaviour, she and Mrs Baines were sentenced to nine months' imprisonment in Pentridge gaol. Her flamboyant courage had made her *the* socialist heroine of the hour. Edgar Ross, the son of R. S. Ross (who was a witness at the wedding), still remembers reciting a poem in her honour written by the socialist 'poet laureate', R. H. Long, after her trial, at which a judge named Notley Moore had presided:

> Adela Pankhurst, what have you done?
> Meddled with poison, handled a gun?
> Nine months' gaol from Notley Moore
> For openly pleading the cause of the poor ...

She was released on medical advice at the end of January 1918, by which time the Government, forced to go to the country on the conscription controversy, had been defeated in a second referendum. 'Reward, not punishment,' *Dawn* commented, 'would have been her portion had our rulers been wise. So it has been throughout the ages: those who labour in a noble cause win scorn and pain as flames draw air ... ' More welcome and more touching to her than such routine party heroics was a letter received from Sarah, the youngest of her three step-daughters, while she was still in prison (for she had married Tom Walsh partly out of compassion for his three motherless children): 'Dear Mother,' wrote Sarah, 'I will not see you on Saturday, so don't worry. You don't know what might happen, you might be out before you can say Jack Frost. I am reading *Oliver Twist*. I think you have read it and it's a very sad story, I almost cried when I read it. But it's nice in the end, how Mr Brownlow adopted Oliver for his son. I think I will close my little letter hoping you will like it, and I also send it with my fondest love, Your loving child, Sally.'

The Rosses could always be relied upon to look after the Walsh girls in emergencies, which in Tom's absence at sea and Adela's on speaking tours, were frequent. Adela's new responsibilities did not dilute her radicalism. In a series of articles for the *Socialist* which closely paralleled

Sylvia's attitude in the *Worker's Dreadnought*, she warned of the dangers of milk-and-water socialism. Rootless, compromise socialism, she wrote, inevitably produced the kind of political apostasy typified by Lloyd George, who in 1900 stood out against the Boer War and in 1917, leagued with the reactionary gutter press and the Tories, was the champion of a fight to a finish involving the murder of millions of innocent workers. Sentimental pacifism, starry-eyed democracy, were useless in what was essentially a class struggle. 'What we want is working-class control, and the basis of this is Industrial Unionism'. All the workers in any given industry or industrial process, skilled or unskilled, should make common cause in a 'hold-all' union, which in turn (as the I.W.W. had preached) would be grouped in One Big Union. Only so could Capitalism be defeated – by the Big Battalions of Labour. 'In Russia the Soldiers' and Workers' Councils rule ... We do not want strong leaders in Parliament, but servants who will carry out the dictates of the industrial bodies.'

Imperialism, she argued, was only capitalism writ large and greedy for raw materials and cheap markets. The League of Nations, damned by Christabel for its enfeebling internationalism, was attacked by Adela (and by Sylvia) because it would be dominated by the Great Powers, intent on clinging to their spheres of influence. It would, in fact, be nothing but a League of Capitalists. When, suffering from mental and physical exhaustion, Adela resigned as an organizer of the V.S.P. in May 1918, she wrote in a farewell message: 'The negation of nationality seems to me so important that I hope the party will ultimately make it the supreme test for socialists. Socialists who are 'loyal' Germans, Englishmen or Australians are co-partners of the capitalist dividers of the human family – Keep the Flag Flying!'

Sylvia too was grumbling at the anaemia of the pseudo-socialists of the Labour Party. 'Somehow or other', she fretted, 'the British Labour movement must be roused to demand the Bolshevik peace terms and the Bolshevik way of dealing with the world.' She criticized the absurdity of preserving and even multiplying the competing nationalisms of Europe. It was all very well for Mrs Pankhurst and Christabel to flow with sympathy for Central Europe and the Balkans. No British interests were at stake there. When they were, it was a very different tale. British troops who were forced to fight for Czech independence might soon be asked to crush Irish or Indian independence.

Small wonder that *Britannia* printed a tart condemnation of the two problem Pankhurst daughters. While in America in 1916 Mrs Pankhurst, being informed of an anti-conscription rally organized and addressed by Sylvia in London, sent a cable to W.S.P.U. headquarters: 'Strongly repudiate Sylvia's foolish and unpatriotic conduct,' it read. 'Regret I cannot prevent use of name. Make this public.'

PART TWO

NEW WORLDS

Emmeline Pankhurst and Dr Richard Marsden Pankhurst in 1879, the
year of their wedding, when she was twenty and he forty

Clacton-on-Sea, *c.* 1890: Sylvia *(top)*,
Adela and Christabel

c. 1910: Mrs Pankhurst leaves a London
railway station on a speaking tour
of the provinces

'Black Friday', November 18th, 1910. Mrs Emmeline Pankhurst and
Dr Elizabeth Garrett Anderson move in deputation to the House of
Commons, London

CHAPTER ONE

FEMINISM'S NEW LOOK

The failure to get a woman into Parliament was a disappointment. Political leaders – all of whom, except Asquith, had, when the vote was granted to women over thirty on a property qualification early in 1918, claimed to have been long-time supporters of women's suffrage – felt able to forget the 'Woman Question' in the priorities of post-war. The press, reflecting an anti-feminist reaction, insisted that women, now that the emergency was over, should return to their true sphere (the home) as wives and mothers or domestic servants. Britain's 'surplus women' were now seen as a menace to returning, jobless heroes.

Individual women and women's organizations prepared to combat this resurgent philistinism. Beatrice Webb, in a brilliant minority report to the War Cabinet Committee on Women in Industry, wrote of the need for 'clearly defined occupational or standard rates for all persons of like industrial grade ... There is no more need for such rates being made to differ according to sex than according to race, creed, height or weight.' The Women's Freedom League (W.F.L.), in which Mrs Charlotte Despard, now seventy-five, continued to take a close interest, and the old non-militant National Union of Women's Suffrage Societies – restyled the National Union of Societies for Equal Citizenship – campaigned for equality of franchise (in 1918 all men over twenty-one had got the vote) and for the removal of the many legal and professional disabilities which still remained. The W.F.L., in its journal *The Vote* (which still bore its old pre-war slogan, 'Dare to be Free'), stressed the need for women prison governors, women jurors and even judges, and demanded that peeresses should sit in the House of Lords in their own right. On this last proposal (not adopted until 1963), Lord Birkenhead, the Lord Chancellor, commented in debate: 'For centuries the constitution of this House has been arranged on a masculine basis. If we are to be abolished, I think I would rather perish in the exclusive company of my own sex.'

The Vote reported in October 1919 that nearly two hundred woman

65

were standing for metropolitan and provincial borough councils – the start of a large and lasting infiltration of local government. To achieve a target of one hundred women M.P.s (necessary to make sure that men did not backslide) it suggested a system of proportional representation, under which some of the rejected women candidates would have been entitled to represent large minorities in various constituencies. It deplored the lack of female representatives to the League of Nations, and also the knighthood conferred on Mr Patrick Rose Innes, the magistrate who, before the war, had earned notoriety in suffragist circles for his lenient view of sex crimes against little girls.

Mrs Despard and Mrs Pethick-Lawrence (who became president of the W.F.L.), had both been Labour candidates in the election of 1918; both opposed the vengefulness of the Versailles Peace Treaty – certain, they argued, to lead to a second world war – demanded the lifting of the blockade of Germany, and criticized intervention in Russia; both attended the International Conference of Women at Zurich in May 1919 (a reunion of those who in 1915 at The Hague had founded the Women's International League for Peace and Freedom), at which a gospel of forgiveness was preached, and French and German delegates embraced on the platform; both spoke up for Irish independence (Mrs Pankhurst and Christabel were demanding that Ireland stay unified under British rule). Mrs Despard returned to her native land as a militant Sinn Feiner, and refused to visit the viceroy (her brother, Lord Ypres), who lived in a state of near-siege in Dublin Castle.

The main trend of feminist activity now was progressive, with a strong tincture of socialism. It had to take account of the wartime revolution in sexual standards. Not only had there been a fantastically high snap-marriage rate, but a sharp increase in gather-ye-rosebuds-while-ye-may promiscuity. The illegitimate birth rate rose by thirty per cent: and it was not restricted to the lower classes, for middle- and upper-class girls, serving in their tens of thousands as factory workers, nurses, drivers and service auxiliaries, shared chaperoneless in this phase of emancipation. The rate of illegitimacy would have risen even more sensationally but for the wider availability of contraceptives, which by the end of the war were being sold by every village chemist. Habits of promiscuity, almost traditional among some sections of the working class, crept upwards, while the practice of birth-control, already established in the middle classes, spread downwards.

The vote, though valuable as a symbol of liberation, could not, argued the new, progressive feminists, reconcile the basic interests of men and women any more than it had abolished the class war. It was urgently necessary to define and promote a healthy sexual relationship. As early as 1917, editing a symposium entitled *The Making of Women*, Victor Gollancz had written of striking a balance between 'the puritanism of Miss Christabel Pankhurst, who regarded every man as a monster, and the even more futile attitude of people who arrogated to themselves the absurdly misleading name of Freewomen'. One contributor, Maude Royden, a celebrated noncomformist minister and before the war one of the ablest of all suffragist speakers, criticized the feminist fallacy that all women longed, or should long, for a career outside the home. The sentimental adulation of the wartime woman-doing-a-man's-job was facile and even insulting. 'A woman who bears children, runs a household and brings up a family is still only an "arrested man" and a perpetual minor; but a woman who can clip tickets on a tramcar is recognized at once as a Superwoman—in other words, a man.' A proper system of family allowances would give motherhood the dignity and security it deserved: and it was up to men to make marriage less of a drudgery by changing their attitude to it. The old notion that women liked to be mastered, that men were active, women passive, was a relic of human adolescence. Sexual partnership was the only wholesome, helpful ideal. Without it, Miss Royden forecast, there would be a disastrous increase in sexual neurosis.

That the sex war was largely the result of sexual tension, itself caused by abysmal ignorance, was the theme of *Married Love*, a remarkable book which first appeared in March 1918, and whose 'frankness' brought its New York publisher a fine for obscenity. The author, Dr Marie Carmichael Stopes, was a strong feminist who refused to take either of her husbands' names, and whose first marriage, to a Canadian botanist, had been annulled for non-consummation. The daughter of an eminent anthropologist, and an outstandingly brilliant student of chemistry at London University, her exotic career had been the pride of women eager to chalk up pioneering achievements. From London she went to Munich to take a Ph.D., and there fell in love with a middle-aged Japanese professor. After three years on the scientific staff of Manchester University, she went to Japan for fossil research, returning to Manchester as Lecturer in Fossil Botany. She also lectured in palaeo-botany at London University.

This steepling academic distinction made Dr Stopes's emergence as the champion of birth control and sexual harmony doubly spectacular.

When she learned of the terrifying frequency of abortion and of infant mortality, especially in the slums, she made it her mission to spread knowledge of contraceptive techniques – the 'Magna Carta of the Poor', as she called it. Her own experience of sexual incompatibility gave her a second grand theme, enunciated in her first book, *Married Love*, a scientific yet lyrical onslaught on the double standard of sexual morality. False modesty, she alleged, was the great curse of the middle classes, banishing pleasure from the marriage bed as an unclean thing, making wives neurotic with frustration, driving men to frequent prostitutes – and all in the sacred name of purity. The answer was not to shut men up in this cage of crippling pseudo-spirituality, but to make men and women realize that they could take pleasure in each other's bodies, experience the joys of mutual satisfaction. This aspect of emancipation had been largely ignored or suppressed by orthodox feminists. Yet political emancipation was, in a sense, superficial. 'The surface freedom of our women', she insisted, 'has not materially altered the pristine purity of a girl of our northern race. She generally has not even the capacity to imagine the basic facts of physical marriage, and her bridegroom may shock her without knowing that he is doing so. Then he is bewildered and pained by her inarticulate pain … '

Man-made pseudo-science had strengthened the hold of pseudo-religious dogma. The widely respected statement of the German gynaecologist Windscheid was typical in its dangerous absurdity. 'In the normal woman,' he had pontificated, 'especially of the higher social classes, sexual instinct is acquired, not inborn. When it *is* inborn, or awakens by itself, there is *abnormality*. Since women do not know this instinct before marriage, they do not miss it when they have no occasion in life to learn it.' Because men had invented this poisonous myth, it was their duty – arduous no doubt, but rewarding – to dispel it. The first necessity was to understand that all normal women *had* sexual desires, and to learn the true law of their ebb and flow – to master, in fact, not women, but the Art of Love. 'Welling up in her', rhapsodized Dr Stopes, 'are the wonderful tides, scented and enriched by the myriad experiences of the human race from its ancient days of leisure and flower-wreathed love-making, urging her to transports and self-expressions … To the initiate she will be able to reveal that the tide is up by a hundred subtle signs … '

Dr Stopes's researches had revealed that it was best to have three or four days of frequent intercourse at the period of strongest desire, followed by some ten days of continence – a fortnight not being, in her opinion, 'too long for a healthy male to restrain himself with advantage'. It was impossible to dogmatize about the frequency of coitus (which she described in close medical detail). That was a matter for individual decision. But she quoted the case of the Queen of Aragon who suggested six times a day as the norm, and commented with roguish relish: 'So abnormally sexed a woman would today probably succeed in killing by exhaustion a succession of husbands.' There was no such thing, she maintained, as a 'correct' position. It was certainly not necessary, though many men, as the upper dogs of society, seemed to think it was, for the man to be on top. Whatever the position chosen, the important thing was for the man to learn to exercise self-control in order to make certain that his partner achieved full orgasmic satisfaction. All husbands should remember that each act of union 'must be tenderly wooed for and won, and that no union should take place unless the woman desires it and is made physically ready for it'. Dr Stopes gave minute instructions as to how a woman should be so prepared.

Birth control—the avoidance of too many pregnancies—would obviously help to keep the vital spark of romance alive. Women must not become dreary domestic drudges. Husbands and wives must not feel that they had to go everywhere together, or they would create an atmosphere of stifling 'fidelity'. Intellectual equality was as important as physical: the man must encourage his wife's mind to develop. It would be a glorious, lifelong experiment, this adventure in delicate, mutual adaptation, but if it was persisted in the joy of that new unit, the pair, 'would reach from the physical foundations ... to the heavens, where its head is crowned with stars'.

Important as Dr Stopes's teachings were to the promotion of a fuller human experience, they could be put into practice only if her pupils had a good deal of money. Without separate rooms (to avoid over-familiarity: separate *houses* were even mentioned) and a quota of servants (what facilities would *they* have for the great quest?), the experiment could hardly be conscientiously conducted. There was a danger, too, that the emphasis on satisfying his wife's desires could condemn a husband to a hell of penitential guilt. The beautiful partnership might turn into a peculiarly unpleasant form of vengeful sex war.

The capitalist distortions of society, wrote Sylvia Pankhurst, must be removed before any true comradeliness, sexual or otherwise, on any but the smallest scale, could be secured. To pretend otherwise was fanciful, selfish nonsense. Dr Stopes's idealization of marriage and her near-condemnation of divorce were suspect. How could love flourish in an institution (marriage) sanctioned by fear of social reprisal and based on the worship of property? Genuine freedom could not prosper in such a prison: there could be only the illusion, or perversion, of it. Particularly awful in her view was the type of middle-class wife who terrorized her husband and talked endlessly about her soul. 'We are not much in sympathy', she wrote in the *Dreadnought*, 'with the typical hustling American business man, but we have often felt compunction for him, seeing him nervous and harassed, sleeplessly, anxiously hunting dollars, and all but overshadowed by his over-dressed, extravagant and idle wife, who sometimes insists that her spiritual development necessitates that she shall have no children. Such husbands and wives are also found in this country; they are a growing product of the upper reaches of the capitalist system. Yet such wives imagine that they are upholding women's emancipation.'

Sylvia was always quick to detect and expose phoney warriors, mealy-mouthed militancy. But she admired the courage of Emma Goldman, the ebullient Russian-Jewish anarchist who, since the 1890s, had been advocating free love—in deeds as well as words—in the United States. After observing the constrictions of some American feminists, hell-bent on staying respectable for fear of tarnishing the cause, Emma Goldman had developed strong views on what she called 'The Tragedy of Women's Emancipation'. In an article published in *The Spur* (an English anarchist weekly) in December 1919, she described how she had seen too many professional female careerists—teachers, doctors, lawyers, engineers—sacrificing themselves on the altar of a stunted conception of independence, scared by 'a horror that love and the joy of motherhood will rob them of their freedom and hinder them in the exercise of their profession ... compulsory vestals before whom life, with its great clarifying sorrows and its deep, constraining joys, rolls on without touching or gripping her soul ... There are too many decaying ruins of the time of the undisputed superiority of man—ruins that are still considered useful.' While breaking old fetters, the women's movement had forged some tragic new ones. Where was the great race of women who could look liberty full in the face, achieving emotional as well as political and intellectual liberation? The narrow, puritanical, spinsterly vision of the bourgeois suffragist banished man, as a disturber and doubtful character, yet women's freedom was inextricably interwoven with men's freedom.

This curiously enough was a point which, throughout the suffrage agitation in Britain, had been made by the well-mannered, ladylike 'constitutionalists' under the leadership of Mrs Millicent Fawcett, who had found herself obliged to repudiate not only the provocative violence of the Pankhursts' militancy, but its stigmatization of men as moral lepers (after all, their husbands, even some of their best friends, were men). Neither Mrs Fawcett nor Mrs Pankhurst, however, were likely to agree with Emma Goldman's belief, shared by Sylvia, that liberty of the body was as important as liberty of the mind, and that only a communist revolution in morals as well as economics could bring true comradeship, the sense of a common cause.

CHAPTER TWO

OLD LOYALTIES

To Mrs Pankhurst and Christabel, licking the wounds of the Smethwick defeat, the sex speculations of Sylvia, Dr Stopes and Emma Goldman were shocking and unseemly. They still believed that women had a mission to cleanse public life. Talk of the joys of sexual harmony, of women's right to the orgasm (subtle part though it might be of a feminist revenge), horrified them. It was a bad example for young women, already, due to the war, accustomed to higher wages, greater mobility and a lamentable freedom from parental restraint. If men would only be decent and control themselves, as women had been forced to do (and a good thing, too), all would be well. It surely could not be right for wives to compete with courtesans. It was women's task to raise men from the mire of carnal passion, not to wallow in it themselves, to shore up a crumbling puritanism, not to disintegrate it completely.

After all, not men but women and young girls were the people who suffered from the so-called comradeship of the sexes. Illegitimate births had increased, and Mrs Pankhurst, though on a small scale, had at least done *something* practical to help. In 1915, in *Britannia*, she had announced the W.S.P.U.'s intention of adopting fifty 'war babies'. In fact, though a War Baby Fund had been opened, money was slow to come in. Obstinate in her good intentions, Mrs Pankhurst herself adopted four little girls who, as she travelled about, were left in the care of Nurse Catherine Pine and of a young woman skilled in the new Montessori methods of child training. Perhaps she wanted to atone for the chaotic yet often harshly conventional rearing of her own children, for the tragedy of Harry which, for the rest of her life, in moments of depression, rose up to torment her. She and Christabel, though damning pacifists, conscientious objectors, shop stewards and internationalists, snipping away at almost every tendril of socialist nonconformity, apparently felt the need for an area of growth, of hopeful experiment, in their lives. They even opened Tower Cressy, a well-equipped Montessori day nursery, in the centre of London, and Jane Kenney, one of Mme Montessori's favourite pupils, was brought over from Washington to run it.

It proved impossible, though, to extend such benevolence into their political judgments or their relations with their own highly individual children. There was Adela in Australia, reportedly on the verge of communism, and Sylvia resoundingly over the verge. It was something to be grateful for that Sylvia did not, like Dr Stopes, talk so freely about penes and vaginas and the erotic importance of stroking one's wife's nipples; but why, oh why, did she have to make a disturbance in the Strangers' Gallery of the House of Commons, calling the Government murderers for spending millions of pounds on intervention against Russia and communist regimes in Germany and Hungary and doing nothing to clear slums or relieve the miseries of the poor? What did Sylvia, poor impulsive creature, *know* of such matters, of the burdens and decisions of *real* power? 'Sylvia', said Mrs Pankhurst in a press statement, 'has the artistic temperament. People with that temperament are peculiarly susceptible to outside influences, and extremists are making use of her because of her name. Now that women have the vote and constitutional means of expressing their political opinions and remedying their grievances, we strongly disapprove of such manifestations. Both my daughter Christabel and I strongly repudiate the action of my second daughter.'

Mrs Pankhurst had been half irritated, half flattered, by a press campaign which hinted that the privileges granted to her by Lloyd George, her special missions to Russia and America and Christabel's prime ministerial backing at Smethwick, had been unmerited, since the Women's Party itself represented an extremism which was now quite out of touch with progressive feminism. Was Lloyd George, demanded the *Sunday Times*, trying by such favours to ensure that there was no resumption of militancy—perhaps to force full adult suffrage or to speed the legislation needed to sweep away the other injustices featured in Christabel's programme?

The truth was simple enough. Mrs Pankhurst believed that women, having won the right to influence political action, should use it to defend and strengthen, not to denigrate or weaken, the country, the way of life, the Empire which was now, in a fuller sense, theirs. Like most rebels, like Lloyd George himself, having fought her way to a position of eminence, she wanted other rebels to have patience, wanted the world to stand still and trust her judgment and be done good to. Her mission must now be to persuade the world—so restless, so childishly rebellious—to have faith in the good intentions and the superior wisdom of its elders and betters; to realize that there always had been, and always would be, Leaders and

Led, Captains of Industry and Followers, Governors and Governed. To her, now a romantic Tory in the Churchillian manner, socialist egalitarianism seemed a mean conspiracy to rob life of its peaks and its blazing personalities. She *had* to resist such anti-heroic drabness with all the vehemence she could still summon.

She too had her vision, her artistic temperament, a strong sense of propriety and composition. So had Christabel. But how could they possibly express themselves if their human canvas was for ever being joggled up and down, or whisked away, or slashed or daubed over by maddening hooligans? It was very cruel, very stupid. So Mrs Pankhurst and Christabel were on the side of those who tried, after the dislocations of war, to bring people back to 'eternal realities', back to a sense of proportion and due station, to restore order in the National Family which Mrs Pankhurst felt she had the right, the vocation, to mother. There were army riots over priorities of demobilization to settle. Tanks and troops had to be brought out to quell the 'Red' Clydesiders, striking for a forty-hour week. Welsh miners had to be disciplined. Britain seemed near to civil war in 1919. Many workers appeared to feel more warmth towards Russia than towards any politician in their own country. Even the police talked of forming their own union, and struck for higher pay. There were many illusions to be destroyed.

It was particularly distressing that not only shop stewards and male socialist rabble-rousers, but women who should have known better, were helping to create those illusions—Maude Royden, for instance, and Mrs Pethick-Lawrence, Mary Macarthur and Margaret Bondfield, the women's trade union leaders (who had both considered the suffrage campaign irrelevant, since the main objective was to get a Socialist Government, which would see justice done to men and women). Margaret Bondfield had even sneered at suffragism as a pastime for frustrated old maids with nothing better to do. Beatrice Webb, too, now so full of socialistic plans and tardy feminist fervour, had been an active anti-suffragist. If these were the women who were considered the new leaders of the cause, then, tired though they were by fifteen years of incessant fighting, it was the duty of Mrs Pankhurst and Christabel to rally the Women's Party for a supreme effort.

Christabel announced that she would stand as Women's Party candidate in the Abbey Division of Westminster, a constituency which would surely relish her anti-Bolshevist, anti-trade-unionist programme more keenly than Smethwick. There was a hope that on the expected retirement of the sitting member, Mr Burdett-Coutts, Miss Pankhurst would be given a clear run. In a series of public meetings she stressed the danger of a return to party strife. A National Government under firm leadership would, by bold and realistic planning, abolish poverty and 'democratize' prosperity. In the concerted strategy of a truly *national* socialism, class warfare, that great waster of human energy, would cease. Rulers would be chosen for their ability and their patriotism alone, whatever their party label or social background. Sentimental snobbery about the virtues of the proletariat was one of the biggest pitfalls of the moment, she thought. Professional people often earned less than so-called working men, and it was monstrously unfair to make special concessions to those who happened to have the horny hands of toil. Instead of bringing more hardship on wives and mothers by striking for higher wages and workers' control, the Miners' Federation should show its social concern by insisting that families were re-housed in dwellings equipped to banish domestic drudgery. Christabel challenged the Miners' Federation to produce a model housing scheme and so prove a constructive interest in social reform: otherwise their womenfolk might be the next to go on strike. In a useful publicity gambit, Flora Drummond was sent to Scotland to present Christabel's challenge to Robert Smillie, the miners' leader.

Christabel was disturbed by reports that representatives of the Big Four at Versailles, and especially President Wilson, were inclined to treat Germany leniently. Women would not tolerate such weakness. What right had Wilson, the man who had kept America out of the war until 1917, to influence European policy? Those countries whose death-roll was the longest should have the loudest voice, and Lloyd George must see to it that they had. 'The Prime Minister', warned Christabel, 'must choose between the great patriotic majority which placed him in power, and the gang of Asquithian pacifists, pro-German money-grubbers who put their pockets before their country, and Bolshevists and cranks of all sorts who compose the unpatriotic minority.'

In April 1919, not content with cross-channel verbal sniping, she, with her mother and Mrs Drummond, went to Paris for a personal interview with Lloyd George. They went armed with the support of Lord Northcliffe, soon to be maddened to the point of insanity by the Prime Minister's wrecking of his political ambitions. 'There are indications', reported the *Daily Mail*, 'that Lloyd George will stop listening to irresponsible pro-Bolshevist and pro-German elements. Miss Christabel Pankhurst had an interview with him the other day and told him frankly that public opinion in Britain would not stand for a policy that puts tenderness for Germany before support of our Allies.' Apart from lecturing the Welsh Wizard, the Pankhursts conferred with their protégés, Masaryk and Benes, rejoicing in the emergence of the desperately vulnerable new state of Czechoslovakia: and renewed contact with 'Billy' Hughes, the Australian Prime Minister, whose main preoccupations (the maintenance of White supremacy in the Pacific and forcing Germany to repay the £364 million Australia was estimated to have spent on the war) probably seemed to them an example of the kind of hard-headed realism which was badly needed in the deceitful corridors of power. There was the pleasure, too, of just being in Paris, their favourite city, and recalling the excitements o Christabel's exile with the Princesse de Polignac, the Baronesse de Brimont, and other people of influence who had befriended her. Mrs Pankhurst showed a flash of her old fire when, with just that suave, unthinking condescension against which she had hurled herself and her shock troops, the French politician Briand remarked that it might be a good idea for his countrywomen to organize a militant suffrage campaign. One did not joke about such things with Mrs Pankhurst. 'I trust', she icily replied, 'that the French Government will take steps to make that unnecessary.'

Her advice was ignored (Frenchwomen did not get the vote for more than twenty years), but this fresh glimpse of male insensitivity may have stiffened her determination to resuscitate the Women's Party. Back in London, she addressed the Kitchener House Officers' Club. Soldiers and women, she said, were the best hope for the future. Women would see that military victory was not thrown away by softness. Germany must be made to realize that poverty and hardship were the price of iniquity. In May, at the Central Hall, Westminster, Christabel stated that the spreading sabotage of Bolshevism, itself the creation of a German Jew, was the work of international gangsters posing as workers and controlled, in some unspecified way, by German financiers – (1919, that year of exaggerated hopes and grandiose fears, was full of such speculations). 'We want none of this scandalous nonsense in this country,' she declared. The League of Nations, so free with pious resolutions, would be powerless, she was sure, to counteract this conspiracy. Only a strong Franco-British alliance, joined by America if President Wilson could be brought to his senses, could do that. If Bolshevism and German militarism were not thoroughly crushed, she foretold (with deadly accuracy, as it turned out) a Russo-German alliance and a second world war in twenty years' time. Signatures on a peace treaty would mean nothing, since Germans recognized nothing but *force majeure*. The price of freedom was eternal militancy.

Christabel found few people to listen to her. The mountebank journalist M.P., Horatio Bottomley, soon to be imprisoned for financial fraud, was preaching much the same gospel of ceaseless vigilance and middle-class woe to a much larger, but fundamentally apathetic, audience of war-weary Britons. The elder Pankhursts were forced to admit that their role as a minor mouthpiece of a waning Lord Northcliffe was not a dignified or even an effective one. The idea of a separate women's political organization found small response. The money was not available to keep the Women's Party going. It was wound up. Tower Cressy was handed over to a committee and converted into a War Memorial Orphanage.

Mrs Pankhurst and Christabel, by some sleight of history's hand, had been shuffled from the centre of the stage. The door of 10 Downing Street was no longer open to them. Lloyd George, so busy ennobling the industrialists whose interests thay had so unstintingly defended, had no honours for them. They had lost, or temporarily mislaid, their *raison d'être*. Their own movement, a spirited but hard-flogged steed, had collapsed beneath them as the trumpets of modified victory sounded; the electorate had rejected them; and they could not easily think of themselves as subordinates. They had never counted costs: they had little money, and it was time to think of making some. Mrs Pankhurst had three adopted daughters (Christabel had taken the responsibility for one) to bring up. True, in March 1920, *The Times* announced that friends and admirers were raising a testimonial fund for them 'in recognition of their work for women's suffrage'. But money trickled rather than rolled in – the middle classes, even the plain rich, were feeling a variety of pinches – and in any case to rely on charity was unthinkable.

Christabel hoped to earn some sort of a living as a journalist. Mrs Pankhurst could still command high fees and big audiences as a lecturer, but only, since it seemed that she was a prophet without honour in her own country, overseas. In the summer of 1919 she rented a cottage at Peaslake in Surrey, near the Pethick-Lawrences, and spent a few months there with the children. Ethel Smyth, who visited her there, found the household a little cloying in tone. Mrs Pankhurst liked to create an atmosphere of quaint innocence as far removed as possible from the harshness of adult politicking. 'In her early youth', wrote Miss Smyth, 'there was a charming witchery about Christabel, and it was Mrs Pankhurst's conviction that the suffrage movement had robbed the world of a great dancer ... Hence it came, I supposed, that the children flitted about like fairies, offered you scones with a curtsy, and kissed their hands to you when they left the room. Having been a tomboy myself, these fairy revels failed to enchant me ... '

But this was a brief, Arcadian interlude. In the autumn, leaving the girls with faithful Nurse Pine, Mrs Pankhurst sailed for New York, bent on earning sufficient money to buy a small house in Surrey and settle down with her family. This, she persuaded herself, was now the limit of her ambition. At sixty-one, she had surely earned an honourable retirement.

As the elder Pankhursts withdrew from the old battlefield, a new and unlikely champion emerged. Virginia-born Nancy, Viscountess Astor, had not exhausted herself in years of agitation and imprisonment. Married to the son of an eccentric millionaire reputed to be the richest man in the world, she had no worries about cash. As her 'war service', she had supervised a specially built hospital in the grounds of Cliveden (the great Astor country mansion in the Thames valley near London), through which twenty-four thousand Canadian soldiers had passed. Used to playing the political hostess on a grand scale, she was already known for her blunt wit and Christian Science to all the leading public figures of the day, including Lloyd George, Arthur Balfour and Winston Churchill. Even the chance to become the first female M.P. fell into her lap. When her father-in-law died and her husband (against his will) succeeded to the viscountcy dispensed by Lloyd George, and had to leave the Commons, she stepped into his shoes at Plymouth — a constituency where she was already popular, appreciated not only for her bracing jollity but for munificent gifts of maternity centres and nursery schools.

Electioneering in November 1919 in a carriage drawn by a fine pair of sorrel horses, she made no pretence of thinking that everyone was equal, and overcame the obvious fact of her wealth by making a joke of it. 'And now, my dears,' she quipped at the end of one speech, 'I'm going back to one of my beautiful palaces to sit down in my tiara and do nothing, and when I roll out in my car I will splash you all with mud and look the other way.' Her press coverage was greater than anything the suffragettes had achieved at the height of their news value. Every antic, every remark, was reported. In America, at the start of the long, earnest grind of her lecture tour, Mrs Pankhurst could hardly open a paper without reading of the success of Lady Astor, a success which she had so keenly coveted for Christabel. And it had come to an American who had not even *tried*, who did not have to think about being a lady or go on about

Germany or work out a statesmanlike programme or live down a suffragette past, who said she did not believe in sexes or classes and that it was only the heart that mattered; a woman who had only marshalled guests and generalled servants entered Parliament between Lloyd George and Balfour, while Christabel faded into the shadows and wrote articles for Lord Northcliffe.

It must have been galling. Yet there were occult consolations. Lady Astor's aggressive platform manner owed much to the example of the Pankhursts. She was fond of quoting Christabel's riposte to hecklers who bawled, 'Don't you wish you were a man?' ('Yes, don't *you*?') She relished Mrs Pankhurst's famous opening to her speeches in the first American tour of 1909 ('I am what you call a hooligan!'), and her reply to the man who shouted, 'If you were my wife I'd poison you', and was silenced with a 'No, you wouldn't. I'd do it myself.' For all her surface flippancy and joyous ego-bashing, Lady Astor was a woman of the Old School, a defender of the Old Moral Virtues none the less outspoken because her own first marriage had ended in divorce, none the less effective because she used the weapon of guffaw as well as the bludgeon of scorn. She even faced ridicule by advocating prohibition, and her parliamentary uniform, a plain well-cut dark-blue suit with a long skirt, worn with a white blouse and a faintly military tricorne hat, set a good example of functional elegance.

And yet ... If only Christabel had possessed some of the easy assurance of all that wealth; if only *she* had been able to give a dinner party attended by the Prime Minister and most of his Cabinet to celebrate her first day in the House of Commons; if only *she* had been able to afford three full-time secretaries ... But the thing had happened. The première had been staged, even though with the wrong star. And Lady Astor herself admitted her surprise that she should be the first parliamentary shot to be fired by the great cannon of the women's movement.

CHAPTER THREE

HANDS OFF RUSSIA!

In almost gleefully cacophonous family counterpoint the Pankhursts continued their attempt to penetrate the wilful, perhaps merciful deafness of the masses. The shafts of their cross purposes, the furious enfilading fire from far Right and extreme Left, were aimed as much at that apolitical, hobby-dulled, sub-human indifference which they could never understand or tolerate, as at each other, or at the ideologies which they seemed to represent. People must not be allowed to wallow in ignorance. They must be forced to take an interest in their destiny. The moral fog in which they loved to grope must be blown away. They must be forced to see, and to choose between, Right and Wrong. For in an age which was busy manufacturing new reasons for inertia in the shape of popularized theories of relativity, comparative anthropology (it all depended when and where one was born), psychological tensions and war weariness, the Pankhursts continued to preach for a decision, and expected human beings to do or die on the old battlefields of absolutism, from which, after a war to end wars and a surfeit of Noble Propaganda, they were in full retreat. Caught fast in the prison of their ingrained, overmastering *concern*, the Pankhursts continued to agonize on behalf of the multitudes outside. Was it possible, they cried through bars of iron sincerity, to live for bread alone? Was it possible to exist without a cause?

But whereas Mrs Pankhurst, in the sacred name of tradition and continuity, made ready to defend the broken ramparts of the *ancien régime*, Sylvia, in the name of a shining future, prepared to blow them up and build a new city. Her vision was one of aesthetic arson, of what she called the 'pure white flame' of communism beautifully devouring the old rubbish, clearing the way for a fresh Creation. The months after the Armistice were full of such longings, the dreams of cultured idealists claiming that they were the dreams of 'the people'. The artist Frank Brangwyn, writing in the *Daily Mail*, insisted that 'our returned fighting men demand ... a new and more beautiful London. But before we can reconstruct we must destroy ruthlessly. We must tear down Slumland

and remodel Suburbia ... Our City Beautiful must be a city of happy homes housed in noble buildings ... worthy of its splendid sons.'

For Sylvia, everything that went on in the Old Establishment, and especially in Parliament, the fraudulent heart of it, was a kind of disgusting, galvanic dance of death. The entry of women into Parliament, and especially of Lady Astor, that offensive reactionary who dared, from her lap of luxury, to lecture the poor on their duties, was but a tiresome charade. She herself, for this reason, had refused an invitation to stand as a Labour candidate in Sheffield in December 1918. Since 1917, though often pelted with refuse by angry East Enders, Sylvia and her small band of disciples had been exhorting the poor not to trust the Government, but to follow the example of their Russian brothers, to rise up and smite it, to form themselves into Soviets; to stop believing the lies of the plutocrat press and realize that their sons and husbands had died in a dirty capitalist squabble; to gird themselves for the *real* fight for freedom, which was just beginning.

Her East London Federation of the Suffragettes had become the Workers' Socialist Federation (W.S.F.), the *Women's Dreadnought* had been renamed the *Workers' Dreadnought*: her objective was no longer equality of franchise but world-wide revolution, the transformation of the denizens of the slums into citizens of the world. Readers of the *Dreadnought* puzzled over the connection between the Bolshevik Revolution, reported at ecstatic length, and a reduction in rent, an increase in food rations or a rise in the old-age pension. Sylvia might be impatient of local and national authorities (who wasn't?), but 'they' would always be there. 'They' might have to be pushed and prodded by the likes of Sylvia or good old George Lansbury (himself, in Sylvia's opinion, too willing to accept 'their' permanence), but 'they' could never be got rid of. That was the long and the short of it. As for the revolution, it would make only a bigger mess. Better the devils one knew than those one did not. What guarantee, after all, was there that the revolution would not throw up an even harsher, because more idealistic, set of taskmasters? Ideals were dangerous things, all right for Sundays (if you went to church) and elections, but only fit, like best clothes, for moth-balls in between times. Frustrated by this attitude, the result (she tried to remind herself) of centuries of capitalist repression and distortion, Sylvia looked for portents of hope elsewhere. The Russian People's Information Bureau which she opened in July 1918 to disseminate, in pamphlet or lecture, the message of the *Dreadnought*, found readier listeners and readers among the miners

of south Wales and the midlands and north of England, and in the dock-
yards and factories of 'Red' Clydeside. David Kirkwood, a leader of
Glasgow engineering shop workers ('the greatest Huns in Christendom',
he had thundered during the war, 'are the capitalist class of Britain'), and
John Wheatley, the brains of the Scottish I.L.P. (soon to be lost, with
Kirkwood, in the harlot toils of Westminster); William Gallacher, the
sharp little Scottish shop steward; John McLean, the fiery Scottish schoolteacher who, with Gallacher, was the driving force of the Marxist
British Socialist Party; A. J. Cook, the militantly Marxist miners' leader;
these were the people who spoke her kind of language, proletarians who
seemed to have struggled free of resignation and brute apathy.

The shop stewards' movement, formed in 1915 in Glasgow to offset the
collaborationism of official trade union leaders, was an important nucleus
of resistance: the fact that the Women's Party spent so much energy
denouncing it was evidence enough of its desirability. As for the Women's
Party—jingo, imperialistic and reactionary though it was—Sylvia recommended her socialist colleagues to imitate it at least in its efficiency,
determination, and refusal to be intimidated by the logic of its own
convictions.

The tactical demands of revolution had belatedly altered Sylvia's
attitude to the war itself. Vile and futile it might be, but by the second
half of 1918 it was doing a fine job of social demolition, *forcing* the workers
of Europe to take action. The Soviet example was being followed in
Hungary, in Poland, in Austria, in Germany itself—crippling industrial
strikes, a growing hatred of bourgeois politicians and pseudo-democracy,
a dawning glimmer of workers' control. If the war could have lasted a
little longer, even at the cost of the death of a few thousand more soldiers,
might it not have done the work of a thousand thousand agitators in
bringing the co-operative commonwealth to life? Might it not, in its last
throes, have redeemed the ugly waste of the previous four years? Christabel's fight to a finish had its baleful attraction on the Bolshevik side
of the fence.

But when the Armistice and the interventionist war against the
Soviets in Europe and Russia were launched, Sylvia switched her energies
into the Hands Off Russia movement. This, though it was a temporary
rallying point for progressive opinion of many nuances, was powered by
a communist core—as yet not organized into a party or bulldozed into
orthodoxy—which alone was willing to make real sacrifices of time and
effort for it. When, at the end of December 1918, President Wilson drove

down Pall Mall on his way to Buckingham Palace, Sylvia's contingent was there with appropriate posters: HANDS OFF RUSSIA! HANDS OFF THE WORKERS' AND SOLDIERS' COUNCILS OF GERMANY! WILSON, STOP YOUR SECRET CONVERSATIONS! Wilson was out of favour with the Pankhursts. To Christabel he was a feeble and enfeebling idealist, to Sylvia he was the man who clapped a hypocritical mask of liberalism over the Allied Powers' murderous repression of true progress. She claimed in the *Dreadnought* that one particularly piercing shriek (perhaps from Melvina Walker) of 'Hands Off Russia!' made Wilson turn his head. But the blockade went on. 'With your armies and navies occupying the ports of a people struggling to establish a new civilization', she raged, 'you seize their ships, stop their commerce, take possession of their railways and factories—then send relief to feed them! What a programme!'

'I am proud', she said, 'to call myself a Bolshevist.' She put no trust in opportunist Labour politicians or Fabian socialists like Ramsay Mac-Donald and Sidney and Beatrice Webb, who were as scared of the possibility of real revolution (which would mean their political extinction) as any Tory. Ramsay MacDonald, who had spent an uneasy war alternately running with pacifist hares and hunting with militarist hounds, was anathema to Mrs Pankhurst. To Sylvia he was just a bogus bogey, whose reputation as a radical was deliberately inflated by the Government, 'lest if it left him to sink into obscurity, the workers should choose heroes for themselves—wild revolutionary fellows like Gallacher and John McLean.'

The precarious hold of militant Marxism, of Soviet resistance, in Germany was broken when in January 1919 its great leaders, Karl Liebknecht and Rosa Luxemburg, were murdered in Berlin by anti-communist, anti-Semitic army officers, murdered (it was strongly suspected) with Allied connivance. Shocked and angered by the news, Sylvia spoke with even more than her usual vehemence at a Hands Off Russia rally in Farringdon Street, London. The meeting demanded industrial action—a general strike to force the Government's hand. Indian and Irish nationalists hotly pressed the injustices of their countries. 'We have only one life in this world,' pleaded Sylvia. 'Can't we see the revolution in our time? Can't we live in it and enjoy it? I want to see the beginning. I want to see something done. When are you going to begin? If the police came here tonight and killed some of us, I think it would do a great deal of good!'

Even that like-minded audience laughed at this Pankhurst martyr urge: and there was no general strike. Sylvia had to derive comfort from sporadic outbreaks of industrial militancy in south Wales and Clydeside.

Discontent in the army and navy over pay cuts and priorities of demobilization also seemed to offer a promising field for propaganda. The *Dreadnought* manager, Harold Burgess, meeting two Irish Guardsmen in a pub
in the Strand and hearing them express some liquored disapproval of
British policy in Ireland, invited them to his home, supplied them with
pamphlets on How to Form Soviets in Britain, and gave them a small
bribe to spread the message in their barracks. The men told their officers
of this attempt to suborn them, and, under instruction, trapped Burgess
into correspondence by writing a letter which said: 'We are getting on
well and have a large number of followers. Pamphlets are being swallowed
up and the men's blood is boiling. We can get hold of some machine-
guns ... ' A week later, Burgess was arrested and tried at Bow Street
police court. The guardsmen described an interview with Miss Sylvia
Pankhurst in the Fleet Street office of the *Dreadnought*, during which they
were informed that the guns would be smuggled to revolutionaries in
Ireland (though they conceded that 'Miss Pankhurst did not seem
entirely happy about the guns'). Amid cries of 'Courage, Comrade!' and
'Dictatorship of the Proletariat!', Burgess was sentenced to six months in
jail, and so became one of Britain's first Bolshevik near-martyrs.

Still, by the skin of her teeth, at large, Sylvia accepted an invitation to
talk to the Irish Women's Franchise League in Dublin, and startled her
audience by urging them not to tinker with parliamentary reformism,
but to make propaganda for direct action, the seizing of farms and
factories by the workers, for instance, and the setting up of Workers'
Soviets. Irish nationalism, she observed, though it might have the *appearance* of being revolutionary (like the pre-war suffragette movement), was
in fact riddled with reaction: it must rid itself of the blinkers of pseudo-
democracy and get into line with the forces of significant radicalism.
Appointed English correspondent of the *International Communist*, whose
editorial offices were in Petrograd, Sylvia contributed a series of articles
on the iniquities of blockade and intervention. This new activity was
widely reported in English newspapers, which also headlined the arrest
of a Norwegian journalist who had brought over three hundred pounds
from Sylvia's Norwegian fans (who remembered her from her suffragist
lecture tour of 1913) to buttress the chronically shaky finances of the
Dreadnought.

At about this time, the tiny band of forlorn hope of which Sylvia was
the most publicized member received a sensational new recruit. Speaking
in Glasgow, the best-selling humorous novelist, Jerome K. Jerome, of

Three Men in a Boat fame, announced his conversion from Conservatism
to Bolshevism. He too was impatient with Fabian socialism. How long,
he demanded, was Labour going to sell its bone and muscle and brain to
the enemies of Labour? If a man got on in the Labour movement he was
usually flattered and bribed by the capitalists into a treacherous tameness.
Women toiled in factories for a pittance, while it took an able-bodied
man and a three-thousand-guinea motor car to take one rich woman
shopping. A miner was lucky to get four pounds a week for his labour,
while another man got two hundred thousand pounds a year for allowing
him to work. It was no use looking to Parliament for radical reform—
Lloyd George, Bonar Law, Sir Edward Carson, and other pirates of the
Establishment, took no notice of it. If they had the financiers and the Press
Lords on their side, they could ignore Parliament, which merely endorsed
their decisions. Parliament was never meant to serve the common people:
it had been fashioned by the commercial classes to secure themselves
against feudalism, not to help the working classes to liberate themselves.
The working classes must forge their own instruments of government.

This was just Sylvia's point of view, and in July 1919 she set it out in a
long letter to Lenin. The socialist movement in Britain, she complained,
was too full of compromisers. Official trade unionists were so rotten with
collaboration that they could hardly be counted as socialists at all. The
I.L.P. was honeycombed with Christian Socialists like George Lansbury
(she was more and more critical of her old comrade) and pathetic office-
seekers like Ramsay MacDonald. The British Socialist Party and the
Socialist Labour Party (whose main strength was in Scotland) were both
inclined to apply for affiliation to the bourgeois Labour Party and put up
candidates for Parliament. Only her own Workers' Socialist Federation,
the Shop Stewards' Movement, and the South Wales Socialist Society
stood out firmly against compromise.

Lenin's reply, though tactfully phased, was critical. The Shop Stewards'
Movement, which at least had direct contact with the workers, and could
foment and exploit strikes, was clearly the most promising group. Some
of the others, including the W.S.F. were, he feared, too small, too
intellectual, too bourgeois in a sense, to be in touch with realities. To
split socialist unity and make difficult the formation of a unified Communist Party over the issue of whether or not to affiliate to the Labour
Party and take part in Parliament, seemed to him mistaken, a sign of
political adolescence. Some would stand clear, some would not. There
was room for both. 'We Russians,' he concluded smugly, 'who have lived

through two great revolutions, know the importance of carrying on Soviet propaganda from inside the bourgeois parliaments.'

Sylvia bristled at the accusation of amateurism. How dare this pedant assume that *Russian* experience was the only experience that counted, that *Russians* were the only people who had thought deeply about the tactics and implications of a new society? Had Lenin ever been forcibly fed or paced a cell for twenty-eight hours, in a state of delirium, to secure release? Had he not heard of the British Chartists, who had striven confusedly but heroically for a New Deal before Russia had begun to stir in her Tsarist sleep? Had he not heard of her two great mentors, William Morris and Edward Carpenter, the conscience-stricken artist and the gentle yet blazing anarchist? Theirs was no slide-rule socialism, obsessed with industrial statistics and petty machiavellian political intrigue. They had seen that people needed beauty as well as mechanical efficiency, had souls as well as bodies to save, that the battle was against the philistine ugliness of capitalism as well as its political and economic tyranny. They had preached the desirability of a clean cut, a frontal, bannered confrontation of good and evil, had described with vivid scorn the snares of gradualism. To maintain that the old political and social institutions were in any sense necessary was (Carpenter had written in his essay on *Non-Governmental Society*) 'the same as to say that because to a Chinese woman of rank foot-bandages are necessary, therefore women cannot exist generally without foot-bandages. We have to realize that our present social forms are as ugly and inhuman as a club foot.' Was Lenin content to use power seized on behalf of the workers to tie them more closely to the machines of a new and crushing industrialism? 'Nature', Morris had written, 'will not finally be conquered till our work becomes part of the pleasure of our lives.' Of course Russia was under siege, fighting for survival, struggling for bread alone. But had Lenin a vision of something more than an ascending spiral of brute material prosperity?

Sylvia's hot resentment was somewhat cooled by a six-month whirl round the socialist centres of Europe. She knew that she left her beloved *Dreadnought* in safe, competent hands. Norah Smyth could be relied upon to supervise the W.S.F. offices, to raise funds or provide them from the private means which she continued to make so generously available. But there was now – and it was a development not entirely to the liking of the ultra-feminist Miss Smyth – a new member of Sylvia's inner circle of trusties. Silvio Corio was an Italian left-wing socialist whose views had forced him into exile at the turn of the century. For nearly twenty years he had waged a bitter propaganda war on the Italian Establishment, first from Paris, then from Holland, then, when the war came, from London. Eight years older than Sylvia, he was a revolutionary veteran used to starving for an ideal, a brilliant political journalist skilled not only in research and writing, but in the setting up of type and lay-outs for a whole succession of clandestine presses. Their meeting in that underworld of agitators and refugees which was the breath of life to Sylvia was a meeting of souls deeply kindred, and one full of consequences for the future direction of her daemonic enthusiasms. Corio it was who took over the management of the *Dreadnought* in her absence, and gave her introductions to the leaders of the Italian, Dutch and German socialist movements.

The authorities, to whom she was a marked woman, had confiscated her passport. She had little money. But she was smuggled over to the Continent by methods perfected by the ingenuity of Corio and his many fellow refugees, and crossed the Alps *on foot* to be present at the Italian Socialist Congress at Bologna in September 1919. From there she made her way to a socialist conference in Amsterdam, and then made contact with the Spartacist communist groups formed in Germany by Karl Liebknecht and Rosa Luxemburg. She came back dismayed at the ineffectiveness of official socialism and convinced that strong forces of reaction, which (unlike the Socialist parties) would take swift and drastic action, were gathering in Italy and Germany. She hurled herself with redoubled zeal into her fight to persuade the East End dockers to refuse to load ships with war material bound for Poland which, now that the official Allied intervention forces had been withdrawn, was being supplied with arms to continue the war against the Worker's Fatherland. Melvina Walker and Norah Smyth, docker's wife and businessman's daughter, were joined in the campaign by Harry Pollitt, later secretary and chairman of the Communist Party of Great Britain, but then London District secretary of the Boiler-maker's Union. Pollitt was sacked for telling men to stop work on the conversion of two large barges into munition carriers. He, Sylvia, Norah Smyth and Melvina Walker spoke day after day outside the dock gates and distributed thousands of secretly printed copies of Lenin's *Appeal to the Toiling Masses*.

Their incessant efforts brought success when in May 1920, with the full backing of the Dockers' Union, men refused to load the *Jolly George* with a cargo of crates labelled 'O.H.M.S. Munitions for Poland'. This action brought a belated admission from Bonar Law that the Government (despite frequent denials) had been sending munitions free to Poland since October 1919. It also resulted in an emergency conference of the Trades Union Congress, the Labour Party and the Parliamentary Labour Party, which warned the Government that 'the whole power of the organized workers will be used to defeat this war'. 'Well done, London dockers!' Sylvia exulted in the *Dreadnought*. 'British Workers Are Waking Up At Last!'

But already there were accusations that Sylvia was too fond of hogging the headlines, that she was using the communist movement as a vehicle for her own outsize personality, and sabotaging the attempt to build a unified party by rejecting Lenin's advice to compromise over 'non-essentials'. She made matters worse by refusing to take part in a unity conference scheduled to take place in the Cannon Street Hotel, London, in July 1920. Not only that, but in June 1920 she jumped the gun by rechristening the W.S.F. 'The Communist Party (British Section of the Third International)', and presenting it in the *Dreadnought*—far the most widely read communist publication—as the only genuine nucleus for an honest, militant communist movement. This heretical stroke was openly rebuked by Lenin in a message to the convenors of the July conference—at which wealthy Dora Montefiore, who had fought briefly alongside Sylvia as a suffragette (and joined her again on the platform in June 1919, this time to lecture the Sheerness Women's Labour Party on 'The Class Struggle from the International Standpoint'), was elected to the provisional executive committee. Ellen Wilkinson, a former suffragist organizer (and Minister of Education in Attlee's Labour Administration of 1945) was a Guild Communist delegate.

Lenin renewed his literary bombardment (with Sylvia and William Gallacher as the two main targets) in a long, heavily sarcastic essay called *Left Wing Communism: An Infantile Sickness*. Noble hatred and sublime intentions, he wrote, were not enough. Politics—the manipulation of public opinion—was an art which had to be learned, and where better to learn it than in the House of Commons from such hardened, subtle professionals as Lloyd George? Lloyd George was not too proud to learn from Bolshevists: they should show the same realistic humility. Britain, like Russia, would have to pass through a phase of bourgeois socialism. To refuse, like Comrade Sylvia Pankhurst, to come to terms with this fact, was to show the petulant impatience of 'an obviously impotent minority'. Experience of a 'Labour' Government would no doubt disillusion the working classes and clear the way for Communism. The point was to hasten the process by persuading electors to vote for Labour candidates, and only to put up Communist candidates where there was no danger of weakening the Labour vote. Also, British communists should apply for affiliation with the Labour Party. If they were rejected, that would be a good propaganda point. 'Comrades Sylvia Pankhurst and William Gallacher are mistaken if they think that this is the betrayal of communism, the abandonment of the struggle against the social traitors. On the contrary, the communist revolution stands to gain a great deal by it.'

Lenin attached considerable importance to the 'parliamentarian controversy', for it threatened to split communism in Germany and Italy as well as in Britain. Here was the start of that insistence on 'monolithic' strength, that labyrinthine, inquisitional pursuit of unity through the liquidation of heretics and 'visionaries', which led to the great purges of the 1930s, the flexibly inflexible adherence to the Moscow line, the bureaucratic apotheosis of Stalin. Yet this vicious onslaught on intellectual vitality was led by the most rigorously intellectual ruling clique the world had yet seen. To fight for an idea while killing idealism seemed to Sylvia a fearful and chilling contradiction in terms. She remembered how Christabel's similar reasoning had twisted the suffrage movement out of all resemblance to its first generous image. She remembered the barren years of heckling and scuffling, and her longing for a straight, clean, open fight appealing to the best, not the worst, in human nature, burned hot within her. She knew that Lenin's thesis would be one of the main items on the agenda at the Second Congress of the Third International opening in Moscow on July 15th; and though denied visas by the embassies of the countries through which she had to pass en route, determined to attend and argue the matter out with Lenin.

She crossed the Arctic Sea in a small Norwegian fishing boat, and was violently sick most of the way. On the train to Petrograd she saw many Russians wearing British and French Army uniforms, relics of the war of intervention against which she had striven so wholeheartedly. The train was besieged at halts by peasants bartering country produce for tobacco, tea, sugar, needles, cotton thread. In Petrograd, between trains, she noticed a superabundance of slogans, shops empty of food and streets so empty of traffic that weeds grew a foot high. In St Isaac's Cathedral, where in 1917 her mother had gone to admire the glowing icons and the marvellous singing and to lament over the agnosticism in which she had reared her children, Sylvia, while enjoying the architecture, noted with approval that there were few worshippers, that the altar cloths looked dirty, that only a few frowsy artificial flowers were placed before the images of the Virgin and Child.

At the entrance to the Hotel Internationale, where Mrs Pankhurst had stayed in the royal suite, a girl sentry with a sunburned face filed passes on the bayonet of her rifle, and Sylvia ate a meal consisting of a small dollop of mashed potatoes and gravy followed by watery tea. Moscow was oppressive, its sultry heat made worse by the drifting haze of a great forest fire on the outskirts of the city. Against her proletarian will, St Basil's Cathedral, with its gilded onion-shaped dome, fascinated her. She wanted to sketch the priests, with their rich robes and long matted hair, but soon plunged into the bustle and chatter of the red-bannered Djelavoi Djor Hotel, where the conference delegates were housed, moving about in national droves, looking rather grotesque in the loose Russian peasant blouses with which they had been issued. The main topic of conversation was Lenin's attack on the anti-parliamentarians, and the lobby buzzed with fresh excitement when the news of Sylvia's arrival spread. The conference was nearly over: only a few days remained. The British delegation of nine, which included Gallacher and Helen Crawfurd (ex-suffragette and leader of the Women's Peace Crusade of 1917-18), had been rebuked in open session by Lenin. What, he chided, was the use of *having* an International if every little fraction was going to decide policy for itself? Was it possible, even at the eleventh hour, that an impassioned plea from Sylvia might sway the decision against Lenin, leave national parties free to develop their own tactics, make the conferences of the Third International democratic debates rather than Russian briefing parades?

Sylvia was not given a chance to speak in open session. Lenin sent for her almost immediately to take part in the Commission on English Affairs then sitting in the Kremlin. She was led through the Throne Room to one of the Tsar's private apartments. Lenin's charm worked powerfully upon her. He greeted her eagerly, and seemed 'more vividly vital and energetic, more wholly alive, than other people'. Short, broadly built, quick in thought and speech, his sheer dynamism was overwhelming. 'Brown hair closely shaved,' she noted, 'beard lightish brown, a rather bright complexion that looks sandy because it is tanned and freckled by the hot sun. The skin of the face and head seems drawn rather tightly. There seems to be no waste material. Every inch of his face is expressive.' The picture of an arrogant, bureaucratic bully which she had formed vanished in the presence of the original. The pathos and courage of the revolution, too, was pressing upon her, changing her perspective. Trotsky had just returned from the still active Polish front. The White invaders were still on Russian soil. Sylvia understood the need for discipline, the obsession with unity, and was suddenly willing to minimize her forebodings. The great clash did not take place. For the moment, Sylvia was utterly disarmed.

Lenin gave her the place of honour on his right at the committee table. She and Gallacher restated their objections to his thesis. Lenin bantered them. Why so heated? It was only a question of tactics, of the most expedient way to put principles into practice. Communism could always use integrity like theirs, but zeal must be tempered with plain cunning. If the decision to affiliate to the Labour Party and infiltrate Parliament proved wrong, it could always be changed. Left wingers like Sylvia would be needed to keep a close watch on the 'tacticians' and see that first principles were not swamped in a sea of expediency.

Sylvia could not quarrel with this. Lenin was able to announce to the conference, assembled in the Throne Room, that agreement was now complete: even the British, even Sylvia, had seen reason. Delegates sprang to their feet singing the Internationale, seized Lenin and hoisted him on their shoulders. 'He looked', wrote Sylvia, 'like a happy father among his sons.' She went on a lightning conducted tour of workers' rest homes, model schools, hospitals, a few factories. She protested about the fly-breeding refuse tips outside a maternity ward, but again reminded herself that Russia was in its seventh year of war and struggling to lift the huge burden of centuries of feudalism. She could not, however, prevent herself from commenting sharply when an American comedy film was shown at a children's party she attended; but was told that 'a shortage of Russian films had prevented the authorities from altogether banishing the capitalist product'. There was such a shortage of leather, too, that many people, she noticed, wore bark shoes—she saw a pair catch fire while a man was hammering red hot iron in a factory forge.

Sylvia did not meet Emma Goldman, whose enthusiasm for the Workers' Republic had turned rapidly sour. Emma, the ardent anarchist, who (with hundreds of other political undesirables) had been deported from the United States, had been given the ludicrous job of touring the provinces to collect exhibits for the Museum of the Revolution in Petrograd. This kept her away from favoured visitors. Otherwise she could have told Sylvia about the fate of Russian anarchists, men and women who had risked everything for a new society, gaoled and even tortured and shot for their opposition to the Bolshevik tyranny. She could have told her about Prince Kropotkin, the great anarchist teacher who returned from thirty years of sedate exile in the London suburb of Bromley to find himself confined to one room, under constant surveillance by secret police, his papers searched, forbidden to write or otherwise communicate with the seething world outside. Emma Goldman could have told her — but perhaps, in the still dazzling aura of Lenin, she would not have listened — that despite all the bloodletting and the fancy scientific jargon, the Bolshevik revolution was just another piece of tricky political scene-shifting.

Unlike Emma, who had intended to make her home in Russia and was now trying desperately to get out and wondering if she would ever be allowed to, Sylvia was just a tourist (her mission completed, her fears temporarily quieted) in a hurry to get back to the fight in England, anxious to make every possible allowance for her comrades. She contrasted education in the Workers' Republic, shorn of the tawdry trappings of monarchy — education for an ideal, with the 'superficial, spurious Empire-worship and snobbery of elementary schools in Britain', and the 'selfish, mercenary cult of "getting on" taught by parents anxious for the material welfare of their children in a cruel, competitive world'. She was impressed with the health of the children she saw, the priority for food and milk which they had. She agreed with the woman in Petrograd who, as they watched communist troops, clad in a weird assortment of old clothes and cast-off capitalist uniforms, entrain for the front, turned to her and said: 'Why do the capitalists fight against us? It is cruel to force the young men of Russia to fight for progress against the entire world ... '

At Murmansk, she and Gallacher and ten other delegates of various nationalities stood on the deck of the Norwegian fishing boat waving goodbye and singing the Internationale. The sea was so rough that the skipper put into a little harbour in the north of Norway. Sylvia and Gallacher were rowed ashore, clambered over sea-weeded rocks on to peaty, springy soil and ate a meal with hospitable villagers. It was idyllic — the warm friendliness, the good, plentiful food, the storm outside and stern spare beauty of the coast. Politics, formulas for unity, seemed a world away. But the storm abated, the boat chugged on, and in a drizzling late August dusk-before-dawn Sylvia landed in Britain, evading officials who had been set to watch for her. It was a dispiriting moment. 'So I returned to the British Empire,' she wrote. 'A pile of dingy, smoke-begrimed buildings ... poor little children, bare-legged, ill-clad and dirty ... a ragged, shoeless dwarf, with legs all twisted, crawling along, supporting himself on his hands and wincing as the sharp stones cut his palms ... '

Faced with that sombre, Dickensian gloom, she may have asked herself if, after all, Comrade Lenin was right. Must one wait and scheme and burrow? Even if one failed, wasn't it worth dying on the barricades of naivety in protest against such dreariness?

CHAPTER FOUR

THE LITTLE WOMAN IN
THE DOORWAY

At the end of September 1920, under the headline SYLVIA'S WORLD REVOLUTION, the *Daily Express* reported her arrival at a meeting of her own controversial Communist Party (British Section of the Third International) held in a small hall in a back street of her home town, Manchester. Perhaps confusing her with Christabel, the reporter exclaimed: 'What a Sylvia! Those who remember the aesthetic face, the smart, beautiful woman of the intense suffragette campaign, would never have recognized her. Her hair was dishevelled, her face drawn, her shoes unpolished and well-worn.' Constantly harassed by lack of money and printing debts, totally absorbed in her task of regenerating the human race, she had lost whatever pretensions (and they were few) she might once have had to smartness. Only the protective Norah Smyth's insistence roused her to take any interest in her personal appearance (her neglect of which had always annoyed her mother). Yet men fell in love with her. In moments of enthusiasm especially, talking animatedly on or off the platform, her pale face with its slightly protuberant teeth, full, soft lips, soulful, droop-lidded eyes and loose mass of fine brown hair, could take on a real beauty, a kind of spiritual glow like her mother's.

Sylvia's colleagues had kept up a fine show of Lenin-defiance in the *Dreadnought* while she was away. 'British workers', ran one editorial, 'are far from being the political babes Comrade Lenin seems to imagine ... The fact that the capitalists *want* the workers to participate in Parliament, *want* them to send Henderson, Thomas and the group of fakers, lawyers, liberals and other political sycophants who constitute the Labour Party, to us is a good enough argument not to want them to do anything so suicidal.' The Manchester meeting was attended by at most fifty delegates – the combined strength of the various sects which made up the Communist Party of Great Britain (C.P.G.B.) was barely two thousand, five hundred – but it showed no awareness of insignificance. A handful of sincere communists, it argued, was worth far more than the hundreds of thousands of nominal socialists in the huge Labour Party. After an earnest

debate, Sylvia's resolution that her party should be represented at the next
and final unity conference, but should refuse to affiliate to the Labour
Party or play the parliamentary 'game', was carried unanimously, the
ex-servicemen in the hall (some of them had lost an arm or a leg in
the war) being particularly vigorous in their agreement. The Left, it
was decided, must preserve its integrity as the conscience of communism.

The *Sunday Express* noted that Sylvia, in getting to Moscow and back
without being arrested, had 'completely outwitted the Special Service
Branch of Scotland Yard'. But the police and the Defence of the Realm
Act, a wartime measure which was still in force, were soon to catch up
with her. The *Dreadnought*, which now bore a hammer-and-sickle emblem
and the subtitle 'The Organ of the Communist Party', was her downfall.
The issue dated October 16th, 1920 contained three articles deemed to
be seditious. The one on the front page, headed DISCONTENT ON THE
LOWER DECK and credited to S.000 (Gunner), H.M.S. *Hunter*, caused
the greatest stir. After listing the pay grievances of Royal Navy ratings –
abolition of free railway passes and of marriage allowances for men under
twenty-five – it urged: 'Men of the Lower Deck: Are you going to see
your class go under in the fight with the capitalist brutes who made millions out of your sacrifices during the war? Comrades, here is fertile
ground for propaganda to win the Army and Navy to the cause of the
workers ... ' Unemployment was rising, ex-servicemen and their families
starving. Ratings must refuse to act as strike-breakers or in any way to
sabotage the sacrifices the miners were making in the fight for freedom.
'To the rank and file of the Navy', the article ended, 'I say: You are the
Sons of the Working Class, therefore it is your duty to stand by that class
and not the class and Government which is responsible for the starving of
your ex-service brothers. Hail the formation of the Red Navy, which
protects the interests of the working class, and repudiate the dirty financial
interests which you are protecting now!'

The other two offending pieces were 'How To Get a Labour Government', by Comrade Rubinstein, and 'The Yellow Peril and The Docks',
by Leon Lopez. The first insisted that Parliament, whether dominated by
Tories, Liberals or Labour, remained 'part of the oppressive machinery
of the bourgeois state'. It was the mission of communists to destroy it and
perhaps (as William Morris had suggested in his Utopian socialist fantasy
News from Nowhere) to turn its building into a storehouse for manure.
Success would be achieved, 'firstly by destroying the faith which millions

of British workers still have in Parliament. Secondly, when we have secured power enough, by dispersing it by the force of Red Guards in the streets and paralysing strikes in industry.' The article about the docks, written by a coloured man, protested at the attempts made by the capitalist press to whip up racial hatred over mixed marriages of white women and Chinese in the Limehouse area. Apart from the fact, said Mr Lopez, that such marriages were often just as happy as double-white unions, both whites and coloureds of the working classes must learn that they had one fundamental enemy in common – the capitalist oppressor. They should not allow themselves to be pitted against each other, but rather demonstrate their solidarity by combining to 'lead the attack on those bastilles, the bonded warehouses'.

The articles were not more subversive or aggressive than many which had appeared in the previous two years. But the *Dreadnought* office, several times raided during the war, was again ransacked by the police. Sylvia was questioned about the identity of the 'Red' gunner, which she refused to reveal, and arrested on a charge of incitement to sedition in His Majesty's forces and the civilian population. The rebellion in Ireland, nationalist disturbances in India, the seemingly uncontrollable rise of unemployment, and the constant threat of a crippling strike by the triple alliance of miners, railwaymen and transport workers, had turned Lloyd George's 'homes fit for heroes' National Government of Reconstruction into an edgy group of alarmists. In 1919 the strike of Welsh miners had been countered by the declaration of a state of emergency, reservists had been recalled to the colours, machine guns posted at the pitheads and troops quartered in the area. Still the workers were restless, the situation seemed to be deteriorating, the war against Soviet Russia had failed, Britain seemed fertile with revolutionary possibilities – and Sylvia, busy sowing her seeds of revolt, could no longer be ignored. According to the press, she was not only Britain's most dangerous Red, but the chosen emissary of Lenin in a new and carefully planned campaign of sabotage.

The Government had apparently forgotten that to bring a Pankhurst into court was to let loose a tigress of propaganda in the arena of her choice. In choosing to make an example of Sylvia it presented her with an opportunity which she took with both hands. On October 28th she was charged, and on November 5th – Guy Fawkes' Day – during the hearing at the tiny Mansion House police court, she treated the magistrate, Sir Alfred Newton, and spectators, including a squad of reporters, to the liveliest display of Pankhurst fireworks since her mother's trial at the Old

Paris 1913: Christabel Pankhurst reads the latest copy of the *Suffragette*, which she edited from exile

Left to Right: Emily Wilding Davison, Sylvia Pankhurst, Christabel Pankhurst and Mrs Emmeline Pethick-Lawrence in a suffragette procession, *c.* 1910

The gracefully eloquent Christabel Pankhurst of the early years of the suffragette campaign as seen by 'Spy', the famous cartoonist of *Vanity Fair*

Bailey in 1913. She thanked the Government for giving the articles such wide publicity: but was it so ignorant as not to know that the ideas contained in them had been put forward in such acknowledged classics as William Morris's *News from Nowhere* and Karl Marx's *Communist Manifesto*, which were freely available in almost every public library? Brought up by a socialist father, she had, she said, been a socialist all her life, though at one time she had been misguided enough to imagine that Votes for Women were an important ingredient of social revolution. She had tried as hard as anyone to heal the wounds made by capitalism. In the East End 'many and many a time women brought their children starving and dying to me. I started four clinics and have sat up night after night with the little ones. I also set up a day nursery, but all my experience showed that it was useless trying to palliate an impossible system. It is a *wrong* system', she blazed, 'and has got to be smashed. I would give my life to smash it. You cannot frighten me with any sentence you may impose ... You will not stop this agitation. The words that are being written in my paper will be as common as daily bread.'

Sir Alfred Newton sentenced her to six months' imprisonment in the second division, and remarked that in his opinion the Government had been very lenient, that only her sex prevented him from sentencing her to six months' hard labour. She was freed on bail pending an appeal, but forbidden to take any part in the production of the *Dreadnought* or to speak in public. Her enforced absence did not abate the paper's pugnacity. Why should the workers wait, it demanded, for a so-called Labour Government to nationalize industries? That would only burden them with a load of bourgeois bureaucrats. The members of the triple alliance should brush aside their feeble leaders and take over direction of their industries themselves. It was madness to trust J. H. Thomas (secretary of the railwaymen's union) and other 'pimps of Labour' ready to sell out to the bosses. Sylvia used her enforced leisure not only to prepare her own defence, but to write a two hundred page account of her visit to Moscow, entitled *Soviet Russia As I Saw It*. Her prospects of success in her appeal, already slender, were not improved when the police found two letters written by her in the possession of a Finnish communist who was to take them to Moscow. Both letters—one to Lenin, one to Zinoviev, head of the Third International—complained of the gutlessness of middle-of-the-road communism and asked for funds to keep her own group (and especially the *Dreadnought*) in existence to activate the laggards.

But probably the only success she aimed at was another *tour de force*

4

of propaganda, which she duly achieved when her appeal was heard
before Sir John Bell and the Bench of Aldermen of the City of London
early in January 1921. She looked very pale, and with an unusual touch
(albeit ideological) of personal adornment, wore a red carnation in her
lapel. The whole historic setting – the ancient, beautiful Guildhall, symbol
to her of the kind of decadent sham-medievalism with which finance-
capitalism liked to cloak its naked greed, inflamed her to a white heat of
oratorical fury. Wasn't this just the kind of grotesque charade to expose
which she had agonized through a dozen hunger strikes, a hundred
unpublicized privations? To help and to rouse the exploited she had been
forced to give up her painting: yet these dull, arrogant exploiters dared,
posturing against a background of beauty created by artisans of the past,
to accuse her of being a criminal! The fight against all that they represented had twisted her as it had twisted the nation, had forced her to acknowledge the necessity for hatred, for destruction, including the destruction of
her own health and her dearest ambitions. On the rejection of her doctor's
plea that, since her patient was suffering from severe internal inflammation
as a result of her many prison ordeals, she should be given first division
status (so that the treatment which she was receiving could be continued)
Sylvia burst out: 'I have gone to war too, and my life will be shortened.
You financial people have good brains and use them looking after your
own interests. I have better brains than some of you, yet I have lived in
the East End and been clothed with garments given to me by friends ... I
am going to fight capitalism even if it kills me. It is wrong that people like
yon should be comfortable and well fed while all around you people are
starving.'

She and her political colleagues were not violent by nature. They had
been made desperate by their sensitivity to suffering. If they were disabled,
other more ruthless leaders might take over. 'I might be squeamish if it
came to killing people, but if you ruin the health of some of us you may
cause the movement to fall into cruder hands.' But whatever happened,
capitalism was doomed. 'It is obvious', said Sylvia, leaning forward and
gripping the rail of the witness box, 'that we are passing from one form
of society to another, from capitalism to socialism and then to something
more perfect'. Her simple, tender yearnings (and her memories of the
Bible, which, as the only book readily available, she had often read in
prison with a rare intensity) fused in a peroration of moving, religious
fervour. 'In Soviet Russia I have seen wonderful things. I know we will
create a society where there are no rich or poor, no people without work

or beauty in their lives, where money itself will disappear, where we shall all be brothers and sisters, where every one will have enough.'

It is doubtful if the Guildhall had ever known such quivering shameless passion—the sort of emotionalism that had embarrassed well-born suffragettes and had made Mrs Pankhurst, seeing herself as it were in a magnifying glass, plead with her daughter for restraint. Stumbling and breathless, it was nevertheless in the true strain of visionary communalism, rather than hierarchic communism. For Sylvia's soul, despite incessant journalism and political turbulence, still shone with a redemptive radiance impossible to hide.

> In every cry of every man,
> In every infant's cry of fear,
> In every voice, in every ban,
> The mind-forged manacles I hear.
>
> How the chimney-sweeper's cry
> Every blackening church appals,
> And the hapless soldier's sigh
> Runs in blood down palace walls ...

She quoted Blake in the *Dreadnought* because he expressed her sense of a stifled world of fulfilment crying out to be born. She dreamed with William Morris of 'the noble communal hall of the future, unsparing of materials, generous in worthy ornament, alive with the noblest thoughts of our time and the past ... such an abode of man as no private enterprise could come anywhere near for beauty and for fitness, because only collective thought and collective life could cherish the aspirations which give birth to it.' She longed with Edward Carpenter for 'a millennium not of riches, nor of mechanical facilities, nor of intellectual facilities, but a time when men and women all over the earth shall ascend and enter into relations with their bodies ... ' She knew (better than he) what Carpenter meant when he wrote in *Towards Democracy*: 'If I am not level with the lowest, I am nothing; and if I did not know for certain that the craziest sot is my equal and were not proud to walk with him as my friend, I would not write another word—for in this is my strength.'

In this strength, in this very British tradition, Sylvia faced the Philistines on the Bench. 'Socialism', she proclaimed, 'is the greatest thing in life for me. You will never crush it out of me or kill it. I am only one of thousands or millions. Socialists make it possible to practise what you say in church, that we should love our neighbours as ourselves. If you work against socialism, you are standing with reaction against life, standing with the dead past against the coming civilization.' She also read long excerpts from a variety of books—from J. R. Green's *History of England* (on Cromwell's rough ways with Parliament), from William Morris, from Marx and Engels—and even a selection of her own editorials in the *Dreadnought*, ignoring Sir John Bell's peevish attempts to keep her to what he regarded as 'the point'.

Her appeal was dismissed with costs. All but a week of her five months in Holloway prison were spent in an infirmary cell. She was given a 'special' diet, but like other prisoners had to submit to a 'general search' (for writing materials and other forbidden articles) on alternate weeks. In a *Dreadnought* article written soon after her release, she contrasted the refusal to allow her, as a communist, to write or to receive literature from outside, with the comparative lenience shown to her as a suffragette. 'Those who stood up for political liberty and free speech when suffragettes were burning buildings seem to be deaf or blind now,' she sneered. 'Was it only the glamour of Albert Hall meetings and smartly-dressed ladies of the middle and upper classes which caused their fervour?' She protested, too, about the treatment of pregnant women and nursing mothers, forced to endure the plank beds, harsh, ugly clothes and mean diet.

Norah Smyth brought processions of sympathizers to Holloway to sing the Red Flag and display banners with the slogan SIX MONTHS FOR TELLING THE TRUTH. On one of her visits, Miss Smyth brought a grandiloquent message from Moscow: 'As free working-class citizens of the first Proletarian Republic of the World, enjoying all social and political rights, we send to Comrade Sylvia Pankhurst our warmest greetings, above the heads of our common enemies, the capitalists, the owners, the rich.' The news from outside was heartening in some respects, disturbing in others. It was to be expected, no doubt, that the Scottish I.L.P. should refuse affiliation to the Third International on the ground that it would split rather than unite the working class and (in the words of Emanuel Shinwell) 'meant working for a civil war'. But what had come over William Gallacher, a few short months ago so vociferous an opponent of compromise and parliamentarianism, but at the Leeds Unity Conference in January eating his words and condemning 'sectarians' as more anxious to impress each other than to co-operate in the great crusade? Sylvia sent a gloomy message to be printed in the *Dreadnought*. She still thought—and Lenin had agreed with her—that a united party must leave freedom for 'leftists' to follow their own line. 'I have not changed my view', she grumbled, 'that there are elements in the C.P.G.B. which are not communist and not revolutionary'. Even in the W.S.F., she darkly hinted, there were too many timid renegades.

Nevertheless, Gallacher was under police surveillance, and in March he too, with eight other communists, including ex-air ace Colonel Cecil L'Estrange Malone, went to prison. Malone, a Liberal M.P., had changed his views after a visit to Russia and announced at a rally in the Albert Hall that he would not mind if a revolution which would free millions required the hanging of Lloyd George and Lord Curzon from the nearest lamp-post.

When, at 8.50 a.m. on May 30th, the moment of release came, the *Daily Herald* (still sympathetic despite the *Dreadnought*'s frequent battering of George Lansbury) reported the scene under the headline THE LITTLE WOMAN IN THE DOORWAY. A crowd had begun to gather at 6.30, singing revolutionary songs and waving little red flags. Then 'the great studded door of the prison swung open, and Miss Pankhurst's hapless figure stood in the aperture. There was a great cheer which died away when it was seen that she was swaying as if about to fall, and that tears were rolling down her cheeks.' Norah Smyth and Jessie Payne rushed forward to hold her. Then other friends, including Melvina Walker, closed round, covering her face with kisses, and she was taken to Eustace Miles's restaurant (an old suffragette rendezvous) for a welcome-back breakfast. In the warm, comradely atmosphere, with a huge Six Months For Telling The Truth banner on the wall, Sylvia's strength and spirits appeared to revive. Yet amid the clatter of teacups and the hearty Cockney congratulations, her face, so pale and drawn, was more than usually melancholy. Perhaps she sensed that a new fight loomed, a fight with the leaders of Britain's brand-new Communist Party, that party chairman Arthur McManus and party strategist William Gallacher (both from Red Clydeside) were about to join Sir Alfred Newton and Sir John Bell and the city aldermen in condemning her refusal to conform.

CHAPTER FIVE

SYLVIA'S WILDERNESS

Always a believer in taking the fight to the enemy, Sylvia opened hostilities with the C.P.G.B. in a *Dreadnought* editorial of August 1921. As she had forecast, the Labour Party rejected the communist request for affiliation to form a 'United Front of Socialism', and she ridiculed the glib optimism of Zinoviev's estimate of the effectiveness of communist 'nuclei' in the trade unions. 'Let us', she taunted, 'hear from you, O communist nuclei!'

Shortly afterwards she received a letter from the party executive committee demanding that she cease to use the *Dreadnought* to subvert party unity and hand it over to an official editorial board within two weeks. After some acrimonious correspondence, she agreed to attend a meeting of the committee early in September. Chairman Arthur McManus informed her that the party would not allow any member to publish a newspaper, book or pamphlet unless it had been officially approved. To this, Sylvia replied that the *Dreadnought* was the only paper in Britain which reported the controversies in the international communist movement; that such controversies were signs of healthy development; that by studying and participating in them members would grow in knowledge and political experience. It was farcical, she maintained, to play at dictatorship of the proletariat while at the same time being afraid to do anything revolutionary. In any case, dictatorship was not an end in itself, but a passing necessity of the transition period. It was, in fact, alien to the true communist ideal, and must wither away with the achievement of real communism. She regretted that there was little sign of such a withering in Soviet Russia, little sign even of a recognition of its desirability. There was no alternative for her but to leave the party, if it persisted in such a tiresome parody of revolutionary discipline.

So she was expelled. The knowledge that the *Dreadnought* was in even deeper financial trouble than usual may have influenced the executive committee's 'toughness', but Sylvia preferred to kill the paper rather than condemn it to what she regarded as a living death. Somehow, though, from a variety of well-wishers, in pennies and in large cheques, she believed that the money would appear, a tribute from those who appreciated her invincible nonconformity. Norah Smyth, Dora Montefiore, and some of their wealthy friends would sell some more shares. Her old friends the Pethick-Lawrences would help. The resources of capitalism would be used to keep in motion the rod which beat it so vigorously, so entertainingly. Sylvia had never failed, after all, to give people a dazzling run for their money. The money was forthcoming, and the *Dreadnought* continued to plague the C.P.G.B. 'I do not regret my expulsion,' wrote Sylvia. 'That it has occurred shows the feeble and unsatisfactory condition of the party; its placing of small things before great; its muddled thinking. I desire freedom to work for communism with the best that is in me. The party could not chain me.' She was an early (though almost eager) victim of the long series of manœuvres which either liquidated intellectuals — the very people who had put communism on the map — or used them as propaganda hacks. Ideas, let alone idealism, were already beginning to be suspect, intellectuals bad security risks.

'I am tired, comrades,' Sylvia confided to her readers. 'I have had a long and hard struggle.' Norah Smyth resigned from the C.P.G.B. in sympathy with her chief, having joined it for the same reason; and Sylvia found magnificent words to express her sense of weariness and injustice. They were not, for once, her own, but those of a Shakespeare sonnet:

> Tired of all these, for restful death I cry,
> As, to behold desert a beggar born,
> And needy nothing trimm'd in jollity,
> And purest faith unhappily forsworn,
> And gilded honour shamefully misplaced,
> And maiden virtue rudely strumpeted,
> And right perfection wrongfully disgraced,
> And art made tongue-tied by authority,
> And folly doctor-like controlling skill,
> And simple truth miscalled simplicity,
> And captive good attending captain ill:
> Tired with all these, from these I would be gone,
> Save that, to die, I leave my love alone.

But this was a passing mood. Sylvia was soon rallying the meagre clans of nonconformist communism with a call to join a Workers'

Communist Party ('independent', as she put it, 'of bureaucratic jacks-in-office') pressing for direct industrial action and affiliated to the Fourth International. This had been formed in Berlin by a breakaway group, the German Communist Labour Party, which hoped to link up with similar groups in Russia, said to be trying to work out an alternative to Lenin's ossifying dictatorship of the proletariat. This move was ridiculed by Gallacher. 'The class-content of the Labour Party', he wrote in *The Communist*, 'is proletarian. To unconditionally repudiate affiliation to it because of its defects leads to the most pitifully barren sectarianism. It brings one close to the position of the bewildered theoreticians of the "Three and a Half International", whose immaculate communist parties and beautiful, but politically impotent, industrial unions are no more a menace to capitalism than is the Primrose League' (a Conservative women's organization). In reply, Sylvia lamented that the Communist Party of Great Britain was not British at all. It took its orders from Moscow. 'It has no policy of its own; it is wandering about in a quagmire, trying to apply a policy made in Russia to a set of conditions to which Russian policy is inapplicable.' This was particularly sad in the case of Gallacher, once so hot an opponent of the Lenin thesis. 'Oh, Comrade Lenin,' she sighed, 'with your tortuous Asiatic tactics you are corrupting these simple Westerners, who do not understand you, and whose metal is softer than yours!'

She noted, too, that Albert Inkpin, secretary of the C.P.G.B. and a vice-president of the Third International, while on trial for subversive activities, not only employed a well-known capitalist lawyer to conduct his defence, but, far from extolling the virtues of revolt in court, pleaded that since he was 'the servant of a committee' he could not be held personally responsible for its decisions. 'Not thus', commented Sylvia acidly, 'does the blood of the martyr become the seed of the Church.' Honest Albert Inkpin, too, presumably, had been misled by Lenin's Asiatic tortuosities; as, to judge by their showing in the House of Commons, had the first two so-called Communist M.P.s, Walton Newbold and Shapurji Saklatvala, a wealthy Parsee who had been a prominent member of the group which in 1918 had met in a Fleet Street café to discuss the formation and progress of Sylvia's Russian People's Information Bureau.

Lenin's chameleon realism was making him, to Sylvia's puritan eyes, almost indistinguishable from any other opportunist politician. First he ended prohibition in Russia and re-introduced the sale of vodka — that evil opiate of Tsarism—as a Government monopoly. Then, short of money and industrial know-how, he launched a New Economic Policy which re-opened the doors to foreign capitalists and their insidious techno-cratic missionaries. It was reported that Trotsky not only assured visiting American Senator King that the Soviet Government would safeguard the investments of capitalist firms, but told him that he need have no fears that Russia intended to blow on the embers of German com-munism. Yet Hitler was already beginning to push for power (the *Dreadnought* was perhaps the first paper in Britain to treat Nazism seriously). 'How art thou fallen, O land of revolution,' moaned Sylvia, 'what have you done, O one-time trumpet of revolution? In your im-patience of the slow awakening of far multitudes, you have turned your face from the world's lowly and enslaved. You have dabbled in the juggleries of capitalist diplomacy. By subtle and specious arguments and by the glamour of the Russian Revolution, you have diverted many from the quest of communism ... '

Expelled from the C.P.G.B. and now quite ignored by Lenin, Sylvia attempted to activate the Poplar Borough Council. Led by George Lansbury, all thirty councillors, including Nellie Cressall and Mrs Parsons (two of Sylvia's 'old girls' of the East London Federation of Suffragettes), had gone to prison rather than levy the cripplingly high rates demanded by the London County Council. They insisted that the burden of rates should be shared by the wealthier London boroughs. Their imprisonment was a national as well as a local sensation, and 'Poplarism' the topic of the day in almost every newspaper. Sylvia, however, was not unduly im-pressed. Going to prison was a fine propaganda gesture, but what positive policy had the council, which numbered two nominal communists (one of them Lansbury's son Edgar) to offer? Certainly it had taken over the administration of the welfare services which she had pioneered during the war, and had built a few excellent housing estates. But cutting local poor relief and council employees' wages was not the right answer to the economic crisis, even if it did help to mitigate their 'militancy' in capitalist circles. Why not sharply increase the rates paid by the owners of factories in the East End, still raking in swollen profits at the expense of their underpaid workers? Why not kick out the landlords altogether and set up Soviets? Why not give a *really* radical lead to the rest of the country?

But not even the Poplar Council would take her advice. So in 1923, with the help of Norah Smyth, she formed an Unemployed Workers' Organization (the forerunner of a larger, but very similar, communist

organization active in the Depression of the 'thirties) to bring pressure
to bear. Her new tatterdemalion army set siege to the town hall and
locked the councillors in. When George Lansbury, whose pacifism in the
class war had exasperated Sylvia, called in the police, who broke a few
heads in a baton charge, the *Dreadnought* was quick to draw the moral.
'One thing stands out clearly: it is that the result of working-class representatives taking part in the administration of capitalist machinery is that
they become responsible for enforcing the regulations of the capitalist
system itself.' But she was tired of scoring easy debating points, ashamed
of the broken heads for which her own impetuosity was responsible. It
was her last and least admirable attempt to force the pace of revolution.
She abandoned her efforts to wean the masses from their low mania for
sport, petty gambling and royalty.

It is doubtful if many of the workers read, or if they read, compre-
hended, the high political tone of the *Dreadnought*, let alone Sylvia's
occasional dithyrambic, Whitmanesque poems. For instance:

> I sing of revolt,
> I sing of the burning sun,
> I sing of thee and thy heat waves,
> Thy heat waves that stir men's hearts to revolt,
> Arousing a storm of passion, barriers overthrowing.

> Burst ye the bonds of wagedom,
> Burst ye the bonds, O people,
> Stirred by the sun that burns,
> O life-giving sun that burneth.

> Why will ye chaffer by the market barrows,
> Or show your wares behind glass when the sun
>   is raging,
> Faded and spoilt are the paltry wares ye are selling.
> Abandon this tedious barter in which ye waste your lives!

Few of her old followers responded to a call to demonstrate for the release
of Sacco and Vanzetti, the Italian anarchists under sentence of death in
America. They could not appreciate the long excerpts from Rosa Luxemburg's densely intellectual correspondence. They, like Gallacher, were
tired of the delights, perhaps sensed the ingrowing dangers, of what
Ramsay MacDonald called, with a careerist shudder, 'the minority mind'.
They had no time or inclination to learn Esperanto, the international

language which the *Dreadnought* warmly recommended as a key to open the cages of nationalism. While having a cynical awareness of the short-comings and absurdities of politicians, electioneering and the Royal Family, they were prepared to enjoy the spectacle of the nobs competing for the favour of the workers, of the King and Queen riding out in state coaches to state occasions. Unlike Sylvia, they did not choke with rage at the contrast between royal palaces and the poor packing ten or more into one room or driven to live in caves and holes in the moors of Northumberland. They had had a surfeit, the masses had, of doom and gloom, and were prepared to take their fun as and where they found it, capitalist or not. Their underlying xenophobia was exasperated by the constant talk of foreign countries and foreign examples. They were resigned to muddling through like sensible Britishers, not to be taken in by a lot of theories. If, in 1923, Sylvia had lain starving on a stretcher on a pavement outside the Houses of Parliament or anywhere else, there would have been few hands to lift her and carry her in triumph or in pity. She was, in fact, becoming a bore.

The sledge-hammer Marxism of the *Dreadnought*'s 'Light on the Old Testament' series of Lessons for Proletarian Schools fell on stony soil. 'We saw', went one lesson, 'that the Hebrews, when a wandering desert people, were communists, that after they conquered Canaan they first held the land in common, but that gradually they established private property with all its attendant evils. The prophets of the Old Testament were agitators who demanded a return to communism.' Little came of Sylvia's project for starting a working-class fiction magazine, though she did publish a letter from a comrade asking for subscriptions to a proletarian novel to be entitled *The Millionaires of Bethnal Green*. This, it was announced, would feature the cruel fraudulence of landlords, the victimization of revolutionary workers, the hypocrisy of the law, the stabbing of a communist – and all would be woven into 'a love story in which the heroine is forced on the streets'.

Yet if the *Dreadnought* had drifted far from its original intention of being a journal of the people, by the people, and for the people, it still contained plenty of entertainment and knockabout Pankhurst idiosyncrasy for the intelligentsia which now kept it in precarious being. Sylvia continued to clash journalistically with George Bernard Shaw, who during the war had advised her to stick to her welfare services and leave politics alone, since she 'could not even convert her mother and Christabel'. When, in a long open letter, she criticized the meanness of the

Labour Party's Unemployment Bill, with its proposal for near-penal 'work colonies', and appealed to him as an intelligent 'reformist' to protest against it, he replied brusquely: 'Of course the Labour proposals would look ridiculous in Moscow. But where would be the sense of presenting Communist proposals to a virulently Capitalist Government? In this world you have to take what you can get or go away empty. If I did what you want me to do and the Labour Party withdrew its proposals, the unemployed would starve or tear the place down until the Government tided over the emergency by doles and baton charges and perhaps a little machine-gunning ... Tell the workers they will be jolly lucky if they get as much as the Labour Party is asking. They made their bed in 1918' (i.e. voted Lloyd George's Liberal–Tory coalition into power) 'quite deliberately; now they must lie on it.'

Labour's success at the polls in December 1923, Sylvia predicted, would achieve little but an exposure of the hollowness of its claims to socialism. The fact that eight women became M.P.s in that election, though marking an advance in public opinion, was far less significant than unenlightened feminists seemed to imagine. 'Women', she wrote, 'can no more put virtue into the decaying parliamentary institution than can men: it is past reform and must disappear. The woman professional politician is neither more nor less desirable than the man professional politician; the less the world has of either, the better it is for it.' As for Lady Astor, with her eternal babble about the value of old-fashioned motherhood and the importance of domestic labour as a form of national service, 'the place for her is in the home rather than in the House'.

It was a sad fact that the Fascists and Nazis were grabbing power because they regarded talk as a preliminary to, and not a substitute for, action. The fascination of direct action, by contrast with the stagnancy of the pseudo-democracies, was shown by the fact that even 'Liberal' newspapers like the *Manchester Guardian* and the *Daily Herald* welcomed Mussolini's 'vitality'. Europe, including Britain, seemed to Sylvia to be faced with the choice of a Fascist or a communist dictatorship. Must the vitality of evil triumph over the anaemia of good? Could not the women of Britain, she asked, clutching in extremity at old feminist straws, show the same passion for true liberation which they had lavished on the essentially bourgeois crusade of the suffrage movement? 'O beautiful communism', she hopefully rhapsodized, 'splendid ideal of complete fraternity which alone can emancipate all men and women, that same spirit of sacrifice shall be thine in full, unstinting measure ere long.'

But more and more, in the *Dreadnought*, she went back to the past for solace, to Ernest Jones, the Chartist leader and poet, to Robert Brough's mid-nineteenth century *Poems of the Governing Classes*, mining deep in the rich vein of British radicalism which was so dear to her. As a comment, for instance, on Labour's rich rabble-rousers, she printed Brough's satire, *A Friend of the People*:

> ... He goes on the hustings in very old coats
> (He's a change at the club) when soliciting votes,
> His beard he neglects and his nails he begrimes
> (His jokes on clean collars are killing at times).
> Hang your wine! Give him beer from the pewter or can —
> Sir Menenius Agrippa's a *popular* man!

The paper took on a markedly literary tone, with stories by Anatole France (described as 'an adherent of the Third International') and poems by Ezra Pound. Yet Sylvia had not set out to produce another leftist cultural magazine. She realized that the people she wanted to reach were not listening. She felt, while she resented, the likelihood that the egregious Ramsay MacDonald might be correct when he forecast 'a century of political stagnation' with no significant shift in public opinion. Even hyper-loyal Norah Smyth, stripped of most of her shares and all of her illusions, finally, regretfully, left—begging Sylvia, in a long and touching letter of farewell, to recover her sense of proportion and, even more important, to cultivate a sense of humour. Mrs Payne died. The W.S.F. headquarters in the Old Ford Road seemed utterly desolate and meaningless.

In July 1924, after a decade of rampaging independence, the *Dreadnought* ceased publication and Sylvia and Corio moved to the comparative rusticity of Woodford Green, where she had first gone as a smuggled suffragette refugee in Willie Lansbury's woodcart. There she bought a small café, called the Red Cottage, and determined to earn a living by serving teas and light meals, and, in her spare time, writing the books which her whirlwind career as an agitator had left her no leisure to attempt. Her friends found it hard to believe that, whatever her intentions, she was through with public controversy. What books did she have in mind? What splintering of the suburban calm of Woodford Green lay in store? Was there a hint of things to come in her recent outburst about the institution of marriage in the *Dreadnought*? Criticizing a bishop's routine lament that many who used 'our lovely marriage service' had already flouted its precepts, she had remarked: 'A large source of unnecessary sorrow and cruelty will be removed when this point of view has been altogether eliminated. Neither legal nor religious forms can make the mating of men and women either right or wrong. The sexual functions must be regarded as natural functions, and freed from the conventions by which the private property system and religious officialdom surround them.'

Sylvia was still a nonconformist, as incapable as ever of nonconforming in silence and obscurity. She was simmering. But it was only a matter of time before she came once more to the boil.

CHAPTER SIX

DOWN UNDER

In March 1917, the executive committee of the Victorian Socialist Party (V.S.P.) had met in Melbourne to consider Mrs Pankhurst's statement that she was 'ashamed of Adela', and resolved that it viewed with sorrow Mrs Pankhurst's apparent 'idolatry' of William Hughes, Australia's renegade socialist Prime Minister.

In the post-war period Mrs Pankhurst's shame must have deepened, even if she no longer bothered to give it public utterance. Certainly Adela did not talk or write about free unions and techniques for sexual self-fulfilment. She was at least married – though the ceremony had been more socialist than Christian – and by 1923 had three children (one son, two daughters) of her own as well as three stepchildren. So far, so good. But all those children and the multitude of domestic chores they implied did not kill Adela's political vehemence. She was as active a socialist as her husband, who, people said, seemed to have been re-energized by Adela, to have taken on a seriousness and an earnestness which made it difficult to see in him the hail-fellow-well-met Irishman, fond of his liquor, of pre-war days. In 1918 he was elected secretary of the New South Wales branch of the Australian Seamen's Union, in 1919 became its general secretary – and so prominent in the anti-authoritarian movement of the period that he was nicknamed 'The Lenin of Australia'. Silvio Corio, an Italian communist, could not even be called a son-in-law. Tom Walsh, a bona fide son-in-law, was also a communist. A fine situation, Mrs Pankhurst may have reflected, for an evangelist of Empire!

As Big Business regrouped itself for the contest with socialism, and the official Australian Labour Party offered at best a dull policy of limited state capitalism, the main impetus towards a radical revolution came from the robust pilosophy of the I.W.W. The simple cynicism of its paper, *Direct Action*, appealed strongly to a strain of anarchic freelance zest, a romantic vestige of pioneering freedoms in Australia's huge open spaces which despised the bureaucratic paraphernalia of central government and had woven a heroic Robin Hood legend about Ned Kelly (hanged in Melbourne in 1880), a cattle rustler and bank robber who killed a number of policemen but boasted that he had never harmed a woman and only robbed the rich. There was still a profound distrust of politicians as city slickers who battened on the innocence of ordinary folk and were parasites on the backs of the real workers. The I.W.W. had expressed this sentiment in doggerel songs, crudely but effectively anti-Establishment (and therefore anti-ecclesiastical, for priests and parsons were regarded as the mealy-mouthed moral police of the ruling class). *Bump me into Parliament*, sung to the tune of 'Yankee Doodle', was a typical example of this kind of thing:

> Come listen all good friends of mine,
> I want to move a motion,
> To get an Eldorado here
> I've got a bonzer notion.
>
> *Chorus:* Bump me into Parliament,
> Bounce me any way,
> Bang me into Parliament
> On next election day.
>
> Some wealthy friends I know
> Declare I am most clever,
> While some may talk an hour or so,
> Why, I can talk for ever.
>
> Oh yes, I am a Lib-Lab man,
> I believe in revolution;
> The quickest way to bring it on
> Is talking constitution.
>
> I've read my Bible ten times through,
> And Jesus justifies me,
> The man who does not vote for me,
> By Christ he crucifies me ...

Direct Action tirelessly hammered home the message that political manœuvring was futile, state capitalism a blind alley. 'The state places its time-servers and toadies in the most desirable positions of authority, by systems of pimping and espionage, while superannuation schemes and sliding wage-scales are used to sap whatever militant spirit there may be among the men.' The arbitration court was a pet device of Labour politicians. 'It has bled the pockets and befogged the minds of the Australian working class, and filled the pockets of the patriotic gang of legal luminaries who are the ablest product of Labour parties and anti-quated craft unionism.' The great necessity was not to drift, but to use every permutation of industrial sabotage to bring the capitalist system to a standstill—a course which had the added advantage of bringing the class war into the open and forcing the issue. The dislocation and discrediting of the reformist, capitalist-lackey Labour movement would make certain a head-on clash: it was for this reason, and not out of any idealistic pacifism, that the I.W.W. had whipped up the anti-conscription cam-paign. The creation of an aggressive class-consciousness was, for the time being, more important than any constructive programme. Once that consciousness was there, its sheer momentum would, reasoned Tom Barker and his followers, force through the revolution and throw up solutions. The I.W.W. leaders (few of whom were Australian-born, a point much stressed by the Government), realized, like the Bolsheviks, that the great mass of dullards had to be picked on by a determined minority. Small craft unions—reactionary fortresses in which skilled workers, the 'aristocrats' of labour, shut themselves away from the plight of the unskilled workers—must be disbanded and re-formed in industrial unions grouped in One Big Union. This would pave the way for a truly industrial democracy, with a central administrative body composed of delegates representing definite industrial interests—and no scope for intriguing careerist politicians.

Such was the strategy, such the objective: itself, despite the studied 'toughness' of I.W.W. terminology, tenderly utopian. By the end of the war, savage Government legislation, police action, and loaded trials of Tom Barker, Peter Larkin (brother of Jim Larkin) and other leaders had extinguished the I.W.W. Yet its influence was still lively, and the agita-tion for the release of the prisoners (most of whom were finally deported) continued until 1920. Tom and Adela Walsh set themselves to revitalize the Seamen's Union, traditionally militant, whose resistance to intimida-tion had led, in 1890, to the formation of the Labour Party, and whose example might now help to rally the workers for a big militant heave.

Adela's old friend and fellow campaigner Jennie Baines, jailed for leading a 'Red Flag' demonstration in Flinders Park, Melbourne, in February 1919, was released after a four-day hunger and thirst strike (thus becoming Australia's first hunger striker), and soon afterwards presided at a meeting of the V.S.P. addressed by Adela. How long, she queried, were people going to put up with unemployment and squalid housing conditions? When would they realize that revolution was the only cure, a complete change of social, political and industrial control – a change, moreover, whose very simplicity terrified office-seeking politicians who 'suffered from chronic inertia, which they call the constitutional attitude'. In May 1919, soon after having her first baby, Richard, Adela moved to Sydney, where her husband took up his duties at the headquarters of the Seamen's Union. Her three stepdaughters who, after leaving a convent school, had been staying with the Rosses, came with her. Under the leadership of Walsh, the union had, in April, begun a long, classic, winning strike for better living conditions on board and higher pay. Combined with an obstinate strike in the coal mines, this was a real threat to industry and public services in New South Wales and, as time went on, in the whole country. The unions, said the *Sydney Morning Herald*, were aiming at nothing less than the defeat of the Government. The Walshes were using their influence for sinister purposes outside the terms of 'healthy' trade unionism. In May, while Adela and Jennie Baines worked frantically to raise money for the strike fund, a compulsory conference of union leaders and employers broke down in Melbourne. In July, Tom Walsh was fined one hundred pounds for continued incitement to strike, and on repeating the offence appeared in court in Melbourne. 'If Melbourne is plunged into darkness,' he had told a crowd of strikers, 'that will force the Government to concede our terms.' Adela travelled from Sydney to be with him, and to help to draft the speech which he planned to make in his own defence.

The seamen's grievances were real, he told the judge. They were sick of being made fools of in arbitration courts which were obviously dominated by the shipowners. Why were the shipowners not prosecuted for *their* anti-social obstinacy? Why should the seamen – and their servants, the union officials – be persecuted for making just demands? The seamen would never go to arbitration again. There would never be peace in the shipping industry until the Government forced the owners to come to terms. Jailed for three months, Walsh, whose treatment brought vigorous protests from the New South Wales Labour Party, was released in September. But the strike continued until the end of 1919, when the owners guaranteed to improve crew quarters and to grant a token – though unsatisfactory – pay rise. In the meantime, Adela darted about doing all she could to keep up spirits and pressure. It was not true, she said in a series of speeches, that the strike had been organized by a handful of professional agitators. Her husband reflected the wishes of the vast majority of the men. He was not influenced by Russian communists or subsidized by them. Was it so difficult to understand that he was protesting against a great and glaring injustice which could be paralleled in every industry—the greed of owners and shareholders who denied to the workers a fair share of the wealth which they produced?

In March 1920, by which time she was pregnant with her second baby, *The Socialist* published a long letter from Adela headed 'The Party and the Crisis'. The fires of purposeful militancy, she warned, were already burning low. Those who should be concentrating on industrial organization were busy poking about in the ashes of theological controversy, sneering at God, priests, Christianity, the family, and wrangling over the interpretation of Marx. There was talk of a new, left-wing socialist party: but in all probability this would only muddle and intensify the already ludicrous scramble for illusory power, that *ignis fatuus* of Labour politicians. It was a sheer waste of time and energy to argue about religion and sexual morality, matters which should be left to the judgment of 'those who after the revolution, freed from the pressure of economic want, will doubtless see with clearer eyes than ours'. Control of industry was the basic need. When that was complete, there would be 'no more need for glib politicians at election time to persuade all the ignoramuses in the country to vote for socialism'. The unions—or the One Big Union—would control the country and its armed forces. 'Try', she ended, 'to build no more rationalist Utopias; but begin the slow struggle of teaching the industrial classes the meaning of economic freedom, and leave their religion and morality to take care of itself.'

A few months later she and her husband took part—gingerly—in the discussions which led to the formation of the Communist Party of Australia. Both were asked to serve on its provisional executive committee, and in February 1921 an article by Adela entitled 'Communism and Social Purity' (tracing the evils of prostitution to the immoral economic pressures of capitalism) was published by sister Sylvia in the *Dreadnought*. 'The wages of tens of thousands of young men', she wrote, 'are such that they cannot possibly maintain a family on them: yet they are herded together in cities under conditions which are most calculated to stir the sexual passions. A large proportion of capitalist activity is directed to stirring up sensuality in mankind; books, pictures, songs and plays are produced for no other purpose, and hotels, houses and other establishments yield large profits to those who cater for their satisfaction ...

Profits and prostitution—upon these empires are built and kingdoms stand ... Communism will abolish prostitution, and will enable young people to attend schools and universities, where the mind will be developed and every influence used to encourage purity and decent self-restraint.' By the time this article was published, the Walshes, whose attitude towards the C.P.A. was sceptical from the start, but who perhaps hoped that it might prove a successor to the thrusting militancy of the I.W.W., were already alienated by the incessant splitting of ideological hairs. Like Sylvia, they resented the manipulation of the Third International by Zinoviev, and felt that the stilted jargon and constipated academics of bourgeois communism would be likely to douse rather than inflame revolutionary ardour. They saw, too, that the conventional Russian-inspired denunciation of the 'racialism' of the White Australia policy—a policy dearer to the Labour movement than to employers—was completely unrealistic, mere sabotage for its own, or for Moscow's, sake. They preferred to choose and to use their own weapons in an open duel with capitalism.

In December 1920 the seamen had struck again. It was not only a question of basic wages, overtime rates, and hours of work, but, as Adela explained in the *Seamen's Journal*, of 'job control'. The union claimed the right to control the recruitment of crews, making sure that the owners did not scale them down in the interests of economy (profits), or introduce 'black' labour. The owners, on the other hand, claimed the right to absolute control of their 'own business'. As the strike spread, bringing inter-state shipping virtually to a standstill, not even newspapers' massive reporting of the cricket test matches between England and Australia could keep it off the front page. In New South Wales alone, unemployment had risen steeply (and was worsened by the side-effects of the strike). The offices of the state governor in Macquarie Street, Sydney, were besieged by angry mobs. Hundreds of passengers were stranded in Tasmania when an entire ship's crew walked off. Firemen refused to go aboard at sailing time, and in one case sauntered into a first-class lounge and demanded drinks. When the purser tried to intervene, they swore at him and said that the seamen were running the ship and would not take orders from owners' pimps. This, primmed editorial writers in high-hat state-of-emergency prose, was getting 'perilously close to Sovietism pure and simple'.

In February 1921 Walsh was elected general president of the Seamen's Union, and at the All-Australia Trades Union Conference continued to

urge the formation of One Big Union. Backed by the T.U.C., he pressed
for a federal tribunal to inquire into the shipping industry. Prime Minister
Hughes, after a long and stormy Cabinet meeting, rejected the demand.
The 'Bolshevik' Walsh and his associates must be taught a lesson. After
two compulsory Arbitration Court hearings, in the course of which even
the Deputy President accused the shipowners of obstruction, the strike
was settled at the end of February. The manning of all vessels in which
disputes arose was to be determined by a committee of eight on which
owners and unionists would be equally represented. This arrangement
worked so well that it was not changed until 1951, and Walsh was congratulated by the President of the Court on his 'able and creditable
presentation' of the seamen's case.

   This flattery, though well earned, did not dim the pugnacity of the
Walshes. In September Adela was in trouble again—especially with
'moderate' Labour politicians—for inciting the unemployed to break the
windows of Parliament House, Sydney, to force attention to their plight.
Early in 1923 she was visited by Dora Montefiore, with whom she had
gone to prison as a suffragette in 1906. Mrs Montefiore, an Englishwoman of conventional Tory upbringing, had married a wealthy
Australian businessman, and had been active in suffragist campaigns in
Sydney in the 1890s. When her husband died she had returned to England, financing her suffragette and (later) communist activities from the
impressive array of stocks and shares which she had inherited. Because of
her wealth and her doctrinal soundness—she was a most meticulous
Marxist—she was kept busy, though now nearing seventy and suffering
from chronic bronchitis, travelling the world to represent impecunious
communist groups at far-off conferences. While in Sydney (partly to
confer with trustees about her investments) she was deputed by the C.P.A.
to represent it at an international get-together in Moscow. She took a
motherly, almost proprietorial interest in the C.P.A., since she claimed
that it was largely formed from 'the remains of the old International
Socialist Party which, with Harry Holland, I helped to form in 1910'.

   For all Mrs Montefiore's undoubted charm and slightly gushing
sincerity, she cannot have been a very welcome visitor in the Walshes'
small and crowded home. But it was fun to talk over old times and old
battles and to hear news of Sylvia (after whom Adela had named her first
daughter, born in October 1920). A second daughter, curiously—even
ominously, to Mrs Montefiore—called Christian had recently been born.
Mrs Montefiore, who had always been able to afford servants, admired

Adela's energy. She had mothered three stepchildren and was now bringing up three children of her own. 'In a climate which is trying in summer
for white women', wrote Mrs Montefiore, 'she cooked and washed and
did the usual daily duties of a workman's wife, besides carrying on a never
ceasing anti-war and socialist propaganda. I was told by someone who
had seen her when she was in bed after one of her confinements, that she
was sitting up writing for and editing the *Seamen's Journal*, with the baby
lying by her side.' Mrs Montefiore found her with 'two little toddlers and
a baby at the breast; the most real, the most plucky little mother that I
think I have ever come across. All honour to Adela Walsh, schoolteacher,
suffragist, wife, mother and communist!'

Communist Adela no longer, in fact, was, since the Walshes had
severed their tenuous connection with the C.P.A. They had even begun
to lose faith in the likelihood of a nation-wide revolution which could
overcome the tight regionalism of Australia's six states, whose watchful
rivalry made easier the anti-socialist manœuvres of the Federal Government. But the running fight with the shipowners continued. By the end
of 1924 sporadic strikes were again paralysing Commonwealth and
interstate shipping in reply to an attempt by the owners to repudiate the
job control agreement of 1921. Their attitude was stiffened by the
knowledge that the Coalition Government headed by Stanley Melbourne
Bruce (who had succeeded Hughes as Prime Minister) was spoiling for a
showdown with militant unionists. A 'Red' scare was systematically
worked up, with Tom Walsh as one of the chief bogeymen. There was
talk of sterner measures, special legislation, a para-military force of special
police. 'In Italy,' observed the *Sydney Morning Herald*, 'the land was only
saved from Red dominance by the heroic remedy of Fascism.'

Walsh, still president of the Seamen's Union, and the union's general
secretary, Swedish-born Jacob Johnson, stood firm. By July 1925 shipping
movement in Sydney harbour was confined to a few foreign vessels and
some coasters manned by 'black' crews. At the beginning of August work
was resumed on the understanding that the 1921 agreement would be
honoured. Then came a new development. The crews of British ships in
Australian ports struck when they heard that their union, led by Havelock
Wilson (the hero of Walsh's seafaring youth), had agreed to a wage cut.
When Walsh and Johnson offered support and financial help to the
British strikers, Havelock Wilson protested that Walsh had deliberately
stimulated the revolt, which was part of a plot to disrupt 'Commonwealth
communications'. In reply, Walsh claimed that he had been invited by

British seamen, sickened by Havelock Wilson's treachery, to come to England and help form a new organization closely linked with the Seamen's Union in Australia.

The Federal Government now rushed through two amendments: one to the Navigation Act, to allow the transport of goods in foreign vessels during prolonged strikes: the other to the Immigration Restriction Act — specifically aimed at Walsh and Johnson (both of whom had lived in Australia for more than twenty years) — calling upon persons not born in Australia and believed to be concerned in acts of hindrance or destruction, to show cause why they should not be deported. Hearing this, Walsh, accompanied by Adela, made a defiant speech in the Domain, a Sydney park noted for the variety of its orators. The speech made headlines all over the world. 'If the Empire', stormed Walsh, 'is to be maintained by such sufferings as British seamen complain of, then I say to hell with Bruce and to hell with the Empire!' Newspaper cartoons showed him jumping savagely on the Union Jack.

Shortly after this, he and Johnson were served with deportation orders. Since the Labour-controlled New South Wales Government refused to allow the state police to be used for strike breaking or deportation, the Government concocted a Bill authorizing the enrolment of a force of so-called peace officers. Recruited mostly from retired police officers, the force was nicknamed 'Bruce's Blue-Bottles' or 'Bruce's Body-Snatchers'. The Government had hopelessly overplayed its hand. Walsh and Johnson were arrested in November 1925 and imprisoned on Garden Island while their case was argued for eight days in a High Court crammed with people and humming with excitement. On December 11th the court reached a unanimous verdict in favour of the prisoners. Their conduct of union affairs was not treasonable or even unreasonable. They were not liable to deportation, since long residence entitled immigrants to be regarded as Australians in every sense of the word.

Taken back to the mainland in a naval launch, the two men were given a rousing welcome by huge crowds. Walsh was reunited with his wife and children. He embraced Adela — tiny, staunch, excited Adela — with jubilant fondness (and the Walshes' affection for each other was notorious: they were often seen walking hand in hand in the streets). He knew the truth of the remark made in the New South Wales Parliament by Miss Preston Stanley (Australia's first woman M.P.) at the height of the deportation crisis: 'Make no mistake,' she had said. 'The power behind Tom Walsh is his wife, Adela Pankhurst.'

It had been one of Mrs Pankhurst's great achievements as a suffragette to prove that power was not necessarily the plaything of the rich, the leisured and the learned. Her rejected antipodean daughter, rich in nothing but a passion for justice and a taste for a tingling fight had, with the same kind of scorching naivety become, at least temporarily, the most influential woman in Australia.

PART THREE

MOTHERS SUPERIOR

CHAPTER ONE

THE READJUSTMENT OF
CHRISTABEL

On January 19th, 1921, those who noticed the item in the personal columns of several newspapers of the better class were surprised to read the following advertisement: 'Miss Christabel Pankhurst (owing to the victorious termination of her leadership in the Cause of Women's Political Enfranchisement) seeks remunerative, non-political work.' Interviewed by a *Daily Express* reporter, she said: 'I am advertising for a non-political post because a sufficient private income is necessary for a political leader. I cannot continue my leadership because I am not financially independent. I am glad I was privileged to do something for the enfranchisement of women, which I regard as one of the greatest changes in human affairs ever made.'

The rather stilted hauteur of these pronouncements was symptomatic of Christabel's difficulty in adjusting to the post-war world, the Smethwick defeat, the collapse of the Women's Party. The war had not only ended the suffragette campaign, but had provided a substantial substitute starring role. She had still been surrounded by the warm, insulating loyalty of the inner circle of Manchester stalwarts—Annie and Jessie Kenney and Flora Drummond—and sustained by the current of her mother's doting love. Now, this very vulnerable goddess, this ageing girl prodigy, shivered in the unaccustomed cold. 'That spirit of air and fire whose name is Christabel' (as novelist-suffragette Elizabeth Robins had called her in 1911) was now nearing forty. The incense clouds had thinned, had blown away, the disciples had dispersed.

She *could* have taken up a career as a barrister (the Sex Disqualification Removal Act of 1919 made this technically possible), but she shrank perhaps from the publicity and the need to work on ungrandiose briefs not of her own choosing. Her legal training had been designed, and used, to outwit cabinet ministers: it would have been a hard descent to use it to defend erring nonentities. An unflattering picture of Christabel at this time of painful transition was painted by her sister Sylvia in a flimsily fictional series which she wrote for the *Dreadnought*. A young man of vaguely socialist yearnings leaves the provinces to earn a living and get a political education in London. Among other relatives, he visits his aunt, described as 'a lady politician'. This aunt had been 'one of the foremost in the fight for votes for women, and had staked her political all on the war: she had flouted the humanitarians and reformers and had come out as a coercionist opponent of the working class. She had started a crusade to save Britain from the shop stewards, and had even (for Sylvia was convinced that Christabel was responsible for Mrs Pankhurst's fall from socialist grace) 'dispatched her obedient mother to save Russia from the revolution'.

Her crusades had, however, missed fire. 'She ought to have been the first woman to enter the portals of Westminster. She had been preceded by one who was her inferior in every respect save wealth. It was her mission to be a political success, to have a career of meteoric brilliance which would demonstrate that women could be, in the political field as in others, the equal of men.'

'Her mental endowments', Sylvia ruthlessly continued, 'and her considerable services to the Lloyd George coalition entitled her to an immediate under-secretaryship; cabinet rank should have followed swiftly, and the premiership before many months had passed ... Her strong, clear brain assured her that socialism would benefit the majority of the population, and that the careerism of the brilliant few was harmful rather than helpful to the masses; but she thrust such knowledge behind her. It was her mission to be the successful woman; politically everything must be sacrificed to that. In her ambition she was not wholly selfish, or at least she thought she was not. She was still obsessed with the idea of sweeping away the obstacles in the way of the advancement of the clever members of her sex, and she told herself this was a worthy object.' But alas her record as a thorn in the side of the Government was too recent, and, just as important, 'her championship of the rich and their war had been a little too violent, a little too viciously extreme to produce the necessary impression of solid respectability.'

Frustrated ambition, reasoned Sylvia, had brought to the surface a streak of indolence in her character. She drifted from the house of one rich friend to another, including her maternal aunt, Mrs Goulden Bach, who was married to an official at the Austrian embassy. For 'in spite of a socialist upbringing, she had acquired, during the fashionable high tide of the suffrage movement, a desire for wealthy and aristocratic society ... She was coldly mundane, with a touch of cynicism, born of the fact that she, the much-adored centre of a dashing movement, had fallen into the background.' Sylvia was not Christabel's only severe critic. Several prominent ex-suffragettes, while appreciating her need to relax and respecting her desire for privacy, found her attitude irritating. Ethel Smyth, never an admirer of hers, wrote to Mrs Pankhurst complaining that Christabel's aloofness, her apparent delusions of grandeur, were not making the task of raising money for the testimonial fund any easier. Her letter was returned unanswered. No doubt Christabel found the whole testimonial process as difficult and embarrassing as her ex-subordinates, and could hardly be expected to make deliberate efforts to be ingratiating. The hot-house 'democracy' of the W.S.P.U. had evaporated, and Christabel, once systematically idolized as the symbol of liberation by women who were her social superiors, was now seen by some of them, with the cruel logic of reasserted class-consciousness, as a jumped-up provincial giving herself airs.

The testimonial fund made slow progress, finally reaching a total of just under three thousand pounds (of which Lady 'Fanny' Houston, the eccentric, fiercely imperialist, and hugely wealthy widow of a shipowner gave one thousand pounds). This was much less than the sum raised for Mrs Millicent Fawcett, the retiring chief of the non-militant suffragists. But then Mrs Fawcett was the widow of a Cambridge professor who had also been a prominent Liberal politician (and who, as Postmaster-General under Gladstone, had, though in favour of votes for women, never voted against his leader on the suffrage issue); she had never savaged the Government; she had wide connections in the worlds of politics and learning; she was less of an outsider; men as well as women of influence and means could pay financial tribute to her ability without seeming to condone arson or countenance the neurotic; she did not badly *need* money, so it was less embarrassing to give it. The poorish response to the Pankhurst appeal was the more galling because when it was launched *The Times* had announced that the aim was to raise at least ten thousand pounds 'with which to defray the cost of a country house for Mrs and Miss Pankhurst, and to secure for them an annuity'. After much discussion, it was decided to carry out this scheme, even though on a reduced scale. A house was bought and furnished at Westward Ho! in north Devon, and the balance of the money—about fifteen hundred pounds—sent to Mrs Pankhurst in Canada.

While this strange arrangement was being debated and made, Christabel was making her first attempt to break into the commercial journalistic market. Lord Northcliffe, an enthusiast for the Pankhursts ever since they had joined forces with him during the war, commissioned her to write a series for one of his papers, the *Weekly Dispatch*. The eyebrows of the title-studded testimonial fund committee and of watchful ex-militants must have been raised when, in April 1921, the first of four long articles appeared under the sensational billing 'CONFESSIONS OF CHRIS-TABEL: Why I Never Married. First of a Candid Series. Miss Pankhurst deals with all the incidents of her amazing private and public career, *omitting nothing.*'

There followed a closely argued, sometimes moving, and certainly far from titillating defence of her celibacy. She had never married, she said, because she had never wanted to: not only because she had not met a man who measured up to her exacting standards, but also because she *had* to stay single in order to be an efficient leader of the women's movement. Her followers would have felt a sense of treachery if she had taken a husband. 'The Government's conviction of the suffragettes' tenacity', she declared with simple, sublime egoism, 'depended on the conviction of my own personal unending unyieldingness as leader. If I had married, the Government would have believed that I was likely sooner or later to abandon militancy.' Her husband would probably have had to face social ostracism and either her children or her work for the vote would have had to suffer.

She had, in any case, always felt that she had a family, the great family of the W.S.P.U. 'In a sense the women were my children. Children indeed they seemed to me, born a pioneer in advance of my time ... I always felt so motherly towards them and took a mother's pride in seeing them develop and gain confidence through working in our wonderful movement.' It had been delightful, too, to see suffragettes' husbands gaining a new respect for their wives as they revealed hidden qualities of intelligence and devotion to an ideal.

Christabel saw no reason to feel ashamed of her spinsterdom. Had not the unselfish work of unmarried women—Florence Nightingale and Edith Cavell to name only two—been one of England's peculiar glories? Nuns, taking religious vows, were honoured for their decision. Honour was also, she thought, due to those who, without taking formal vows of celibacy, lived up to the same ideals. Celibacy, contrary to popular belief, did not mean a life without passions or emotional fulfilment. She had had the supreme satisfaction of fulfilling her destiny; the great happiness of living a life of inspiration. 'I have known passion,' she affirmed, 'passion that strengthens one for endurance, shakes one with its mighty force, makes humans god-like, fills them with creative force. The passion of my life has been for the freeing of women, not only for reasons political and economic.' She had always sensed that 'a struggle such as ours had its highest significance elsewhere, was simply the dim reflection of a far struggle on some celestial battlefront where greater hosts than ours clash in the eternal struggle for light.' She hoped that as equality between the sexes increased, men and women would become, as it were, 'the two wings to lift humanity heavenward'.

Subsequent articles, dealing with the W.S.P.U.'s suffrage and wartime campaigns, were more prosaic. Christabel rebuked those who held that women's massive war effort rather than the suffragette guerrillas, had secured the vote. This would not have been granted, she was convinced, if politicians had not been afraid of a resumption of militancy. She dealt firmly with the suggestion that the Pankhursts had made a fortune out of militancy. Both she and Mother (she always spelled it with a capital 'M') were poorer in everything but a sense of duty done. Why, otherwise, would she have advertised for a job? Her advertisement, though it brought many replies, did little to solve her problem. Mr Selbit, a well-known music hall illusionist, offered her five pounds a performance, or twenty pounds a week if she accepted a long-term engagement, to take the leading part in his act, 'Sawing Through a Woman'. The work, he stressed, was of a non-political nature, as Miss Pankhurst had stipulated, and all expenses would be paid. There were several offers from film companies: but as Christabel (with tongue in cheek or heart on sleeve?) told the *Daily News*: 'This is not the sort of work I am looking for. I want something that will be permanent and progressive.'

The few people who were really close to her knew that she was moving towards a permanent, if debatably progressive, solution, a solution made more attractive by the levity of such offers. The spiritual bloom of the *Weekly Dispatch* article had its roots in the missionary zeal of the militant crusade. In August 1914, writing in the *Suffragette,* she had interpreted the war as 'God's vengeance upon a man-made, woman-subjecting civilization'. In 1917, she had told an audience in London that, rather than have a peace which made any concessions to Prussianism, she would be willing to see London destroyed. Humanity, she rapped, was not the final expression of the divine will. Women realized the truth of those words in the Bible — 'Fear not those that kill the body but have nothing more that they can do.' The war, she maintained, was 'in very truth a conflict between God and the Devil, and women's part must be to keep the spiritual side of the conflict uppermost'. Yet even as she continued to speak and write in terms of a millennium of pervasive feminism, she began to distinguish a small, still inner voice telling her that men and women were not like that; that both were incorrigibly imperfect, that there could be no final balance struck by them. Yet the need for an apocalyptic finality, for a Last Judgment, remained. Towards the end of the war she happened, during a chance visit to a bookshop, on a volume dealing with biblical prophecy. The vision of the Second Coming of Christ as the ultimate and only answer, the sole gateway to a really new dispensation, began to beckon her with a power which increased with every setback to her political ambition. Could it, she asked herself, be her mission to put human strivings into a heavenly perspective, to take the murderous edge off human perfectionism by setting forth the promised perfection of the reign of the Son of God on earth? Could it be that lesser employers had rejected her because the Great Employer had a task for her? It was a pleasing, a humbling and yet a dignifying thought, falling like balm on the wounds inflicted by Mr Selbit, the perfidy of statesmen, and the indelicacy of editors.

For she had strongly objected to the *Weekly Dispatch*'s souped-up presentation of her articles, and had refused the offer of a contract for a further series. It was a sad fact, and matter for serious reflection, that the mind of her patron, Lord Northcliffe, had been unhinged by the frenzy of frustrated political ambition. She did not intend to allow her resentment against Lloyd George—who could, after all, if he had really wanted to, have got her into Parliament—to poison her whole life. As a Second Adventist she could, like Sylvia, despise the pitifully inflated hopes of mere reformism; and she could be certain that the revolution which she would preach would, however long postponed, be a revolution to end all revolutions. More than that, her keen and irrepressible talent for political analysis could be employed in relating trends of the times to the great architecture of Revelation. No longer the goddess of the suffragettes, she could at least be the impresario of a *deus ex machina*. She could offer the shining clues of a divine clarity to those who walked in darkness. While escaping from the dreary toils of a vulgar careerism, she could find a job for life, scope for a new, even more sublimated, motherliness. It remained to be seen whether there was a modest livelihood to be earned.

Christabel decided to go to Canada, where Mrs Pankhurst had settled, to talk things over with Mother. She had time for only a short stay in the

Sylvia Pankhurst speaks to an East End audience outside the newly opened suffragette headquarters in Bow, *c.* 1912

May 1921: the release of Sylvia Pankhurst from prison

Sylvia Pankhurst with friends and supporters at a 'welcome back' breakfast in May 1921, after her release from Holloway Prison

house at Westward Ho! before selling it. Early in August 1921 she crossed the Atlantic with Betty, her adopted daughter, and Grace Roe, once her understudy in the W.S.P.U. and now her closest friend.

CHAPTER TWO

THE ANTI-BOLSHEVIST

On September 13th 1919, less than a year after her controversial wartime visit to the United States and Canada, Mrs Pankhurst arrived in New York on the White Star liner *Adriatic*. Again she was to lecture on the evils of Bolshevism and the part which women should play in combating them. In so doing, she was ploughing no lone furrow. She joined, however unwittingly, a raucous band of hectic and often sinister harrowers. America was at the height of an hysterical Red Scare, deliberately fostered by financiers and industrialists who were determined to break the back of militant unionism. They had the active approval of federal, state and municipal government and the wild co-operation of the big-circulation press. A wartime scarcity of labour and the need to keep vital industries in uninterrupted production had, despite an 'emergency' veto on strikes, enabled organized labour to wring some concessions on pay and hours. It had hoped to exploit this tardy trend. But when the war ended, employers' and citizens' associations had begun to behave like so many extensions of the rapidly reviving Ku Klux Klan in their bid to reassert what J. P. Morgan Jr called 'American principles of freedom' in industry.

Mrs Pankhurst was surely unaware of the complex rights and wrongs of this murderous contest, or of the extent to which American trust capitalism, with its huge ramifications, private armies, agents provocateurs, and bought political power differed from British capitalism even at its most reactionary. Her message of social service as the ideal for all sections of the community was intended for Wall Street as much as for Union Hall. So with conscience clear and wits alert she sallied forth from her cabin, clad in a long Edwardian gown, her thick grey hair meticulously coiffured, a velvet band with a cameo brooch around her neck (for she had evolved an idiosyncratically regal fashion reminiscent of that heyday of Empire in which she had been such a notable rebel) to receive the reporters on deck.

She had, she briskly informed them, little time for President Wilson's pet, the League of Nations: and America had shown that it shared her opinion by refusing to have anything to do with it. She too preferred to deal in realities. Britain, France and the United States should immediately form an alliance for the preservation of the peace of the world. As the three most powerful nations, they alone could guarantee it, and they should make their alliance quite openly, irrespective of the criticisms of other nations. In America, where Mrs Pankhurst was still, despite the meteoric rise of Lady Astor, considered a 'world figure', she blossomed. She looked much younger than her sixty-one years, addressed several meetings in New York, and floated on a stream of interviews as in her own warm and rightful element. 'Parlour Bolshevism,' she told the *Evening Post*'s representative, with that faint, ironically disdainful smile which had quelled many a dissident and made English judges sweat under their horsehair wigs, 'parlour Bolshevism seems to be quite prevalent here. Men and women during the war were awakened as never before to an interest in labour conditions.' A sentimental attitude towards 'the workers' had made well-meaning people an easy prey for Bolshevist propaganda. It was her mission to put them right, and—at a fee ranging from 250 to 500 dollars a lecture—she could continue to trumpet the programme of the now-defunct Women's Party.

'I have spent my life with the masses,' she claimed. 'I know and love them. But because they work with their hands I do not think they are so much different from other people. I do not believe they have a direct revelation.' She believed in the necessity of government by those classes— 'the leisured classes if you like'—which had the experience, the education and the training, and, most important, a sense of *noblesse oblige* and of the urgency of making a strong and reasoned defence of the values of a Christian civilization. Full-scale military intervention in Russia was part of that defence; for there were many 'loyal' Russians who longed, given support, to overthrow the Bolsheviks. Mrs Pankhurst's graphic descriptions of Bolshevik bureaucracy, crushing free enterprise in any form, were particularly calculated to appeal to American rags-to-riches psychology and resistance to federal interference.

After leaving New York she headed south, travelling through a country where feminist rejoicing was at its height. Only two weeks before her arrival the Nineteenth Amendment to the Constitution had been adopted, granting to twenty-six million adult American women the right to vote in all elections on equal terms with men. This victory was the climax of a prodigious marathon of persistence and organization. The suffrage campaign had lasted over fifty years and had had to win its way state by state.

The fact that its leaders had been trained in techniques of reform in the anti-slavery and temperance movements, and that its first successes had been gained in the Middle West (where women's votes proved a bulwark of fundamentalist Christianity in its struggle with the saloon bar), had given the movement a flavour of spiritual superiority and militant puritanism even stronger—because often officially recognized and encouraged—than in England. American women, or at least the middle- and upper-class females who had, in their frustrated leisure, formed the vast majority, if not the entirety, of the suffrage movement, were, they felt, the superiors *as well as* the equals of men. They were the rightful leaders of the national family. This rule of the matriarchs had no need to send women into politics to guard its power, which remained in the home. 'I disclaim all desire to meddle with vulgar politics,' wrote Elizabeth Cady Stanton, the most vigorous suffragist of the nineteenth century, 'or to sit in council with rum-drinking, tobacco-chewing men, with thick-lipped voluptuaries who disgrace our national councils with their grossness and profanity. Until a new type of man be placed at the helm of the ship of state' (and under matriarchal pressure he gradually was) 'rest assured we women shall decline all nominations for office.'

Mrs Pankhurst, until the British Parliament had been opened to women in 1918, had shared these views. She found the matriarchal atmosphere— the very antithesis of that free co-operation between the sexes preached by Emma Goldman and Sylvia Pankhurst—stimulating. She could claim to have had a considerable influence on suffragism in the United States. Not only had her three pre-war lecture tours given American women an example of evangelistic aggression in which their own movement (partly because of the indifference, or even friendliness of most American males) was lacking, but several American suffragists had spent several years in Britain on active commando service with the W.S.P.U. They had tasted the full range of suffragette experience, including imprisonment and forcible feeding. In 1907 Harriot Stanton Blatch, the daughter of Eliza- beth Stanton, had returned to America to set up her own Women's Political Union, using the shock tactics and spectacular publicity parades that she had seen so effectively pioneered by the Pankhursts. In 1913 Alice Paul (who in 1909 had entered the Mansion House early in the morning disguised as a charwoman and waited twelve hours to make a Votes for Women protest at the Lord Mayor's Banquet) and Lucy Burns, veterans of many a desperate Pankhurstian exploit, came back to rouse American women to a new•pitch of militancy in the push for the federal amendment. They merged their organization with Harriott Stanton Blatch's to form the *Women's Party*. This kept up such a constant furore by deputation, picket and poster during the war on President Wilson and the Democratic Party that harassed politicians referred to its members as 'Bolshevists' and over a hundred were imprisoned. A number of these hunger struck and were forcibly fed, thus tacking on to the tail end of the orderly, organizational suffragist progress an exotic pennant of Pankhurst extremism.

There were many old friends to meet, many reminiscences to make. But a note of controversy was soon struck, and this no doubt was to Mrs Pankhurst's liking: for she had been worried in the past about the obstinate lack of male opposition in America, and thoroughly gratified when the Women's Party finally slapped American politicians into open resentment. Tension was not only the lever of reform but the soul of publicity. Miss Mary Kilbreth, president of the American National Association to Oppose Woman Suffrage, now at its last desperate gasp, obligingly provided a touch of it. In a wildly misinformed press statement she questioned whether Mrs Pankhurst was a fit person to teach American women their patriotic duty. 'You will recall', she wrote, 'the reign of terror and the frenzy of depredation by bombs, kerosene and vitriol throwing which paralysed society and law in England … of which Mrs Pankhurst was the guiding spirit, and which was believed to have been the symptom that convinced Germany of England's impotence.' Even in her present phase Mrs Pankhurst could not be considered sound. 'The purpose of her visit to the United States, as of her previous visits, is apparently to meddle in our national politics.'

This outburst brought a rejoinder in the form of a long letter in the *New York Times* (headed 'Militant Suffragist as World Reconstructor') from Rheta Childe Dorr, an American suffragist who had helped Mrs Pankhurst to write her autobiography, *My Own Story*, published in 1914. After detailing the patriotic activities of the Pankhursts, carried out at a time when Americans were busy keeping out of the war, she ended: 'If the Germans counted on British militant suffragism as a symptom of British impotency in war, they simply made one more of their notorious and Gott-inspired mistakes. If the "antis" are counting on that long-past fight between the suffragettes and Mr Asquith's Government to prevent Mrs Pankhurst from doing a one hundred per cent efficient piece of reconstruction work, both here and in Europe, they are making another mistake, quite as Teutonic and unavailing.'

The echoes of this skirmish had barely died away before it was time for Mrs Pankhurst to come north, travelling by ship to Halifax, Nova Scotia, to begin her long transcontinental tour of Canada. She landed with a group of English war brides, who were welcomed by a committee of local women and given a canteen meal before being routed to their various destinations. In the cold winter weather, Mrs Pankhurst's optimism temporarily froze within her. She felt, as she did from time to time (it is a tribute to her resilience that she did not feel it more often), a twinge of resentment at the people in England, many of whom should have known better, who persisted in seeing her as a suffragette pure and simple, a woman of one role whose usefulness was now virtually exhausted. What about all her hard and brilliantly effective work in local government in Manchester? Did that go for nothing? Why should she allow herself to be buried, smothered with flowery tributes, when she was still so very much alive? 'Christabel and I', she wrote to Ethel Smyth, 'kept our noses to the grindstone for a long time because *someone* had to do it, not because, as people think sometimes, we are women of one idea, obsessed by it ... There are many things I would have liked to be and to do.' Now that she had to earn an independence for her old age and provide for the children (who had been left in England under the care of Nurse Pine), she was only too glad that in doing it she could 'help a little to keep the Empire together and defeat the Bolshevists and defeatists who are hard at work here trying to destroy the victory our armies won in the war'. Sometimes she wished that she did not have to keep on and on lecturing, but she had to accept the necessity. Apart from the children, she had never been a devotee of thrift. 'I cannot', as she put it, 'reduce my standard to one of constant pinch and save.'

This was her fourth trip to Canada. She had been there in 1911, stirring up the suffragists (who had been battling for the provincial and federal votes since the 1880s), and twice during the war: in 1916, when she spoke on women's war service, and in 1918, when she launched a shortlived Women's Party on Christabel's model. By the end of 1918 Canadian women had the federal vote, and had been enfranchised in all except three provinces (they had to wait until 1944 to get the vote in Quebec). But events in 1919 seemed to give special significance to her warnings about Bolshevism. All through the spring and summer there had been a succession of parades and civic welcomes as most of the four hundred thousand Canadians who had served overseas came home. Over sixty thousand had been killed, and Canadian troops had distinguished themselves at Ypres, in the Battle of the Somme, and in the offensive of 1918 which finally broke German resistance.

Yet, as in Britain, the bands and the bunting, the fireworks and the frolicking searchlights, the noble sentiments of thousands of speeches, masked a profound discontent which was at least partly inspired by the example of the Workers' Republic in Russia. People were tired of the two-party see-saw of Liberals and Conservatives, and of the evident blindness of the wartime coalition, led first by Sir Robert Borden, then by Sir Arthur Meighen, to shifts of economic power and gross profiteering. In 1919 Winnipeg was brought almost to a standstill by a general strike intended as the first blow in a widespread movement of socialist liberation. There was talk of forming Soviets, but this surge of vaguely revolutionary idealism was quickly and completely crushed by federal police and troops called in by the civic authorities. Between 1896, when the vast prairies ('the last, best West') of Canada began to be explored and settled, and 1911 more than three and a half million immigrants had entered the country. Though British and Americans were still in a majority, many of these were Germans, Scandinavians, Ukrainians, with small minorities of Russians, Austrians, Poles and Italians. There were also curious religious refugees from Russia, the Mennonites and the Doukhobors—theocratic, separatist and puritanically austere—who hoped that the wide open spaces of Manitoba and Saskatchewan were big enough for them to be forgotten and left alone by secular governments. Even they had been roused by attempts to enlist them in the armed forces, and resisted eccentrically by appearing naked in the streets of raw prairie townships in protest against this and other violations of their privacy.

Already in 1918 Mrs Pankhurst had advised a strict embargo on non-Anglo-Saxon immigration, a theme to which she now returned. But even the normally conservative farmers of the prairie provinces were in revolt. Wartime food shortages in Europe had enormously boosted their production: but this had been overmatched by an even more startling expansion in mining and industry. By 1917 Canada, rich in nickel, copper, lead and zinc, was turning out almost a third of the huge quantities of shells used by the British forces in France. Apart from the old-established urban centres of Montreal and Toronto, a string of towns—Regina, Saskatoon, Calgary, Edmonton—had grown rapidly from board-shanty trading posts to sizable industrial towns. Farmers began to organize themselves into a political pressure group to demand government intervention to protect their interests against a post-war slump and the machinations of city-slicker financiers. The United Farmers Organization gained power in Ontario in 1919 and was influential in other provinces. In 1920 at Winnipeg it launched a new federal party—the National Progressive Party. Its socialistic programme—taxes on business profits, public ownership of utilities, legislation to break the stranglehold of big business—was not motivated by a study of Marx but by a fear of political venality and of the dominance of industry and finance capitalism. Canada's new wealth and importance must be matched by a new unity which could only be achieved by bold, definite action by the Federal Government. This could no longer be content with holding the ring, but must take the responsibility of shaping an economic future which would do justice to all sections of the community.

With this kind of patriotic doctrine, administered by a National Government purged of the irrelevance of party strife, Mrs Pankhurst had strong affinities. If the responsible sections of the community could forestall the Bolshevists by in effect 'abolishing the proletariat' (this had been one of Christabel's favourite Women's Party slogans), by the provision of adequate educational and health services, a rational housing programme, and a sense of national urgency which would appeal to and employ all classes, then all would be well. The British Labour Party's notion of re-housing the workers was, she maintained, hopelessly out of date, and did nothing to relieve housewives of the traditional horrors of domestic drudgery. The answer, she urged, was not 'an inferior imitation of a middle-class villa for each individual family', but large community blocks, where families, without sacrificing privacy, could share a number of 'luxury' services hitherto monopolized by the rich. Lighting, heating, cooking, laundry should be communalized, and each community should have day nurseries, crèches, infant schools, libraries, gymnasia and infirmaries.

So eloquent did she wax on this theme that by the time she reached Victoria, British Columbia, in May 1920, Mrs Pankhurst was being billed as 'the eminent economist'. During the next three months she lectured to an estimated total of some seventy thousand people in summer educational camps in western Canada. She emphasised the part which a dedicated spirit of national service could play in enlisting the natural enthusiasm of youth, which otherwise might be in danger of seduction by the specious idealism of the Bolshevists. 'Our sons and daughters', she proclaimed, now in the full flow of her recognition as the Mother Figure of a revitalized Imperial Ideal, 'must be trained in national service, taught to give as well as to receive. The daughters of the rich, for instance, should be taught nursing, so that in time there might be developed a vast national organization which would ensure that every woman, in no matter how remote a district, would receive proper care and attention in time of childbirth or illness.'

By August she was back in Victoria, a city to which she had taken a great fancy. Small (in 1920 the population was only thirty-eight thousand), intensely and exclusively British, it was, with its well-gardened, tennis-courted villas, the essence of well-to-do suburbanity. Founded as a fort in 1843 by officials of the Hudson's Bay Company, its garrison flavour had been heightened by the establishment of a naval base in the 1860s, and by the fact that the Royal Engineers, in its early period as a crown colony, had built roads, acted as a police force, and when disbanded had remained as settlers. Victoria warmed to the imperialist fervour of Mrs Pankhurst, which in its eyes quite obliterated her suffragette peculiarities. She was accepted at her own current valuation. Pleasing zephyrs of respectability caressed her soul. She stayed for a while at the St James's Bay Hotel, then rented a villa in Hollywood Crescent, a select residential area with a glorious sea view. She sent for Nurse Pine to join her with the children, Mary, Joan and Kathleen Pankhurst, now about four years old. Victoria, she wrote to Ethel Smyth, was 'a lovely spot and very cheap'. It suited her so well that she had gained too much weight and was taking a course of slimming massage. She was reluctant, she said, to do anything but potter about, sewing for herself and the children, and reading—at least until December, when she was due to resume her anti-Bolshevism in the United States.

Yet even in Victoria, among her roses and her family, Mrs Pankhurst's busy Fate would not leave her alone. She received an invitation to a dinner party at the Empress Hotel from Mrs Neville Rolphe, secretary of Britain's Social Hygiene Council, formed primarily to campaign against venereal disease (on the increase partly as a result of the return of infected soldier 'heroes'). One of the other guests invited by Mrs Rolphe—who was on a world fact-finding tour—was Dr Gordon Bates, recently demobilized from the Canadian Army Medical Corps. Dr Bates had formed a National Council for Combating Venereal Diseases to aid the Dominion Council of Health in a campaign of preventive education and curative treatment. Special clinics had been opened by provincial authorities with the help of federal grants; films and literature had been prepared, and a team of medical lecturers recruited. The one thing lacking was a speaker who could appeal to the people's conscience and breathe life and the ardour of a moral crusade into a collection of statistics. Mrs Pankhurst, with her well-known belief in a high moral standard as the only true preventive, seemed providentially designed for this role.

CHAPTER THREE

THE SOCIAL DISEASE

When Mrs Pankhurst left Victoria for the United States, she was full of the prospect of a new career, a new cause. She had been anti-Bolshevizing since 1917, and there were plenty of others now on the same tack. She kept in constant touch with Dr Bates in Toronto. From Raleigh, North Carolina, she wrote asking him to send specimen literature of his association to an address in Chicago, whence it could be forwarded while she was lecturing in the Middle West. She enclosed a cutting from the Raleigh *News and Observer* about a case in which the State Supreme Court had upheld the decision of a jury in Mecklenburg to award a woman damages because her husband had infected her with venereal disease. 'More and more,' was the editorial comment, 'the same purity is required of men that is required of women. There is less and less toleration for men who feel they must sow their wild oats before they settle down for life.' This, thought Mrs Pankhurst, was encouraging. It showed that even in backward southern states a better public opinion was growing. How could she get into this fight? Commercial agencies would not commission her to lecture on what was still euphemistically referred to as 'the social disease', so she hoped to link up with Dr Bates and the National Council for Combating Venereal Diseases (N.C.C.V.D.).

In March 1921 she wrote to Dr Bates from the Hotel Pennsylvania, New York. This was her base for the next month, during which her speaking assignments included a visit to Bryn Mawr Girls' College. In New York, she said, she had met officials of the American Society for Combating Venereal Diseases, had seen some of its educational films and read its literature. She felt that much could be done to interest the mass of people in the subject if it was brought to life by actual examples of personal tragedy, such as the Raleigh case. 'It is always the concrete case that prepares the public for general reform,' she remarked, and recalled the effective play which the W.S.P.U. had made with the 'Queenie' Gerald case in 1913.

On her own initiative she had arranged—at a reduced fee of one

139

hundred dollars—to speak to women's institutes in Edmonton and else-where on her new theme. But she wanted to speak under the auspices of the N.C.C.V.D., and hoped that Dr Bates would be able to fix other engagements, beginning in Toronto, so that she could pitch straight into the campaign on her way back to Victoria. Dr Bates asked her for a summary of the kind of address she would give, perhaps to quieten any misgivings there might be about the celebrated Pankhurst frankness. She replied that she would not give a standardized speech. There were so many facets to the question that she could easily give a different speech every day. But she could say that she would appeal for a higher standard of public health and public morals, and would illustrate the need for both from her experience of local government in Manchester. She preferred to leave medical details to medical men: but if no expert was present she would undertake to speak in general terms about venereal disease. She was, she concluded, an extempore speaker. 'Your council must trust me to say the right and tactful things in the right way if I am to speak under their auspices.'

On April 20th Mrs Pankhurst, due to speak in Massey Hall, Toronto, two days later on 'Social Hygiene and the World's Unrest', showed all her old flair for what she called 'working up interest in a meeting'. She startled reporters at her press conference (and provided sub-editors with some juicy headlines) by stating that the subject of her talk was closely related to the infectious mental disease known as Bolshevism. Both were the result of a mistaken and promiscuous flouting of traditional decencies. Women, she added, had the power, if they would only use it, to raise men to their own level of sexual morality. The *Toronto Daily Star*, while pointing out that Pankhurst combativeness took different forms ('if memory is not deceptive Sylvia is this day in prison as a consequence of sympathizing with the dictatorship of the proletariat'), gave Mrs Pank-hurst a lyrical buildup. 'She has been a woman of sorrows and acquainted with grief. As she was escorted to a seat in the House of Commons at Ottawa in 1916, when the war was at its depth, the little fellows who crowded the chamber that day felt the presence of motherhood clad in shining armour. The armour is still there, and motherhood also, as to-night will show. So lights on, and hats off.'

Massey Hall was full to overflowing. Mr Justice Riddell, president of the N.C.C.V.D. and chairman of the meeting, declared that forty-thou-sand people in Toronto alone, and half a million in the Dominion as a whole, had venereal disease, and that most of the surgical operations on

women were due to it. Dr Marlow, who followed him, stressed that venereal disease was preventable, and spoke of the need for healthy recreation.
It was left to Mrs Pankhurst to provide the guts and the moral fireworks of
the evening. As the *Toronto Globe* put it, 'she lifted the question from the
purely medical to the realm of the spiritual.' This was a question, she said,
which had occupied her for a long time. In fact—though this might
surprise her audience—the main motive behind the suffragette campaign
had been her horror at the prevalence of filthy sexual disease and moral
squalor, and her determination to empower responsible women, through
the weapon of the vote, to end such a state of affairs. In an old, crowded
country like Britain it might take a long time to do this, but in a young
country like Canada, with its small population, it should be possible to do
it much more quickly. She and her daughter Christabel were just as convinced now as they had been in 1905 that prevention was more important
than medical cure, necessary as that was. Men must learn to control
themselves. Despite all the 'modern' ridicule, chastity was still a cardinal
virtue. Women were not happy 'to have as husbands men who are merely
physically cured. Christabel and I knew that good women have ever
wanted to give their best when they bestowed their hand in marriage, and
that they would never be satisfied till men had the same feeling.'

The knowledge that Christabel was soon to join her buoyed Mrs
Pankhurst on the long, loquacious journey westward. On May 18th, from
Medicine Hat, Saskatchewan, she sent a bustling progress report to Dr
Bates. She had addressed meetings at Windsor, Ontario, at Winnipeg and
Brandon in Manitoba, and at Regina. She was en route for Alberta, where
meetings were scheduled at Lethbridge, Calgary and Edmonton. Response, she considered, had been good; but she was still worried by the
lack of popular appeal—it was no use preaching to the converted. Most
people shuddered at the very thought of going to a 'lecture'. Would it
not be better to call meetings 'Public Health Demonstrations' or 'Mass
Meetings to Support a Campaign Against Venereal Disease'? She could
personally rouse a lot of interest and make many influential contacts if it
was arranged for her to arrive in a place a day or two before she spoke in
public. Most of the seating should be free: but there should be a charge for
reserved seats, a collection to defray expenses and for the council's educational work, and literature should be *on sale*—not given away—at every
meeting. One had to be prepared for invitations to hold extra meetings in
churches and a whole range of institutes ... So the accumulated wisdom
of a decade of militant suffragism was poured out upon Dr Bates.

A further report and more advice followed when, after a twelve-day tour of Vancouver Island, Mrs Pankhurst returned to Victoria for her summer holiday. Even in the excitement of reunion with her own adopted family and with Christabel and Betty and Grace Roe, she did not slacken, nor cease to put forward suggestions for the big N.C.C.V.D. drive planned for Toronto and Montreal in the autumn. She could never be idle for long – and domestication, to her, was a form of idleness, a pretty haven into which one put for refitting. She had to know that there was a series of platforms, a string of audiences, ahead.

Christabel, interviewed in Montreal on her arrival, had given no public hint of Second Adventism. The *Montreal Star* described her 'graceful, girlish figure, merry blue eyes, musical voice and curly brown hair – the redoubtable Christabel, as she was familiarly known to everyone from street urchin to cabinet minister'. She was, she said, in Canada for a holiday and had no plans for speaking engagements. Woman suffrage had justified itself so completely, had so utterly disproved the wild fears of male politicians, that it was no longer a matter for controversy. The question which now most interested her was the abolition of poverty. She hoped that Britain would lead the way in the development of natural resources by scientific methods. She also hoped, while in Canada, to study the possibility of settling Canada's extensive under- or even unpopulated areas with immigrants from crowded Britain, and to present a report on her findings.

When Christabel got to Victoria she found, though affectionately greeted, that the bustle in the house (Mrs Pankhurst had moved to Beach Drive, Oak Bay, and there was a resident governess to teach the children) was more connected with Mother's impending departure for Toronto than with her own arrival. It was not, one imagines, the ideal atmosphere in which to discuss at any length her spiritual ambition, still a tender plant. Mrs Pankhurst was more concerned to feel God's blessing on her current endeavours than with a facet of Christianity which could, if widely and blindly believed, lead to a partial or total paralysis of human effort. She was focused, as always, on the next stage rather than on the reign of the Prince of Peace.

After quite a short visit, Christabel and Grace Roe left for the United States. For all her devotion to her mother, Christabel was not inclined to be drawn into the vortex of the V.D. campaign. She, too, wanted to strike out on a line of her own, and the wealthy women's clubs of California were keen to meet the great Suffragette Pin-Up in the flesh (drawings and photographs of the youthfully impudent Christabel had adorned the rooms of tens of thousands of women). The two friends stayed first in Santa Barbara, then at a cottage, aptly called 'The Little Mission', in Hollywood. Once more she was unsuccessfully approached to take part in a film about her own exploits. She enjoyed the sunshine and the social climate: she was, for the moment, the prime attraction for every hostess of ambition in the area. Grace Roe, as in the old days, organized her engagements and sifted her visitors. She did not entirely agree with Christabel's religious views—she herself, like Annie and Jessie Kenney, was soon to become a theosophist—but felt that she must help in her struggle to reorient herself.

Grace Roe, an Irishwoman of gentle birth, was training to be a nurse in London when she first saw Christabel. It was at the mammoth open-air demonstration (there were twenty platforms and newspapers estimated the crowd at five hundred thousand) staged by the W.S.P.U. in Hyde Park in the summer of 1908. She had pushed her way through to where Christabel was speaking. 'It was warm', Miss Roe remembers, 'and she had taken off her bonnet and cloak and was wearing a green tussore silk dress. She was so graceful, had lovely hands, and a wonderful way of using them. The men in the crowd were swaying about, singing a parody of some popular song:

> Put me on an island with a beautiful girl,
> But not with a blooming suffragette ...

Yet she soon had them quiet and eating out of her hand. I said to myself: "She's all sincerity from the top of her head to her fingertips. I would follow her anywhere." It was curious to watch her at a meeting. While other people were speaking, she would sit, apparently dull and listless— almost lumpish: but when her turn came, she would light up. I adored her, and had a dozen different pictures of her in my room at home ... '

Christabel's Second Adventism, which she now began to deploy, rather shyly, in public, did not seem likely to bring her a financial competence (for she was no more resigned to pinching and saving than her mother). Collections taken at her lectures did not amount to much. Her audiences were not pleased when she ended a stirring account of bygone battles, or a shrewd analysis of the international situation, with a sudden, rather jerky paean to the Great Clue. Oh, she knew that Christ's coming had been expected all through the centuries since His crucifixion and resurrection, but that was no reason to sneer at the belief. The divine time scale was different from human reckoning. Was it not true that in any household, when the return of a beloved, long-absent traveller was expected, the family rushed again and again to the door at the sound of footsteps or a knock, only to have their hopes dashed. Yet the traveller would come at last.

This unsophisticated stuff was slightly embarrassing: but Christabel's implication that women were just as twisted by sin as men was positively offensive, and anachronistic. For many years American men had shown themselves almost masochistically eager to accept the fair sex's estimation of itself as a superior race. No less a person than the hard-drinking, he-man writer Jack London had asserted that 'women are the true conservators of the race. Men are the wastrels, the gamblers, and in the end it is by their women that they are saved.' Since 1917 Los Angeles had resounded with the bizarre, sex-shot gospel of Aimée Semple Macpherson, and was already the happy hunting-ground of a colourful spectrum of religious charlatans dispensing the exotic, cocktailed essences of oriental faiths. American women were used to shopping around for a formula which suited their egos. The more militantly feminist of them had not been content to accept the Bible, which they regarded as a kind of exultant manual of male domination. Elizabeth Cady Stanton, with the help of some collaborators, had actually produced a Woman's Bible, dismissing the Old Testament as the uninspired history of an ignorant, underdeveloped people. The myth of Adam and Eve was clearly the product of an insane patriarchal malice. Incidents such as that of the drunken Lot sleeping with his daughters were typical of a degenerate male attitude. The New Testament had a more acceptable tone. Christ had suffered for his pioneering feminism. But the misogynist Paul had so completely distorted his message that Christianity in its present form was no religion for any self-respecting suffragist. Mary Baker Eddy had gone further by founding her own religion, ordaining her own priestesses, and writing her own Bible, *Science and Health, With a Key to the Scriptures*. She had insisted that God was at least half Female, and was believed by many devout Christian Scientists to be a Second Incarnation of the Christ.

Lady Astor had shown her sex loyalty by becoming a Christian Scientist. Yet here was Christabel, of all people, not only taking the Bible at its face value, but talking as though Zoroastrianism, Hinduism, Yoga, the various permutations of Buddhism, and the new world faith of Baha'i, had no relevance whatsoever. It really was quite incomprehensible, and acceptable at best as one more example of the well-known, obstinate eccentricity of the English.

When Mrs Pankhurst, who in January 1922 moved to Toronto to join the staff of the N.C.C.V.D. as chief lecturer, wrote asking Christabel to join the family, Grace Roe urged her to accept, and escorted her back. A sudden decision by Mrs Pankhurst to electioneer on behalf of Conservative Prime Minister Sir Arthur Meighen and the continuation of a national coalition had caused a momentary panic at N.C.C.V.D. headquarters, and she had with some difficulty been persuaded by telegram to abandon the project. It was just as well, since the Conservatives were crushingly defeated in the general election of December 1921, and government grants (from which the N.C.C.V.D. benefited) were then controlled by a Liberal-Progressive Government. But Mrs Pankhurst's handling of a fund-raising-cum-educational campaign in Toronto, Ottawa and Montreal during the autumn and early winter was a spectacular success. Profiling her in a feature article, *Maclean's Magazine* reported that she worked like a slave at her social hygienics, travelling and speaking tirelessly, and showing a remarkable talent for adapting herself to different audiences. In the space of six weeks she had addressed the Masonic Lodge, Rotary Clubs, the Canadian Manufacturers' Association, the Daughters of the Empire, many women's institutes, the Women's Law Association, the Women's Press Club, men and women factory workers, university students, church congregations, women in reformatories, printers on strike, and a string of drawing-room gatherings in the homes of social leaders.

The National Council's publicity concentrated heavily on her patriotic, anti-Bolshevist record, for there had been a disturbing tendency in some quarters to confuse Mrs Pankhurst with her daughter Sylvia. But by the time she set out for a tour of Ontario and the eastern provinces, this misconception had been effectively dispelled. Thousands of people were to be seen wearing the N.C.C.V.D. badge (in the old W.S.P.U. colours of purple, white and green) which she had designed. Provincial prime ministers with their entire cabinets were proud to appear on the same platform with her. Local officials basked in her approval, and sometimes writhed under her reproofs. When the Mayor of Bathurst, New Brunswick, during a perambulation of the town, told her that the most impressive new building was a Home for Fallen Women, Mrs Pankhurst witheringly demanded: 'And where, pray, is your Home for Fallen Men?'

Her eminence was such that in April 1922 she was chosen as one of

Canada's main representatives at the Women's Pan American Conference held in Baltimore. Lady Astor was the guest of honour and principal speaker, but Mrs Pankhurst's glamour and audience appeal was still so powerful that, though she had only five minutes to summarize Canada's social hygiene campaign, she had most of the three thousand delegates standing on their seats, cheering and waving their handkerchiefs. She and Lady Astor talked about prohibition. Lady Astor, though an out-and-out prohibitionist, had been forced to realize that liquor could not be enacted out of circulation in Britain. Mrs Pankhurst had heard too much of the evils of bootlegging to approve of restrictive legislation. Reform had to come, she thought, from within, not from without. Nevertheless, she told the annual convention of the influential Women's Christian Temperance Union in Toronto a little later that the three greatest evils in the Empire were materialism (the lack of an ideal of service), intemperance, and sexual immorality: and she hoped that the W.C.T.U. would soon be able to turn its efficient wrath against the last-named foe.

In the early summer of 1922 Christabel arrived in Toronto, and soon found that her services as an orthodox evangelical and Second Adventist were much more appreciated in that almost oppressively Protestant city than in California. When, by special invitation, she gave a series of sermons in the Knox Presbyterian Church in November, the congregations were so large that the doors had to be locked long before the service began. 'Without Me ye can do nothing' was the text of her first talk. Legislation, however well-meaning, the grant of political power to women, however just and necessary, could not be expected to cure the radical depravity of human nature, the universal cancer of original sin. Only the Son of God, when He returned in His power and glory, could do that. Despite the attempts of the so-called Higher Criticism (a product, like so much else that was undesirable, of Germany) to kill belief in the literal inspiration of the Bible, she was convinced that it was 'not the Bible which was on trial before us; but we who are on trial before the Bible'. At subsequent services she spoke on 'Signs of the Times' and 'The Sin Question'. It was fashionable, she said, but quite mistaken, to talk of a 'new morality'. This was simply a current manifestation of the age-long rebellion against the morality of God as exemplified by Christ. It was natural, when absolute Christian standards were everywhere being undermined, for the young to snatch at pleasure. But she felt that if the issue were put squarely before them they would, with their 'fresh, untainted minds', find a *real* challenge in a study of the prophetic writings of

the Bible, which offered great intellectual excitement and a new dimension of understanding — 'to see in this preliminary turmoil the oncoming
of the Kingdom of God fills the heart and soul with comfort.' Some
observers complained that her manner was too much that of a barrister
manquée addressing a recalcitrant jury. Others pointed out that her conversion was not as radical as might at first appear. Had she not merely
replaced the vote by Christ as the panacea for all human ills? But her actual
congregations found her urgent lucidity a pleasant and stimulating change
from the soporific shibboleths of routine evangelical oratory.

With her first book, *The Lord Cometh!*, about to be published in New
York, she began work on her second, entitled *Pressing Problems of the
Closing Age*. In *The Lord Cometh!* she listed the Old Testament prophecies
already fulfilled — Christ's birth at Bethlehem, His crucifixion and
resurrection. She was not, she emphasized, writing on a sudden impulse.
For several years her faith had seemed 'too fragile a flower to expose to
the cold wind of other people's possible scepticism. I felt that I must go
slowly, study more, become better qualified to defend the faith that is in
me.' Drawing perhaps on her Californian experiences, she denounced the
current fad for synthetic religions which left out the awkward facts of sin
and Christ's atonement for it. This selective toying with truth was another
symptom of the drift towards a religion of humanity in which man was
his own measure. Out of this, as Nietzsche (a Hun again, you see?) had
hoped, would grow the worship of Superman, and Supermen, as history
showed, were liable to turn into devils incarnate — very limbs of that
Prince of Darkness whom Christabel, in her somehow rather toytown
cosmos, believed to have a very real existence.

In *Pressing Problems* she fixed the return of the Jews to the Holy Land,
and Mussolini's attempt to reinflate the arrogance of the Roman Empire
in Europe, as two signs of the near approach of Armageddon. The world
was plunging, she was sure, into 'the scientific barbarism which will mark
the end of this age'. Already in the last war this barbarism had struck at
civilian populations. That human lust for power which produced the
great wars of the past was bound to produce one greater than all the rest,
a contest that would be truly final. She appealed to philosophers and
politicians to 'renounce human speculation in favour of the study of
prophecy as it applies to the dangers and perplexities of today and tomorrow'. But her reasoning, as clipped and cocksure as it had been in
1905, ended on the horns of a hopeless dilemma: which was the most
virtuous course — to strive by all means to settle human differences and so

postpone the Second Coming, or to hasten by a deliberate and insensate iniquity the Divine Intervention?

In December 1922 the New York correspondent of *Truth* reported that 'the Pankhursts have brought forth fruit meet for repentance. It was quite an unexpected pleasure to run across Mamma in Toronto, of all places, where the Most Protestant of all cities pays her a salary to preach hygiene to her younger sisters in the community. She exerts a wise and restraining influence over their manners which is much appreciated by conservatives. Christabel is also there, and has been converted to Christianity of a somewhat rigid type, which brings her into great demand as a lecturer in churches on literal inspiration.' Nurse Pine at least remained impervious to Christabel's gloomy logic, and was apt to make irreverent jokes to the effect that if the Second Advent was liable to come at any moment, it seemed hardly worthwhile educating the children or cooking dinner. Undeterred by such homely nudges, Christabel continued to prosper on the Protestant circuit. In the summer of 1923 she carried the fight across the border, taking part in a series of Bible conferences and appearing as one of the main evangelists at tented but staid revivalist meetings in New York. 'Those who remember the fierce crusades for Votes for Women', said one report, 'are surprised to see a quiet, slender figure in demure grey' (her favourite green silk gowns had, with other childish things, been put away) 'acknowledging that she has lived in a fool's paradise and thanking God her eyes have been opened.' In March 1924, from the pulpit of Calvary Baptist Church, she assured listeners that the world's unrest was due to the absence of its True King.

Soon after her return to her home in St Mary Street, Toronto, Mrs Pankhurst began to show symptoms of physical and mental exhaustion. For four and a half years she had imposed upon a frame already weakened by incredible exertions and ordeals a schedule calculated to sap the stamina of a woman half her age. Now a vice-president of the Public Health Association, she had recently carried out a motor tour of northern and eastern Ontario, travelling more than four thousand miles and speaking in some thirty towns. Following this, she had spoken several times a day during the annual National Exhibition in Toronto, and had delivered a fervent plea to the delegates of the Federated Women's Institutes, assembled at Ottawa. 'Help us', she said, 'to educate the people of the Dominion to the necessity of a single standard of morals – that of the highest. Teach your children reverence for the marriage vow of men and women. Instill into their minds the belief in purity of body, mind and soul.'

She was given six months' leave from her work with the N.C.C.V.D. (which in 1923 had been rechristened the Canadian Social Hygiene Council). At the Toronto Exhibition she had been attracted by the Bermuda stall, and now decided to visit that island with Nurse Pine, Christabel, and the four girls. Though she had become a Canadian citizen, the idol of Canada's organization women, and the soul of the war on the social disease, she never went back to Toronto.

PART FOUR

MRS PANKHURST'S
LAST STAND

———— ◆•••◆ ————

CHAPTER ONE

THE LONG WAY HOME

Bermuda, with its balmy climate and leisurely, parochial social tempo – it was not then high-geared to the American tourist trade, but as imperially British as Victoria – had its charms for Mrs Pankhurst. She stayed for some months at Glencoe, a guest house in Salt Kettle, then rented Roche Terre, a pleasant house on a slight hill overlooking the Sound near Buena Vista. She went swimming with the children and was soon restored to health. She went visiting and charmed the islanders (who expected a leathery battle-axe) with her fragile beauty and her pleasant, uncombative conversation.

But she soon became bored and restless. Christabel was away for long periods in the United States. In January 1925 she preached at the Ascension Memorial Church, New York, predicting that the nations of Europe would soon be grouped under a dictator who might well be a forerunner of the Anti-Christ. In March, still in New York, she declared that the earth tremor which had shaken that city was God's warning to abandon the worship of the false gods of materialism. In May she was telling students of the National Bible Institute in the Church of the Stranger to use the Bible not just as a source of spiritual comfort, but as a political guide-book. Her visits to Bermuda were few and fleeting. When she *was* there she spent most of her time working on a third book of Second Adventist exposition. With Christabel so active, so absorbed, it was increasingly intolerable to be idle, to be just a fond mother.

It was a welcome diversion when she was asked, by leaders of the local agitation for woman suffrage (a long-standing joke in Bermuda) to speak in support of a Suffrage Bill which was about to be introduced (though with little hope of success: Bermudan women did not get the vote until 1944) in the Assembly in Hamilton. She consented to address a meeting in the Mechanics' Hall in Queen Street. Never before had the island feminists drawn such a crowd, of both sexes. Mrs Pankhurst was bantering rather than aggressive. She was glad, she said, to be in Bermuda, but astonished to find that women's franchise should still be a matter for argument.

'Really, gentlemen,' she remarked, amid laughter, 'Bermuda claims to be the oldest British colony and to have the oldest colonial parliament. What are you afraid of? I wonder you haven't more courage! Even Spain is thinking of giving votes to women!'

It was an amusing little skirmish, but curiously enough it did not stir her to renewed thoughts of public service. The very memory of the Canadian winters chilled the marrow of her bones. She was in an Emersonian mood. Wouldn't it somehow, she wondered, be possible to start a small family business, just her and Christabel and perhaps a close friend or two? It must be in a place with a mild all-the-year-round climate. Not in Bermuda: it was too much off the beaten track. But there should be a suitable spot somewhere on the Mediterranean coast, where she would not be so far from England. Christabel would prefer that. She could continue to write her books and do some preaching, but a business would give her something to fall back on, a bit of financial security; and it would provide a sort of anchor, a home, for both of them.

Christabel showed little enthusiasm for the scheme, perhaps remembering the fiasco of Emerson's, and more willing to admit that the Pankhursts had no talent for commerce. But Mrs Pankhurst persevered. She wrote to Mabel Tuke ('Pansy' to her friends), an old intimate of W.S.P.U. days who, she thought, might be just the person to join forces with them in this new, as yet unspecific, venture. Mrs Tuke, now in her fifties, was a widow of private means. Her husband, a captain in the South African Constabulary, had died in 1905, and on returning to England Mrs Tuke, a tiny, pretty little Kentishwoman whose deceptively frail appearance (she did not die until 1963 at the age of ninety-two) was the origin of her nickname, had joined the W.S.P.U., of which she was honorary secretary for six years. Christabel had been particularly fond of her: and Mrs Pankhurst perhaps felt that her participation would help to overcome Christabel's objections.

Mrs Tuke was keen. She even suggested the form which the enterprise might take. Why not a tea shop on the French Riviera? It was full of British expatriates who would no doubt appreciate such an amenity, and the climate was pleasant. Mrs Pankhurst seized on the suggestion eagerly, and her daughter gave a grudging consent. There was an important point, though, to be settled before the idea was put into practice. If Mrs Pankhurst's savings were to be invested in the tea shop and she was to abandon her income as a speaker—for at this point, characteristically, she thought in terms of a drastic severance—they could no longer afford the expense of a nurse and a governess for the children. Betty, of course (Christabel's girl) and Mary (Mrs Pankhurst's favourite) must stay. But Joan and Kathleen would have to go. Through friends in England Mrs Pankhurst found a good, permanent, well-to-do home for them. It would be fairer to them, she reasoned, to make the break now. So, in those days of lax, almost non-existent adoption laws (in an interview in Toronto Christabel had spoken of adoption as the duty as well as the pleasure of wealthy, childless, married women), Joan and Kathleen, accompanied by Nurse Pine, now ending nearly fifteen years of selfless devotion to Mrs Pankhurst, went to their new foster parents.

Soon afterwards, Mrs Pankhurst and Christabel, with Mary and Betty, left for London. There they collected Mrs Tuke and, in the late summer of 1925, just when the industrial deadlock in Britain seemed to be crying out for a burst of Mrs Pankhurst's fiery conservative eloquence, set out for the south of France. Juan-les-Pins was the place, and 'The English Teashop of Good Hope' the name, chosen for the business. Christabel had her writing and renewed intimacy with Mrs Tuke to occupy her. Mrs Tuke, who did most of the marketing and made the cakes and scones, was busy. But for Mrs Pankhurst the French Riviera, and especially the Britons there, must have come as a rude shock. The retired stockbrokers and civil servants, the businessmen who had made a quick pile during the war, the bogus majors and phoney baronets, the well-born crooks and genteel spongers were patriots to a man – but only in the sense of praising Mussolini, hating the working classes, and living in constant fear of a 'Bolshevik' revolution in Britain which might play havoc with their incomes. This terror was magnified by the presence of a horde of penniless White Russian refugees. But far from going back to the old country to grapple with this imaginary revolution, the British residents' main pastimes were heavy drinking, golf, malicious gossip, getting their names and photographs into the local papers, and manoeuvring for invitations to the right parties.

The social atmosphere in the graceless jerry-built villas along the Côte d'Azur was as stifling as that of an Indian hill station, without the excuse of being an outpost of Empire. It must have been infinitely depressing for Mrs Pankhurst, if she penetrated these circles to any extent, to hear the petty debasement of that imperial sentiment which to her was an ideal of service. Nor, with the exception of a few elderly ladies of straitened means, did resident Britons patronize the Teashop of Good Hope. They, like the literary and artistic colonies at Cagnes and elsewhere, favoured hard liquor: and perhaps, with a final touch of grotesque irony, some of them still thought of Mrs Pankhurst as a Scarlet Woman, a sex hooligan. Much more attuned to the livelier aspects of the Riviera was the flamboyant ex-anarchist Emma Goldman who, at the age of fifty-six, had just married a sixty-five-year-old Welsh miner in order to get British nationality, and came to Nice to stay with Frank and Nellie Harris before settling down to write her very piquant memoirs – at St Tropez.

Old colleagues were horrified to think of their leader in such a depressing situation. In November 1925 Lady Rhondda, a former suffragette, wrote to Mrs Pankhurst asking her to work with the Six Point Group. Founded soon after the war, this was concerned not only with getting equality of franchise, but with the long and detailed fight for social, legal, economic, political and moral equality. Lady Rhondda guaranteed Mrs Pankhurst an income of four hundred pounds a year for a minimum of three years. A little stiffly, Mrs Pankhurst refused. It was not merely that she had been used to earning almost as much as that for two or three talks in America, or disliked the idea of being 'rescued' by former subordinates acting on an impulse of generosity. She was not really convinced of the wisdom of agitating for full womanhood suffrage at a time which (especially perhaps after listening to the wild gloom of some expatriate conversations) seemed to her a crisis involving the whole future of the nation. The flapper vote could surely wait awhile. Women had, in her view, all the voting power they needed to get the reforms they wanted. Surely the immediate priority was to educate women to use the votes they *had*, wisely and constructively? Even before she had left England in 1919, Mrs Pankhurst had been concerned at the leftist, progressive tone which seemed to be dominating the women's movement. It was not a tone of which she approved. If she returned to England, she would have to find her own level.

Towards the end of January 1926 a *Sunday Express* reporter gave an account of a visit to the teashop. 'From the aggressive championship of women's suffrage', he wrote, expressing a truism which no doubt had become increasingly and even odiously apparent to poor Mrs Pankhurst, 'to the secluded backwater of a rustic teashop in Juan-les-Pins seems an incredible step ... I went in, sat down, and a gracious lady asked me whether I wanted Indian or China. It was Mrs Mabel Tuke of suffragette fame. I said I would have Indian if I might, and a toasted scone. "Certainly," Mrs Tuke confided, "that is just what we have. Plain scones and shortbread. I make them every morning." My tea arrived minus milk, served daintily and in a most charming manner by Miss Ursula Finch, aged nineteen, daughter of the Vicar of Mitcham, Surrey.' Miss Finch apologized profusely: but still, after the reporter had eaten his scones and cakes, the milk had not appeared. 'Then came the chance of a lifetime. I asked again, and this time the milk was brought to me by Miss Christabel Pankhurst. She had been presiding at the adjoining table over a party which was deeply immersed in solving half a dozen world crises, and my milk had lain forgotten there ... Later Miss Pankhurst, as though entertaining in her own drawing-room, came and chatted with me. She told me how she had come out to write a new book, and out of kindness of heart had been helping an old comrade of militant days ... '

Mrs Pankhurst was not there. The Côte d'Azur had been too much, or too little, for her. It was only too plain that not even a fraction of Christabel's heart was in the business. It was doomed, and with it most of the money Mrs Pankhurst had put into it. Just before Christmas she had gone to London with Mary to stay with her sister, Mrs Goulden Bach.

She now had to grapple with the problem from which she had fled in 1919, the problem of finding some sort of employment in England, where it had seemed that she was virtually unemployable.

CHAPTER TWO

'GENERAL' DRUMMOND
SOLDIERS ON

While Mrs Pankhurst had been working her way to the virtual, virtuous position of Canada's First Lady of Moral Uplift, convalescing in Bermuda, and fretting on the Côte d'Azur, the list of women's premières in Britain (as recorded in *The Vote*) had been gradually, relentlessly lengthening. In 1921 Miss Helen Kyle, the first woman barrister, had been called to the Irish Bar. In England in 1922 came a womanslide of thirty barristers: newspapers, with heavy coyness, began to irritate male lawyers by focusing attention on the newcomers as 'our latterday Portias'. In 1923 appeared the first woman solicitor. Jurywomen had come on the scene in 1919, though, to the fury of women's organizations, judges were still apt to insist that they should retire while cases of criminal assault on children were being heard.

The general election of December 1923 saw the return of eight women M.P.s, and Margaret Bondfield became a junior minister in the Labour-Liberal coalition. Earlier in the same year *The Vote* had hailed the achievements of Miss Allen Cust (first woman to qualify as a veterinary surgeon); Miss Muriel Lloyd (first woman to be elected a Fellow of the Royal Numismatical Society); Miss Lilian Barker (appointed Governor of the Women's Prison at Aylesbury); Mrs Oliver Atkey (first woman pilot to enter for an air race—the Grosvenor Challenge Cup); and Dame Edith Lyttelton, already a justice of the peace, and now first British woman delegate to the League of Nations (where she stoutly advocated the use of women police to suppress the white slave traffic). There had been, it was noted, a gratifying increase in the number of women mayors, and the formation, in December 1924, of a British Women's Symphony Orchestra, conducted by Miss Gwynne Kingston, was enthusiastically received. The Anglican Church was still lagging. At the 1920 Lambeth Conference it had decided to allow women to become deacons—which meant that, in emergency, they could preach and conduct services, but could not give the blessing or administer the sacraments. This concession, fumed *The Vote,* was quite inadequate, for 'was it not a woman to whom the Master gave the first message after the Resurrection— "Go thou and tell thy brethren"? Christ intended women to occupy an equal place with men in the Church.'

Legal inequality had been shorn of some of its more bizarre features. That section of the Larceny Act which assumed that a woman living with her husband could not steal from him was deleted. The Matrimonial Causes Act of 1923 provided that the adultery of either spouse was sufficient reason for divorce (previously wives had also been obliged to prove cruelty or desertion). The 1925 Criminal Justice Act did away with the presumption that a wife who committed a crime in her husband's presence did so under his influence. Something had been done to give women more, though by no means equal, rights in the guardianship of their children.

To Mrs Pankhurst the picture was by no means of clear and unexceptionable gain. Mrs Fawcett had, in 1925, been made a Dame in recognition of her public services as 'constitutional' leader of the suffragist movement. Mrs Pankhurst might have been pardoned for thinking that her services and Christabel's should have been simultaneously honoured. But this was a passing consideration. There were more far-reaching developments to be deplored. The sanctity of the family, as well as male arrogance, was in danger of being undermined by easier divorce; the so-called leaders of society were popularizing the view that marriage was not a sacrament but a social convenience. Women were being eased down a slippery slope to the level of male immorality. This, in her view, was an insidious, a disruptive kind of equality.

Moral leadership—that seemed to her the great lack. Of course it was right for women's organizations to protest against the reactionary attitude of the trade unions, the refusal to grant anything near equal pay for equal work, the insulting proposal to force 'surplus women' (the excess of women over men, partly due to war casualties, was estimated at about two million) back into domestic service or to ship them to the Dominions. But basic spiritual values must be upheld, the old moral medicines preserved from specious dilution. Mrs Charlotte Despard (now, in her eighties, numbered among those republican extremists who sought to overthrow the government of the infant Irish Free State) was still the acknowledged saint and oracle of the Women's Freedom League: yet she used her authority and perennial newsworthiness to trumpet her opinion that women, if they wished to create a truly just society, must align themselves with the forces of radical socialism. Mrs Pethick-

Lawrence, the W.F.L.'s new president, was also a socialist (her husband, standing as a Labour candidate, had defeated Winston Churchill in an election contest at Leicester in 1923). Ellen Wilkinson, the only woman M.P. to have been an active suffragist (and then only as a non-militant) had only recently left the Communist Party. She also maintained that women had a common cause with men to further the victory of socialism: it was, she insisted, a sheer waste of time and energy to perpetuate the sex war — in some respects nothing but a capitalist smokescreen which hid the realities of the class war — or to pretend that women M.P.s should have 'women's policies'.

All these women, Mrs Pankhurst noticed, were always talking a lot of modish cant about women being great natural pacifists and referring to the League of Nations as if it was a Holy of Holies rather than a product of wishful thinking and (not to mince words) sheer cowardice. Even Mary Richardson, one of the wildest of the W.S.P.U. militants, who in 1914 had slashed the Rokeby Venus of Velasquez in the National Gallery in protest against the persecution of Mrs Pankhurst ('the most beautiful personality of this age') — even Mary Richardson had stood — unsuccessfully — three times as a Labour parliamentary candidate. Lady Astor, admittedly, was in a different category: but only just. Even she did not stand up to close scrutiny. Certainly she had put that frightful old anti-suffragist Sir Frederick Banbury in his place, tugging at his coat-tails to make him sit down when he tried to talk out her Intoxicating Liquor (Sale to Persons under 18) Bill. Certainly she had given as good, or even better, than she got in parliamentary repartee, and had shown a pleasing contempt for the man-made flummery of parliamentary procedure (who else would have dared to offer the Speaker a juicy peach to quench his thirst and humanize his attitude during the stifling heat of a summer session in the House?). But her lively defence of the old moral virtues was a trifle too knockabout, a mite too flippant. And there were other flaws. Her militancy was sadly tinged with the spirit of appeasement, with over-reverence for the League of Nations. As a celebrity-collecting political hostess, she showed a lack of proper discrimination, inviting vulgar Labourites like J. H. ('Jimmy') Thomas — the 'h'-dropping, champagne-guzzling railwaymen's leader — and intellectual playboys like George Bernard Shaw. Mrs Pankhurst had never forgiven Shaw for his refusal, despite a theoretical belief in the equality of the sexes, to take part in a suffragette rally at the Albert Hall. He not only, he had said, believed in woman suffrage, but in the duty of women to fight for it, and added: 'If

A press shot of Mrs Pankhurst taken in early 1926, soon after her return to England after an absence of more than six years

Sylvia Pankhurst (aged forty-five) and baby Richard (aged four months), April 192

you or anybody else thinks that I am going to become the tame Tomcat of the suffrage movement or any other women's movement in this country, you will find yourself mistaken.'

Dr Marie Stopes, in her bruising championship of birth control, was the one true militant in the Pankhurst tradition, battering away at prejudice with a fanatical, blinkered sense of divine mission. Clad in a green flowing gown and leather sandals she stormed into Westminster Cathedral and chained to the font a copy of her latest book, exposing the cruel folly of Roman Catholic obscurantism. The royalties of her best-selling books — *Married Love* had been followed by *Wise Parenthood* and *Radiant Motherhood* — had been used to finance the opening of birth control clinics in working-class districts in the East End of London, in Leeds, and (bravest of all) in granitically puritan Aberdeen. In the East End, as she revealed in her book *Mother England,* she had, in three months, received more than twenty thousand requests for abortions from ailing, overworked, pregnant-for-the-umpteenth-time women. Her second husband, aircraft pioneer Humphrey Verdon Roe, campaigned with her. She had to endure virulent opposition from the Churches, and when, in court, she claimed a divine inspiration for her work, prosecuting counsel sneered: 'Dr Stopes will have you believe that God sent down this beastly, filthy message!' Yet she prevailed. By the end of the 1920s acceptance of contraception was general: even the royal physician Lord Dawson of Penn gave it the respectability of official backing.

It was a tremendous victory: but one likely to appeal to the progressive Sylvia rather than to the conservative Mrs Pankhurst. She would probably have been inclined to agree with the professionally censorious lawyer, or with the Bishop of Woolwich, who condemned birth control because it 'facilitated the exercise of a spiritual faculty for the satisfaction of a physical desire only'. Freedom to emulate the sexual irresponsibility of men was not an aspect of liberty to be encouraged. Yet it seemed the one aspect which was widely appreciated, and incessantly reported in newspapers. There was, she understood, a growing readership for novels — some of them written by *women* — about middle-class girls, tired of the abnegations of feminist apartheid, succumbing rapturously, in showers of asterisks, to the cave-man charms of apache-type anti-feminists. There was even a neo-Victorian vogue, whose devotees thought it much more fun to manipulate men — the poor, silly darlings — with their fluffy charm than to lecture them about women's rights.

There was, too, a growing revolt among the intelligentsia against the

6

aesthetic repercussions of feminism: a revolt soon to be given its most
brilliant expression by Virginia Woolf in *A Room of One's Own*. Poets
and novelists, both male and female, lamented Mrs Woolf, had been sadly
inhibited by the stridency of the sex war. This incessant striving to prove
one's equality or superiority was a bore, and witheringly hostile to genuine
creativity in the arts. Thank heaven Jane Austen and Emily Brontë had
been born before the women's movement began. If the great writers of
the past had been raked by the batteries of the Pankhursts, English literature might have been robbed of most of its glorious heroines, Shakespeare's
androgynous genius crippled. Attempts to write 'pure' feminist books
were only matched in their aridity by efforts to produce purely masculine
books. 'Some collaboration', wrote Mrs Woolf, 'has to take place in the
mind between the woman and the man before the act of creation can be
accomplished ... There must be freedom and there must be peace ... The
writer, once his experience is over, must lie back and let his mind celebrate
its nuptials in darkness ... ' The pitting of sex against sex, of quality against
quality, was a relic of schooldays when it was vital to win and to receive
from the headmaster or headmistress 'a highly ornamental pot'. Surely,
though, as human beings matured they ceased to believe in 'sides' or the
importance of prizes? Oh for a truce to the tedious journalistic clichés
about women disliking women or 'being hard on' women, and to those
endless, obtuse, useless books about women by men which cluttered the
shelves of the British Museum. Oh, in fact, for a final calming of the back-
wash of feminism. 'Women, women – but are you not sick of the word? I
can assure you I am.' An adequate private income and a room of one's own
did more to make one the equal of men, in the sense of being indifferent
to or magnanimously tolerant of their opinions, than an avalanche of
levelling legislation.

This was clever enough, no doubt – Mrs Pankhurst, like Christabel had
always distrusted 'mere' cleverness (she would probably have agreed with
Stanley Baldwin's dictum that 'intelligence is to the intelligentsia what the
gentleman is to the gent'). But she knew that the intelligentsia was not
very large or even very influential except among its own members, that
the great mass of sensible, right-thinking Britishers, men and women,
despised cleverness as much as she did. In any case, there were more hopeful trends, more robust attitudes, among women in which one could take
comfort. Miss Rotha Lintorn-Orman, for instance, seemed to be aiming
at the correct targets, trying to uphold the responsibilities of her class. A
spinster of thirty-seven who dressed mannishly and ran a dairy farm in

Somerset, she was the granddaughter of a field marshal and had been a motor transport driver in Serbia during the war. In 1923, alarmed by the spread of 'Bolshevism', she had advertised in *The Patriot,* a news sheet owned by the Duke of Northumberland, for recruits to fight the Reds. She received many replies, from the kind of people who still thought of Ramsay MacDonald as a revolutionary and believed that a Labour Government would be the prelude to an onslaught on private property and gentlewomen's virtue. Miss Lintorn-Orman's enemy was 'Bolshevism' in all its imaginary ramifications—free love, pacifism, atheism, trade unions, contempt for the sanctity of the family: the vague complex of progressive myths which Churchill had in mind when he preached a holy crusade against 'the foul baboonery of communism'. Miss Lintorn-Orman was also suspicious of Big Business, Lloyd George's dreadful *nouveau riche* nobility, and that fifth column of Jewish financiers who, by lending money to Edward VII, had bought their way into Society. It was a pity the field marshal's granddaughter should have taken her inspiration from abroad, but that in itself was an indication of the feebleness of Britain's present leaders. Miss Lintorn-Orman's British Fascisti wore no uniform, but members carried black handkerchiefs and wore badges on which the words For King and Country encircled the ambiguous initials 'B.F.' They were taught to salute (notably during the playing of the national anthem) by flinging the right hand across the chest and touching their badge.

But the most truly heartening patriotic development was the success of the Women's Guild of Empire (W.G.E.). Founded by Mrs Flora Drummond (nicknamed 'The General' because of her pugnacity and her habit of riding at the head of suffragette processions in pseudo-military garb) and Miss Elsie Bowerman (a suffragette and the daughter of a suffragette), it had continued the work of the W.S.P.U.'s wartime industrial campaigns, in which both Mrs Drummond and Miss Bowerman had been prominent. It had been a solace to Mrs Pankhurst, in her long exile, to know that the Pankhurst tradition was being carried on by such capable and uncompromising disciples. It was gratifying, now, to learn that the guild had prospered—thanks to generous contributions from leading industrialists—to the extent of having more than thirty branches in England, Scotland and Wales, and a membership of some forty thousand women, most of them the wives of working men.

Flora Drummond, the guild's controller-in-chief, had joined the W.S.P.U. in 1905 and been nine times imprisoned. Born in Manchester of Highland Scottish stock, she had spent her childhood on the Isle of Arran. Both she and her first husband had been among the earliest members of the I.L.P. and the Fabian Society (her son was christened Keir after Keir Hardie); but like Mrs Pankhurst she became disillusioned with the Labour movement because of its refusal to do more than pay lip-service to the cause of women's suffrage. Her first clash with bureaucracy came when she was refused permission to work as a postmistress because she was not of the minimum height specified in the regulations. Later, she had run a typists' pool in Manchester, and had also, that she might learn at first hand the conditions of a working woman's life, worked in a clothing factory. There she had discovered that wages—four shillings a week was not uncommon—were so low that many girls had to rely on part-time prostitution. This knowledge of the seamier implications of women's inferior status had filled her with anger, and with a determination to seize the political power to do something about it.

Her message to the workers, and especially to the militant miners of south Wales, Scotland and the north of England, was that capital and labour must co-operate. She admitted that obstructive, cheese-paring management was often as much to blame for labour troubles as short-sighted trade unionism influenced by the foreign doctrine of workers' control—which, she assured the workers, was 'for export only' (this had been one of Christabel's favourite themes), for if Russian workers behaved as some misguided Britons did, they would soon be put up against a wall and shot. Strikes and lock-outs, which only increased misery and unemployment and lost customers, were not the answer. Whatever exponents of the class war, such as A. J. Cook, secretary of the Miners' Federation, might say, the real struggle was for survival in a highly competitive world. The word 'Empire', Mrs Drummond emphasized, had been featured in the guild's title as a protest against the growing and regrettable tendency to sneer at patriotism and worship the mad mirage of international working-class brotherhood. 'It used to be said', she boomed, thrusting her plain, shiny, pug-nosed face at her audiences, 'that a Britisher's word was his bond. This is no longer so when the foreign buyer has to go to other countries because our manufacturers cannot keep to their delivery dates. This lies at the root of the unemployment difficulty.'

Trade unions, harped the W.G.E., should keep out of politics; genuinely secret vote by ballot should be the rule, to avoid the possibility of intimidation by the strong-arm squad; all trade unionists should make a point of attending branch meetings in order to prevent the conduct of their affairs from falling into the hands of a minority of busybody extremists; and it would not be a bad idea if workers' wives attended meetings to make sure that their husbands kept a due sense of proportion and did not allow themselves to drift on a tide of proletarian fantasy. It was the wives, after all, who had to bear the brunt of the poverty caused by prolonged strikes, trying to feed hungry children, facing landlords and tradespeople with empty purses. What was the use of having votes if the real power was in the hands of industrial organizations in which women had no say? Women should agitate for representatives of management and labour to get together *on the spot* instead of referring everything to government and trade union bureaucrats in offices in London.

State welfare was suspect to the W.G.E. Family allowances ('young-age pensions') were described in the Guild's *Bulletin* as 'the thin end of the wedge, the thick end of which is government control of marriage and parenthood'. Harder work, higher production, and higher wages should be the aim of all those who valued their independence. Not only socialist politicians were guilty of fostering the idea of the state as a universal provider. Conservatives too were guilty of a dilution of values. 'Vote for me and see what you will get is far too common an attitude.' Wizards of all parties were busy weaving their materialistic spells. Yet, said the *Bulletin,* 'the crass materialism of Marx and Lenin means a farewell to all idealism and love.' Governments existed 'to enable us to work in peace and security to develop those talents with which Nature has endowed us. It is not there to work for us or to enable us to escape our responsibilities ... British people have more than once saved the world from materialistic despots. Let us demand a higher standard from our representatives, and they will then realize that bread and circuses will not satisfy a free-born people.' The *Bulletin* approvingly reprinted a letter to *The Times* by Dame Millicent Fawcett on the subject of family allowances. 'I am one of those', she wrote, 'who regard the responsibility of parents for the maintenance of their children as an invaluable part of the education of the average man or woman. To take it away would dangerously weaken the inducements for steady industry and self-control ... and would at the same time involve the country, already overburdened by enormously high taxation, with an annual charge running into hundreds of millions.'

When it came to the industrial Battle of Britain, women who in the years of the suffrage campaign had denounced each other as over-violent or excessively timid found themselves on common, solid, laissez-faire, middle-class ground. During the 'unofficial' British seamen's strike of

1925-6 (which was backed by the sympathetic action of the Australian Seamen's Union led by Tom Walsh), the W.G.E. formed a Seamen's Wives Vigilance Association, which vowed to 'give a warm welcome to Mr Walsh' if—as he had announced he would if he could obtain leave from his duties in Sydney—he came to England to preside over the foundation of a rival, left-wing seamen's union. The association was particularly active in the docks of London's East End, heckling strike leaders so ferociously, reported the *Bulletin,* that their meetings broke up in disorder.

This attack on Sylvia's old battleground may have impressed Mrs Pankhurst as a way of vindicating the family honour, and so have influenced her future actions. But delightful as it was to meet Flora Drummond again and to see the vigour of the W.G.E.'s campaigning, Mrs Pankhurst was too occupied by the immediate anxieties and distractions of home-coming to take any part in it. Amongst her anxieties was a report in the *Evening News* headed PANKHURST REUNION IN ENGLAND? Mrs Pankhurst, said the item, was already in London. So was 'Red' Sylvia. Christabel was said to be about to come to London, and if Tom Walsh arrived to confer with the rebel seamen, no doubt he would bring his wife Adela, who had done so much to help him in his socialist agitation, both as a speaker and as a journalist. 'All four', the report ended, 'are remarkably effective public speakers, and were they all to appear on one platform, it would be one of the most interesting meetings ever held in London.'

A regular Pankhurst circus, in fact, for the amusement of the idle-minded multitudes. Even if Adela had come to London, such a grotesque concatenation would, of course, have been out of the question. Mrs Pankhurst had not forgiven or corresponded with her wayward daughters. She had not lifted her wartime excommunication. But it was distressing to be exposed to such flippant speculations. And there was no denying that Sylvia *was* in, or very near, London. The hot breath of her unfortunate reputation had reached even unto Toronto, temporarily curling the edges of her mother's respectability. It was a fair bet that she would (even though she was in her forties and should know better) find a new way to shame Mrs Pankhurst. Just what way time alone would tell.

CHAPTER THREE

TRUE BLUE

For the first few weeks of Mrs Pankhurst's stay in London, press inquiries about her were referred to Mrs Drummond, who gave a summary of her activities since she had left England six years previously and added, in one bulletin, as though she was talking about convalescent royalty: 'Mrs Pankhurst is alert and in good spirits. She looks not a day older.'

It was true, or truer than most royal bulletins. Her hair was white, her face more deeply lined, but the bone structure kept it beautiful and shapely. It had a wistful, yearning quality too, something between a revered headmistress and a compassionate saint of many martyrdoms. Sometimes, especially when she toyed with the eyeglass which hung on a long ribbon round her neck, and looked straight at a questioner, she had a formidable look of suffering seniority, of one who has had to march through a morass of human stupidity and is half amazed, half amused that she must still bear with it. At the end of January 1926 newspapermen got their first look at her when she held a press conference in the home of her sister, Mrs Goulden Bach. 'She looks stronger', reported the *Manchester Guardian,* 'than the wasted wraith of the last frantic stages of militancy. She has the same erect bearing, the same bright, watchful eyes, and the old skill in answering or turning difficult questions.' Of course, she said, the younger women should have the vote ('they must be irritated by the fact that they are not considered to be grown up'), but she herself would not be pressing their claims. She would leave that to others. It had always been a great grief to her to have to set aside wider interests for the sake of a single object – the breaking down of the sex barrier. She thought she had earned the right to work for general questions – slum clearance, for instance, a properly planned rehousing programme, the right to employment of married women, unstinted professional opportunities for women. She also hoped that, in the present state of the nation, with the threat of near civil war in industry, she could help those who were striving for industrial peace and try to awaken Britain to a sense of her responsibilities overseas.

Her stay in Canada, she said, had intensified her faith in the mission of the British Empire. More should be done, she thought, to interest Canadians in Britain and to counteract what she regarded as the unfortunate influence of American books and films. Why not, for instance, send distinguished British lecturers to travel Canada? Why not, also, arrange to loan collections of British art? Though she was not a member of the Women's Guild of Empire, she considered that Mrs Drummond was 'doing splendid work, and that hers is one of the most useful movements of our time'. A strike used for political purposes was a form of irresponsible militancy: she had always maintained that men, having the vote, had no right to make what amounted to war on society, since they were able to use constitutional methods to redress their grievances. 'I believe', she said, 'that we have reached a stage in human affairs when we need more than ever to get together, to emphasize the points of unity, not the points of difference.' Was she satisfied with the way women had used their votes? 'I don't think they have done badly,' she replied, 'considering that it is so hard not to get wrapped up in the mere struggle for existence. Of course we expected a great deal from our enfranchisement. But so did men when they fought for theirs. It is the only way – to keep fighting, to believe that the miracle is going to happen.'

Rumours that Mrs Pankhurst intended to become a parliamentary candidate were confirmed when at the beginning of March she was the guest of honour at a gathering held by the Six Point Group at the Hyde Park Hotel. The primary purpose of the meeting was to concert plans for a big equal-votes-for-women demonstration in July, in which more than twenty women's organizations were to take part. But the presence of Mrs Pankhurst and, it may be, a lingering sense of guilt about her, raised a comparatively routine occasion to a high pitch of emotion. Lady Astor declared that she was only present to pay her humble tribute to Mrs Pankhurst. 'There is no sacrifice', she said 'that any woman would not make to get her into the House of Commons.' She was willing to resign her seat and offer it to the greatest women's leader of all time. She felt that she had been in the House 'as a sort of preliminary canter, waiting for a real horse to come along'. Mrs Pankhurst was that horse. Her place was in Parliament, and neither she nor the country should rest until she got there. In reply, Mrs Pankhurst confirmed that she wanted to become a Member of Parliament, but declined to accept the sacrifice, touched as she was by it. She must fight her own contest. She admitted, in reply to questioning, that she was 'a constitutionalist of constitutionalists', but

denied that she intended to become a Tory. Her present intention was to
stand as an Independent when opportunity arose.

In the meantime she needed to earn some money. Despite constant and
highly lucrative offers, she had nearly always refused to write for the
press. She found it hard to express herself on paper. She was an orator, not
a writer, needing the response, the sounding-board of an audience to
bring out her almost mediumistic powers. An American syndicate had
asked for a long series from her, but finally, with reluctance, she consented
to produce one shortish 'Women Today' piece for the *Evening News*. Its
findings were not original, but her anecdotes of the bad old days were so
telling as to make one wish that a sympathetic interviewer could have
recorded her in full, recollective detail. 'Sixty years ago', she generalized,
'any woman in England, with one exception – the Queen upon the throne
– could be described as a compulsory feminine Peter Pan, a human being
who politically and to a great extent legally never grew up.' The plight
of a married woman was well described by the husband who said: 'My
wife and I are one, and I am that one.' She remembered how her own
mother had helped one unfortunate woman with four children, who had
been deserted by her husband, to start a small shop – which prospered
until the husband, briefly returning, exercised his legal right of possession,
sold the business, pocketed the proceeds, and again vanished. Men even
collected their working wives' weekly wages. Only the lack of such
knowledge, the lack of comparison, could make it possible for people to
go on asking if having the vote had made any difference.

But the approach of the General Strike of May 1926 (which after seven
years of sub-revolutionary rumblings, was now, with a deal of almost
therapeutic governmental encouragement, ejected, like some foreign
body, from the British proletarian system) temporarily eclipsed all other
considerations and impressed upon Mrs Pankhurst the need for party allegiance. In April she witnessed the W.G.E.'s enormous demonstration – the
'Great Prosperity March' as it was called – at which thousands of working
women from all over Britain, headed by 'General' Drummond, marched
through the streets of London to the Royal Albert Hall to demand an end
to the industrial disputes which were ruining the nation and thrusting
the wretchedness of poverty into millions of homes. Housewives had
never gone on strike, but if matters did not improve they might have to,
to bring men to their senses.

In the weeks which followed the miners' rejection of the Samuel
Report of March 1926 – which recommended wage cuts or the working

of longer hours for the same wages—and the mineowners' posting of
lock-out notices at the end of April, the government completed its
preparations for a state of emergency. It was secure in the knowledge that
not only were the trade unions (and the Parliamentary Labour Party,
under the leadership of Ramsay MacDonald) hopelessly divided or even
fundamentally hostile to the strike, but that the British middle classes
were raring to prove their loyalty to King and Country and to come at
last to grips with the class enemy. The 'unofficial' Organization for the
Maintenance of Supplies (O.M.S.) under the command of Lord Hardinge,
a former Viceroy of India, and Lord Jellicoe, the ex-chief of the Royal
Navy, claimed to have recruited a hundred thousand volunteers to act as
special constables, transport drivers, messengers, clerks, or wherever they
might be needed to maintain public services. Miss Lintorn-Orman's
British Fascists, now headed by a retired brigadier-general, merged with
the O.M.S., and even kidnapped Harry Pollitt in a raid on Communist
Party headquarters. The W.G.E. offered its quota of strike breakers, and
Mrs Pankhurst felt constrained to take some part in the symbolic, nine-
day mock battle between the Forces of Decency and Stability, represented
by the Prime Minister, Stanley Baldwin, and the Forces of Disruption, led
by her old wartime opponent A. J. Cook. 'During the war', said the
W.G.E. *Bulletin,* 'Mr Cook was a convinced pacifist. Wars between
nations he abhors, but a class war, which means horror, misery and starvation undreamt of in any international struggle, is to him a goal to be
desired. Could even the changeable female, with all her whims and
caprices, be more illogical than this?'

But it was not to the W.G.E., but to the Women's Auxiliary Service,
headed by another ex-suffragette, the crop-haired, monocled, impressively
jack-booted Commandant Mary Allen, that Mrs Pankhurst lent her
prestige. During the war Miss Allen (who had once smashed windows in
Whitehall and had thrown W.S.P.U. leaflets at Asquith as he crouched
under a blanket at the bottom of a carriage on his way to a political
meeting in Scotland) had helped to found the first uniformed force of
women police in Britain. Since the war, as the Women's Auxiliary
Service, this had seen service in Germany and Ireland. In response to the
appeal of Mrs Stanley Baldwin for women to provide relief services during
the strike, Commandant Allen, after consultation with Mrs Pankhurst,
offered to arrange lectures and entertainments for the wives of East End
dockers, with the object of keeping the women off the streets and away
from agitators' meetings.

The strike ended before the scheme had time to get into its stride, but the short contact with the Baldwins, and her growing admiration for Stanley Baldwin's handling of the 'crisis' and for his political philosophy in general, almost certainly influenced Mrs Pankhurst in her decision, announced in June, to stand as a Conservative parliamentary candidate. Here, it seemed to her, disillusioned as she was by her experience of Tory 'patriots' on the French Riviera, was a man of ideals, a truly national figure (whose integrity was freely acknowledged even by socialists), a man who had stood firm against the bitter hostility of Tory diehards such as Churchill, Birkenhead and Neville Chamberlain, a man genuinely dedicated to industrial peace and class unity. Had he not in 1919, when he was Financial Secretary to the Treasury, donated one hundred and thirty thousand pounds representing twenty per cent of his personal fortune (derived from the family steel business) to the Government to liquidate war debts, and urged other men of wealth – alas, unavailingly – to do likewise? Had he not, by his simple, manly pleas for moderation and understanding, reduced M.P.s of all parties to tears and at least temporary repentance? Had he not travelled the country to warn well-banqueted industrialists of the danger of provoking class warfare, and to stress the equal responsibility of management and labour, especially now that huge industrial combines and vast conglomerations of trade unions brought the risk of a cripplingly massive confrontation of masters and men? Had he not, in reply to a rabble-rousing tirade from Walton Newbold, the Communist M.P. for Motherwell, prophesied with quiet emotion that 'there will never in this country be a Communist Government, and for this reason – that no gospel founded on hate will ever seize the hearts of our people. It is no good trying to cure the world by spreading out oceans of blood, or by repeating that pentasyllabic French derivative, Proletariat. The English language is the richest in the world in monosyllables. Four words, of one syllable each, contain salvation for this country and for the whole world, and they are Faith, Hope, Love and Work ... '

There were other facets of Baldwin calculated to appeal to Mrs Pankhurst's romantic sense of allegiance. He was not an office-seeker, a mere careerist. In fact (like Mrs Pankhurst latterly) he claimed to have been forced into the political arena by a sense of duty, not by a natural relish for the job. He was, he said, a Worcestershire man, who would have preferred to spend his leisure on his country estate, savouring the incomparable pleasures of the English countryside (did she not, too, intermittently hanker for a cottage in the country?). Then there was his deep, oft-proclaimed love of England, not only of its physical beauty but of its psychological peculiarities. These two themes were summarized in a speech made in 1924 at the annual dinner of the Royal Society of St George. The Englishman, he had told applauding guests, was preserved by a sense of humour from the solemn absurdities of dogmatists. He might be a bit of a muddler, a slow starter, but when it came to staying power he was supreme. As a nation, England was 'to some extent impervious to intellectual impressions' and equally impervious to criticism – a most useful thing for English statesmen, 'which might be the reason why they last longer than those who are not English'. But for him – and at this point Baldwin eschewed flippancy, spoke with quasi-religious solemnity: the laughter stilled, faces grew serious and one could have heard a cigar sucked – England was the countryside. It was 'the tinkle of the hammer on the anvil in the country smithy, the corncrake on a dewy morning, the sound of the scythe against the whetstone, the sight of a plough team coming over the brow of a hill, the wild anemones in the wood in April, the last load of hay being drawn down a lane as twilight comes on ... '

This kind of lyrical fireside chattery, when gathered into book form by an enterprising publisher in 1926, ran through five large editions in as many months. Baldwin, who when he became Prime Minister in 1923, had been petulantly described by the frustrated Lord Curzon as 'a person of the utmost insignificance', had proved himself a past master of public relations – an art which the multiplication of mass media made increasingly important. The darling of the whole rapidly expanding range of the middle classes, his books, his pipes, his broadcasts, his reassuring, but always gentlemanly, mateyness had, within three years, made him the best-loved as well as the best-known politician of the century. Even intellectuals succumbed to his charm. Asquith, when he left the Commons in 1926, said of him: 'I have never found one who more completely satisfied my ideal of an English gentleman.' The socialist pundit Professor Harold Laski complimented him on the 'human directness' of his leadership. Neville Chamberlain welcomed the change from what he called the 'superficial brilliance of an essentially inferior nature like Lloyd George'. Baldwin had got himself accepted as the Kindly Head of the National Family – just the image to catch at Mrs Pankhurst's maternal loyalty. Clever people might sneer at his anaesthetic nostalgia and refuse to swallow his mind-blurring bromides, but Mrs Pankhurst respected his attempt to take the malice out of Parliament, to make politics *wholesome*. This, surely, was social hygiene at its noblest.

Though careful not to trumpet his prejudices, Baldwin was known to dislike the League of Nations and the tedium of foreign affairs in general (to the extent of dozing off when they were discussed at Cabinet meetings), and to have a wistful hankering for the good old days when, as he once put it, 'if the Japs were cheeky, one showed them the guns of the China Squadron, and no more was heard.' Baldwin might be a scaled down, half camouflaged John Bull: but a John Bull he nevertheless, though hintingly, haltingly, was. He realized how valuable Mrs Pankhurst, with her imperial sentiment, could be to the Tories. Also, at a time when the Conservative Party was, for the first time, intent on wooing the female electorate (soon to be greatly enlarged by the grant of the flapper vote), the adherence and advice of the old suffragette leader might be a considerable asset. Furthermore, it was nice, for once, to be able to combine political adroitness with genuine pleasure. For Baldwin honestly liked Mrs Pankhurst, a magnificent Englishwoman if ever there was one, and a worthy Mother of his National Family.

Her 'conversion' to Conservatism (of her own grand and idiosyncratic brand), though it had obviously begun at least fifteen years before, was the subject of much comment, particularly in American and Canadian newspapers. The *Philadelphia Public Ledger* and the *Toronto Star Weekly* carried a long interview. 'Women, you know,' she said, referring to Lady Astor's offer, 'do stand by other women most beautifully, in spite of the old slander to the contrary. Women are not envious or petty.' If she got into Parliament, she would certainly work for full adult suffrage for women ('everybody admits that a girl of twenty-one is usually years older in common sense than a boy of the same age'). She would also press for the improvement of prison conditions for both men and women. Here, she said, she spoke from inside experience. She had been put into solitary confinement, she remembered, for speaking to Christabel in the exercise yard, and penalized for refusing to wash out her cell every day. 'A daily washing sounds all right, but it means that your cell is always damp. So I offered to *sweep* the floor every day.'

Though in some ways her ideas were still advanced, her clothes were not. 'In any crowd of fashionable women', wrote the interviewer, 'you would pick Mrs Pankhurst out immediately. She would be the most quietly dressed woman in the room, probably the only woman whose hair was not bobbed, and certainly the only one whose clear complexion remained free of artificiality' (none of the Pankhurst women ever used cosmetics). She was by no means dowdy, though hopelessly behind the times in the matter of dress length. 'The other day in the drawing-room of

her sister's London home she wore a black frock which was very smart
without being at all extreme. It came a trifle more than midway to the
ankles. Her grey hair, beautifully waved and coiffed, was crowned with a
Spanish comb of conservative design.' To her two young nieces, Enid
and Sybil Goulden Bach, then taking part enthusiastically in demonstrations for equal suffrage, she appeared kind, gentle and almost awe-
inspiringly immaculate. She specially liked lace, fine French kid gloves
and delicate kid shoes for her small, exquisitely shaped feet. She still
delighted, as had genteel militants of pre-war days, to have pretty tea sets
made in the purple, white and green of the W.S.P.U.

She did not like the short skirts and heavy rouging then in vogue ('for
the average woman nothing could be more unbecoming than the very
short gown and the very red face'). It wasn't, she hastened to add, that she
was narrow-minded, but simply old-fashioned enough to feel that there
might be a wide difference between style and good taste. The emancipation of women had inevitably brought a new freedom and experi-
mentalism in dress. Even short skirts and excessive lipstick, said Mrs
Pankhurst, with noble tact, were really 'an expression of one of the finest
things in human nature – a groping toward beauty'. She did not expect
young girls to dress like her. 'The post-war girl', she loyally stated, 'may
do and wear things that shock her grandmother. But she is still just as
sweet and moral and fine as the average girl has always been. I believe in
women, you know. Completely.'

The reaction of the British press to the 'conversion' tended to be sour.
No doubt, commented the *Daily News,* Mrs Pankhurst, if and when she
was 'safe in the precincts of the constitutional temple, would be able to
exchange some interesting anecdotes with Lord Birkenhead and Sir
William Joynson-Hicks' (who had been willing to risk civil war to preserve Ulster's separatism) 'of the days when all of them were plotting its
downfall.' The *Evening Standard* remarked that her announcement was not
really surprising. Her methods of running the W.S.P.U. had been anything but democratic, and Christabel had allowed herself 'to be treated by
her staff with a deferential adulation such as might surround a princess'.

Such cavillings only helped to confirm Mrs Pankhurst in her course. In
subsequent press interviews and in two further newspaper articles (a
triumph over her natural inclinations which was a sure sign of bristling
loyalty) she exceeded Baldwin's most sanguine expectations. The General
Strike, she said, had convinced her that anyone who had the true interests of women at heart should stand firmly behind Mr Baldwin and the

Government. Industrial peace was necessary to expand the home market and regain foreign trade. The class war – 'that foreign importation' – must go, and be replaced by unity and co-operation between hand and brain. This was a truth the force of which women, being realists, must feel. They should stand forth as, under the inspiration of the Women's Guild of Empire, thousands of working-class wives already had, to protect the representative institutions in which they were now included.

Women, the child-bearers and home-makers, knew in their hearts that socialist regimentation in Russia – and in Britain too, despite the moderation of some Labour leaders, who would soon be brushed out of the way, as Kerensky had been, by hard-core Reds – aimed at the liquidation of the family unit, that characteristic and sacred product of centuries of Christian civilization. When they realized this, women voters would see to it that the socialists, in however apparently innocuous a guise, were never allowed to form another Government. Speaking, at the Ladies' Carlton Club, with a reckless sweep of generalization to which its members, in an age of discreetly muffled Toryism, had long been unused, she proclaimed: 'I joined the Conservative Party because I believe that today there are only two parties – the Constitutional Party, represented by Mr Baldwin and the Conservatives, and the Revolutionary Party. If you can only convince the ordinary woman that her home is threatened, her religion is threatened, and even her security in marriage is threatened, then we shall have her support ... '

Wasn't it, some of her hearers might have been pardoned for asking, a trifle over-cavalier, even unconstitutional, to dismiss what, after all, however deplorably, was now His Majesty's Opposition as a gang of crypto-subversives? Wasn't Mrs Pankhurst, laudable as her intentions might be, somewhat ludicrously alarmist in her interpretation of socialism's attitude to the family and to religion? Even in Russia the family had received a fresh, Bolshevik blessing and persecution of the Church had been considerably modified. Were working-class women very *concerned* about religion? Did they indeed, have any? Was it necessary, was it *advisable,* to paint the enemy in such crude colours? Had Baldwin, that Man of Peace, been altogether *wise* to encourage this elderly but still vigorous tigress to enter a fold which might occasionally bleat alarm but was too prudent to roar defiance?

To those who entertained such misgivings it was a relief that instead of (as several newspapers had predicted) being offered a safe seat, Mrs Pankhurst chose (my dear, *chose*) to ask the local Conservative Party in the invincibly Labour East End constituency of Whitechapel and St George's, Stepney, to adopt her as prospective candidate for the general election due in 1929. Her plea to be allowed to attack the Dragon of Socialism in one of its main London lairs was granted. When she left the party offices in Cable Street after the adoption meeting, held early in February 1927, a Jewish member of the audience rushed after her shouting 'Mazeltov!' (Yiddish for 'Good luck!').

Loving a fighter, the East Enders warmed to Emmeline as they had warmed to Sylvia. If anyone could make an impact on the huge Labour majority, she could. But though, to some Tories, it was a relief that Mrs Pankhurst was to tilt at the windmills of her melodramatic imagination in the obscurity of Stepney with an almost guaranteed lack of success, to Sylvia it was a direct provocation, a wilful assault on her old kingdom (which possibly it was), a doubly painful act of treachery to the memory of the radical Dr Pankhurst. Wilfully or not, Mrs Pankhurst's action brought the family feud to a flashpoint of tragic-comedy.

CHAPTER FOUR

A WOMAN OF PRINCIPLE

Towards the end of January 1927 soon after news of her mother's intentions reached her, a letter from Sylvia was published in the socialist periodical *Forward*. 'Dear Editor,' it rather pompously ran,

> Permit me, through your columns, to express my profound grief that my mother should have deserted the old cause of progress ... For my part I rejoice in having enlisted for life in the socialist movement, in which the work of Owen, Marx, Kropotkin, William Morris and Keir Hardie, and such pioneering efforts as those of my father, Richard Marsden Pankhurst, both before and during the rise of the movement in this country, are an enduring memory. It is naturally most painful to me to write this, but I feel it incumbent upon me, in view of this defection, to reaffirm my faith in the cause of social and international fraternity, and to utter a word of sorrow that one who in the past has rendered such service should now, with that sad pessimism which sometimes comes with advancing years, and may result from too strenuous effort, join the reaction ...

This letter, summarized in several national papers, signified that the Pankhurst family sparks could be expected to fly furiously once more. Sylvia, of course, did not see the matter in this vulgar light. For her, the departure of Mrs Pankhurst and Christabel to North America had been a relief. Her fiercely loyal fixation on her father, and her equally fierce, though frustrated, love for her mother, had made it easier to accept, or forget, Mrs Pankhurst's activities while Atlantic distances thinned their impact. Distance, too, had dulled the pain of the knowledge that Christabel, whom she persisted in regarding as the prime family traitor and the corrupter of her mother's better instincts, was still Mrs Pankhurst's chosen, if not always entirely willing, companion.

But to have them both back in London, Mrs Pankhurst as an out-and-out Tory and Christabel preparing to begin a series of widely publicized lectures as the star Cassandra of the (to Sylvia) antediluvianly ludicrous

Advent Testimony and Preparation Movement—the grief and shame of such proximity, made more odious by her mother's eruption into the East End, was well-nigh intolerable. The period since Sylvia had left the East End and extinguished the barely glimmering ashes of the once fiery Workers' Socialist Federation had not been an easy one. She could endure the inevitable local gossip about her and Corio and the social ostracism of Woodford Green (though in fact the mingled fascination and revulsion of residents gradually turned into a kind of perverse pride in their strange 'bohemian' celebrity). But there was not much of a living in the Red Cottage café—though it was more successful than the Teashop of Good Hope at Juan-les-Pins, and at least catered for a respectable working-class clientèle, mostly bus and lorry drivers. Sylvia left most of the café work to the adaptable Corio and a girl help, and spent her time writing books and articles: this brought in enough money to enable her to buy the Red Cottage and the small plot of land on which it stood, and to build a wooden hut at the back in which she could work in peace away from the steam and the clatter of the counter.

India and the Earthly Paradise, over six hundred pages long and the result of months of research in the British Museum (research so meticulous that in later years it was often stated that Sylvia had visited India to write the book) was published in Bombay in 1926. Sylvia had taken a close interest in the Indian nationalist movement, and was particularly attracted by Gandhi's emphasis on the need to preserve, in an age of large-scale industrialization, the co-operative way of life of village communities. Indulging now in the rare pleasure of dreaming noble, *News from Nowhere*-like dreams after a decade of gruelling controversial journalism and reluctant immersion in the soul-killing *minutiae* of party politics, Sylvia, after sketching the history of religion and politics in India, the development of the caste system, the rise and decline of foreign empires (including the British Raj), let her idealistic imagination run riot. Could India, she wondered, whose primitive village communism had survived so many hostile pressures, find a formula for that earthly paradise of unstinted humanity for which she still longed, and which Soviet Russia had so signally failed to satisfy? Could the blessings of the machine be used to enrich, but not to oust, the vitality of that hardy communism? Industry and forms of government, she advised, should be scaled to meet the needs of regional units, thus avoiding the dehumanization of remote bureaucracies and the divisive tedium of place-seeking politicians.

She visualized, sitting in the British Museum or writing away in her

wooden shack, the good-life-in-miniature of the Greek city states or
William Morris's guild socialism bejewelling the dusty hugeness of India.
Industrialization would be used to save labour, to release those millions
of villagers for a splendid orgy of creative craftsmanship. In her manage-
able, almost suburban units (for Sylvia's flights of bucolic imagination,
like those of most town dwellers, had an incurably suburban tinge), the
neighbourhood assembly would need to meet only occasionally. 'Its
members', she wrote, 'will gather as comrades and practical people,
making plans for common needs to be carried out mainly by common
effort. The most primitive people can play their part intelligently in the
assembly of producers. The most cultured can be but slaves – or auto-
crats – without it.' How sad it would be if Indian independence, when it
came, should mean only exploitation by native capitalists instead of
foreign ones, should release a frenzied surge of imitation of Western
industrial methods and parliamentary techniques ...

In a slightly mocking notice of the book, the *Manchester Guardian*,
while praising the range and depth of Sylvia's research, questioned
whether an agnostic communist was really qualified to grapple with
India's stubborn religious complexities. 'One can easily see', smiled the
reviewer, 'that when Sylvia Pankhurst is vicereine she will change the
face of India in a year or so. But one is not quite sure whether she will
begin by abolishing child marriage, the caste system, private property and
the monetary system, or by granting full adult suffrage and full liberty to
India to govern herself according to her own ideas. And will Sylvia
Pankhurst's Empire be a land of self-governing, self-contained villages
each producing for its own needs, or will her experts distribute the
products of monster coal mines over an endless network of railways, while
the cultivators are instructed to preserve the droppings of their cattle to
fertilize the fields commanded by gigantic irrigation works which shall
bring the snows of the Himalayas to water the sands of Cape Comorin?
In spite of her forceful intellect, Miss Pankhurst fails to keep in touch with
the hard conditions of the Indian problem.'

The same tendency to soar impatiently from the particular to the
stratospherically general was shown in another, smaller book which she
was writing at this time for one of those 'Shapes of the Future' series for
which there always seems to be such an insatiable demand. *Delphos, or the
Future of International Language* was the title. After a lucid and careful
listing and analysis of the main proposals for an international language –
Esperanto, Ido, Interlingua, Romanal, Occidental, Medial European and

Pan Roman—since Leibniz first worked on the problem in the eighteenth century, Sylvia plumped for Interlingua, a kind of flexionless Latin. Esperanto, already taught in schools in seventeen countries and used in a monthly circular issued by the International Labour Office, was not, in her view, entirely satisfactory. The 'interlanguage' of the future should be based on existing languages, which had 'deep echoes of meaning folded within them', and not on scientific symbols; it should use the Roman alphabet and consist largely of words common to the Indo-European speech family from which modern thought and science had sprung. Spelling should be etymological, and not follow 'the false trail of simplification, which leads to deformation and the obscuring of meaning and origin'. An ideal combination, thought Sylvia, might be a Latin vocabulary and a Chinese-type grammar, since this was the simplest and least formal known.

The creation of a satisfactory interlanguage would surely facilitate the creation of a co-operative commonwealth of the world. It would be the fine and final flower of a socialist revolution which would usher in the day when 'newspapers will no longer fill their columns with accounts of larceny, intemperance' (Sylvia did not drink, and was a vegetarian) 'wars, industrial disputes and the speeches of party politicians.' Only pages devoted wholly to national literature would be printed in the national language. The news and all scientific and technical journals would be written in Interlanguage. In fifty years time, she hoped that schools would be completely bilingual, using the national language only to teach national literature, history and geography. 'The Interlanguage', she concluded, 'will play its part in the making of the future, in which the peoples of the world shall be one people; a people cultivated and kind, and civilized beyond today's conception, speaking a common language, bound by common interests, when the wars of class and of nations shall be no more ... '

But the weaving of socialist fantasies from the bowels of the British Museum could not cure Sylvia's itch for public, aggressive action, nor banish the pain of those withdrawal symptoms from which she had been suffering since she retreated into her self-created wilderness. Harry Pollitt and William Gallacher, now zealously toeing the Moscow line, had been sentenced to one year's imprisonment in October 1925 for incitement to mutiny. They were still busy with their niggling sabotage, and had formed what they called a National Minority Movement in the mining and other industries. But where was the vision? For what did they risk their liberty?

For a group of neo-nationalist Russian gangsters who had not only ended prohibition and grabbed a state monopoly of the manufacture and sale of vodka, but had even increased the alcoholic strength of the pernicious stuff. 'As one of the earliest and most ardent in welcoming the Russian Revolution in a sincere belief that it was a great movement of liberation,' she moaned in the *Daily Herald*, 'I must express my deep sorrow and indignation. All the great Russian liberators deplored this poisonous drink in Tsarist days, and it is reputed that a great increase of drunkenness has come with forty per cent vodka. What next shall we expect from a Government miscalled Communist?'

The British Labour Party had fulfilled her worst expectations. That it should have taken office while in a minority in the House of Commons and dependent on the good will of the Liberals ('it is we who govern,' said Asquith) was a measure of its lack of principle. George Lansbury and a few wistful but ineffectual dissidents might lament the facile, corrupting fraternization of Parliament, with its assumption that the capitalist social and economic system, though it might be tinkered with from time to time, was essentially sound and sacrosanct. They might bemoan the way in which the party machine crushed individuality and made mincemeat of personal integrity. But the fact remained that the Labour Party had delivered itself into the palsied hands of Ramsay MacDonald, and that his attitude of 'constructive' compromise had infected the leadership of the trade unions. MacDonald's version of classlessness was the same as Baldwin's — a vague equality in the sight of a lay preacher's God. As early as 1905, in his booklet *Socialism and Society,* he had condemned the revolutionary approach. Just as Baldwin insisted that politicians, like careful gardeners, should leave the roots of society undisturbed, so MacDonald had written of the need for 'organic change ... which must proceed in stages, just as the evolution of an organism does'. He and his cronies (O tormented, honest shade of Keir Hardie!) seemed intent on demonstrating that they could rise above their humble origins and wear court dress and grace Society functions as to the manner born. MacDonald, though he did not dare to follow Lloyd George's example of selling knighthoods for up to ten thousand pounds, baronetcies for up to forty thousand pounds, and peerages for a great deal more, was known to have accepted a 'gift' of thirty thousand shares in the thriving Edinburgh biscuit manufacturing firm of McVitie & Price, and to have rewarded its managing director with a baronetcy. He drove about, cigar in hand, in an expensive car paid for by wealthy 'socialist' M.P.s, including Sir Oswald

Mosley. It was, to Sylvia, a picture of unrelieved ignobility. No one had summed it up better than Churchill (who at least had the merit of not bothering to conceal his contempt for the workers). 'The socialists', he jibed, 'dreamt that they were clearing a pathway along which the toiling millions were to advance towards Utopia, but they wake up to find that all they have been doing is to set up a ladder by which the honourable baronet' (Mosley, who in 1926 became M.P. for Smethwick, Christabel's old constituency) 'can climb to place and power.'

With such leaders the General Strike, which might have stood some chance of success if it had taken place six or seven years earlier – before the creeping paralysis of MacBaldwinism had set in – was bound, thought Sylvia, to fail: or to succeed only in strengthening the repressive powers of the Government. In any case, the cut-price capitalist trade war could not be ended by a national skirmish. It could only be ended, as she had constantly insisted, by a world revolution of workers. In 1922, in the *Dreadnought,* she had condemned the mad, vicious circle of capitalism. British coal exports to American markets in the West Indies, Honolulu, and South America, for instance, had been boosted by cutting British miners' wages in order to reduce prices. American coalowners had replied by cutting their employees' wages – 'to compete with the starving miners of south Wales,' Sylvia wrote, 'who are collapsing in the pits for lack of food, and whose wives and children plead for Poor Law relief. When,' she had cried then, and still, though with decreasing hope, cried, 'when will the workers break down the barriers which shut them out from a life worth living?'

The whole weight of bourgeois Fabian socialism was against the General Strike, whose foredoomed failure was welcomed by a woman whose superior, pseudo-scientific frigidity had made her one of Sylvia's pet aversions. Beatrice Webb noted in her diary, with a near approach to joy, that the strike should teach both sides a lesson and have the desirable effect of cooling what she called 'the proletarian distemper' and of killing 'the pernicious doctrine of workers' control' (which, she was glad to see, had never been allowed to exist in Russia). With the melancholy satisfaction of one whose predictions have been proved horribly correct, Sylvia watched the strike collapse like a carnival monster, heard of the humiliating finale at 10 Downing Street, where Ernest Bevin and J. H. Thomas, representing the General Council of the Trades Union Congress, shuffled apologetically before the National Father Figure. 'I do not know whether I am overstepping the bounds,' faltered Bevin, 'but I would like you to give me an idea of what a just settlement means.' Thomas was even more abject. 'You answered us', he wheedled Baldwin, 'in the way we knew you would answer us—namely, that just as you recognize we have done a big thing in accepting the responsibility, we felt sure the big thing would be responded to in a big way. I never liked the word war ... '

It was some comfort, perhaps, to know that in the East End women had emptied slops and showered broken glass and blistering abuse on the heads of special constables, those hated symbols of middle-class reaction. But the fact was that in the spring and summer of 1926 Sylvia was prevented by more intimate concerns from knocking too long on the hollowness of official socialism. At the age of forty-four she believed that she was pregnant. Excitedly she telephoned her old friend and W.S.F. aide Charlotte Drake, who now had a draper's shop at Custom House, by the East End docks. When they had first met in 1913, Mrs Drake, the mother of four children, had told Sylvia bluntly: 'You should breed. We need more like you.' To which Sylvia had replied that she was too busy to have children: her work for the movement came first. Later, perhaps ... But then the war had come, and the terrific era of the *Dreadnought,* and the move to Woodford Green, and starting the café and writing her books, and the feeling that perhaps she was too old, her body too broken by the repeated gruellings of an agitator's life, to be able or (in her estimation) worthy to conceive and bring forth new life.

But now that the pace had eased, her health had improved. She felt stronger. She *wanted* to have a baby, to tackle the challenge of being a mother (and also to put into practice—since her motherhood, like nearly all the Pankhursts' undertakings, would be didactically public—her theories on how to bring up children); she wanted to defy Mrs Grundy, to prove conclusively that she was no spinster-type feminist, or one of those female busybodies who, as Mussolini (among others) put it, embraced humanity because they were afraid to embrace a man. But the multiple exhilarating experience was not yet to be. When she went, after shop hours, to Custom House, where Mrs Drake—who thoughtfully provided her with a wedding ring to avoid any possible embarrassment— had arranged for Sylvia to be examined by a midwife, the verdict was that hers was a 'phantom' pregnancy. She wanted to have a child so much that she had developed the symptoms. But she was no more truly with child than she had been twelve years earlier when, to disguise her from watching detectives, Mrs Drake and other disciples had not only smeared her pale face with unaccustomed (and detested) rouge, but had stuffed a large cushion under her clothes to simulate pregnancy.

Sylvia, however, was not through with motherhood. Some time in February 1927 Mrs Drake had another phone call. 'There's no mistake this time,' announced Sylvia jubilantly. 'I can feel the baby kicking.' Again Mrs Drake summoned the midwife, again slipped on the anti-scandalistic ring. 'I said to her', Mrs Drake remembers, ' "What about a son in December then?" But the midwife contradicted me. She thought it would be a girl. Sylvia was very upset. "But Mrs Drake said it would be a boy," she complained – she was very naive in many ways. So I said to the midwife, "You're only guessing. My guess is as good as yours." When she had gone, Sylvia asked me what I thought of her being an unmarried mother. I just told her, "Friends are friends. You accept them. You don't start catechizing them … " ' In all her vicissitudes, Sylvia had the gift of retaining the loyalty – the generous, protective loyalty – of people from widely differing social backgrounds who sensed the painful vulnerability of this self-giving Fury. Mrs Drake told Sylvia that she could stay with her while she was having the child. Lady Sybil Smith offered to arrange for her to enter the Hampstead nursing home where her own children had been delivered. Unwilling to hurt Mrs Drake's feelings, guilty perhaps about having a baby in such unproletarian style, yet conscious that at her age giving birth would be a difficult process needing the best possible medical attention, she asked Mrs Drake's advice. What should she do? Why, said Mrs Drake, whatever she thought was best for the child, of course. So Sylvia accepted Lady Sybil Smith's offer: and the Pethick-Lawrences, those childless, diligent benefactors who loved her as they might have loved a brilliant but unpredictable daughter (as indeed they had loved, and still loved, Christabel), sent her a substantial and much needed cheque.

Gradually the news filtered through the circle of her friends and acquaintances: though somehow, for the time being, it was kept from Mrs Pankhurst. Sylvia wrote to her mother (she had been deeply, if illogically, hurt that Mrs Pankhurst had made no attempt to see her): but the letter was intercepted. Norah Smyth, who was still struggling to pay off debts incurred during the East End campaigns, heard about the baby from an old colleague of the now defunct Workers' Communist Movement. 'I know', she wrote, 'that S.P. had often longed to have a child of her own. With her it was less "free love" than premeditated action for a definite result.' Corio's intellectual companionship had gradually become a necessity to Sylvia. 'Mine was not intellectual enough,' said Miss Smyth wistfully, 'partly because she had the effect of stultifying what little I had, partly because I was always overworked and never had the time or energy to think.' She was sure that Corio would make an excellent father, and fortunately 'many people who used to be horrified at the thought of illegitimacy now take a broader view, realizing that women have a right to satisfy their maternal instinct even if they are unable to marry. Sexual psychology', she added, 'is curious. There are some things one has to accept, however much one dislikes them.'

On December 3rd Mrs Drake received a short note from the nursing home in Fitzjohn's Avenue, Hampstead: 'Have just had a son—S.' It had been a hard birth. Sylvia, says Mrs Drake, was badly torn and could not sit down for weeks. But she carried her nonconformity through to the last detail. The birth certificate described Estelle Sylvia Pankhurst as a journalist: but the column headed 'Name and Surname of Father' was left blank. That was Miss Pankhurst's business. On December 23rd several newspapers contained a short item: 'Sylvia Pankhurst announces the birth of her son, Richard Keir Pethick Pankhurst'—Richard after her father, Keir after Keir Hardie, Pethick in gratitude to the Pethick-Lawrences, with whom Sylvia and her baby stayed for some weeks after leaving the nursing home. While she was there, Mrs Pankhurst happened to telephone. When Sylvia answered, she immediately replaced the receiver—not because she knew about the baby, but because, as she had already re-affirmed, she had severed all connection with her unworthy daughter and was resolved never to speak to her again. The two halves of the family had drifted too far apart to be able to speak to, rather than harangue, each other.

Under the whole-hearted influence of Corio, an acknowledged leader of Italian socialist exiles in London, Sylvia had already begun the anti-Fascist crusade which was soon to eclipse even her propaganda for free unions and progressive motherhood as the ruling obsession of her life. In January 1928 the *Manchester Guardian* printed some lively corres-pondence between her and Bernard Shaw. She had asked him to use his prestige to intervene with Mussolini in a case of political persecution. 'My dear Sylvia,' he replied, 'I am afraid I can do nothing to help. As I am a socialist, and the socialists in Italy are persecuted by the Fascists, my advocacy would do more harm than good.' In any case, he teasingly added, 'Mussolini seems to be almost as arbitrary a despot as if he had been born a Pankhurst, and the slightest kind of foreign interference puts his back up at once.' He was tired, he complained, of having his motives twisted. 'According to our indignant Liberals I am a Fascist, because I tell them to stop spitting in Mussolini's face and look at home for subjects of agitation. When I claimed the same consideration for Lenin, I was a Bolshevist. Heaven knows what I shall be next.'

To which accomplished prevarication Sylvia hotly retorted: 'I should certainly have thought that a request from you to the Fascist authorities would receive a most cordial assent, for none has defended the Fascists and their leader with the vigour and ingenuity shown by yourself.' How did Shaw reconcile his letter with his recent declaration that Mussolini was in effect 'a socialist doing socialist work?' Mussolini might pose as a socialist and deceive Shaw, but he had deliberately and viciously crushed the Italian working-class movement. 'Meanwhile', Sylvia snapped, 'you stand by and applaud the instrument of this destruction, and sneer at those who have suffered for their heroism, their ability and their faith. You call them disgruntled Liberals. Wherein is your policy more socialist than theirs? It is time you declared what you mean by socialism.'

Like her mother, Sylvia loathed lip-service and mere word spinning. It had grieved her to watch Shaw, the socialist street corner orator of the 1890s, turn first into a bourgeois Fabian and then into a fashionable entertainer and the prime pet and collector's piece of Lady Astor. The attack on Shaw, the wealthy, paradox-mongering playboy socialist, was a defence of Corio, a man who had truly suffered for his convictions, had shared the brunt of the *Dreadnought* battle with her, and preferred to remain anonymous (though he could have earned money and even a measure of notoriety as a journalist) in order the more efficiently to carry on his anti-Fascist work, and because he was incapable of that egocentric attitudinizing in which Shaw revelled, and which the commercial press demanded. But though respecting and fiercely defending Corio's desire for privacy, Sylvia did not hesitate to release the bees in her bonnet to buzz, with a maximum of publicity, in the popular press. A long interview about her baby, granted to an American journalist early in April 1928 and first published in New York, was featured exclusively in Britain in the *News of the World* under the headlines 'EUGENIC' BABY SENSATION— SYLVIA PANKHURST'S AMAZING CONFESSION—'SOUL-MATE' OF 53—THE BREAK WITH HER FAMILY. Looking rather straggle-haired and wan, she was photographed in her book-crammed shack behind the Red Cottage café. She had wanted a baby without the ties of marriage. Her 'husband' (who was not available for comment) was 'an old and dear friend whom I have loved for more than ten years. Since I have retained my name and personality, and he is of a retiring disposition, I will not bring him publicity by naming him. My friends know him: that is sufficient. I wanted a baby, as every complete human being desires parenthood, to love him and cherish him, to see him grow up and develop, and to leave behind me a being who will, I hope, carry on the best that is in me and my stock.' Was the baby eugenic? 'It is good eugenics', she answered, 'to consider if one is of sufficient general intelligence, bodily health, and freedom from hereditary diseases to produce a healthy and intelligent child. I believe that of myself. I believe that, also, of my baby's father. Indeed, I consider that he has many gifts with which to endow our child, and much aptitude and patience as a teacher.' Like any proud parent, she pointed out her baby's perfections. He already weighed fourteen pounds and everyone told her he was months ahead for his age. His hands seemed to her remarkably artistic—just like his father's.

Then came the propaganda punch lines. Love and enthusiasm, Sylvia announced, were the two factors which made life worth living. She believed that as society tended away from individualism and production for profit towards co-operation and mutual aid, marriage (though she stressed that the family would remain the fundamental unit of society— 'an institutional upbringing can never compensate a child for the absence of parental love') would become more perfect, freer. It ought not to be the subject of a legal contract. 'It is better, more dignified, and more sane to part by mutual consent than after nasty, hypocritical proceedings in the divorce court. Love and freedom are vital to the creation and up-bringing of a child. I do not advise anyone to rush into either legal or free marriage without love, sympathy, understanding, friendship and frank-ness. These are essentials, and having these, no legal forms are necessary. Indifference, hostility and compulsion are the factors to be feared, and the influences that lead to sorrow for the individual and danger to the progress of the race.'

Other reporters hastened to Woodford Green for further dogmatic pickings. But while Sylvia was dispensing her unconventional but highly proper wisdom, the father of the young Welsh girl who was serving in the café, horrified at the thought that his daughter was not only working in a Red Cottage but employed by a Scarlet Woman, arrived in haste to snatch her away from such moral contagion. And while Sylvia, carefully tidied, wearing a loose white dress, holding plump little Richard naked in her arms, and looking years younger and even beautiful (as she often did in the regenerating thick of a good fight), was posing for a formal portrait in a Woodford photographic studio, the press was already firing the inevitable salvoes of moral indignation.

Most women, wrote a columnist in the *Daily News,* would have shunned publicity in such circumstances, even if public opinion had become more tolerant. But Sylvia was different. 'She glories in her experiment. She wants us all to know. Henceforth Richard will be known as the illegitimate son of a very famous woman. Hard lines on him!' Her attempt to boost the 'modern movement', which was based on 'jungle ethics', had labelled her child for life. Most good mothers would sigh and say, 'I don't think much of her.' It was monstrous to make a baby born out of wedlock the excuse for a sermon subversive of hallowed values. 'Still (thank God!) we all recognize that marriage is a high and holy thing, and is the normal and rightful way of bringing a child into the world. For some women there is an excuse. They are trapped or fall from weakness. This has been done in the light of day, and is an offence to the laws of man and God.'

There could hardly have been a fruitier example of the kind of falsely chivalrous knight-errantry to challenge which Sylvia had thrown down her baby-gauntlet. Nor, perhaps, a much more accurate summary of the kind of sentiments which Sylvia's action aroused among her estranged relatives—and especially in her mother, now at last obliged to face the latest facts of her daughter's serially outrageous life.

CHAPTER FIVE

ROADS TO GLORY

Christabel at least was ranged unequivocally with the forces of preservation, the battalions of decency. As a conservative evangelical she was busy rallying Protestant clergy and churchgoers to the defence of bourgeois values. Since 1917 evangelicals had been tireless in anti-Bolshevism, backing intervention against the Soviets, lambasting the blasphemy of Socialist Sunday Schools, habitually referring to Lenin as 'this criminal, this assassin, this precursor of Anti-Christ', well-armed with lantern slides of Bolshevik atrocities. In Parliament, conservative evangelicalism had a powerful leader in Sir William Joynson-Hicks, Home Secretary from 1924 to 1929, who was fanatically steadfast in his determination to suppress communism, night clubs (and pleasure in general), and attempts by Anglo-Catholic intellectuals to 'Romanize' the Anglican Book of Common Prayer.

In September 1926, under the auspices of the ultra-evangelical Advent Testimony and Preparation Movement, Christabel had started a six-month lecture tour which took her all over the British Isles. In Birmingham, Bristol, Ipswich, Cardiff, Liverpool, Manchester, Edinburgh, Glasgow and Dublin—and most notably in London—she attracted immense audiences and wide press coverages. On-the-spot 'decisions for Christ' running well into four figures, due largely to Christabel's allure, were reported by the *Advent Witness,* which was encouraged to anticipate that

the whole kingdom will be raised. The Lord's people cannot fail to see that the long-prayed-for revival has already begun, not only by pointing back to Calvary but forward to the Coming Glory ... No doubt thousands have gathered out of curiosity to see and hear Miss Christabel Pankhurst: but curiosity has changed to wonder that one so recently called to the higher service of proclaiming the Coming of the Lord should have grasped not only that glorious truth, but the facts of His Diety, His true incarnation. His atoning death and triumphant resurrection. Miss Pankhurst has no reservations as to any of the sublime doctrines of Grace. Our prayer must now be not only that she may be used, but kept.

She was as two-dimensionally black-and-white and cheer-leaderly confident as she had been during the war or the suffrage campaign, when as early as 1908 she had declared that militant methods, distasteful as they were to those who were forced to practise them, had made votes for women 'one of the burning questions of the day' and would shortly lead to the sweeping away of politicians' excuses and the attainment of complete success. It was piquant to hear her state in the Free Trade Hall, Manchester (where in 1905 she had created the first suffragette disturbance) that women's emancipation was no more capable of righting the world than any other human reform. In Wales, she predicted that Britain would soon have a woman Prime Minister. Only a few years ago, she said, the prospect would have filled her with delight and pride. Now her rejoicing would be tempered by the knowledge that women were no less fallible than men (a truth to which she had refused to listen when it had been preached by Mrs Fawcett and the non-militants).

At the Queen's Hall, London, while a massed choir sang Second Adventist hymns and a score of black-suited clergy waited sombrely on the platform, Christabel entered late and passed with characteristic shyness to her seat. There she remained in her slumped, pre-speech posture, head bent, face hidden by the wide picture hat which she still affected (no more than Mrs Pankhurst did she make concessions to passing fashion). 'When she rose to speak,' reported the *Manchester Guardian,* which always did the Mancunian Pankhursts proud, 'the audience rose to greet her – an indication that it included a great number of suffrage women, who perform this simple rite when they wish to show special honour.' The chairman, the Reverend F. B. Meyer, deplored the demonstration, reminding the audience to keep their thoughts on the true object of the meeting, though gallantly admitting that Miss Pankhurst *was* a most comely ambassador of the King of Kings. 'If she were a little older,' he coyly quipped, 'I might call her Deborah, a real Mother in Israel.'

Christabel's voice, shriller than her mother's, less supple, had nevertheless the same power of projection. But she did not try to dramatize her message. Her object was rather to avoid drama, to present the fulfilment of Biblical prophecy as something to be taken for granted, not ooh-ed and aah-ed over, a matter of simple facts. In the ten-thousand capacity Royal

Albert Hall, which she twice filled to overflowing, the audience again rose to greet her. She was radiant with optimistic gloom. The portents of the Coming were, she said, thickening on every side for those who had eyes to see. The impotence of the League of Nations, war in China, the fear of war in Europe, the worsening of Franco-German relations, the world-wide sabotage of Bolshevism, earthquakes and other major natural catastrophes: all augured the nearness of the Final Solution. As she was fond of saying: 'I go about with the Bible in one hand and a newspaper in the other. The two go well together, for the concentrated study of the newspapers is a Christian's duty as this Age draws to its close.'

Of course she had her critics. The *Church of Ireland Gazette* complained that she overstated her case. 'She paints the present conditions of the world in quite unnecessarily dark colours,' it said. 'To say that none of the efforts of men to improve the world are of any avail, that even, as she would seem to imply, *Christian* men can hope to accomplish no real improvement so long as this dispensation continues, is simply not true. It is also dishonouring to God. Has Miss Pankhurst ever heard of the successes of Foreign Missions?' The fact that her inflated hopes of women's suffrage had been disappointed was no reason why 'everyone should be called upon to join her in disillusionment'. But this, and similar carpings, were minor crosses, easily borne. Christabel was happy. Hers, moreover, was a happiness (and a job) which, if the prayers of her fellow-believers were answered and she was kept in the faith, would last her lifetime, whatever the date of the Lord's Return. It was a great relief to Mrs Pankhurst to see her so settled, so lively, so eminent in her chosen field.

Not long after Christabel's triumph at the Albert Hall, Mrs Pankhurst was asked to make a speech there, at a mass meeting of Conservative women, proposing a vote of thanks to Mr Baldwin, then at the height of his power and popularity as leader of the party. She refused to use a microphone — 'I shall not need that. I spoke here often in the old days when such things did not exist, and I think I still know how to pitch my voice.' Even at her most emotional, she had never shouted, always relying on her magnetic presence and charismatic face to achieve absolute quiet. The extraordinary resonance of her voice and the purity of her diction were such that her softest whisper (and she habitually dropped her voice for dramatic effect) floated to the farthest gallery. Once more the huge audience rose in ovation to a Pankhurst. Emmeline, now sixty-eight, had need of such encouragement. Her health was fragile, and, reckoning that electoral victory in Whitechapel was unlikely, she overextended herself by answering calls to speak in other constituencies and at many large – and even not so large – Tory gatherings. The Conservative Central Office took full (some thought too full) advantage of her eagerness to be used wherever it was considered that she might be useful. At least once, when she spoke on behalf of the Conservative candidate in Southwark, London, she had the unique and unpleasant experience of being shouted down. Even when she descended among the audience to plead for order (had not she gone to prison, she cried, for freedom of speech?) a claque at the back of the hall continued to yell, cat-call, and sing 'Tell Me the Old, Old Story' and the Red Flag.

By Easter 1927 she was, quite visibly, a wasting asset. Her friends were alarmed, and Mr and Mrs Marshall (he had acted as solicitor to the W.S.P.U., she had been a suffragette) took her on a Mediterranean cruise, and then to the quiet of their country house in Chipping Ongar in Essex, to recuperate. In the late summer, looking stronger but with her stamina still dangerously low, she undertook an extensive, exhausting speaking tour. She would rush to catch a train straight from a series of meetings in the East End, and come back to London sometimes in the early hours of the morning. Often she arrived at her temporary host's house, grey with tiredness, and flung herself into an easy chair. Yet on the platform, even if it was only to open a bazaar or launch a garden party, she would appear transfigured.

To every speech she brought a sense of missionary urgency and earnestness out of tune with times flaccid with drift and plain bewilderment. She hated to see the grass growing between the British Lion's recumbent paws. In the Free Trade Hall, Manchester (where, as Lancashire's most famous daughter, she was an even bigger draw than Christabel) she stoutly defended Baldwin – 'a splendid man, perfectly honest' – against his Tory critics, and told how she was trying to hold up the flag of Empire and the cause of King and Country in one of the 'Reddest' constituencies in England. She could not, she said, understand the assumption that because she was now a Tory she must, by definition, be less democratic than she had been when she was a socialist. She certainly felt no different. In fact it was her concern for, and faith in, parliamentary democracy which had made her a Conservative. (Shortly before this, on her eighty-third birthday, Mrs Despard had told a meeting of the Women's Freedom League: 'I have no confidence in the future of parliamentary democracy. The workers will not continue to tolerate present-day conditions. I can

A 1929 portrait of the Second Adventist Christabel

Sydney 1926: Mrs Adela Pankhurst Walsh, her husband and his colleague, Jacob Johansen (*right*)

Adela Pankhurst Walsh speaking in Macquarie Place, Sydney, in the 1930s

see a great upheaval coming. What I think will come is an Economic Government, with industries, professions and agriculture represented.')

There was, thought Mrs Pankhurst, a great need for more women in politics. It seemed to her that the men were too often harassed and enfeebled by the heavy business anxieties which had followed the war, and that they should 'lie fallow for a while and let the women take over'. Frequently she demanded that the barriers against the employment of women (re-erected by many trade unions after the wartime truce) should be torn down, and she condemned protective legislation for women in industry. It was very convenient for men to kill women's competition by kindness, but wartime experience – and the experience of working widows with children to provide for – showed that there were very few jobs which women could not do, very few strains which they could not (and were not often forced to) endure. In many cases they stood up to stress better than men. Any attempt to treat women like children must be sternly resisted. To limit women's range of experience by restricting their opportunities of earning their living, while at the same time giving them political power, was, in her view, dangerous and certain to breed thoughtlessness and irresponsibility.

She took a close interest in the activities of the Women's Guild of Empire. Towards the end of 1927 she attended a welcome-back luncheon given to Mrs Drummond on her return from a three-month tour of Canada with a group of W.G.E. delegates and their husbands. Mrs Drummond agreed with Mrs Pankhurst that British emigration to Canada should be increased, not only to ease unemployment in Britain, but to offset the influence of non-British immigrants. She intended, she announced, to open an emigration office for this purpose, and had arranged for representative women in various Canadian provinces to be available for help and advice. Once more, as in its still lively industrial peace campaign, the W.G.E. had acted as the willing and efficient executive of Pankhurst projects. Mrs Drummond had performed another valuable service. Just before leaving for Canada she had put her old chief in touch with Mrs Nellie Hall-Humpherson, who from the early autumn of 1927 worked as Mrs Pankhurst's secretary. As a suffragette, Nellie Hall had, in 1914 when she was barely twenty-one, been forcibly fed for three months (together with six other women, including Grace Roe) in Holloway Prison. Her mother Pattie Hall – one of the six original members of the W.S.P.U. when it was first formed in Manchester in 1903 – and her sister Emmeline, named after Mrs Pankhurst, had also been to prison as

7

militants. Her father, Leonard Hall, had been a close friend of Dr Pankhurst, and a prominent member of the I.L.P. in its early days.

These associations, and the knowledge of Nellie's utter loyalty and vigorous capability, made Mrs Pankhurst pressing in her request. Nellie, now married to a schoolmaster working in Warwickshire, had two children. But she forthwith turned her life upside down, found a cheap flat in London and a nursemaid to look after the children, and took up her new and unexpected duties. Every morning at nine o'clock she arrived at 35 Gloucester Street, where Mrs Pankhurst was staying with her sister Mrs Goulden Bach. The first task was to go through the mail, while Mrs Pankhurst sat in front of the fire eating breakfast in her dressing-gown. 'We discussed the day,' Mrs Hall-Humpherson remembers, 'then sometimes we would go on to a weekly meeting of women in Whitechapel; or go canvassing together, visiting houses, shops, even pubs, and perhaps holding an outdoor meeting. We also organized tea parties specially for Jewish women (said to be particularly resistant to electioneering). Sometimes there would be a session with the local Conservative committee, sometimes an evening meeting. In addition to all this a London County Council election was in the offing, and Mrs Pankhurst was zealous in her support of the Conservative candidate, Commander Venn, the husband of a niece of Dr Ethel Smyth. The Hon. Edith Fitzgerald and Barbara Wylie, friends from prewar days, were wonderfully helpful, and brought theatrical friends to entertain at our tea parties. Lady Katherine Japp came too – a Canadian ex-actress who had married Sir Henry Japp, a well-known engineer. The East Enders adored Mrs Pankhurst. She was a lovely person to them. She never talked down to them, and was interested in *them* rather than expecting them to be interested in her.'

But since she combined frequent sorties for the Conservative Central Office with this strenuous schedule, Mrs Pankhurst's energy was always liable to flag. The heavy London fogs of December 1927 did not help her health or spirits. During the Christmas holiday Mrs Hall-Humpherson telephoned her every morning. One morning she was in tears. 'I went dashing round. Christabel had given her a toy dog, very highly bred, with ancestors a mile long and a constitution resembling a snow-flake – and it was not well! It had been seen by a vet, but was not getting better, and Mrs Pankhurst was afraid that Christabel would think she had neglected it. The dog died, and instead of enjoying Christmas frivolity with my family I wandered about with the body until I could find a place where it could be decently interred.'

Life, in fact, was nigglingly filled with minor frictions. Used until 1919 to undisputed joint control, with Christabel, of her own party machine, treated in Canada as a near-oracular celebrity, Mrs Pankhurst and her idiosyncratic methods did not go down well with some of her new associates. Despite her almost frantic zeal, the bureaucrats (both male and female) of the Central Office increasingly regarded her as an awkward, if magnificent, cuckoo in the Tory nest. She had no money, not even a motor-car. She was simply not one of them. Her emphasis on spiritual values and imperial horizons seemed to them ill-timed in a period of rocketing unemployment and economic dislocation. The kind of propaganda which the Central Office was preparing to catch the flapper vote must surely, if she was aware of it (and as a member of the Women's Advisory Committee of the National Union of Conservative and Unionist Associations she probably was), have disgusted her. 'When you put on your very best pair of artificial silk stockings with extra-strong toes and double cotton tops,' ogled one pamphlet, 'does it ever occur to you that not only are you clothing your shapely legs in beautiful silk stockings, but that you have also found one of the many things for which you should say thank you to the Conservative Government?' Mutual disapproval extended to the branch office in Cable Street where, as Mrs Hall-Humpherson puts it, 'the staff may have been devoted Conservatives, but they were not devoted to Mrs Pankhurst, her candidacy, or me. In the end we only dealt with them when it was absolutely necessary.'

It may have been an added offence in official eyes that Mrs Pankhurst was liable to steal even carefully prepared governmental thunder. When, at the end of March 1928, the Flapper Vote (technically Equal Suffrage) Bill got its second reading in the Commons, Mrs Pankhurst's presence in the Ladies' Gallery received much sentimental attention in the press ('What a record of direct achievement in a single lifetime! Is there any equal to it in the public life of today?'), and her photograph appeared on the front pages, together with that of the Home Secretary, Sir William Joynson-Hicks, who moved the reading. For Mrs Pankhurst it was an occasion full of historical echoes and instructive entertainment. Prim, ebullient Joynson-Hicks, with his black silk tailcoat, high starched collar, black cravat and buttonhole carnation (HE DIED AS HE HAD LIVED, A PERFECT OLD WOMAN was the epitaph suggested for him in the debate by Brigadier-General Sir George Cockerell, one of the tiny group of diehard opponents of the Bill), had owed his first return to Westminster to massive suffragette intervention in a by-election in Manchester in 1908, when Churchill was defeated. Why, demanded Sir George Cockerell, should women—more than five million of whom were about to be enfranchised—be placed in a perpetual majority? Was not this to replace one injustice by another? Unless some new electoral system could be devised to right the balance, he could see only two alternatives: a massacre of the female innocents at birth, or the bearing of more male children by women.

How often, in the old days, from behind the oriental-type grille which then hid the ladies in their gallery, had Mrs Pankhurst been forced to listen to such facetiousness as members talked out yet another private member's bill to give the vote to less than two million women? It was pleasant, too, to see for the first time Lady Astor in parliamentary action, treating Sir George's mock flippancy with the mock flippancy it deserved, shuddering and flinging up her hands in simulated horror while he spoke, and afterwards quipping: 'The preponderance of women is an unfortunate provision of Nature. You can't change Nature, but you can change the law.' Mrs Pankhurst admired Lady Astor's touch. It was excellently judged. She may have longed to join her in the House. But apart from any political considerations that prospect now seemed increasingly remote. 'She looked', reported one newspaper, 'very frail and old, not even the shadow of an Amazon.' Yet she had resolved to live among her constituents, even in a hopeless cause. It would save her many tiring journeys and be a gesture of identification. Mrs Hall-Humpherson had already searched the constituency for suitable lodgings. The best she could find were some furnished rooms over a barber's shop in the Ratcliffe Highway, Wapping. Mrs Chipperfield, the barber's wife, was a good cook, cheerful, and a great fan of Mrs Pankhurst. The rooms were light and airy and clean, but the sitting-room wallpaper was pseudo-Chinese in rather garish royal blue and gold. Throwing herself with childlike zest into the move, Mrs Pankhurst chose a black carpet to cover the floor and subdue the impact of the wallpaper. Her own desk and a few small pieces of furniture and ornaments were moved from her sister's house to add a personal touch.

At Eastertime, early in April that year, she went to stay with the Marshalls at Chipping Ongar. She talked about her schooldays and the times she had spent with Christabel in Paris, spoke of her husband, and grew sombre at the memory of the death of Harry and of her baby son Frank. In the midst of these family reminiscences the news of Sylvia's baby and of her sensational press interview burst upon her. In her already weakened condition, it had a devasting effect. She wept for hours on end, sobbing that she would never be able to speak in public again. But after going to church on Sunday she grew calmer and resolute to face the music of Sylvia's orchestration. On April 11th she was driven to her rooms in Ratcliffe Highway.

She spoke again, but was cruelly heckled about her daughter's 'carryings on'. She said it was not her custom to discuss private matters in public, and somehow finished her speech. But it was her last effort. Suddenly the East End adventure seemed less gay. It was as if a moral as well as a physical slum had opened to engulf her, its curs snapping at her fastidious heels. It seemed as though Sylvia's conduct had been, not a matter of perverse principle, but a blow deliberately aimed at her: just as, to Sylvia, it seemed that Mrs Pankhurst's Whitechapel foray was a calculated personal affront. A burning shame shrivelled the last shreds of her pugnacity. The jaundice which, since her hunger strikes, had recurrently plagued her, struck with unusual virulence. She took to her bed, and cancelled such engagements as Mrs Hall-Humpherson, the Hon. Edith Fitzgerald and Barbara Wylie could not, between them, fulfil. She apologized to Mrs Chipperfield for being such a bother, and thanked her for her kindness and excellent food. Racked with painful nausea, she could not digest anything. 'If I could only get my strength back,' she kept saying, 'I know I've got five years of good work in me yet.' The noise of the shop, the Cockney chatter, the roar of the traffic, which in better health would have been part of the fun, the four musketeering, now became a trial. Dr May Williams, also an ex-suffragette, was called in and constantly attended her. Lady Japp brought fruit and flowers and being, like the other three disciples, lively and amusing, helped to relieve the gloom.

Soon Mrs Pankhurst was saying that she did not need a nurse, that she had had this kind of attack before and got over it. She began to sketch future tactics and listened eagerly to the reports which her lieutenants brought back to her. Sometimes she would ask Mrs Hall-Humpherson to sit on her bed and read aloud the long letters, crammed with political comment and advice, which Christabel wrote regularly. She was genuinely delighted to get a letter from Adela, full of tenderness and regret for the long rift, and announcing that she and her husband had come round to Mrs Pankhurst's way of thinking. Class warfare, the destructive pitting of labour against capital, was, after all, a blind and murderous alley, and the Walshes meant to start a movement to promote – militantly, of course – the message of industrial peace. Mrs Pankhurst immediately despatched a letter of whole-hearted reconciliation. But still, despite several requests, she refused to see Sylvia, and gave instructions that she was to be refused entry. Fifteen years earlier Mrs Pankhurst had gone to the East End to ask Sylvia bluntly: 'Are you staying with these women or coming with us?' Sylvia's wounds were too recent, too lethal and too intimate to be forgiven. There was almost, perhaps, a superstitious sense that the fantastic ghost of the Sylvia of the East End, along whose streets she had been carried fasting and agonizing like a holy woman, had risen in wrath to smite the intruder: and Mrs Pankhurst was not a good loser.

When she failed to rally, she realized that there was one more melancholy duty to perform. She could no longer afford, even if she lived, to give Mary Gordon, now twelve, the care or the education she had planned. A new home was found for Mary, with an eminent, kindly and cultured civil servant and his wife. Here was another defeat, it seemed to Mrs Pankhurst, another admission of weakness, of failure. Frank, Harry, Joan and Kathleen, and now Mary, had been taken from her. She was very lonely, very chastened, and all the love, all the ingenuity, of her three lieutenants was needed to raise her from a horrible slough of despond. The circle of concern was widening. It was known that she received no more than a pittance from the Conservatives for all her touchingly willing work, and now an illness fund, another dole of pity for the old and battered Queen, was opened, with Lady Astor and Lady Rhondda prominent and Mrs Baldwin said to be sympathetic. News of this seemed to make her a little easier. There was talk of staying with the Marshalls, and perhaps another Mediterranean cruise.

Then at the end of May came a steep and alarming relapse. Christabel took her mother to a nursing home in Hampstead, not far from where she was lodging (and also, ironically, not far from where Sylvia had had her baby). Christabel also called in Dr Chetham Strode, a well-known physician who, during the war, had given his services as honorary medical adviser to Mrs Pankhurst and her adopted children. Hurrying back to London from a brief Whitsun holiday, Mrs Hall-Humpherson learned that neither Dr Williams, Edith Fitzgerald nor Barbara Wylie had been able to see Mrs Pankhurst. She herself was told by Christabel and Mrs Goulden Bach that no visitors were allowed. Yet it was rumoured that Mrs Pankhurst had been subjected to drastic stomach pumping, the shock of which, Dr Williams thought, was bound to weaken her. Determined to break what seemed an over-possessive family barrier — Christabel had deplored her mother's slumming from the start — Mrs

Hall-Humpherson phoned the matron of the nursing home (Mrs Pank-hurst had been moved to Wimpole Street), and was told that Dr Strode had been trying to contact her for several days. On June 12th, when she was shown into her room, Mrs Pankhurst burst into tears. She could not understand why Nellie had not been to see her before. She had been asking for her ever since she was taken away from Mrs Chipperfield's rooms. The following day Mrs Hall-Humpherson visited Mrs Pankhurst again. She was very weak but still conscious. On June 14th when Barbara Wylie went to the nursing home, she was only partly conscious and unable to understand a somewhat tardy message from the Conservative Central Office that 'it would be all right about money'.

When Mrs Hall-Humpherson went to a call-box to phone the nursing home for news, she saw the midday papers arriving at the Underground station on the other side of the road. (Mrs Pankhurst had a horror of Underground trains and would never travel on one.) The newsvendors began to fit new placards into their lean-up frames. Each of them carried the headline MRS PANKHURST DEAD. She was just a month short of her seventieth birthday. Sadly, Mrs Hall-Humpherson hung up the receiver and stepped out into the cruelly indifferent noise and bustle of the pavement. Mrs Chipperfield must be told. All but a few of the Conservatives at headquarters and in Cable Street would be relieved. They would be able to choose a new candidate, no doubt a man, no doubt wealthy (the Hon. Loel Guinness, as it turned out). Sylvia must be feeling pretty dreadful. How lucky that Mary had been settled. Thank God that Mrs Pank-hurst was finally at rest, beyond the reach of malice and meanness, beyond the necessity for testimonial or illness funds or canvassing constituents or defending Baldwin ...

CHAPTER SIX

THE CANONIZATION OF
MRS PANKHURST

While, at the Marshalls' London house at Gayfere Street, Smith Square, Westminster, the venue and details of the funeral – who should be flag bearers, who pall bearers, who chief mourners – were, under the chairmanship of Christabel, minutely discussed, and questions of priority and precedence settled diplomatically though not without argument, obituary impressions from a dozen different hands tumbled from the press. Hasty death masks, they added up to an interesting composite portrait. 'Mrs Pankhurst is dead,' wrote George Lansbury in the *Daily Herald,* 'the once fiery spirit is at rest. She has been likened to Joan of Arc: but to me, who knew her well at the height of her powers, she was just a supersensitive soul, seared so deeply by what life had revealed to her that the rebel spark was quickened into action fated to mark an epoch.' The militant suffrage campaign, said the *Daily News,* was 'perhaps the most brilliant piece of electioneering of our times'. Occasionally, as in Emily Wilding Davison's death on Derby Day, the campaign had turned into tragedy. Often it produced rollicking farce. 'But always it was played at high speed before record audiences. Mrs Pankhurst had a remarkable fertility of resource, an unequalled sense of the right moment to strike. She had, moreover, a superb courage, and with it that white-hot enthusiasm which gave to the campaign, with all its hysterical excesses, a kind of wild dignity. Within six months she and her followers had turned women's suffrage, until then a subject for academic or facetious discussion, into a question for which men as well as women were ready to fight to the last ditch.'

She was a person, wrote another obituarist, who seemed, like Joan of Arc or Florence Nightingale, to have been providentially designed for her mission. She had been, actually as well as symbolically, 'the very edge of that weapon of will power by which British women freed themselves from being classed with children and idiots in the matter of the franchise'. Even her beauty had possessed a divinely imperishable quality, undiminished by suffering. Always that tautly resolute face had carried like a clarion call, always it had remained 'finely, if unsensuously feminine':

and that had been a tremendous asset to the cause 'at a time when its opponents claimed that only unfeminine freaks could want a vote or brave the rigours of fighting for it'. One newspaper tabulated her fantastic prison record—sentences totalling over four years, of which, at reckless personal cost in hunger, thirst and sleep strikes, she had served perhaps eight months. If she had been born in the great days of ancient Rome, said one tribute, she would have a mother of the Gracchi. If she had lived in the middle ages, she would have rivalled St Catherine of Siena or made herself famous as a Poor Clare. She was 'a spiritual descendant of all martyrs and fanatics who have ever worn themselves out in pursuit of an ideal'. Yet she was the very opposite of what many people believed her to be, this little woman of delicate prettiness, with a soft voice, an elegant taste in clothes, and a horror of sentimentality. It was almost laughable to see her as a 'general' giving orders to her 'soldiers', as she called them. She had possessed, said the *Times,* a power of oratory unrivalled by any other woman of her generation, a power which stemmed from the fact that she had been utterly convinced that she was working for the salvation of the whole world as well as of her own sex. Despite her autocratic methods (themselves significant of her burning certainty that *her* way was the *only* way) and her grievous mistakes, she was 'a humble-minded, large-hearted, unselfish woman'. Quite deliberately, knowing the cost, she, a widow in her forties, had undertaken a warfare against the forces of law and order which had overstrained her fragile body. 'It will be remembered of her that whatever peril and suffering she called upon her followers to face, she herself was ready to face, and did face, with unfailing courage.'

Christabel, to whom Mrs Lucy Baldwin had sent a letter of official condolence, gave her version in the *Daily Mail.* The greatest sacrifice her mother had made for women was, she insisted, that she had been willing 'to be falsely reckoned an eccentric, a virago. To break into the closed circle of citizenship she was ready to seem the thing that she was not ... She disliked eccentricity, she was reserved, sensitive, above all she had a wonderful, innate dignity. Uninvited, unexpected, she came among women with a great gift for them. The gift conferred, she now leaves them with her own quiet dignity, nay, with majesty ... ' Mrs Drummond, writing in the Women's Guild of Empire *Bulletin,* picked out Mrs Pankhurst's 'divine gift of distinguishing reality from sham, sincerity from hypocrisy', as her outstanding quality. She had seen with a devasting clarity that as long as women remained politically impotent, society would be out of balance and social reform would languish. For Mrs Pankhurst, the subjection of women was 'the epitome of the greater subjection of the spiritual to the material which is at the root of all wrong and injustice. The standards which held the bodies of women and of little children as of less account than money and property were intolerable to her.' She had regarded Prussianism, Bolshevism, pacifism (and its corollary, a flabby internationalism) as the same materialistic enemy in different guises, and had fought them with all her strength. Mrs Despard, herself a militant socialist and pacifist, summarized in *The Vote*: 'To me, her great service to women lies in the fact that she discovered, stimulated, and through her personal initiative, harnessed for action, the Spirit of Revolt. For this we owe her a debt of gratitude that nothing can repay.' The Bill for Equal Suffrage had been approved in the House of Lords as Mrs Pankhurst lay dying. 'I am full to the brim,' Mrs Despard exulted, 'but how I wish that wonderful woman Mrs Pankhurst was with us. This is only the first victory in a long battle before us. I am very, very proud of the young generation. I like to see these young girls with their long legs and short skirts. When I was a girl we were not allowed to show our ankles. Women have discovered one another. They are no longer rivals, but comrades.'

On June 17th, the night before the funeral service, which was to take place in St John's Church, Smith Square (chosen because of its nearness to the Houses of Parliament, the scene of the great suffragette demonstrations) Mrs Pankhurst's body lay in state in a small *chapelle ardente* in the West End. In the queues of friends and comrades and ordinary, curious members of the public, Christabel appeared several times; unable, it seemed, to believe that the strange partnership in which her revered mother had put herself so humbly, so proudly, at the head of a suffrage army directed by her precocious daughter was, at least in this dispensation—so full of partings and incompleteness—at an end. The undertakers had carefully arranged Mrs Pankhurst's soft, silvery hair about a face magnetic even in death. A subdued light fell from a lamp placed by a small golden cross above her head. Men and women, surprised by the daintiness of the immaculate corpse, murmured pityingly, often with tears in their eyes: 'The poor little woman.' Hearing which, one ex-militant snorted indignantly: 'Poor little woman, indeed!' In those two insights, those two emphases, was contained the secret of Mrs Pankhurst's subtle double grip on public sympathy and feminist frustration.

Late that night the coffin was taken to St John's Church, where a suffragette guard of honour kept vigil round it. As they stood there in the

Valhallan candlelight, temporarily united in the noble ritual of soldierly homage, fighting back the impulse to shift or cough, determined to rival the silence and immobility of their dead chieftain, an aeroplane – 'The Friendship' – carrying a young female pace-setter of the new age of machines and Flying Fools was nearing touch-down at Burry Port, near Llanelly, in Wales. Next day, the arrival of Amelia Earhart – The First Woman to Fly the Atlantic – blew Mrs Pankhurst off the front pages of the evening papers of June 18th. Even the morning papers of June 19th, still gushing over 'Girly Lindy' were content to let the dead bury their dead. Mrs Pankhurst, an inveterate headline filcher, would no doubt have appreciated the irony of the situation. But however curtailed the press reports, Smith Square was jammed with people to witness something of what the *Daily News* called 'the most impressive public funeral for a social pioneer since the death of General Booth, the founder of the Salvation Army' – an apt comparison, since Mrs Pankhurst, too, had seen her women as warriors of Salvation.

The church was heaped with flowers, huge bouquets in the purple, white and green of the suffragettes, thousands of purple irises, which in the old days had been used to decorate the platforms and drawing-rooms of the militants. Waiting there, in uneasy proximity to Christabel (Mrs Drummond in a press interview had spoken of a 'private grief' which had hastened Mrs Pankhurst's end, and the *New York Times* had sub-headed its obituary REVOLUTIONARY ATTITUDE OF DAUGHTER SADDENED DAYS), Sylvia, looking anything but a Scarlet Woman in clothes as un-fashionable as, if much less expensive, than those of her sister, was flanked by her accuser, Mrs Drummond, and by the seven other chief mourners: Annie Kenney (now Mrs Taylor); Robert Goulden, one of Mrs Pank-hurst's brothers; her sister, Mrs Goulden Bach; her nephew, Mr Edward Goulden Bach; and her nieces, the Misses Enid, Lorna and Sybil Goulden Bach. Mrs Despard was there, sibylline in a flowing black gown, her hawk-like face and dazzlingly white hair framed in a black mantilla. So were Mr and Mrs Pethick-Lawrence; Commandant Mary Allen, with several uniformed officers of the Women's Auxiliary Service; the Hon. Edith Fitzgerald; Dr (later Dame) Laura Knight, the painter, who had been a suffragette in the Women's Freedom League; Dame May Whitty, representing the Actresses' Franchise League; Mrs Victor (now Lady) Gol-lancz (who in 1914, before her marriage, had 'stormed' Buckingham Palace with Mrs Pankhurst and risked imprisonment by cutting telegraph wires on the outskirts of London); Lady Rhondda; Lady Sybil Smith; and

Lady Astor. There, too, were Miss Helen Fraser, an ex-suffragette who had been the first woman candidate adopted by a parliamentary constituency in Scotland; and Miss Helena Normanton, one of England's first women barristers. Heading the Conservative Party delegation were Mrs Baldwin and Lord Curzon, that erstwhile pillar of anti-suffragism. Miss Eleanor Rathbone, one of the most effective women M.P.s, came as president (in succession to Millicent Fawcett) of the National Union of Women's Suffrage Societies; George Lansbury and Henry Nevinson, the journalist, represented the many men who had been moved by Mrs Pankhurst to fight alongside the suffragettes. The Canadian High Commissioner and Mme Draga Ilich (representing the women of Serbia, on whose behalf Mrs Pankhurst had raised funds in her tour of the United States in 1916) were reminders of other facets of the dead woman's tireless and multiple crusading.

As the organist played 'O rest in the Lord', Mrs Hall-Humpherson, bearing the W.S.P.U. flag, and Miss Elfreda Acklam (a young Conservative Party worker who had sometimes driven Mrs Pankhurst about) bearing the Union Jack, walked slowly down the centre aisle, dipped their colours at the chancel steps, and took up positions at either side of the bier. After the entrance of the choir and clergy, the congregation rose to sing Mrs Pankhurst's favourite hymn, 'Sun of My Soul, Thou Saviour Dear'. The staunchly agnostic Sylvia, however contrite, must have squirmed slightly at the unction of such lines as:

> When the soft dews of kindly sleep
> My weary eyelids gently steep,
> Be my last thought, how sweet to rest
> Forever on my Saviour's breast.

('a strange contrast', commented the *Daily News,* 'to public memories of this indomitable fighter. It was a revelation of gentleness drawn out of bitter waters'). The address by the Reverend Geikie Cobb, an old suffragette supporter, recalled the tragic yet exhilarating spectacle of 'the irresistible force impinging on the immovable object' as Mrs Pankhurst hurled herself against the Liberal Government. Mrs Pankhurst's soul was now with God, but it would go marching on, and she would expect new generations of women to build on the foundations she had laid, to strive for economic equality and (a congenial flash for the pale and suffering Sylvia) to change the obsolete and barbaric conditions of marriage.

As the ten pall bearers (all ex-suffragette 'jailbirds'), among them

Barbara Wylie and Mrs Marshall, lifted the coffin, draped in purple, and carried it down the aisle to the strains of the exquisite *Nunc Dimittis* and Chopin's Funeral March, emotion broke loose. An elderly man ran out into the aisle, kneeled and raised a fold of the pall to his lips. Women fell on their knees. One old woman in the gallery buried her head in her arms and sobbed heartrendingly. Outside the church, women lowered flags over the coffin and crowded round the hearse, delaying the start of its long journey to the grave. The policemen on duty on the steps of the church saluted. Some of them wept.

Thirty cars followed the hearse. The coffin was laid by the open grave in the great sooty necropolis of Brompton Cemetery, while Mrs Drummond hurried to a side street to marshal a procession of women and get them marching along the Brompton Road in a last tribute. More than a thousand women, with W.S.P.U. standards fluttering above them, and the purple, white and green ribbons (and the prison medal which Sylvia had designed) pinned to their coats or hats, linked arms and swung along, the Old Contemptibles of the suffrage war. They were middle-aged and elderly; wearing, some of them, the actual clothes, the flared, ground-sweeping skirts, in which they had done their desperate deeds; tired, many of them, from long journeys, for they had rallied from all over Britain by an instinct of love, loyalty and discipline which the years had not atrophied. Mrs Minnie Baldock, an East Ender and one of the first women to join the W.S.P.U. in London, led the procession. Behind her came cars piled with flowers. Some of the working-class women (from the dingy streets of the area) who lined the pavements had waited for five hours to catch a glimpse of the coffin and the march past. They held up their babies to see the sight, and, in hundreds, joined the suffragettes as they turned through the archway which led into the cemetery.

The surge of curiosity was such that the police had difficulty in preventing the chief mourners and the officiating clergyman, the Reverend Hugh Chapman, from being shoved into the grave. Christabel, her eyes red with weeping, had to be supported. Sylvia, wearing a large black hat, stood a little apart, glancing now and then towards baby Richard, who was being looked after by some friends. The short address pleased those who were set on 'spiritualizing' Mrs Pankhurst. Her violence and rebellion were, said Mr Chapman, 'palliated' for those who 'looked beyond the letter to the spirit'. Mrs Pankhurst had been a truly holy woman, and 'we men are dominated more by winsome holiness and self-eclipse than by individualism and forcefulness.' He agreed with Christabel that Mrs

Pankhurst, though essentially modest and retiring, had steeled herself to endure misrepresentation. The mere thought of uncleanness had fled before her. Men and women, hearing her speak, had been inspired with a yearning to find the Holy Grail of a companionship 'without the smallest danger of soilure'. She had, with all her divine indignation, a patience, a tenderness and a piety which were 'the marks of a saint in its broadest meaning'. He regarded Mrs Pankhurst as 'the incarnation of the spirit which has brought about the Girl Guides and other bodies in which religion and athletics are blended'.

There was much truth, no doubt, in all this. But some of his listeners felt that the Reverend Chapman had left out truths which were just as important. They resented this spiriting away of their leader. They were angered by what seemed to them a presumptuous male bowdlerizing. It was a wonder, as Ethel Smyth said (and later wrote) that Mrs Pankhurst did not rise up from her coffin in protest. The conversation and letters of the woman she had known (and had given up two years of her professional life to follow) had crackled with gleeful and unsaintly pugnacity. 'The *Daily Mail*', she had written in 1913, 'credits us with half a million damage during the year, exclusive of golf links, letter boxes etc. Not so bad for pin pricks!' Or again: 'Whatever happens will hurt the Government. If I get away they will be laughed at. If I am taken, people will be roused. The fools hurt themselves every time ... ' Nor had she been the intolerable, priggish bore Mr Chapman had made her sound. She had enjoyed, for instance, reading George Moore's *Tale*. The part about bosoms, she had said, particularly amused her. *What* a beast he was, but *so* amusing ...

After the address, the mourners, holding purple cords, lowered the coffin into the grave. Filing past, women piled flowers high as a W.S.P.U. standard was slowly dipped. The sound of their grief could be heard in the street above the traffic's murmur. Most certainly they were grieving for the death of a fighter, not for the passing of a stained-glass, palliated man-charmer. True, Mrs Pankhurst died about as poor as a church mouse, leaving estate valued at eighty-six pounds to Christabel. But the Conservative Central Office evidently did not agree with Mr Chapman's version of her character. When Mrs Hall-Humpherson, at Christabel's suggestion, applied for a job there and mentioned her organizational experience with the W.S.P.U. she was sharply told that that kind of experience was not considered an asset; that Mrs Pankhurst's methods were not necessarily those of the party; and that there had been much concern at headquarters about the way in which party directives had been ignored during Mrs Pankhurst's campaign in Whitechapel.

Mrs Hall-Humpherson, like Mrs Pankhurst, emigrated to Canada. Women's organizations in Britain continued to interpret the Pankhurst spirit by a detailed struggle for equality – in public swimming baths for example. 'At certain baths', commented *The Vote,* 'the absurd rule is in force that a woman may not enter unless accompanied by a man, but a man is at liberty to do so without a woman! Women are tired of such galling inequalities. They are determined to have equal facilities at all swimming baths ... ' The initiative of a Miss Dart, a member of the Women's Freedom League, who was fined and publicly reprimanded for breaking the ban on women swimmers in the Serpentine, Hyde Park, was applauded. Female premières, some of them highly exotic (like the achievement of Miss Norah Johnston, the first woman pupil to enter the School of the Master Carillonneur of Malines) were still eagerly chronicled; and a campaign (of which Mrs Pankhurst would surely have approved) was carried on, under the banner headline WHY RAILWAY CARRIAGES SHOULD BE RESERVED FOR WOMEN, with many a lurid report of lewd approaches and indecent exposure by men.

Meanwhile the process of public ennoblement and embalming of Mrs Pankhurst continued. A portrait of her was purchased from the artist, Mrs Georgina Brackenbury, an ex-suffragette, and presented to the National Portrait Gallery. A Mrs Pankhurst Memorial Fund was launched to pay for a statue. This, hoped Mrs Drummond, the chairman of the committee, would be erected either in Whitehall, at the end of Downing Street, or in Victoria Tower Gardens, hard by the Houses of Parliament ('after all,' said Mrs Drummond, 'it is only eight feet square we are asking for one of England's greatest women'). The sculptor, Mr A. G. Walker, who had recently completed a bronze of Florence Nightingale, worked from hundreds of photographs of his subject. The result closely resembled Mrs Brackenbury's portrait, showing Mrs Pankhurst in a rather languid, quizzical, elder stateswomanly pose, bare-headed and with the coiffure and features of her later, Tory-Imperialist phase.

In Toronto, on the first anniversary of her death, a memorial service was held, and floral wreaths laid at the foot of a replica of Mr Walker's statue. On December 8th, 1929 (despite the spreading gloom of the great Wall Street crash), the chief feature of the annual convention of the National Women's Party in Washington, D.C., was a memorial service for Mrs Pankhurst, held in the crypt of the Capitol. Christabel, back on the American lecture circuit, took time off from lecturing on 'The Christian Interpretation of Present World Problems', to speak briefly in reply to the many tributes. The fight for women's suffrage on both sides of the Atlantic, she declared, was 'one of the most beautiful things we have in common'. As well as representatives of forty women's organizations, congressmen and senators and members of the diplomatic corps and their wives attended the ceremony. 'With the processional', reported the *New York Times,* 'there came into the gray walls of the crypt a line of brilliant colour which suggested the vivid, eager personality of Mrs Pankhurst.' Behind the American flag marched a double line of girls in white dresses carrying garlands of purple, white and green, followed by a guard of honour bearing the purple, white and gold standards of the Women's Party.

The finale and pinnacle of commemoration was reached when, on March 6th, 1930, Stanley Baldwin unveiled the statue of Mrs Pankhurst in Victoria Tower Gardens. The audience included representatives of American and Canadian women's organizations. A few of the five hundred suffragettes present had travelled great distances: Grace Roe, for instance, from California, and Mrs Cruikshank from India. The B.B.C. broadcast the ceremony for three quarters of an hour. All traffic along the Embankment was diverted between eleven a.m. and one p.m., and building operations on near-by Lambeth Bridge were suspended during the same period—so that the public could listen to the music and the speeches relayed through loudspeakers. Proceedings opened, gallantly enough, with a selection of works by female composers played by the Metropolitan Police Central Band, and ended with Dame (as she now was) Ethel Smyth, in her Doctor of Music robes, conducting the same band in a spirited rendering of her own 'March of the Women'. The surpliced choir was drawn from St Paul's Cathedral, Westminster Abbey, the Chapel Royal and the Temple Church. Mrs Drummond, a few days earlier, had given a swingeing press interview ('In the beginning there were only four or five of us. You could have put the whole suffragette movement in a taxi cab! Eventually, over eighteen hundred of us went to prison. We set fire to churches and houses to force the insurance companies to put pressure on the Government to give us the vote. There was a good deal of method in our madness'). In Victoria Tower Gardens she confined herself to a few pious remarks about Mrs Pankhurst's love of and devotion to humanity. Mr Pethick-Lawrence and Lady Rhondda made short speeches. But the *pièce de résistance* was Baldwin's elegy. He was no longer Prime Minister. The general election of 1929 had resulted in a second Labour administration. Under MacDonald, dependent on the support of the Liberal rump, and harassed by the onslaught of a world economic depression, this could be counted on to be thoroughly constitutional. In any case, the Opposition needed to have an innings now and again, that was only cricket. And being in office would have the salutary effect of teaching the so-called socialists, already pretty well tamed, that they could never hope to be (in Baldwin's own phrase) more than 'the left wing of the Tory Party'.

Mrs Pankhurst was an excellent subject for Baldwin's euphoric magnanimity. With unfailing drama and a shuddering sincerity she had acted out the age-old dilemma which he was so fond of contemplating: the dilemma of the idealist forced to acknowledge the virtues of authoritarianism, of the emotional socialist recoiling from the ugly brink of regimentation. There was something, said he, peculiarly consonant with the English character and tradition in such a ceremony, commemorating a woman much of whose life had been spent in bitter political controversy. He admitted that he had for many years been opposed to her work, but feared no contradiction in claiming that Mrs Pankhurst had won for herself a niche in the Temple of Fame which would last for all time. There would no doubt have been a Reformation without Luther, a Renaissance without Erasmus, a French Revolution without Rousseau, and there had been a woman's movement without Mrs Pankhurst. But if she did not make the movement, it was she who had set the heather on fire. The cheers that greeted this true if hackneyed statement had scarcely died away before a grave corollary dropped weightily into the silence: 'And as is the way of all conflagrations, good and evil were consumed in it. That is part of the eternal human tragedy. The wheat and the tares grow together unto the harvest.' Mrs Pankhurst, a woman of exquisite sensibility, had been enraged by the brutalities of 'a certain type of callous man'. It now rested with women to tread worthily in the way which she had opened.

In the *Daily Herald,* the day before the unveiling, H. N. Brailsford who, with Henry Nevinson, had resigned from the *Daily News* in protest against Asquith's treatment of the suffragettes (and whose wife had been to prison for the cause), had framed a tribute so moving and so trenchant that Baldwin might have done well to substitute it for his own tired composition.

There are literal minds [wrote Brailsford] which suppose that Mrs Pankhurst faced obloquy and prison to win votes for women. She did a greater thing than that. She suffered to remove from the mind of every young girl the sense that she is born to a predestined inferiority. The strength of this woman was in her torrential emotions ... For me it was Mrs Pankhurst's voice that revealed her. She spoke very quietly and simply, but her voice could give to the plainest statement an almost intolerable power to move. Others did the thinking and piled up the armoury of argument. She alone had the genius to act as if nothing else in this wide world mattered ... Physically she seemed almost youthful; it was when she spoke that all the bitterness that came from powerlessness, all the thwarted movements of pity and sympathy which women had felt for centuries in vain, were audible at last. One never thought of her as an advocate in her own cause. She was Maternity pleading for the race.

Sylvia Pankhurst, the only daughter who watched the ceremony of the statue (Christabel was still in America, Adela in Australia), had herself written a piece for the *Evening Standard*. While acknowledging Mr Pankhurst's dynamic power of evangelism, and her knack of doing the outrageous thing without appearing outrageous, Sylvia still lamented her switch from revolt to reaction. 'Her interest in dress and shopping,' she puritanically sniffed, 'her desultory reading, mainly confined to novels, were surprising in one whose life was so largely given to public causes.' But, she conceded, her mother had had the courage of her convictions. She would be remembered as *the* Suffragette, not as a Tory Imperialist. 'We do not make beams from the hollow, decaying trunk of the fallen oak. We use the upsoaring tree in the full vigour of its sap.'

Sylvia wrote from a plenitude of recent research and cogitation. She was already nearing completion of two thick volumes in which she tried to make her own kind of sense of the women's movement and Mrs Pankhurst's part in it. She may have laid a wreath at the foot of the statue, but she was nursing a literary bombshell which was soon to explode with devastating effect in suffrage circles.

Adela alone was now fighting Emmeline's kind of battles with Emmeline's fanatical vigour; exalting the Empire and smiting the communists so furiously that it seemed as though Mrs Pankhurst's soul must have migrated to her body.

PART FIVE

SISTERS THREE

CHAPTER ONE

ADELA'S GUILD OF EMPIRE

Neither Adela Pankhurst Walsh (for she continued, talismanically, to treasure and feature her maiden name) nor her husband had been able, any more than Sylvia, to stomach for long the ideological charades of the Communist Party or its constant trimming to the winds of the Comintern. Nor did they relish its bourgeois intellectual airs of superiority. At close quarters, Australia's would-be dictators of the proletariat seemed a rum, bickering, unattractive lot, with about as much warmth or mass appeal as the segregationist feminism from which Adela had fled in 1917. After a brief absence, Adela rejoined the Socialist Party of Victoria, of which in 1923 she was appointed honorary organizer, with the right to sit as a member of the executive committee. Though mildly Marxist, the V.S.P. at least had a sturdy home-grown vision of social justice.

She was active in the Women's Socialist League, which aimed to overcome the traditional conservatism of workers' wives—a trait which such middle-class organizations as the National Association of Women or the Progressive Housewives' Association were intent on preserving. Women, thought Adela, must be made to understand how much fuller and more dignified life would be when workers were 'part of a huge co-operative enterprise for human benefit and not cogs in a profit-making machine'. They should realize that as long as vast sums of money were spent on arming for future trade wars, and as long as it was assumed that the aim of schooling was to enable a child to 'rise' out of the working class and become a white-collar snob, education would be stunted. The Socialist League tried to interest women in public health and child welfare, showing that (as Adela pointed out in the *Socialist* in 1924) the health weeks and fly-swatting campaigns recommended by the capitalist press were 'so much nonsense so long as slums and semi-starvation continue to exist'.

But even in un-Muscovite socialism and in the way trade unionism was developing in Australia, there was disillusion for the Walshes. The surge of wartime idealism and optimism about workers' control, about One

Big Union shaping a truly democratic society out of the ruins of the old, bogus parliamentary system, had spent itself. Labour parties, whether state or federal, had settled down to an uninspired reformism. The hour of destiny—if there had ever really been one—had passed. In Russia, the torture of human beings in the name of progress had spelled out the horrors of enforced communism for all except the wilfully blind to see. Of course employers could be almost insanely obstinate, but so could a decadent, visionless, strike-happy trade unionism. Both sides were locked in a grapple of sheer, degrading nihilism, both were prisoners of out-of-date doctrines of class war. Both, while vowing eternal hostility, bowed their backs (Samsons obedient to a voice from the grave) to bring down the pillars of society upon the heads of the innocent. The Walshes believed (as Christabel had proclaimed in 1917) that it was time to burn the misleading books of discredited nineteenth century prophets and start thinking for themselves.

Industrial sabotage, which ten years before in the hectic heyday of the I.W.W., had seemed a gay defiance of the capitalist juggernaut, now looked very different. All, then, had seemed fair—even fun—in the ding-dong class war: even the recruiting of ex-criminals (some of whom had used their skill in forging banknotes with merrily disruptive effect), who, after all, had defied the laws and morality of capitalist society. The cynical slogans (opponents quipped that I.W.W. stood for I Won't Work)—'Fast Workers Die Young', 'The Right to be Lazy (like the boss)', 'A Little Sugar in the Concrete Makes More Jobs for the Un-employed'—had once had a boisterous, snook-cocking, neo-Ned Kelly ring. But in an atmosphere of industrial stalemate, when the unions, with the Walshes in the vanguard, had wrung most of the concessions which could reasonably be expected, and there was no conceivable prospect of a revolutionary upheaval on the grand scale, it was time, surely, to put away such gaudy proletarian toys; and high time that adult workers, with wives and children to provide for, stopped playing with them at the instigation of Moscow-line communists. It was time, in fact, for the die-hard but powerful minorities of labour *and* capital to grow up, come to terms with realities, and accept that they were part of the community and responsible to it. There was even, as was often the case with extremes, a certain affinity between them. Had not unscrupulous profiteering capitalists been willing, in the past, to bring in cheap Asiatic labour? And were not communist trade unionists, fresh from conferences of the Pan Pacific Secretariat in Moscow, busy denouncing the White Australia policy, which alone had preserved the country's civilization and living standards, as base racialism? Yet traditionally, and rightly, the Australian Labour Party was both nationalist and 'white'.

Tom Walsh, president of the Seamen's Union, and Jacob Johnson, its secretary, had been given a tumultuous welcome on their release from prison after the collapse of the Federal Government's attempt to deport them as undesirable immigrants for their leadership of the strike of 1925. Walsh was still assumed to be the 'Reddest' trade union chief in the British Commonwealth. Yet only a few months later he and Johnson were at loggerheads. Walsh wanted to drop the tactics of sporadic strikes which always threatened to accelerate into a major stoppage when sufficient grievances had been accumulated and the shipowners took disciplinary action. Johnson, though not in the Communist Party, belonged to the rigidly Marxist British Socialist Party. For him it was axiomatic that the class war must be kept alive: if it was allowed to die, socialism would give up its very ghost. All through 1926 and 1927 the feud between the two men intensified. By the beginning of 1928 the powerful Sydney branch of the Seamen's Union was demanding Walsh's resignation. In the elections which followed Walsh was returned un-opposed as general secretary, only to find that Johnson's supporters had forced through a motion disqualifying him from holding office. In May Walsh issued press statements alleging communist infiltration of the union, and followed this up with a manifesto, circulated to all branches of the union, explaining his new convictions. The labour-management war was a phoney war which could no longer, he said, bring advantage to anyone but professional wreckers.

The wretchedness of Mrs Pankhurst's last weeks were brightened by the news of Adela's conversion. In June 1928 she revealed her plans to start an Australian branch of the Industrial Peace Union of Great Britain. Havelock Wilson, the British seamen's leader with whom the Walshes had clashed in 1925, sent a telegram of congratulations and an offer of funds. Adela would now, she announced, take the message of reconcilia-tion to the wives of workers. Industrial peace simply meant that workers of all grades – and after all employers and executives were workers too – would co-operate in the task of increasing the wealth and prosperity of the nation. Communist sabotage must be exposed and halted, and, equally, employers must cease to regard industry primarily as a means of making profits. This theme was taken up by Tom Walsh in a speech on which he and his wife, drawing on their wide experience of the Labour movements and on wide historical reading (any spare money was always spent on books), worked with great care.

Delivered to the New South Wales Constitutional Association, it was a closely argued plea for an end to the Marxist dog fight. There had been a time, when he was a young man (he had gone to sea as a cabin boy), when it had been necessary to fight tooth and nail to wrench the merest decencies of life from employers. He had been for a whole nine months on board without a bite of fresh vegetable, nothing but salt beef and pork. He had been disgusted by the prostitution and drunkenness in ports which seemed to be considered the only fit relaxation for brute seamen. The thought of his own daughters being exposed to such in-sulting viciousness had made him, he confessed, 'a red revolutionary of the reddest order'. His devotion to the Labour movement, of which he was proud, had been motivated by a desire to raise himself and his fellow workers out of this bestial rut of ignorance. Now, after fifty years of struggle, the time had come for co-operation, not for the reign of a new shut-minded ignorance. The Russian experiment had proved the im-possibility of workers' control. The Bolsheviks had been forced to call in the hated capitalists to save their industries from ruin, at the same time excusing all the miseries and bloodshed of their regime as mere incidents of a 'transition period'. Both workers and employers must agree to think in national terms, to expand industrial output to provide full employ-ment not only for the existing population but for the millions of Euro-peans who must ultimately arrive to strengthen the power of a White Australia. Communists, of course, would prefer to fill the land with Chinese and Indian coolies who had so little to lose that they would make no resistance to communism. Every sabotaging trade unionist and 'every employer who treats with anything but sympathy his employees' aspiration for a higher and fuller life' were accomplices of the enemies of the country. He hoped for a conference of workers and employers which would formulate a plan for co-operation in industry, put the wreckers out of action, and tackle the problems of unemployment, already serious (especially in the coal and steel industries). Surely this could be better done in 'an atmosphere of concord and in an era of prosperity rather than of ruin and despair'.

Walsh made a similar speech to the Melbourne Constitutional Associa-tion: it was the beginning of a decade of addresses to mildly applauding groups of civic and commercial notabilities. Then he went to Adelaide to explain his views to members of the Seamen's Union. The fact that he was leading in the contest with Johnson for the general secretaryship seemed to show that his attitude was acceptable to a majority of unionists. Adela provided a brisk covering fire for her husband. In Macquarie Place, Sydney, she mounted a fruit-box to appeal for the support of women to form an organization, and to launch a monthly propaganda magazine, in support of industrial peace. Her brisk, urgent oratory, backed by alarming statistics showing the threat to the national economy of irresponsible strikes and reactionary management, soon attracted support and funds from wealthy professional and business men. At her home in Miller Street she, who nerved herself to read, as opposed to merely reviling, communist publications, held a press conference to expose the iniquities of the Pan Pacific Secretariat, to which some Australian trade unionists, including the Johnson faction in the Seamen's Union, were proposing to affiliate. Baulked in Europe, communists were, she said, busy trying to mislead 'the untrained minds of Orientals' and to foment revolution in China, India and Japan. They aimed to destroy the British Empire, and to establish Soviet republics 'after a maelstrom of blood and bestiality'. They would, of course, call the resultant slave states 'newly liberated countries'. The object of the Comintern was to end the very existence of unions, some of which foolishly imagined that it would strengthen their hand.

This forceful and, as the Walshes' children remember, deeply devoted husband-and-wife team bore a curious resemblance (as, ironically enough, did the partnership between Sylvia and Silvio) to Emmeline and Richard Pankhurst's burning unity of personal love and public concern. Even the age discrepancy, particularly in Adela's case, followed the parental pattern. And, like her mother, Adela stoutly denied that her change of political direction had made her an enemy of the true interests of the workers. So (she said to a crowd of heckling miners during a strike in Cessnock, a coal town near Sydney), so she had joined the class enemy, had she? It would be more accurate to say that any worker who followed the lead of communist saboteurs was an enemy of his class. The men should concentrate on clearing such parasites out of the labour movement, and turn their scorn against those wandering agitators who never did an honest day's work but, like vultures, followed the carrion smell of human failure and human bewilderment.

Even when Tom Walsh, after a long dispute about his fitness, as a 'boss's toady', to take office, was confirmed in his election as general secretary by a court decision—no doubt influenced by the fact that his

rival Johnson had been sentenced to six months' imprisonment for intimidation of pro-Walsh seamen—he was unable to carry out his duties.
Hundreds of angry Johnson supporters picketed the King Street headquarters of the union. When, under police escort, Walsh forced an entry,
the chief clerk refused to work with him. Headquarters accounts and
records, which, he alleged, would reveal serious misuse of funds, had
been transferred to the offices of the Johnson-controlled Sydney branch
of the union on the opposite side of the street. Still under police escort,
Walsh crossed the street and returned with the missing ledgers. He was
jostled and jeered at by hostile demonstrators. After four days of this
Walsh, hearing that in a clash between strikers and strike breakers on the
Melbourne waterfront, shots had been fired, applied for a licence to carry
a gun.

There were yells from some demonstrators that he and Adela had been
heavily bribed to betray the workers, and had for three years been busy
undermining union solidarity from within. When Adela addressed the
Sydney Renascent Society, police were on duty to keep out interrupters,
five of whom, all Johnson men, were allowed in after the speech to make
short statements. The Walshes, they said, were doing well out of the
Industrial Peace movement. They would 'get' Tom Walsh in their own
time. Feeling ran higher when Walsh announced his intention to apply
for the registration of a new seamen's union. He himself would not stand
for office, but a substantial number of seamen, frightened by the way in
which a small clique of left-wing officials had gained dictatorial control
of union policy, had applied for membership. The ensuing faction fight
lasted until the end of 1929. Members of the 'official' union refused to
sail with Walsh's 'blacklegs'. Walsh accused Johnson, who was released
from prison in May, of being financed from Moscow. Johnson accused
Walsh of being financed by class enemy industrialists, and of 'having
taught the seamen all they know about communism'. Far from promoting
industrial peace, Walsh's attempt to form a breakaway union caused
open, brawling warfare which threatened to cripple Australian shipping
almost as devastatingly as any of the strikes led by him and Adela in their
militantly socialist days.

Alarmed by the growing chaos, the Arbitration Court refused to
register the new union because it did not represent a majority of seamen,
and Walsh had to abandon the project. From now on the Walshes were
probably the most effective, and often the most bizarre, preachers of the
need for national unity—a theme seldom absent, in a deepening economic

depression, from pulpits, newspaper editorials, and politicians' speeches. Panicked by the slide in wool and wheat prices, the withdrawal of English capital (a phenomenon which disgusted the Walshes), and unemployment (which rose to more than thirty per cent of the normal labour force), the Labour Government of 1929–32, like the MacDonald Administration in Britain, fell back on orthodox deflation – featuring cuts in wages and in welfare and relief rates. In 1932 Joseph Lyons, a former Labour politician, headed a National Government of the United Australia Party, pledged to respectability, decency and honesty, with the slogan 'All for Australia and the Empire'.

Adela had not lost her distrust of politicians or her dislike of empty, soothing phrases. She knew how derisive they sounded to families half starving on the dole, living in shack or canvas settlements and scratching out a living on allotments. She knew how powerful was the lurking violence of frustration, how doubly attractive the class war, with its illusion of purposeful action, must appear. She even had her own highly individual ideas of the causes and solution of an era of drift. The decay of family life was an important factor. The emancipation of women, she argued in two long articles published in the *Sydney Morning Herald* in May 1931, should not mean an abdication of family responsibilities. Bad homes and ignorant parents were, in her view, the only excuse for day nursery schools and kindergartens. Women 'should be ashamed that they have failed so far in their duty as to permit either of these evils to exist'. Schools could only supplement the work of the parents in handing on a right set of values, courage and personal responsibility: they could never supersede it. The very initiative of men, who in the past, in the ceaseless effort to provide for their wives and children, had 'spilled their blood over the whole surface of the earth, and strewn their bones thick beneath every sea in the interests of future generations', had been sapped by women's growing insistence on the right to self-fulfilment outside the home.

This maladjustment of human relationships had led, insisted Adela in a zanily partisan Pankhurst analysis, to a radical corruption of moral and economic values. Girls were now seen, and alas saw themselves, as 'beach beauties, popular typists, society queens, champion swimmers, tennis players, footballers and aviators' – almost anything but home makers. They filled the time which they gained by having no, or few, children with trivial pleasure, personal adornment, even so-called social work which would be better applied to their own, larger families. Women, in their vain folly, were largely responsible for the monstrous growth of the leisure, or entertainment industries. In a fountain of economic utopianism, Adela reasoned that the money spent on sport in Australia would, if properly used, 'wipe out every slum and rehouse the people'. The money spent on drink in New South Wales 'would clothe every child in beautiful and healthy garments', the tobacco bill (she herself was a very heavy smoker, her only self-indulgence apart from buying books) 'would refurnish every ill-supplied home'. If people would limit their cinemagoing to one performance in two weeks, she calculated that (apart from the moral gain of watching less maudlin, sex-mad nonsense) the saving would 'open up thousands of acres to immigrants from older countries, who would set the wheels of industry turning to supply their wants'. Finally, if wives would return to their proper sphere and stop being mere playmates, they could be trained to give their children elementary education up to the age of eight; and the saving in school costs would pay for a really adequate state medical service.

Adela — who had brought up three stepchildren and was now caring for her own four children, as well as being a prolific journalist, an avid reader and a bustling political organizer — forgot that few people have the intellectual equipment or the physical stamina to undertake such a task. Miraculously, she never neglected her own family: though after his departure from the Seamen's Union Tom Walsh, now sixty-six, did much of the housekeeping and cooking. Adela herself cared little about food, existing largely on slices of bread and butter and cups of tea. Her absence of mind was almost legendary. Her children remember how she would get into comic tangles when trying to take her apron off over a wide-brimmed hat while talking vehemently about some topic of the day. 'She was', they say, 'gentle and tough. We were strangely unaware of her political engrossments, and one of our earliest impressions is of Mother, ready for an outing in a suit and hat, giving a last-minute poke to a copper of washing. We loved and respected her and had a strange desire to protect her.' Tom Walsh could be even more abstracted than his wife. Once, when greeted by his daughter Christian on the pavement, he raised his hat in formal acknowledgment and walked straight past her. He was liable to carry sudden decisions to awkwardly logical conclusions. For some weeks, after an argument with the gas man, he refused to use gas and cooked meals in an old kerosene can over a fire in the back garden.

Only a considerable power of abstraction and a blinkered sense of mission can have enabled Adela for nearly ten years to co-exist with the bourgeois women who formed the financial and organizational backbone of the Australian Women's Guild of Empire, which she launched in 1929. She found a few kindred spirits, but on the whole it must have been an uneasy partnership. By November 1931 the guild had become sufficiently well-known to fill Sydney Town Hall with supporters who passed a resolution calling on State and Federal Governments to convene a conference 'representative of all sections in the community, in order to end industrial and class strife and to restore industry on a basis of co-operation and goodwill'. Two months earlier a number of women's organizations – the women's section of the Sane Democracy League, the Feminist League, the National Association of Women, the Women's Christian Temperance Union, the Women's Country Clubs and the Progressive Housewives' Association – had held an anti-communist meeting in the town hall, and had resolved that 'this meeting of women citizens considers communism as the first enemy of the Commonwealth, and expresses the solemn conviction that unless the state destroys communism, communism will destroy the state.' They suggested the banning of the Australian Communist Party, the deportation of communists, an industrial and political boycott of Russia. Quoting from a communist training manual, a Mrs Glencross excitedly alleged that marriage itself would be smashed if 'these fiends' had their way. Women must take the offensive to defend Country, Religion and Morality. Speeches tended to be hysterically indignant. 'If we wished', shrilled one delegate, 'to send anyone to everlasting perdition, we would not send them to Hell, but to Soviet Russia.'

It was Adela Pankhurst Walsh's remarkable achievement to give some intellectual vitality and cohesion (*and* a glimmering awareness of the humanity and grievances of the working classes) not only to her own Guild of Empire, but to the jittery ranks of middle-class feminism generally. The guild, which now had offices in Reiby Place, Sydney, and issued a monthly paper, the *Empire Gazette* (edited by Adela, who was also its chief speaker and campaign director) declared its objects to be (1) to combat communism and all forms of class government, (2) to establish industrial co-operation and peace, (3) to uphold the Christian ideals of life and safeguard the family, (4) to awaken the people to a sense of responsibility for the well-being of the community, (5) to deepen the realization of the value of British citizenship, and (6) to assist in the development of Australia as part of the British Empire.

In her town hall speech, Adela brushed aside suggestions that the

industrial and social crisis had been created by the Communist Party
(which never created anything, merely exploited what already existed),
or could be cured by the suppression of communist literature or the
deportation of communists. After a brilliant and concise description of the
course of the industrial revolution, with its inevitable phase of class war,
she stressed the danger of ignoring the great revolution which, without
any doctrinal fanfare, had happened, and which demanded some fresh
thinking. Industry now depended largely on working-class consumers,
who, she estimated, possessed sixty-five per cent of the community's
purchasing power. The new generation of workers was supplying the
whole complex range of technical specialists needed by industry. Yet
because of party politicians who perpetuated the worn-out concept of
class war, thousands of willing workers were rotting in idleness. 'It is a
mockery to tell the workers not to follow any leaders who will promise
them security, and to denounce those who jeer at religion and family life,
while there are in the world millions of young men who have no prospects of finding a useful work to do on God's earth, or providing a
better shelter than a tent as a home for those they love, of being the
father of any but pauper children.'

It was vital, she said, to put before the workers, who were the majority,
the choice between establishing a system of co-operation between the
investing public, the employers, and themselves, or 'handing over everything to the control of the Government and placing the resources of the
country, their own livelihood and the future of their children in the hands
of politicians'. That—whatever party the politicians belonged to—was
communism. What reason was there to put such confidence in politicians?
'Their most outstanding characteristic, I should say, would be their
inability to manage anything properly. What industry have they ever
promoted but the gambling industry? What have they ever produced
but strife and deficits? What resolve have they shown but a determination
to grab for themselves, their friends and supporters whatever is available
to grab?' Adela's political drift was as impatient of parliamentary democracy as it had been in 1918, but her vision of an industrial parliament now
included employers as well as employees, since both (she now acknowledged) were workers. Once the apparatus of parliamentary democracy
had been dismantled, organized labour and employers' associations could,
free from government intervention, regulate industry and taxation.
Community morality would replace class consciousness, social service
would be the motivating force of all activity. Governments, national and

non-party, would be powerless to make mischief or, indeed, to do anything but what they were told to do by the real powers in the land. 'Capital and labour in alliance', Adela predicted, 'will require neither government control nor political interference, and the vast network of government activity which is impoverishing us today will become useless and will shrivel up and die away'. Trade union leaders would cease to be 'students of Marx, who lived and wrote a hundred years ago' and would become instead 'students of modern industry capable of entering into the management of any business concern on equal terms with the employers'. There would be no need for union funds to be spent on political battles, no payments for strike relief. The money could be used to enrich and protect members by investment and insurance.

Lady Rhondda, who had first admired Adela's ability when they were suffragettes together, consented to become overseas patroness of the guild. Lady Gordon was Australian patroness, and Mrs Jean Maughan, wife of Sir David Maughan, an eminent lawyer, was president. Branches were opened in the industrial suburbs of Sydney, and in near-by industrial centres such as Wollongong. At 'industrial tea parties', wives of unemployed men were supplied with material at cheap rates: this they made into clothes, curtains and cushion covers which the guild arranged to sell. There were weekly meetings, special entertainments, excursions, youth clubs and children's circles, relief funds, Christmas gift funds, and indeed a miniature welfare organization. Wherever there was a strike (and there were plenty) within a hundred-mile radius of Sydney, Adela, accompanied by an aide, would appear in the ramshackle guild car, plonk down a fruit box, and exhort the workers, while leaflets and copies of the *Empire Gazette* were distributed. Employers asked her to speak at lunch hour meetings in shops, in factories, and at the docks, and got into the habit of sending for her whenever there was a whiff of a strike in the air. By 1936 she was addressing thirty different audiences a month, and speaking every Sunday in the Domain. Once, during a wharf labourers' strike, she was drenched by a bucket of water; but, remarking that a sailor's wife was not afraid of getting wet, imperturbably finished her speech. When the guild car finally broke down, it was replaced by a new one (a gift from grateful industrialists), and she set off on a thousand-mile tour of industrial and agricultural areas.

With the help of her husband, she made the *Empire Gazette* not merely a chronicle of guild activities, but a wide-ranging and controversial commentary on world affairs. British capital and British enterprise had (the *Empire Gazette* often stressed) given Australia her free institutions, and British military and naval power was the only sure guarantee of Australia's independence. Adela disliked talk of breaking up the Empire and scrapping national alliances in favour of an international super state. This idea was typical of communists and of superior progressive persons such as H. G. Wells or the Webbs, who longed to transform the world into a huge socio-political laboratory, controlled by a master caste, which would have complete freedom – the only freedom that would be left – to perform their cruel experiments. Ever since Plato, she warned, this idea had been the darling of 'egotistical types who feel contempt for those beliefs and loyalties which move ordinary men and women'. A constant theme was the need to develop Australia's great natural resources, the hunger for which, apart from considerations of national prestige, was the driving force behind Italy's occupation of Abyssinia and Germany's expansionism. Australia must not – for lack of vision, immigrants and sheer hard work – be allowed to find herself in the position of Abyssinia. Wealth of resources and poverty of development offered a standing temptation to powerful, ambitious nations.

On the radio, as well as at public meetings and in the *Empire Gazette*, Adela ceaselessly attacked the attempts of what she regarded as communist-inspired peace movements (for instance, the Australian Movement Against War and Fascism, and the International Peace Campaign) to exploit a natural if naive idealism. Moscow's conception of pacifism was not a total abandonment of violence as a solution of human problems, but a refusal to fight communism and a determination, either by industrial sabotage or open civil disobedience, to weaken the will to resist it. It was sad to find not only young people but experienced organizations such as the Women's Christian Temperance Union, the National Council of Jewish Women, and even ex-servicemen's groups, being bamboozled by such propaganda. Adela made it clear that she still, as she had in 1914, loathed the stupidity and waste of war, but that she now believed that war might, in some circumstances, be the lesser of two evils. As a result of her sturdy defence of Australians' right to fight, or at least to make up their minds if or whom they were to fight without Comintern nudging, she was ejected from several 'peace' gatherings, and the Guild of Empire's representative, Mrs Vera Parkinson, was asked to leave the press table at the grandly styled Everywoman's Conference for Peace, held in Sydney in April 1938.

But despite the *Empire Gazette*'s staunch support for the Empire,

Above: c. 1936, Sylvia Pankhurst dictates an anti-Fascist *New Times and Ethiopia News* article to her secretary in the study at 'West Dene', Woodford Green
Below: Sylvia Pankhurst with the exiled Emperor Haile Selassie

Adela Pankhurst Walsh and Tom Walsh on board ship on their departure for Japan, December 1939

Adela Pankhurst Walsh, in Japanese-style gown, presides benignly at a youth club dance in Redfern, Sydney, in early 1941

Britain and the British monarchy (King George V was praised for his role in unifying the national and Commonwealth 'family': and in 1937 Adela was awarded a George VI Coronation Medal), the Walshes began to have serious misgivings about Britain's ability or even willingness any longer to guarantee the security of Australia in time of war. The ignoble flight of British capital from Australia in the early 'thirties, and the fact that Britain expected Australia to repay all her debts while at the same time spending less on Australian imports, was not encouraging. The Japanese navy had played an important part in defending Australia's coastline in 1914–18; yet, largely under American pressure, the Anglo-Japanese alliance had been terminated in 1921. There had even been talk, at the Canberra Conference of 1938, of jettisoning the White Australia policy and of encouraging Indian and Javanese immigration in order to cut industrial costs and compete in the markets of Asia. The Women's Guild of Empire had started out in 1929 to help build Australia as part of the British Empire: yet within a few years the definite, clear-cut concept of the Empire had been replaced by the vague formula of the Commonwealth, the main function of which, seemingly, was to enable Britain to shed her traditional responsibilities with indecent rapidity.

This may have been inevitable, but to Adela it appeared as part of a depressing trend in which Britain was losing authority, faltering ignominiously while Fascism and Nazism took the initiative in Europe and in the fight against communism. While deploring the persecution of the Jews, she was inclined to discount much of the vilification of Hitler and Mussolini as an attempt by communists and fellow-travellers to discredit their two most formidable enemies. She could not help contrasting the achievements of Germany and Italy in the attack on unemployment, the creation of a dynamic national idealism, and the capturing of the energies and imagination of young people, with the deplorable ineffectiveness of so-called National Governments in Britain and Australia, which had succeeded in stifling not only party bickering but any generous and vital spark whatsoever. Was there not, she asked, a great deal of cant in the Western democracies' claims to enjoy a monopoly of liberty? This liberty was supposed to consist of a free press, free speech and freedom to organize politically. Yet in practice these freedoms were the monopoly of those who could afford to manipulate them – the Western democracies (as Shaw was fond of saying) were in fact the Western plutocracies.

Adela's shallowly submerged socialism was more and more liable to surface, to the embarrassment of many of her Guild of Empire colleagues.

8

'Many of us', she grumbled in the last issue of the *Empire Gazette* on October 1st, 1939, 'might be inclined to think that less freedom for the wealthy might give more freedom to the ordinary people. The Guild of Empire in New South Wales may have the same right to a free press as, say, the Astor interests in the United Kingdom or the Pierpont Morgan interests in the U.S.A. — but which is the more likely to be attended to?' Such Mosley-like sentiments, combined with her ambivalent attitude to Hitler and Mussolini, and her feeling that it was a mistake to go to war with the Nazis when Germany had already got almost all it wanted and was about to turn and rend Soviet Russia, shocked the conventional patriotism of most of the guild's members. The news that Adela and Tom Walsh had accepted an invitation to visit Japan as guests of the Japanese government confirmed such yellow peril patriots in their impression that they had been nourishing a weird viper, a bad security risk, in their midst. The offices of the guild were closed, the *Empire Gazette* ceased publication, and Adela, half comically remarking 'Oh dear, I see I've done the wrong thing again!', resigned. Like Mrs Pankhurst, she could not help exasperating the domesticated creatures into whose preserves she had masterfully, disturbingly strayed.

CHAPTER TWO

MOTHER IN ISRAEL

Untroubled by committees, under the august protection of the Bible, exonerated, as it were, by her cloth, Christabel continued to indulge her taste for the realism of revelation and what she called 'heavenly politics'. She could sound almost as weary as Virginia Woolf herself when interviewed eagerly about the results of women's emancipation. The signs of Armageddon multiplied almost daily – wars and rumours of wars, the return of the Jews to Zion, the blasphemous self-deification of the European and Russian dictators, the ungodly arrogance of Science, the decay of faith and moral standards, the worship of Mammon and Pleasure. But Christabel wisely refrained from putting a date to the Second Coming. *That* it would happen was a dogmatic certainty: *when* it would happen was a dogmatic uncertainty. It might occur in her lifetime. It might be delayed for centuries, by which time, perhaps, as a punishment for their infidelity, the Western Powers might have been overrun by oriental hordes.

The tendency to welcome, almost to gloat over, actual or potential disasters, is inherent in all apocalyptic religions. It gave to Christabel's speculations a certain resemblance to the hilarious Second Adventist sermon in Aldous Huxley's *Crome Yellow*. 'Earnest Christians', the bitter Rector of Crome had thundered to his empty pews, 'regarded the war as a true sign of the Lord's approaching return ... Famine tightened its grip on every country in Europe ... disease of every kind, from syphilis to spotted fever, was rife among the warring nations.' And the best of it was that the episode of 1914–18 was a mere skirmish. War was still smouldering in Siberia, in Anatolia, in Ireland. The Chinese boycott of Japan and the rivalry of that country and America in the Pacific might be breeding a great new war in the East. The prospect was reassuring ...

Yet there is little doubt that in Britain, Canada and the U.S.A. – her gigantic parish as a travelling evangelist – Christabel performed much the same service for Second Adventism as her sister Adela did for semi-Fascist bourgeois anti-Bolshevism in Australia: raising it almost single-handed from its back-street fundamentalist rut, lending it a dull gleam of intellectual prestige. She had not, and did not wish to have, the same swingeing entertainment value as Aimée Semple Macpherson or even Annie Besant, the former feminist and atheist who had become the head of the theosophical movement, had founded a Hindu college near Benares, insisted on the spiritual superiority of Eastern religions, and in the late 1920s took her adopted son, a young Madrasi named Krishnamurti, on a world tour, claiming that he was the latest manifestation of the Godhead. But Christabel managed to deploy, in the dim and musty setting of evangelicalism, something of the impudence which had shone out in the genteel listlessness of the moribund feminism of 1905. No politician worthy of the name, she insisted, could afford to neglect the study of biblical prophecy unless he was content to remain a blind leader of the blind. All who had won their spurs in public life should use their prestige to proclaim the Divine Message. It was disappointing that bishops and archbishops and leaders of the various denominations should be neglecting the great and heartening doctrine of the Second Coming.

Her debut as a preacher in Britain took place at the very climax of the long struggle, which had begun with the challenge of the Anglo-Catholic Tractarians almost a century earlier, to keep the Established Church Protestant—at least in its formularies and official appearances. The 'prayer book crisis' of 1927 and 1928, which, like the abdication 'crisis' of 1937, was one of the great pseudo-events with which Britons chose to divert themselves between the wars, had brought churchgoers—and the House of Commons—to a boil of indignation. Twice the Commons, in which the Hot Protestant hosts were led by the Home Secretary, Sir William Joynson-Hicks, rejected insidious attempts to de-Calvinize the Book of Common Prayer. The second victory, which was front-page news, occurred on the day of Mrs Pankhurst's death (and eclipsed it almost as completely as Amelia Earhart's transatlantic flight eclipsed her funeral).

Christabel, though no intolerant anti-Romanist, may have felt that her own intensive Back-to-the-Bible campaign had played a modest part in Sir William's triumph. Certainly she admired his holy war on D. H. Lawrence and relaxed moral standards in the arts in general. During a series of addresses in the Aeolian Hall, New Bond Street, she congratulated Sir William on his vigorous campaign against indecent books. 'I have not the least patience', she snapped, sounding—and in her sombre Edwardian-esque clothes, looking—the quintessential grand governess of a naughty human family, 'with those flappers who sit down with a piece of blank white paper before them and proceed to put down all the filthy things which they can think of. *This* is not the sort of freedom we women fought for' (did it never occur to her that perhaps *some* of those gallant young suffragette saboteurs *had*, secretly, been fighting for this kind of freedom, among others?). 'It is not the kind of liberty Mother and I ever started out to get. We do not consider that art justifies the writing of books which even men are horrified to read. The books which these young women' (she did not, alas, name names) write are scandalous. Men writers started the tendency, but they had not the audacity to go as far as these young flappers.'

In September 1929 Christabel, whose success as a speaker depended at least as much on such reactionary quotability, and upon her suffragette curiosity value, as upon her religious *idée fixe*, left England for a six-month lecture tour of Canada and the U.S.A., which began in Montreal and included her appearance at the memorial service for Mrs Pankhurst in Washington, D.C. The returned Christ, she confidently told reporters, would regulate the affairs of the world from Palestine. In the late summer of 1930, after a brief stay in England, she was back on the more lucrative and receptive North American circuit. Her books sold better in America, too, bringing in quite a tidy income; and there was another reason why she liked the country. So many people there spoke to her about Mrs Pankhurst that (as she put it) she almost felt that Mother was alive in America. She addressed church and club audiences in New England, New York, Chicago, Ohio, Kansas, Arizona and California. Children, she said, should be taught 'the simple and beautiful doctrine of the Second Coming of Christ while they are young and can accept it without cynicism'. In Los Angeles, a woman reporter, while admiring her clear complexion and vivid blue eyes, complained of the anti-modernity of her clothes, and especially of the large black lace hat which she habitually wore. 'I wish you'd burn that hat,' said the reporter, 'it libels you.' 'All right, I'll burn it,' said Christabel, with the mildness of utter indifference – and continued without a pause to expound her theme. 'We are suffering today from a greed for knowledge of evil. Moral disease and sin is rampant. Groups here and there are striving to keep us from slipping back into barbarism. But nothing can save us but divine intervention ... '

A little later, she was telling an audience of Philadelphia businessmen at a luncheon club of the dangers of materialism so crass that on the eve of the Wall Street crash of 1929 the *New York Times* had carried an advertisement luring the public to invest in the National Waterworks Corporation

in the immortal words: 'Picture the scene today, if by some cataclysm
only one small well should remain for the great city of New York – one
dollar a bucket, a hundred dollars, a thousand, a million. The man who
owned that well would own the wealth of the city.' Economic depression,
catastrophic unemployment, and a drought then causing concern, were all,
she said, fulfilments of prophecy, and urged her audience to get out their
Bibles and search for guidance in the chapters which she thoughtfully
indicated.

The earthquake which, not very drastically, shook parts of England
shortly before she recrossed the Atlantic in May 1931, provided her with
an obvious Adventist opening. 'This English earthquake', she solemnly
told the pressmen who still included her on their list of disembarking
celebrities, 'is full of significance, because it comes in a land which had
scarcely known one on such a scale before. I look upon it as a fulfilment
of prophecy. We are coming to the end of an age.' However that might
be, Christabel was certainly about to strike a rich personal patch. In July
1931, the Welsh Baptist chapel in Eastcastle Street, near Oxford Circus,
London, was crammed to hear her and the great, though toppled, idol,
Lloyd George. Both had flourished in the climate of wartime heroics and
pseudo-spiritual rhetoric. Both had wilted when the climate changed. But
Christabel had revived herself by enlisting in the heavenly host. Lloyd
George, having failed to restore his (or the Liberal Party's) fortunes, now
spent much of his time (though still hearty in his wooing of nonconformist religious backing: hence his presence at Eastcastle Street) fighting
over old battles in the interminable, self-justificatory prose of his *Memoirs*.

Christabel, who in her articles for the *Weekly Dispatch* in 1921 had
singled out Lloyd George as the subtlest foe of women's suffrage, and had
deplored his fatal tendency to play to the gallery, his obsession with
personal power and popularity, believed, like all the Pankhursts, that the
decline of the Liberal Party was due largely to its illiberal vindictiveness
towards women. But in the Baptist chapel the voice of criticism was
silent. 'We two veterans in the pulpit today', she said in camaraderie,
'have each won a war. Mr Lloyd George won the world war, and I had a
hand in winning the suffrage war. It is not enough. I was brought up on
the *Manchester Guardian* and peace and reform movements. I read books
and speeches that told me the world was safe, full of loving kindness,
getting better every day, becoming too sensible and civilized (just as
optimists say it is today) to have another war. You post-war young people,
don't suppose that we pre-war young people did not love peace and pursue

it.' Science was widening the scope of man's greed and lust for dominion. There was already talk of taking possession of other planets. Perhaps soon a man, or, it might be, a woman would reach the moon ... (Here Lloyd George interposed, laughing, that 'the presence of the traditional Man in the Moon would no doubt be a special inducement to enterprise on the part of women') ... But the hope of Christ's return and the heart-searching fear of its imminence were the best, in fact the only guarantee of lasting sanity.

Lloyd George, who listened with the same apparently intent courtesy with which he had received so many suffrage deputations, endorsed Christabel's sentiments. As national armaments piled up and tension grew, it was time, he felt, that 'there should be some new thought, some arresting appeal to Someone above and beyond transient mankind'. He agreed with Miss Pankhurst that the Covenant of the League of Nations, Geneva and Locarno pacts, agreements to outlaw war, all were useless without a complete change of heart among the peoples of all nations. It was through such a message as Miss Pankhurst's, bringing the people back to the fear of the wrath of God, as well as the certainty of His love, that endeavours for peace might find a new vitality.

Even if she realized (as in her shrewdness she probably did) that Lloyd George was seeking to borrow some of her pious plumage, just as once he had sought to furbish his reputation as a progressive Liberal by encouraging the hopes of suffragists, Christabel enjoyed the sense of excitement which flowed from renewed contact, however fleeting, with the fading, but still dimly sparkling man of destiny. There was more such excitement to come. In September she renewed acquaintance with another seemingly crippled political titan, paying the first of several visits to Winston Churchill at Chartwell. He had been a special target for suffragette fury. But during the war, as minister of munitions, he had revised his opinion of the elder Pankhursts. Since the war, his rumbustious anti-Bolshevism, his pugnacious distrust of Germany and of facile assumptions that the 'mistake' of 1914 could never be repeated, had forced him into the same wilderness (a pastel-toned National Government having no place for his hot imperialist colours) from which Mrs Pankhurst and Christabel had cried to a people unwilling to be reminded of the need for eternal vigilance. Chartwell was a rallying point for all those with a pride in Empire and a hatred of appeasement. As early as 1926 Christabel, in her book *The World's Unrest, or Visions of the Dawn*, had detected in Britain and France a growing tendency to acknowledge the justice as well as the expediency of making concessions to Germany and Italy. Behind this weary realism, she held, lay the certainty that the peoples of the world were being shaped into the great power blocs which, armed with the means of scientific extermination, would clash in the struggle to decide who should emerge as the true and ultimate Anti-Christ, the challenger of God Himself, the provoker of Armageddon. This was just the kind of immense, twilight-of-the-gods perspective in which Churchill loved to expand and gambol. These two almost heraldic creatures, as they paced the lawns of Chartwell, entered the emblazoned lists of Right and Wrong, and sniffed the sulphurous yet bracing air of conflicts yet to come.

Christabel's next absence in America lasted for more than two years. When she was not lecturing, she was often the guest for long periods of wealthy American women, many of whom had been prominent in the suffrage campaign. Her pleasant wit, uncompromising Britishness, odd but immaculate clothes and unique status as a living and surprisingly youthful monument of an age and a struggle which already seemed so remote, made her a notable catch for hostesses of the older generation: and one had to admit that her talk about international politics was as well-informed and a good deal more lively than the columns of Walter Lippmann and other professional commentators. It was as good as a book, too (in fact, she probably *was* quoting from one of her books) to hear her analyse the relation of science and religion. The *reading* the girl must have done, and the neat way she marshalled her arguments! The findings of contemporary archaeology, she proved, were confirming the authenticity of the Bible as History, while the discoveries of Einstein and other physicists were demolishing the smugness of the mechanistic science of the nineteenth century and opening huge vistas of mystery where the God of Creation could rule more impressively than ever.

In 1934, when she came back to London, Christabel commanded enough subscribers and financial backing to publish a small monthly journal called *Present and Future* (edited by 'a member of the Church of England', as she modestly called herself), as a vehicle for her more intellectual Adventist essays, especially on the theme of Christianity and Science. In *The World's Unrest* she had already begun to exploit the implications of the new scientific diffidence, which refused to make the unscientific, because unproven, assumption that the unknown was governed by the same laws as the known. Did not this admission shed some light on the possible 'mechanics' of the Second Advent? God could break His Own Laws to reappear in an unprecedented way. Christ, the

Original, Uncreated Light, would far outstrip the speed of created light, travelling at 'His Own absolute velocity', and His all-penetrating rays would make Him visible, as He had promised, to everyone everywhere simultaneously. If the televisual use of electromagnetic rays made it possible to transmit events to other places while they were happening, Christ could surely make the Supreme Event universally available? Similarly, when the Anti-Christ sought, possibly by radio-active explosions, to make the upper atmosphere impassable to the Returning One, He, the Fount of All Knowledge, would annihilate such barriers with ineffable ease. Professor Arthur Eddington's exposition of the theory of relativity and the fourth dimension made it easier, argued Christabel, to think of Heaven as a *place*. Might it not be located in a dimension as yet unexplored by science?

In *Present and Future* she quoted Eddington and J. W. Dunne on new concepts of time. The theory that events did not *happen* but were just *there* waiting to be happened upon, seemed to validate the forecasts of such dream-seers as the prophet Daniel and others endowed with a gift of supra-temporality. Could it be that time was our relation to God's predestiny? Sir James Jeans, in his presidential address to the British Association for the Advancement of Science, spoke of 'the motion of something which does not move in space and time' as a scientific fact. Did this not confirm the existence of a God in His Own Element, and the possibility of His Son's return literally at any moment, as in the miracle reported in St John's Gospel, when (the doors being shut) Jesus came and stood in the midst of His disciples? Such speculations seemed to plunge Christabel into a millennial delight almost as vertiginous as Sylvia's when, in 1919, she rapturously hailed the portents of a Soviet Britain. Yet Christabel schooled herself to caution. 'The whole international picture is there which Christ Himself prophetically pencilled. The open question is whether it is a shadowy sketch of the final picture; whether the outlines are yet as strong, the colours as deep, as they may be on the very eve of the Coming Again of the Divine Artist who will efface this dire world picture and paint in its stead the perfect picture of a world filled with heavenly righteousness and peace, a world made at last the Kingdom of God ... '

In 1937 and 1938 Christabel was one of the main speakers in a nationwide campaign organized by the Bible Testimony Fellowship to commemorate the four hundredth anniversary of the royal approval of the English translation of the Bible, and (in 1938) the quatercentenary of the Reformation. She had noticed that modernists and Anglo-Catholics, who jibbed at what they called bibliolatry, were inclined to tinker with communism and produce 'Red' deans and vicars and men like Dr Barnes, the Bishop of Birmingham, who claimed that the Church 'had never made the unguarded statement that Jesus is God'. Evangelical Protestants, from the time of Wesley onwards, had been mercifully proof against such temptations, and against the sort of wishy-washy compromise represented by the so-called Restatement of Faith published, after lengthy deliberations, by a committee of Anglican divines. Faithful to the prevailing spirit of appeasement, this assigned to angels and devils (and to the Devil himself) a 'symbolic value', thought the 'geographical' concept of Hell anachronistic, was dubious about miracles, the Immaculate Conception (a doctrine perhaps dear to Christabel) and the Day of Judgment. It was a duty and a pleasure to combat such underminers of faith. For surely what people, and especially young people, needed was not a committee's evasive if scholarly memorandum, but the definite Word of God; not the Historical Jesus, but the Divine Jesus, God and Saviour and Lord? Christabel firmly informed a gathering of the Anglo-Catholic Church Congress that, while it was their duty to pray that the world's politicians might be guided to wise decisions, they should refrain from meddling in politics – except to the extent of asking God to hasten the moment of His all-unravelling return.

She continued to urge Christians to use the Bible as the one sure guide to world affairs. Her own studies enabled her to predict a victory for Franco in the Spanish Civil War, since Spain was destined to be part of the Roman (and Holy Roman) Empires then being revived by Hitler and Mussolini. She could probably have earned a good living as a political columnist. But she had no inclination, and no financial need, to do so. She was not rich, but had a fairly elegant sufficiency; she had many wealthy friends on both sides of the Atlantic who treated her like a princess incognito; known and unknown admirers from time to time declared themselves in the most practical way – by leaving her money in their wills. Between 1929 and 1940 she figured as principal beneficiary in at least three wills, a wind (or death) fall amounting to several thousand pounds. To the end of her life, there were women (often spinsters) who, stirred to their depths by Christabel's defiance of male tyranny, by her public lashing of men's sexual irresponsibility, continued to regard her as *the* feminist saint, to remember her as the graceful, pin-up symbol of their secret desires, and to offer her their belated maiden tributes.

In *The Strange Death of Liberal England,* published in 1936, George Dangerfield gingerly hazarded a guess at the reasons for such extraordinary devotion. Mrs Pankhurst ('a fragile little woman, not more distinguished in appearance than other pretty little women who have worn well') had embodied the idea of straightforward revolt in a just cause. So, in a different way, had Sylvia. But Christabel had released a less obvious, but very powerful force among middle- and upper-class women doomed, resentfully to spinsterdom (with its minor, honorary public works) or to marriage with the 'male stranger' of Florence Nightingale's passionate complaint. Christabel gave the maiden life a new prestige and dignity by her message that women should strive to preserve their moral and spiritual superiority (as well as their health) by avoiding the tainted embraces of men. The vote might give women the power to cleanse public life, but even without it they could, if they would, force men to observe the standards of chastity which they imposed on women. Christabel sanctified and focused the 'lesbianism' which, in women of leisure and education, was a legacy of Victorian prudery. 'It is the custom', wrote Dangerfield, 'among certain primitive tribes for marriageable girls to spend some time in the Woman House, to learn the wisdom of women, and it was from some secret yearning to recover this wisdom that the homosexual movement first manifested itself in 1912' (when Christabel set up her shrine in Paris) 'among the suffragettes. But,' he added, 'there was nothing decadent about it.' It might be arrogant, childish in a way, and melodramatic, but not perverse: for 'perversity, if it means anything at all, means the conscious preference of something low before something high, of death before life. And this pre-war lesbianism, which in any case was more sensitive than sensual, was without any question a striving towards life.'

Dangerfield's book had been preceded, and (in its sections on the Pankhursts) much influenced by Sylvia Pankhurst's two bulky volumes, both superb corrals of derring-do and agonized filial impiety, *The Suffragette Movement: An Intimate Account of Persons and Ideals* (1931) and *The Home Front* (1932). The former, enlarging on the lethal sketch printed in the *Dreadnought* in 1921, presented Christabel as the corrupter not only of Mrs Pankhurst but of the suffragette movement as a whole, which, according to Sylvia, she had bent, with diabolical cunning and determination, to her wicked, snobbish, anti-socialist will. *The Home Front*, while giving a detailed account of Sylvia's prowess in the East End during the war, hotly ridiculed the hyper-patriotic behaviour of Mrs

Pankhurst and Christabel and the rump of the W.S.P.U., and lamented their betrayal of the ideals of Keir Hardie and Dr Pankhurst. The appearance of these books had caused much anger and dismay amongst the relatives and admirers of the elder Pankhursts, and Christabel found herself under considerable pressure to take some sort of action: preferably, since it was unthinkable to drag the Pankhurst feud into court, to write an *official* version of events – the more so since, within a few weeks of her mother's death, she had advertised in *The Times* for material to be used in a biography of Mrs Pankhurst. What, people were beginning to ask, had happened to this project? Christabel was, in fact, at work on a carefully documented but (by comparison with Sylvia's nuggety landslides of intimacy) aloofly impersonal account of militant suffragism. But her progress on this was so slow that in 1935 Sylvia again beat her to the punch with a short, affectionate biography of Mrs Pankhurst which repeated, in only slightly modified form, her strictures on Christabel.

Christabel may have realized that she could not begin to compete with Sylvia in sheer literary vitality, Dickensian eye for detail (one reviewer complained that nearly a third of *The Suffragette Movement* was devoted to an account of the Pankhurst family in the period before the W.S.P.U. was even founded), or her ability to convey the sheer, raw excitement of being a suffragette. As for attempting to get Sylvia to retract or revise her indiscretions, Christabel had painful memories of her one effort, made not long after Mrs Pankhurst's death, to deflect her sister from the chosen course – a visit to Woodford in which she had urged Sylvia, for the sake of the family and of the child, to forget her principles and allow Richard to bear his father's name. Her reception had not been such as to encourage any further personal intervention.

A highly sympathetic, almost defiantly protective, study of Mrs Pankhurst by Rebecca West which appeared in 1933, though by no means uncritical of Christabel, did something to repair Sylvia's damage. But when later in the same year Dame Ethel Smyth's long essay on Mrs Pankhurst, based largely on letters which Mrs Pankhurst had asked her to return (and which she had omitted to ask Christabel, Mrs Pankhurst's literary executrix, for permission to use), was published, Christabel felt obliged to seek redress. In her determination to present Mrs Pankhurst as a magnificent but fallible human being, and to demolish the 'plaster saint' image set up by Christabel and the Reverend Hugh Chapman, Dame Ethel had indulged not only her undoubted gift for bludgeoning wit but her equally undoubted aversion to Christabel – at whose insistence

Female Pipings in Eden (the book which contained the essay) was withdrawn from circulation. Early in 1934, soon after her return from the United States, Christabel met Dame Ethel in the office of the publisher, Peter Davies. It was a stormy encounter. Coming from a military family and used all her life to battling tigerishly for fair play as a woman composer, Dame Ethel, in her mannish tweeds, set upon the black-gowned Second Adventist not only with the gruff voice with which she awed orchestras in rehearsal, but (and here the publisher was forced to intervene) with upraised umbrella. Quite shattered by the scene, Christabel agreed to allow the book to be re-issued after certain passages which she regarded as libellous had been removed. In a foreword to the revised edition Dame Ethel noted: 'Unwilling that Mrs Pankhurst's letters should be lost to the world, Miss Pankhurst, while not, of course, committed to all I have written in this monograph, has most generously made me a gift of the copyright in these particular letters, and now permits their publication.'

Blessed oblivion soon closed over this unpleasant episode, and in the New Year Honours of 1936 Christabel was created a Dame Commander of the British Empire (D.B.E.). 'Mother', she told reporters, 'would have been so pleased. This honour is a recognition of the cause of women, and a reminder that they have the power and privilege of taking part in the national unity of which the King spoke at Christmas. Women', she continued, quick as ever to make a propaganda point, 'recognize the limitations of human wisdom, and the more thoughtful of them are looking to more spiritual assistance, relating religion to politics and so helping to find new approaches to our problems.' Dame Ethel may have snorted, Sylvia may have paused in mid-torrent to smile sardonically, but at least Christabel's Dameship had, though belatedly, made honours even with the non-militants (Mrs Fawcett having been Damed ten years earlier). And Sylvia would have recognized, even in its bizarre setting, the true monomaniac Pankhurst spirit in some of Christabel's pieces in *Present and Future*. The firm way, for instance, in which she dealt with the question of whether human beings ought to feel 'insignificant' before the vastness of the universe revealed by astronomy. 'This', wrote Christabel briskly, 'is fallacy, a confusion of quality and quantity! Not only are the crises of human history of vastly greater significance than the crash and clash of those gaseous globes we call stars, but one single sin of the least of men matters more in God's sight than the annihilation of some immense but merely inanimate galaxy.' That was a sentiment with which any

Pankhurst could agree. One needed such high-stepping certainty to win votes for women, converts to Second Adventism, working-class recruits to an industrial peace campaign, fair play for Ethiopia (Sylvia's new obsession), or indeed victory for any single cause in a world raucous with highly competitive injustices.

CHAPTER THREE

THE ORACLE OF
WOODFORD GREEN

The period from 1928 to 1931 had been one of intense and richly diversified literary activity for Sylvia. In an article in a 'The World I Want' series in the *Daily Express*, she reaffirmed her allegiance to the socialism of William Morris and Edward Carpenter. The spectacle of modern industrial techniques (in the comparatively rare cases where penny-wise, shareholder-cosseting British capitalists had introduced them) being used merely to step up the trade war was, she thought, depressing. But this was not the only failure. Why should art and industry be kept apart? Why could not the nation's factories, where millions of men and women spent the best part of their lives, be centres of culture, entertainment and fun as well as of inhumanly repetitive toil? 'I would,' she wrote, 'have art and industry organized more as they were in the craft guilds of the middle ages.' Such a revolution, however, must be a revolution of the soul, forced through by people who had learned the lesson which she had learned in her youth—'that the most satisfying thing in the world is service motivated by love'.

Motherhood, for Sylvia, was a call to arms as well as a deep personal satisfaction. The doctor who had attended her in the nursing home had told her that if she had not had the best of medical care in the nick of time, she would have lost her baby. 'The words came to me as a challenge—"Seek to obtain for others the care you had!"' she wrote in her marathonly titled book, *Save The Mothers (A Plea for Measures to Prevent the Annual Loss of about 3,000 Child-Bearing Mothers and 20,000 Infant Lives in England and Wales and a Similar Grievous Wastage in Other Countries)*. Full of minutely researched statistics about the rapidly improving maternity services in Scandinavia, Holland, France, Germany, Soviet Russia, Poland, the U.S.A., Canada, and even the Irish Free State, and backed by impressive testimonies from medical authorities (for the proprietress of the Red Cottage Café was still a power in the land), its peculiar strength lay in its Mayhew-like vignettes of pregnancy and childbirth among the poor.

The working-class mother (she observed) comes to her travail worn with toil, in a home, perhaps only one overcrowded room, lacking even basic comforts. The cheap flock mattress has gathered into lumps, the slack springs of the old bed creak and groan ... Her eyes are dull, her limp hair falls neglected. She is dressed in shabby, ungainly clothes ... tortured by a varicose ulcer ... But there is work to do. She rests her knee upon the seat of a chair, dragging herself on this cumbrous crutch about the room, dressing the children, washing up the crockery ...

Yet, as Sylvia well knew from her long sojourn in the slums of the East End, the provision of maternity wards was hopelessly inadequate – there was accommodation for only 50,000 of the 750,000 mothers who gave birth annually – home births took place in appallingly crowded and unhygienic conditions, and midwives were meagrely trained. Indeed the study of obstetrics had been shamefully neglected. 'This contempt of the mother's needs and her all-important function', she stormed, 'is as grievous an injury to women as anything she suffered under in the period of political and social subjection.' Hundreds of avoidable deaths were due to lack of proper ante-natal care, errors of judgment by doctors or midwives, or lack of facilities for treatment. Abortion was terrifyingly common among married women with three or more children who dreaded another bestial ordeal, and National Insurance benefits (ten shillings a week for four weeks and a maximum grant of two pounds towards the cost of confinement) were quite inadequate to cover a working mother's loss of earnings.

Home help services, she urged, should be greatly extended; midwives should be recruited in greater numbers and properly trained; a national midwifery service, locally administered, should be provided free of charge; hospital maternity accommodation should be increased; instructions on ante-natal care should be regularly featured on the radio; and (an important point still consistently ignored) 'the person who made the pre-natal examination should attend the patient in labour.' Knowledge of contraception should be widespread, and legalized abortion less frowned upon, but the true need was for moral, economic and obstetric conditions which would assure a happy and successful motherhood.

Sylvia's bitterest scorn was reserved for the treatment of unmarried mothers, whose children were twice as likely to die in infancy as those of the well-to-do. Unmarried mothers had a double load of anxiety to bear.

Yet many hospitals discriminated against them, only admitting them if they were willing to put on a show of penitence, or if it was their first pregnancy. Then there was the question of women who like herself had ethical objections to marriage. She quoted the case of a friend, who 'as a philosophical anarchist disapproves of legal marriage, and was refused admission to a hospital because she was still cohabiting with the father and therefore did not deserve official care'. Sylvia considered that the money used to pay for her mother's statue could more fittingly have been used to open a maternity endowment fund or a child welfare centre; and in a newspaper article stressed that her own decision to be an unmarried mother was in part a protest against a system which encouraged unmarried fathers to dodge their responsibilities. 'I always loathed Mrs Grundy', she declared, 'and I knew that I would meet at close quarters her lascivious curiosity. But I did not mind fighting. I knew that those wretchedly unhappy girls I had met in prison and in the East End were not sinners. So I joined their ranks, ready to battle by their side. In practice, my life at home is just the same as other people's. We have the same economic obstacles, the same community of interests, the same affections, the same anxieties, the same joys.'

From time to time, as Britain's most distinguished unmarried mother (and one of her most prolifically articulate progressives), Sylvia was asked to write on how to bring up children: and was, of course, whole-heartedly in favour of the contemporary trend towards unrepressive parenthood. 'I agree', she said, 'with such thinkers as Bertrand Russell that every child's character can be marred by repression in the early years. Richard is never told "You must not do that!" He works when he wants to and plays when he wants to. He is a free baby: he should be a free man.' She was disappointed that women were not doing more to protect their own interests and to usher in a new era of radical reform. 'The emancipation of today', she lamented in 1934, 'displays itself mainly in cigarettes and shorts. There is even a reaction from the ideal of an intellectual and emancipated womanhood, for which the pioneers toiled and suffered, to be seen in painted lips and nails, and the return of trailing skirts and other absurdities of dress which betoken the slave-woman's sex appeal rather than the free-woman's intelligent companionship.' Women M.P.s had shown no great initiative. The torrential pre-war women's movement had dwindled to a tired trickle. Yet, with the mothers' death rate mounting, the promised maternity service mouldering in parliamentary pigeon-holes, re-housing shirked, and the anti-feminist threat of Fascism spreading over Europe, there was a dire need for a rebirth of the suffragette spirit.

Somehow, while battering away at officialdom with undiminished gusto, Sylvia managed to air the more purely literary side of her nature. In 1930, the same year in which *Save The Mothers* was published, appeared her rendering (in collaboration with I. O. Stefanovici) of the poems of Mihail Eminescu, the Rumanian romantic of the mid-nineteenth century. Already, in her own poems in the *Dreadnought*, she had shown a facility for archaically stately verse, as for instance in her comment on Horatio Bottomley's downfall in 1922:

> ... A futile swindler of a futile world.
> Now he's in prison they of vilest sort,
> Who battened on his bounty, caught the crumbs
> Flung from his bold extravagance,
> Hasten like carrion to the Street of Ink
> To earn some pounds by selling confidence,
> And writing large his follies that they shared
> When Fortune's winds plumped out his pirate sails ...

Eminescu's high-flown democratic sentiment and Tennysonian magniloquence suited her genius perfectly. In her translation of the long poem *Emperor and Proletarian* she was able to give vent to that tearing impatience with social injustice and parasite tradition that had gushed over her judges in the Guildhall ten years earlier. Again, in the stronghold of her study, lined and piled with books like her sister Adela's (about whose apostasy she kept silence), she lashed the idle rich as resoundingly as the suffragettes had once lashed cabinet ministers and prison doctors:

> ... By their own laws encompassed, they take their fill of treasure,
> And drain earth's sweetest juices till sweets, from surfeit, cloy,
> Calling in gay carousals and revel-sated leisure,
> For your fair daughters virgin as tools to serve their pleasure;
> Their foul, lascivious ancients our lovely youth destroy ...

> Demolish all, unsparing, that pruriency engender,
> Raze palaces and temples that crimes from light defend;
> Statues of lord and tyrant to mother lava render,
> Wash out the senile footprints of those who basely pander,
> Fawning behind the mighty unto the wide world's end.

Why, oh why, she asked with Eminescu, was generous idealism always thwarted or distorted?

> ... The yearning for perfection, the universal essence,
> Immutable it lurketh within the hearts of all;
> 'Tis sown at large by hazard; the tree in full florescence
> Seeketh to find fulfilment in every blossom's naissance;
> Yet ere its buds are fruited the greater part will fall.
> Thus frozen in its ripening, the human fruit grows rigid,
> One to a slave, the other to emperor congealed.

Unconcerned for the moment with political means, unhampered by the infuriating lethargy of capitalism's victims, she was free to summon rip-roaring thunderbolts of vengeance on a world of decadence:

> ... Yea, shiver into atoms all pomp and ostentation,
> And from its granite clothing our human life disrobe.

But Sylvia came through strongest in stanzas of lyric sensuality unencumbered by political undertones:

> O'er the hill the moon ariseth, as a hearth of embers golden,
> Staining red the ancient forests, and the lovely castle olden ...
> Lo! Behind that spangled cobweb sleeps the Emperor's daughter, blanched
> By the drowning flood of moonlight that her maiden bed hath drenched ...
> Here and there her robe, unfastened, falleth open and exposes
> Nude her body in its fairness, virgin purity discloses ...
> Throb the life-blood's measured pulses 'neath the eyelids veiling torpor;
> One fair arm extending idly from the couch in heedless languor;
> Warmth of glowing youth the strawberries of her snowy bosom ripen,
> See the ardent fire of breathing stirs her budding mouth to open ...

Bernard Shaw, to whom despite their periodic tilts, Sylvia sent the poems before publication, felt able for once to relax his Pankhurst-baiting and wrote an enthusiastic letter which was used in facsimile as a preface to the volume. 'Sylvia,' he bubbled, 'you are the queerest idiot-genius of this age ... the most ungovernable, self-intoxicated, blindly and daftly wilful little rapscallion-condottiera that ever imposed itself on the infra-red end of the revolutionary spectrum as a leader ... That you had this specific literary talent for rhyming and riding over words at a gallop had hitherto' (apparently Shaw was not a reader of the *Dreadnought*) 'been a secret. The translation is astonishing and outrageous: it carried me away.'

In *The Suffragette Movement*, apart from rattling family skeletons like castanets in a swirling *danse macabre* (and thereby earning the gratitude of future historians), Sylvia dwelt on her student days with rich nostalgia for her abandoned profession, and especially on the few wonderful months she had spent in Venice in 1902 on a travelling art scholarship. Eager as always to make the most of her time, she had risen every morning at five and worked through the day, copying the mosaics in St Mark's and the Carpaccios in the church of San Giorgio degli Schiavoni, setting up her easel in the streets to paint the gay crowds in the Rialto or the vendors by their stalls. She had even, she remembered, in her greed to possess the beauty around her, tried to paint on her balcony by moonlight. The crazy tempo of her work in Venice, she wrote, had been partly due to her anguish at parting from her mother, to the need to dull the feeling that she should be back in Manchester, helping in Emerson's, the fancy goods shop whose wares offended her artistic sensibilities, and whose aesthetic tone she tried to raise by designing furniture and cotton prints. The strength of her loyalty to Mrs Pankhurst and to the suffragette movement was proved by her tigerish vigilance, far exceeding Christabel's in its tenacity, over publications and even stray statements concerning the militant campaign. In 1927 she had forced the temporary withdrawal of *The Cause* (an excellent book about the women's movement by Ray Strachey, a follower of Mrs Fawcett), for the deletion of a paragraph about Mrs Pankhurst's handling of W.S.P.U. finances which might have been construed as libellous.

In February 1932 she was in action again, this time obliging Hutchinson (the firm which later that year published *The Home Front*) to withdraw for amendment a book called *From Information Received*. In this the author, a former Scotland Yard detective, described how early in 1914, while guarding the Prince of Wales (then an undergraduate at Magdalen College, Oxford), he received notice of a suffragette plot to kidnap the prince and hold him as a hostage until the Government gave votes to women. The idea, he asserted, had originated with, and was to be carried through by, 'the East End group led by Miss Sylvia Pankhurst'. Sylvia, challenging this statement, admitted that in 1914 the air had been thick with rumours of suffragette plots, but denied that she had ever hatched such a scheme, and objected to 'the suggestion that I am the sort of person who would kidnap a young lad at college'. She got three hundred pounds damages as well as putting author and publisher to the expense of amending the book. A month later she was publicly defying Megan Lloyd George (the ex-Prime Minister's daughter) to substantiate a statement that the suffragettes had threatened to kidnap *her*. In 1934 Sylvia associated herself with Christabel in her protest against Dame Ethel Smyth's portrait of Mrs Pankhurst. Her biography of Mrs Pankhurst, published in 1935, though still harsh about Christabel, was even harsher about Dame Ethel, whose intimacy with her mother she had always deplored, and whose temerity in writing about the Pankhursts and the W.S.P.U. after a mere two years of dilettante adventuring seemed to Sylvia, as to Christabel, impertinent.

Sylvia did not find it easy, what with her commercial cares and the chores of motherhood, to keep up her tremendous literary output. She poured out her troubles in letters to Mrs Norah Walshe, a suffragette who had worked in a London hospital and had helped in Sylvia's mother-and-child clinics in the East End during the war.

I am in despair about my writing (she confided in 1929). 'Richard wakes early and keeps me on the go till eleven or so. If I can get him to sleep from then till one p.m. it is the best I can hope for ... In the afternoon he won't sleep unless he has not slept in the morning, and if I do make him sleep I have more trouble at bed time. If I get him to sleep at six thirty I am lucky ... and I have to sing and rock him to accomplish it. By that time I seem tired to start my day's work. Some days I have managed to work between eleven thirty and twelve thirty a.m. and again from eight to eleven p.m., and once or twice until one a.m., but I can't keep that up. I break down after a day or two. I find myself so irritable and jaded that when I sit down to write I am often unable to frame a sentence for some time. Yet in the old days the words used to pour out without difficulty at any odd moment in bus, train, everywhere ...

Mrs Walshe, who lived near by, was able to help by taking the baby out in a pram for several afternoons a week. Other friends and acquaintances also rallied round, and for a few precious months Sylvia, leaving Corio in charge of the Red Cottage, went to stay with friends in the Lake District. Soon after her return, she left the Red Cottage and moved to a

large, old-fashioned house called West Dene, in Charteris Road, Woodford Green. It had been vacant for some time, but when she approached a
local estate agent he, chary of her still lingering reputation as a wild,
communist bohemian, demurred: whereupon she tackled the owner
directly. He could see nothing subversive of local morals in this earnest,
quiet-speaking, simply dressed woman. Her face, as it fattened, had
taken on, with its heavily lidded eyes and rather pouchy cheeks, more and
more the expression of a benevolent bloodhound, or, more exactly, of a
fine old British bulldog. He agreed to rent her the property (she later
bought it: and it was her home and campaign headquarters for more than
twenty-five years). Mrs Charlotte Drake, who, at Sylvia's invitation,
stayed at West Dene for some weeks while recovering from a serious
illness, remembers the atmosphere of that dedicated, immensely purposeful, yet in some ways chaotic household. An upper floor had been
converted into a flat which was rented by an American couple. There was
a German au pair girl, a member of the Pioneer Movement, who helped
with the domestic chores. Corio, a small neat man with cropped grey
hair, grew vegetables in the garden and did most of the cooking ('We had
boiled lettuces once, and I *was* ill. So was Sylvia. She ate a lot of lentils,
and oh, they *did* give her wind!'). But once or twice a week Corio would
put on his best clothes and go to London to meet his Italian anti-Fascist
friends.

He was always kind and considerate, bringing meals to Mrs Drake in
her room or in the garden. 'Sometimes', she says, 'my old man used to
come over to help him in the garden. He used to say they'd be sure to get
first prize for weeds and thistles.' Anxious that Richard should have the
companionship of children of his own age, Sylvia started a Montessori
group at West Dene. Three other children attended the classes, which were
held three times a week under Sylvia's supervision. Morris dancing was
her speciality, but she made time to throw herself heart and soul in the
children's play. Some years later, guests to an evening meal were surprised
to see Richard, then eight, absorbedly playing chess with Corio, who left
the game from time to time to serve the next course and clear the plates
away. He was very fond of his son, and after his visits to London would
nearly always return with a small present. Despite his unobtrusiveness in
company it was clear that there was a deep affection between him and
Sylvia. Sylvia's friends had never known her so happy. Corio supplied
the sense of security, the intellectual support, which enabled her, in her
fifties, to blossom with a marvellous, even riotous, intensity. He was, says

Mrs Drake, in no sense a hen-pecked husband, a tame trophy of an Amazonian feminist. He and Sylvia had their points of difference, their heated arguments. Corio had not been put in his place. He had chosen his place and filled it, not with resignation, but with dignity and with pleasure. He had his own friends, his particular mission, his dream of retribution and justice. By secret routes and from fresh refugees he built up a detailed picture of Mussolini's regime, analysed its relations to Nazism, and watched the development of Britain's peculiar brand of Fascism under the leadership of Sir Oswald Mosley. Corio too was on the verge of an Indian summer of activity in the cause which was closest to his heart; and he had the satisfaction of knowing that, gradually, it was engrossing more and more of Sylvia's zeal and energy.

She still, however, had several skins of righteous indignation to shed. She had helped to found a Socialist Workers' National Health Council, of which Mrs Drake was honorary secretary, to agitate for better medical services and to badger the War Office about widows and other relatives of men killed in 1914–18 who were not receiving adequate pensions. She wrote long letters to the press about the cruelties of the extensive traffic in stolen dogs (the Women's Guild of Empire, apart from lobbying M.P.s about the injustice of women losing their British nationality if they married foreigners, was also busy exposing the evils of the Irish horse trade), and defended the Sunday opening of cinemas against its 'religious' opponents — a matter of abstract principle this: for she detested the American films which formed the staple attraction in most picture palaces. She publicly condemned the celebration of Empire Day and Armistice Day as tending to glorify war and the kind of sentiment which made war inevitable. Why, in any case, focus attention on the past, when (as she told a meeting of the British Anti-War Council in 1933) Hitler's rise to power meant a second world war and millions more dead within a few years? She was the first speaker at the H. G. Wells Society, an intellectual discussion group whose aim was nothing less than 'the reorganization of the world'. Reorganizing the world was a game which, hoisted on a variety of moral stilts, everyone from Hitler and Mussolini to Winston Churchill, Neville Chamberlain and Frank Buchman played with reckless abandon. Sylvia distrusted it, sensing (like Adela) that, in one form or another, all this quasi-scientific laboratory-mindedness, even when it did not, as in Hitler's case, speak of ordinary people as worms who must learn the thrill of becoming part of 'a great dragon', certainly treated them like worms who had little significance except as part of some kind of collective monster. She was through with collective monsters (though not with dreams of co-operative bliss), and confined her talk to the H. G. Wells Society to an analysis of the suffragette movement and of the anti-feminist thinking of 'modern' totalitarianism.

She herself was at this time, after her own run of successful prosecutions, under the threat of a libel action arising from certain passages in *The Home Front* — a threat which does not seem to have materialized but which for some months oppressed her. It involved her in a voluminous correspondence with Norah Smyth, who was to have been her main witness, and who was then staying with her brother in Florence (he was an artist and secretary of the British Institute there). 'Oh my dear,' wailed Sylvia, between discussions of financial details and dates of committee meetings of the Workers' Socialist Federation, 'why am I always in trouble? What hideous fate draws me to difficulty as surely as the sun rises?' She steeled herself to the prospect of yet another appearance in court, where, as she half gloomily, half gleefully forecast, 'prejudice against me as a revolutionary, communist, visionary, jailbird etc. will be used with judge and jury. Well, I must fight with my back to the wall — if only my health does not let me down!'

Early in 1934 came what promised to be a pleasant interlude. She was invited by the Rumanian Ministry of Fine Arts to be present at the unveiling of a statue to Mihail Eminescu on the shores of the Black Sea. Corio and the five-year-old Richard accompanied her. Mrs Drake (who had taught Sylvia to cut her own hair by placing a basin over her head and snipping the protruding ends) had made her a smart black lace dress and Richard a blue velvet suit. It was a festive excursion, though strenuous. Sylvia insisted on covering a maximum of ground, visited many churches and schools, and later almost completed a travel book about Rumania. But the journey through Germany, where Hitler had succeeded Hindenburg as Chancellor and swastika flags were flying everywhere, was depressing, and social contacts in Rumania hardly less so. The Fascist Iron Guard was gaining power in the country, and Sylvia was shocked to learn that Fascist ideas had even penetrated the women's movement. In conversation after a luncheon party at the magnificently appointed Women's House in Bucharest, Princess Alexandrina Cantacuzino, president of the National Council of Rumanian Women and once prominent in the feminist international, revealed that she and her colleagues welcomed the attempt to fashion a corporate state which would 'get things done' and rouse the country to new heights of self-sacrifice and communal effort. Such phrases fell ominously on Sylvia's experienced ear, as did the princess's explanations that corporativism did not necessarily mean an end to liberty, since Rumania was so essentially democratic.

What, after all, did the princess, with her expensive clothes and jewellery, her palace full of art treasures and every kind of luxury, know of democracy? 'Whether you realize it or not,' said Sylvia, in tones of bitter distress, with that intensity which at such moments invested her, short and dumpy as she now was, with an unmistakable authority, 'whether you realize it or not—and I think you do—you are working to bring in a Fascist dictatorship which will destroy all that the women's movement has gained!' Sylvia's 'hideous fate' had turned a cultural outing into a political nightmare.

CHAPTER FOUR

THE EMPEROR AND I

As early as 1932 Sylvia had formed a Women's International Matteotti Committee to agitate for the release from house arrest of the widow of Giacomo Matteotti, the wealthy Italian socialist who in 1923 had been murdered for his outspoken opposition to Mussolini. On her return to Charteris Road after the painful scene with Princess Cantacuzino she plunged headlong into a regular anti-Fascist crusade. In Hyde Park and in Trafalgar Square (fellow speakers were Norah Smyth, just back from Italy, and Charlotte Despard, now ninety) she urged women to force the Government—whose head, Ramsay MacDonald, that Pankhurst *bête noire*, drunk with magnanimity, was talking of the need 'to keep in touch not only with progressive but with retrograding movements in our advance'—to take a firm stand against totalitarianism. France, she warned, was honeycombed with defeatism, and Britain was 'the last bulwark among the great nations so far as democracy, and especially democracy for women, is concerned'. Only a real show of determination by nations which still possessed, and truly valued, freedom could encourage the resistance which still existed in Germany and so prevent 'that bruiser Hitler' from aggression. Shortly afterwards she led three hundred women in a 'peace march' past the Houses of Parliament. By the end of 1934 the evident intention of Mussolini to provoke war with Ethiopia by means of an 'incident' on the undefined boundary between that country and Italian Somaliland had given her and Corio the precise target they needed to focus and popularize their hatred of Fascism and their misgivings about the dangerous vagueness of the League of Nations' formula of collective security.

The Ethiopian crisis was the acid test case not only of Italian treachery but of the sincerity of the high-minded liberalism of Britain's intelligentsia. Since the early 1920s Ras Tafari, the Regent of Ethiopia (who in 1930, with more than medieval pomp, had been crowned Emperor as Haile Selassie I) had been an Italian protégé. He had visited Rome with acclamation and had been congratulated on his strenuous efforts to

modernize his country and to stamp out its slave trade. In 1925 he had
been made an honorary member of the Italian Anti-Slavery Society, and
three years later Mussolini had made a treaty of friendship with him.
Britain, on the other hand, had objected to the admission of 'this barbar-
ous country' to the League of Nations in 1923 – an admission sponsored
by Italy largely to check potential British encroachment in the area.
Haile Selassie had spent much of the period of his regency (which began
in 1916 when he was only twenty-four) in a series of bloody wars against
powerful chieftains determined to keep their independence. Seizing on
this point, the preliminary Italian propaganda bombardment claimed that
Ethiopia was not a genuine sovereign state but merely a collection of
warring tribes, that Italian colonization would establish modern administration, end the slave trade, abolish tribalism, build roads and set up an
efficient system of communications, and raise the standard of living – just
as Britain had done in other parts of East, Central and West Africa. Three
leading British newspapers – the *Daily Mail*, *Morning Post* and *Observer* –
backed the Italian case for modernization from the start. But public
opinion was strongly in favour of the primitive underdog. In autumn
1934 the so-called Peace Ballot had shown that ten million people in
Britain favoured economic sanctions, and six million supported military
sanctions against an aggressor condemned by the League.

Sylvia and Corio (who remembered seeing soldiers returning from
Italy's first disastrous attempt to subjugate Ethiopia at the Battle of
Adowa in 1896) set out to mobilize this opinion and to act as its militant
mouthpiece. They knew they were working against time, the calculations
of statesmen, and the class prejudices of senior military and naval officers.
Foreign affairs experts in France and Britain were willing to barter
Ethiopia for Italian support against Germany. Hitler reasoned that a
military campaign in Africa would prevent Mussolini from taking any
effective action against a Nazi coup d'état in Austria. A Foreign Office
committee reported that an Italian conquest of Ethiopia would not affect
Britain's imperial interests, and in June 1935 Anthony Eden travelled to
Rome to bargain on the basis of this report. Britain would give Ethiopia
access to the Red Sea through British Somaliland ('a corridor for camels,'
The Times called it), and in return Ethiopia could no doubt be persuaded
to surrender some territory to Italy. The offer was rejected: but was later
revived in more drastic (to Ethiopia) form by the Hoare-Laval proposals
('a beautiful example', as A. J. P. Taylor puts it in his *Origins of the
Second World War*, 'of using the machinery of peace against the victim of

aggression'). Even Winston Churchill, so vociferous about the Nazi menace, stayed out of Britain in the autumn of 1935, as Italy completed preparations for invasion, to avoid having to commit himself. The Blimps struck back at their progressive baiters. Determined not to go to war for the League of Nations, which to them stood for an anti-militarist leftism (which had set public-school children against their parents, and which, in extreme terms, Sylvia herself had propounded in the *Dreadnought*), British generals and admirals grossly overestimated Italian power on land and (especially) sea, and firmly advised against military intervention. Alternatively, it was alleged that after an exhausting and perhaps inconclusive campaign in the mountains of Ethiopia, both Mussolini and Haile Selassie would be readier to see reason and reach a compromise. So it came about that in October 1935, when Italy invaded, the only army sent by the nations of the League was a horde of journalists, squeezed uncomfortably into Addis Ababa's one very unluxurious hotel.

Every layer of Sylvia's rich simplicity was outraged by these manœuvres, all her generosities and animosities volcanically activated. There was her instinctive compassion for the underdog – whether Soviet Russia in the years immediately after the revolution, the cultureless proles of industry, unmarried mothers or bullied children. There was her inveterate Pankhurstian setting of Principle (All White) against Expediency (All Black); and her shrewd certainty that though principle and expediency might in fact be hopelessly entangled, ideally they must be separated, for only by the tension of ideal opposites could men and women be shoved into action. There was her deep suspicion of political 'experts' and wire-pulling bureaucrats; her scorn for the appeasing antics of Lady Astor and her high-faluting Cliveden set, whom Lady Rhondda, in her magazine *Time and Tide*, had accused of being fascinated by the surface tidiness of the totalitarian regimes; and her contempt for the smooth diplomatic jugglery of Soviet Russia (as performed by Maxim Litvinov) after its admission to the League of Nations in 1934. She had argued with Lenin and seen great jets of expediency douse her pure white light of revolution in Russia. These self-styled experts were always eager, so it seemed to her, to do a deal at the expense of the supposedly sub-human working classes or 'natives'. The 'realism' of Eden and Hoare and Laval reminded her strongly of the 'realism' of Neville Chamberlain who, weeks after the end of the General Strike of 1926, when the miners were still stubbornly resisting, noted in his diary (and he then, forsooth, Minister of Health): 'They are not within sight of starvation, hardly of under-nutrition. They are not living too uncomfortably at the expense of the rate-payer.' If this cold-blooded anti-humanitarianism was civilized, then she wanted no part of such civilization. Despite all the casuistry in the world, justice was justice, injustice was injustice, and must be fought to the last ditch, and there was an end of it. The sooner people realized this, the better for their own souls and for the survival of common decency and any kind of self-respect. Just so had her mother, thirty years before, risen in her apparently puny wrath against the false yet overwhelming logic of the anti-feminist 'experts' and the counsellors of compromise and gradualism.

From the end of 1934 Sylvia bombarded most newspapers and many politicians and leading public figures, in Britain and abroad, with letters about the long term advisability as well as the moral necessity of defending Ethiopia against Italian aggression. Her estimate of Italian military power was more accurate (though probably just as emotive) as that of the experts. Italy, she stated, was 'a dwarf among nations of any size'. If the economic sanctions which the League had voted to apply were stringently enforced – and women should refuse to vote for any politician who failed to promise that he would see that they were – then Italy's bluff would soon be called. If military action proved to be necessary, then it must be taken as the lesser of two evils. In a series of articles for the *Manchester Guardian* (now, to Sylvia's relief, redeeming its lapse of the late 1920s, when it had described Mussolini as 'the greatest statesman of our time'), she argued, often with editorial backing, that if Italy was allowed to get away with it, a second world war was inevitable. Italy she wrote in a letter published by the *News Chronicle*, 'will use the present conquest as a step to others ... In any case, as it was when Hitlerism came to power, Italy's aggression will be Germany's example. The powers which desire peace and right in Europe must act now before it is too late. The League has dallied too long.'

With Corio and his anti-Fascist exiles she produced propaganda leaflets which were smuggled into Italy, Ethiopia and Eritrea and secretly distributed.

While all the world is longing for peace [said one leaflet], Mussolini, for his personal glory, unlooses war. Fascism has already given to the Italian people enormous reductions of wages, now the lowest in Europe; taxation higher than in other countries; complete destruction of all forms of liberty, of speech, press, public meetings and popular representation. Italian prisons are full of persons of noble mind, tortured morally and physically. Italian exiles are everywhere. Now Fascism will give you: A colonial adventure, a war in Africa in which thousands of young Italians will lose their lives and which will prejudice, for years to come, Italy's relations with other countries. Every hand will be raised against Italy and the Italians. Italian mothers, rise up against this monstrous war! It is to Italy that we Italians ought to restore civilization, by destroying the Fascist reactionaries and resurrecting freedom. To Italian workers: The hour is solemn! We must arise! Italians of free mind, we appeal to you! Either in silence or openly, with the means that are readiest to your hands, get to work immediately, unceasingly, for the downfall of Fascism ... Boycott, sabotage the war!

Britain and France, though applying an embargo on arms to both Italy and Ethiopia (a sanction which clearly favoured Italy), refused to take the only two actions which would have seriously hampered Italy's war effort—cutting off oil imports and closing the Suez Canal. In March 1936, at a Stop The War In Abyssinia meeting in Trafalgar Square, Sylvia demanded that the Government should 'get on with its oil sanctions or get out', and also that the Home Secretary should imprison Sir Oswald Mosley and other leading members of the British Union of Fascists—among whom, she was saddened to note, were ex-suffragettes Mary Richardson (who not long before had come to Sylvia with a scheme for starting a communist nunnery) and Norah Dacre-Fox—for incitement to violence. If she, Mrs Pankhurst, the Pethick-Lawrences and George Lansbury had been sentenced on that charge, why should Fascists, with their virulent anti-Semitism, be exempt?

But she was tired of speech-making and letter-writing alone. These must be supplemented by some influential, less ephemeral action. The Italian 'rape' of Ethiopia had produced, in Britain's fertile soil, a plethora of competing societies—from the Ethiopian Minister's Defence Fund and the Abyssinian Association to the Nile Society and the Red Cross Aeroplane Unit for Abyssinia (no one was quite sure whether to call the country Abyssinia or Ethiopia: it was only learned later that Ethiopia was the name preferred by the Emperor). It was time, she and Corio decided, to bring out a weekly newspaper which would, though primarily concerned with the Italian usurpation in Ethiopia, comment on the evils of totalitarianism wherever they manifested themselves. On May 5th, 1936—Sylvia's birthday and the day on which Italian troops, after a six-

month campaign, marched into Addis Ababa—after a rapid and brilliantly successful canvassing for support and funds, the first issue of *New
Times and Ethiopia News*, edited by Sylvia for the next twenty years,
appeared.

> *New Times and Ethiopia News* [she wrote in her first editorial]
> appears at a time when the fortunes of Ethiopia seem at their lowest
> ebb: the greater the need for an advocate and friend ... The cause of
> Ethiopia cannot be divorced from the cause of international justice,
> which is permanent and is not to be determined by ephemeral
> military victories. As friends of Ethiopia we must solemnly and
> vigorously protest against the attack on her millennial independence;
> we must condemn the atrocious barbarities employed against her,
> the bombing of her undefended villages, the use of poison gases by
> which thousands of innocent women and children have suffered
> agonizing death ... We shall set ourselves resolutely to combat
> Fascist propaganda, to secure the continuance and strengthening of
> sanctions ... and persistently urge that Britain take the responsibility
> of initiating an active League policy on these lines ... *New Times* is
> opposed to the conception of dictatorship. It understands that
> Fascism destroys all personal liberty and is in fundamental opposition
> to all forms of intellectual and moral progress.

Sylvia—her stamina boosted to suffragette pitch by the whiff of battle—
and Corio often stayed up all night twice a week preparing copy and
layout. She had two secretaries to deal with her ceaseless flow of dictation.
Her own office-study at West Dene had portraits of Dr Azaj Martin,
the Ethiopian minister in London, and of Carlo Rosselli, the murdered
Italian anti-Fascist leader, on the walls. Other rooms were filled with
voluntary workers addressing and filling envelopes. *New Times*, which
reached a circulation of over forty thousand, went every week to all
British Members of Parliament, among whom Ellen Wilkinson, Eleanor
Rathbone, Reginald Sorensen (now Lord Sorensen), Philip Noel-Baker,
Arthur Creech-Jones, and (after 1945) Peter Freeman, were particularly
useful allies, and to many politicians and influential figures in other
countries. Several special issues were prepared in Amharic and smuggled
over the frontier to Ethiopian resistance forces, and in 1937 extensive
coverage was given of the Japanese aggression in China.

The journalistic standard was extremely high, and contributors represented more fully than perhaps any other publication of the period, the non-sectarian unity of the Popular Front of the 1930s. Dr Martin wrote a weekly article; Nancy Cunard, Professors F. L. Lucas and Berriedale Keith, Arthur Creech-Jones (then the Labour Party's leading expert on colonial affairs) appeared side by side with Henri Robin, a Belgian senator, African nationalists chafing at various colonial yokes, a squad of distinguished Italian political exiles (including Professor Gaetano Salvemini, then in the United States, and Professor Francesco Frola, then in Mexico), articulate refugees from Hungary, Russia, and Spain, and Harold Moody, founder of the League of Coloured Peoples. Sylvia's house, as well as her columns, was open to refugees of all kinds, and to such up-and-coming African politicians as Jomo Kenyatta. The *New Times* advisory board included Nancy Cunard, the elderly Quaker Isabel Fry, Professor Lucas, Colonel Maurice Spencer, Rosika Schwimmer (the veteran Hungarian socialist and feminist leader), and the Reverend V. Ziapkoff, president of the Union of Young People's Evangelical Associations in Bulgaria. The paper's intelligence of happenings in occupied Ethiopia was probably unique. From Wazir Ali Baig, an Indian who was in close touch with the Ethiopian consul in Jibouti, French Somaliland, came regular news of the movements of Ethiopian guerrillas, who fought on long after the Italian occupation was nominally completed, and in fact (as *New Times* constantly emphasized) never ceased resistance. Contacts in Kenya, British Somaliland and the Sudan supplied further information; and from a Hungarian doctor in Addis Ababa came a harrowingly detailed account of the decimating massacre which followed an attempt in February 1937 to assassinate Marshal Graziani, the Italian viceroy.

Sylvia now emerged, from the tangled thicket—almost forest—of her luxuriantly rebel past, as a *grande dame* of the Popular Front, organizing charity bazaars, rallying people of good will (for was not good will, the sense of common humanity, if only it could be released and set to work, the essence of the matter?) even if, by some contingency which now seemed unimportant, they happened to be duchesses, archbishops, Tories, Fabian socialists, or Captains of Mismanaged Industry. Their money and their influence was useful—and used, if not gratefully, then realistically, just as Mrs Pankhurst and Christabel had taken contributions to the W.S.P.U. from wealthy sympathizers who never fired a pillar box in anger. She swam energetically with the tide, lobbying M.P.s instead of agitating for the abolition of Parliament. She could even appreciate, now,

Asmara, November 1944: Sylvia Pankhurst listens to an address of welcome from Eritrean Reunionists

lvia Pankhurst and supporters on a poster parade outside the House of Commons, 1946

Adela Pankhurst Walsh in 1951, aged sixty-six. Though retired from public life, she was still an avid reader and lively thinker

such patriots as Lady 'Fanny' Houston, who in her *Saturday Review* constantly protested against inadequate rearmament, which had 'made the British Lion a toothless old lap dog that can yap but cannot bite', sent a cheque for two hundred thousand pounds to the Chancellor of the Exchequer to be spent on weapons of war, and had her yacht illuminated at night with the slogan MACDONALD IS A TRAITOR.

Had not the proletarian priggishness and middle-class anti-bourgeois crankishness of the Labour movement managed to make even Mosley's Fascism seem attractive, sane, constructive and healthily patriotic? Mosley could talk as dreamily about the British heritage as Baldwin himself, while armchair socialists (as Adela had complained in 1918) put people off by sneering childishly at religion, tradition, generals, the monarchy, sexual fidelity, and ordinary, dogged decency in all its many —and often touching—forms. Sylvia hated the sniggering type of progressive, a phenomenon which roused the gargantuan sarcasm of Percy Wyndham Lewis and the earnest anger of George Orwell. She would surely have agreed with Orwell's lament over the corpse of a faith which in the early 1920s had seemed capable of enlisting the generosity and idealism of a whole generation. 'Socialism', he wrote in *The Road to Wigan Pier*, 'does not smell any more of revolution and the overthrow of tyrants; it smells of crankishness, machine-worship and the stupid cult of Russia. Unless you can remove that smell, Fascism may win. I suggest that the real socialist is one who actively wishes to see tyranny overthrown, not a tedious heresy-hunter. You have got to make it clear that there is room in the socialist movement for human beings or the game is up.'

There was room in Sylvia's movement for any human being who was capable of counting spiritual blessings and willing to help her do battle with the Fascist Anti-Christ. For (luckily for Ethiopia) she lacked Christabel's cripplingly long perspective. To her, Mussolini and Hitler were Absolutely Bad and must be overthrown. She was not concerned with whether they were *the* Anti-Christ, or only foreshadows of the Ultimate Horror. She gladly laid aside her thorny crown of republicanism (though, unlike the reformed Adela, she wasted no editorial comment on the jubilees, deaths, betrothals, coronations and abdications of the British Royal Family) to pay tribute to her own especial man of destiny— Haile Selassie, Elect of God, Conquering Lion of the Tribe of Judah, King of Zion, King of Kings, Emperor of Ethopia, Chevalier sans peur et sans reproche, and Epitome of True Nobility. He was no feeble monarchic symbol, tacked on like so much derisive, expensive tinsel to the grey

9

fabric of economic depression and mass unemployment, but the father of his country, which (though it was as big as France and most of Spain put together) he ruled—as he had to—like a kindergarten. He had been the commander of its brave but pitiful defenders, and was the soul of its resistance. How could Sylvia's romantic ardour, patent in her whole quixotic life as well as in her translations of Eminescu's poems, fail to be captivated by the rare spectacle of a benevolent despot battling not only with the neo-feudalism of Mussolini, but with the tenacious feudalism of his own subjects, who in their remote mountain fortress had contrived for centuries to let the world go by? Interviewing the Emperor shortly after his arrival in England, she wrote ardently (certain of having found a father figure worthy to stand beside Dr Pankhurst in her personal pantheon): 'In those irresistible eyes burns the quenchless fire of the hero who never fails his cause. One sees in his build and bearing, those features full of meaning, those fine and eager hands, the worker who toils unceasingly for the public weal, untouched by personal ambition or material desire for wealth and safety.' How could she not be thrilled by the prospect of helping him to till that almost virgin socio-political soil, to lift Ethiopia into the right kind of twentieth century? How could she not be fascinated by that towering kingdom of volcanic crags which, until the Italians assaulted it with aeroplanes, armoured cars, motorized artillery and poison gas, had for three thousand years repulsed foreign invaders and in 1896 had routed an Italian army with barefoot troops?

During the five years of his exile, Sylvia became the trusted if importunate adviser of an Acceptable Emperor as well as the mate of the admirable, steadfast Corio. Her bliss was complete. She tasted the joys of apotheosis in her lifetime. Photographed, as she sometimes was, beside her Emperor, she looked as radiant as a bride. He had need of allies. Few, at least in official circles, shared her estimate of him. All was embarrassment. Should he be treated as a monarch in exile or a visiting sovereign? Should he be received by royalty or would this offend Italy? Discretion—or, as Sylvia thought, cowardice—won the argument. Haile Selassie was met at Victoria station by a minor official from the Foreign Office. Edward VIII refused to invite him to Buckingham Palace. Stanley Baldwin, who had once more succeeded MacDonald as Prime Minister, was said to have hidden behind a table in the House of Commons restaurant to avoid meeting the Emperor, who, at the end of June 1936, when he went to Geneva to make a personal plea to the Assembly of the League of Nations, was booed, catcalled and whistled at by Italian journalists. Three months

later Sylvia, pausing en route to deliver a message from Dr Martin to a
World Peace Conference in Brussels, went to Geneva to report, with
deep gloom and disgust, the League Assembly for *New Times*. It was like
walking into a morgue. *Rigor mortis*, a galloping paralysis of total un-
reality, had set in after the betrayal of Ethiopia.

At the beginning of the Spanish Civil War, which Corio forecast would
provide, literally, a field day for Hitler and Mussolini, *New Times*
commented: 'We are in the world war of Fascism against democracy.
The war began in Ethiopia: it has spread to Spain. The troops which
Franco relies on to defeat the Spanish people are mainly Africans,
mercenaries from Spanish Morocco. The evil which Mussolini did by
taking mercenary black troops to exterminate the Ethiopians is now
being done in Europe.' But Sylvia was more immediately, and personally,
concerned with the activities of Mosley (who had stated that the quarrels
of Spaniards were not worth the spilling of a drop of British blood) in the
East End of London which, full as it was of Jews who had escaped from
the pogroms of eastern Europe and Tsarist Russia, was the only place
where he attracted anything like a sizable following. It infuriated Sylvia
to see her old kingdom disrupted by race hatred; to know that British
Union of Fascists' loudspeaker vans blaring anti-Semitic slogans toured
streets where she had fought for better things; and to stand by while
six thousand policemen, a patrolling helicopter, and an entire mounted
division protected marching blackshirts from the wrath of the public –
in Cable Street, where Mrs Pankhurst had been adopted as a Conservative
candidate. Wrenching time from her herculean schedule, Sylvia hastened
to Victoria Park, Bow, the scene of many of her suffragette and wartime
rallies, to speak at anti-Fascist meetings held by the Jewish Ex-Servicemen's League, formed to protect Jewish residents from Mosley's strong-
arm squads. During a scrimmage with blackshirt interrupters, her face
was hit and cut by a stone. But she had the satisfaction of knowing that
she had done her bit to help towards the total and humiliating failure of
the British Union of Fascists' East End candidates in the London County
Council elections of March 1937.

Towards the end of 1937 she staged another public argument (in an
article in the *Sunday Referee*) with Bernard Shaw, whose playful Fascist-
fancying continued to exasperate her. 'One of Shaw's greatly advertised
successes', she smouldered, 'was his *Black Girl in Search of God*, a plea, so it
appeared, for the freedom and self-expression of the African people, and
a claim that in their candid simplicity they have something of virtue and

kindness we in Europe have lost in the struggle for wealth and power. But despite all the sweet moralizing of the *Black Girl*, Shaw was on the side of the great battalions of Fascism against the peaceful Abyssinians.' He had written to her that he agreed with the Fascists and communists that 'the British Parliament, with its party system, is the worst organ of government ever devised, except for the purpose of preventing anything being done for the people', and that the dictators could 'do in six months what would take our Parliament thirty years, and then be only half done, and bungled at that' — an opinion with which Sylvia might have agreed in the early 1920s, but which she now regarded as immature. Parliamentary democracy was the means, imperfect (like human beings) as it might be, by which the mass of people had, after a long struggle, managed to get a say in the way the world was managed. 'At your time of life', she snorted, 'you really owe it to the younger generation to probe more deeply into matters, and not to assist the dark forces which are opposed to the decent life of the community, and which impose their pretences on a credulous world.'

Sylvia, now a celebrity of undeniable stature, was asked by Margot, Countess of Oxford and Asquith, to contribute to her symposium *Myself When Young*, published in 1938 with the aim of encouraging young women to make more ambitious use of their new freedoms. A catholic selection of famous women contributors included Ellen Wilkinson, Maude Royden, Irene Vanbrugh, Amy Johnson, the aviatrix ('Had I been a man I might have explored the Poles or climbed Mount Everest, but as it was my spirit found outlet in the air'), and even Gabrielle Chanel ('What figure shall I cut among these priestesses ... a mere woman unable to express myself except in the most feminine and commonplace manner'). Sylvia's piece, a re-write of her family saga in *The Suffragette Movement*, followed, in ironical (yet, granted her new Popular Front *persona*, apt) juxtaposition, a gaily prattling essay by Mary, Countess of Minto ('It was my privilege to be born at Norman Tower, Windsor Castle ... in those historic surroundings I spent the first eleven years of my childhood ... '). Sylvia concentrated on the years in Russell Square, where she remembered having Dickens read aloud to her ('he made real for me the cause of the People and the Poor, though he kept me awake at night'), and going often to the British Museum. There, she had particularly been fascinated by the Egyptian Rooms ('oh, the powerful harmony of those pigments, those large and mystic shapes'). She ended on a note of clarion optimism: 'My belief in the growth and permanence of democ-

racy is undimmed. I know that the people will cast off the new dictatorships as they did the old. I believe as firmly as in my youth that humanity
will surmount the era of poverty and war. Life will be happier and more
beautiful for all. I believe in the GOLDEN AGE.'

There was little in the contemporary situation to justify such glowing
confidence. While Germany and Italy poured armaments, troops and
technicians into Spain, the British Government, with that parody of
etiquette which had made Baldwin dodge behind the table cloth, stuck
to non-intervention. In Palestine, Arab guerrillas were being financed by
Italy. In May 1938 Haile Selassie, who had settled with his family and
his entourage at Bath, sent his children to English schools, spent summer
holidays gazing out to sea from his balcony at Warne's Hotel, Worthing,
and become resigned to what was, by imperial standards, a genteel
poverty, went to Geneva to hear the Great Powers, in their realism,
recognize Italian *de facto* rule in Ethiopia. The British representative, Lord
Halifax, squirmed in his seat with embarrassment—as well he might,
knowing (as he must have done if he read his *New Times*) that large areas
of Ethiopia were still unconquered, guerrilla bands still active, and
Ethiopian refugees refused asylum in Kenya and the Sudan. They were
given the alternatives of internment, return to Ethiopia, or a further
journey to other, less sensitive, territories.

In September 1938 came the debacle of Munich; the spectacle of the
House of Commons in a pandemonium of hysterical gratitude at
Chamberlain's announcement that Hitler had agreed to meet him; the
sight of the whole nation (or at least, almost all its newspapers) grovelling
in relief when Chamberlain returned with another instalment of non-war.
In March Sylvia had led a procession of protest to the German embassy,
and had observed that Britain (with powerful prodding, she might have
added, from Mrs Pankhurst and Christabel) had been more responsible
than any other nation for creating the new, hopelessly artificial, state of
Czechoslovakia. But in 1919, during the deliberations at Versailles,
Britain had not had 'a Prime Minister influenced by the 'vision' of
Fascism. Mr Lloyd George, with all his faults, was not, like Mr Chamberlain, in the armaments ring.' After Munich, *New Times* was bitter. In an
article headed THE BASEST DAY IN BRITISH HISTORY Professor Lucas
wrote:

The flowers piled before 10 Downing Street are very fitting for the
funeral of British honour. For sheer degradation, the frenzies of last

Friday beat even the night of Mafeking. In any country, no doubt, there are people who would throw confetti at a crucifixion. But leaders should have some touch of finer mettle. Any really great man who had felt forced to sacrifice a small nation that trusted in him would at least have returned, not smirking and grinning, but full of anguish and shame. We have lost the courage to see things as they are. Yet Herr Hitler has kindly put down in black and white in *Mein Kampf* the programme which he is so faithfully carrying out.

Czechoslovakia had joined Ethiopia, Spain and China on the list of victim nations, said Sylvia. 'We ask, as often before, when Britain will wake to the knowledge that her place is on the side of world democracy and international justice. If', she darkly added, 'the interests which put oil and other war material before justice had not broken the peace front in 1936, the hideous crisis of today would not have been. Chamberlain must resign.'

The year 1939 brought more gloom. Franco's victory in Spain (accurately predicted by Christabel) and the British Government's prompt recognition of his regime; the Italian occupation of Albania; twenty-five thousand refugees in Britain alone from Nazi persecution (for some of whom Sylvia busied herself to find jobs and homes); the Nazi-Soviet pact (again foretold by Christabel, in 1918). There was a further instalment of flesh-creeping appeasement from Neville Chamberlain, who flew to Rome to talk with Mussolini, burst into tears when English residents sang 'For He's A Jolly Good Fellow' as his train drew out of the station, and submitted to the Duce the text of a speech which he intended to make in the House of Commons.

Yet for Sylvia there were a few personal compensations. The Duce admitted the insecurity of his rule in Ethiopia when, in August 1939, he invited Haile Selassie to return to the country as King of Amharaland (the central province), to help control the guerrillas who were harassing the Italian army of occupation. Her own nuisance value and that of *New Times* had been recognized in the form of several specific attacks in newspaper articles written by Mussolini himself. Later, she revealed that Mussolini had 'impertinently' approached the British Foreign Office demanding the suppression of *New Times*. The Foreign Office went so far as to prohibit the export of the paper to neutral countries, other than the Americas, until Mussolini declared war. Sylvia's name was included on what to her was a roll of honour – the Nazi blacklist of people to be imprisoned or liquidated in the event of a German invasion of Britain. And when war was finally declared (WHY SHOULD YOU DIE FOR POLAND'S 3,500,000 JEWS? asked huge Mosleyite slogans whitewashed on East End walls), Sylvia and Corio rejoiced with a special rejoicing.

'The British Government', wrote Sylvia in *New Times*, 'announces that it is preparing for a three years' war. We shall win through if we have a tithe of the courage of brave Ethiopia, who has fought during the past four years.' Already after Munich she had forecast the certain defeat of the dictatorships in a world war, and more particularly the speedy crumbling of the new, gimcrack Roman Empire and the liberation of Ethiopia. Britain and France had failed to provide a brisk wind of intervention in 1935. They must now reap the whirlwind of their own creation — to which, deeply filling her journalistic lungs, Sylvia prepared to add the huge huff and puff which would help to blow the Italians clear out of Africa.

PART SIX

SECOND WORLD WARS

CHAPTER ONE

CHAMPION OF JAPAN

While Sylvia was busy condemning Japan as a Fascist yellow peril, her sister Adela, viewing the scene from an Australian distance, saw Japan — and the dictatorships of Germany and Italy — in a very different light. In the last issue of the *Empire Gazette* in October 1939, she grumbled that the Anglo-Japanese alliance, made by Empire-minded leaders, had been jettisoned by politicians who cared more for American susceptibilities than for the welfare of the Empire. She distrusted, too, the facile ranting about the evils of dictatorship, and pleaded for a serious effort to understand the conditions which had made them possible and even inevitable, and to evaluate the success of Hitler and Mussolini in realizing the legitimate ambitions of the German and Italian peoples. Just as the cause of Ethiopia drew the floating strands of Sylvia's liberalism into a tight unity, so the plight and the aspirations of Japan had a peculiar attraction for Adela's temperament, equally opposed as it was to the chaotic greed of uncontrolled capitalism and to the calculated sabotage of international communism.

Japan had a record of national independence almost as long, and certainly more impressive, than Ethiopia's and had made a marvellous recovery from the traumatic mid-nineteenth century impact of American, British and Russian strategico-commercial rivalry. After valuable naval and military help during the first world war, Japan had been faced with the combined hostility of the European Powers and the U.S.A., concerned simply to protect their commercial interests in the Far East and persistently underestimating the potential strength of Soviet Russia. Since the militarist coup of 1931 had forced through the creation of the state of Manchukuo out of the rulerless muddle of Manchuria, Japan, which had defeated Tsarist Russia on land and sea in 1905, had been the one power to face the new Soviet imperialism with a determination which was not afraid of war. The Anti-Comintern Pact between Germany and Japan seemed to Adela a logical move in the only confrontation that really mattered — that of the fatherland of communism and those non-communist countries which were prepared to cut away the frills of parliamentary democracy in order to strip down for serious action. If only Britain and France had been willing not merely to *appease* Germany, Italy and Japan, but to *join* them, the 'mistake' of the European war of 1939 would have been avoided, and the *real* tasks—the de-Bolshevization of Russia and the settlement of the problem of China (that huge, frightening vacuum which had to be filled: but by whom?) could have been tackled with maximum efficiency.

The attempt to establish a New Order in China by an Asiatic power which had proved its ability to deal on equal terms with the white races had its attraction, and a powerful propaganda appeal, throughout East Asia. Economic and political stability in China was of vital importance to Japan, and between 1937 and the end of 1939, despite spasmodic resistance from Chinese nationalists (themselves split between the U.S.A.-oriented forces of Chiang Kai Shek and the U.S.S.R.-oriented forces of Chinese communism), Japan came within sight of total conquest of China. In August 1939, at Nomonhan on the frontier of Manchukuo and Outer Mongolia, Japanese troops suffered a sharp defeat in a major clash with the Soviet army. But this was only a check. The Japanese nation, increasingly dominated by an army junta, had been pared down to a war economy (under which industry expanded and prospered) since 1931. Party politics were taboo, the Emperor a prisoner of his own military devotees, the nation committed to face the full might of Soviet Russia—whose European flank was temporarily secured by the Nazi-Soviet Non-Aggression Pact and by Hitler's preoccupation with Poland, the Low Countries, France and Britain. America, though aiding the discredited Chiang Kai Shek, was still neutral. The period of the 'phoney war' in Europe was an anxious one for Japan.

So when, early in December 1939, with the European war a distant rumble significant only (to them) of tragically wasted anti-communist energy, the Walshes set sail for Japan, it was in an atmosphere heavily charged with tension. Their views, based on temperamental inclinations but buttressed by solid reading, were well known to the Japanese Government which sponsored their trip. Pearl Harbour was still two years away. Britain had lost the capacity, if not the will, to play a big role in the Far East; America had the capacity but not the will; Japan alone seemed to have both: with the considerable disadvantage, from White Australia's point of view, of being inhabited by people with yellow skins. It was a challenge to visit the country of which they had read and thought so much, and, if their favourable opinion was confirmed, to try and swing the Australian public over to it. It was, on a simpler level, a sheer pleasure, after so many years at the domestic political grindstone, to have a break, to get away from the sad wreck and the bourgeois bickerings of the Women's Guild of Empire and the industrial peace campaign. Standing on deck to face the cameras the Walshes, in their rather heavily formal clothes—Tom with dark top coat, grey trilby, stiff white collar, pale grey tie and dark suit: Adela with long grey overcoat, polka dot blouse, dark skirt, stout shoes, bulky handbag and crammed-on helmet of a hat: he so tall and gaunt, she short and rather squat—had the look of two family retainers, perhaps a saturnine butler and a formidable housekeeper rewarded, after long years of faithful service, with a hard-earned holiday. No one, looking at them, stiffly, utterly and touchingly together, could have imagined that they would startle officialdom in Australia (and to some extent in America and Britain) by the knowledgeability and passion of their advocacy of Japan's New Order. In what was to be their last fling of public partnership Adela, at fifty-three, reached the peak of her very considerable powers as a controversialist.

They wasted no time in getting down to business. On December 5th they told Japanese pressmen that Australia's embargo on Japanese iron ore represented a policy of shortsighted obstruction which, if persisted in, would 'give a good case for the forcible opening of Australia to Japan's teeming millions'. Australia, they added, should make an alliance with Japan, a country which, if Britain succeeded in crushing Germany, would 'be the only protector against communism'. Three days later the *Sydney Morning Herald* reported that at a banquet given in their honour at the Foreign Federation in Tokyo, Mr Thomas Walsh (ex-cabin boy, ex-communist) had reproached the Australian press for 'playing the Comintern's game' by its constant vilification of Japan, and that Mrs Walsh had urged closer friendship between the two countries and 'co-operation between Japan's millions and Australia's unused wealth'. The Walshes visited public shrines, private homes, factories, schools, craft workshops, and theatres, and talked with leading industrialists and civil servants. All the time they took detailed notes and early in January 1940, at the Imperial Palace Hotel, Tokyo, completed a six-thousand-word booklet—*Japan As Viewed By Foreigners*—on their impressions. Japan's hotel and tourist facilities were, they found, better than Australia's. Australian resorts often had nothing but 'a commonplace tea room, which is a blot on the landscape', whereas the country hotels at Kyoto, Nara, Miyanoshita, Kamakura and Nikko were 'very beautiful, and the proprietors take a personal interest in preserving the beauty of the country, rather than in making as much money as possible'. Japan, they thought, should make a big effort, since substantial tourism might do much to break down existing prejudices and misconceptions, to advertise the attractions of their land more widely, especially at a time when the war in Europe was bound to kill tourism there. Much more could be done to interest Australian women in the better quality Japanese furniture, materials and dresses, if suitably – but not too drastically – modified. Japan might in this way 'give Uncle Sam a healthy reminder that he is not the only person on earth with business ability'.

The Walshes were impressed by the (literally, in so crowded a land) compulsive tidiness of the Japanese, and by the fact that even among tens of thousands of troops home on leave or embarking for the Chinese front, they had seen no drunkenness. They approved of the vitality of a traditional family life, and the absence of that worship of 'individualism' which, in Australia and other 'advanced democracies' had made the family seem an obstacle to progress and 'self-expression'. The survival of the small-farmer class, they considered, gave society a solidity and a sturdy pride which was lacking in nations dominated increasingly by large, impersonal, capitalist enterprises. Even the most powerful industrialists were expected to show a sense of social responsibility and there was an admirable refusal to bow down before mere wealth. The level of employment compared more than favourably with that in Australia, where there were 'many thousands of boys idle on the coal fields, and young men of twenty-five who have never worked. They have been reared and married on the dole. With all our vast territories, they cannot even have a living on the land, and receive no training for a useful occupation in life. Our hills are stripped of forests, and we have no funds for reforestation – yet we have money to wage war against Germany, which was once Australia's second best customer.'

This, however, was but a light-hearted sketch of what was to follow when the Walshes returned to Sydney in February 1940. There was, said Tom Walsh, nothing to fear from Japan, who simply wanted to increase her trade with Australia. Mr Suma, a Japanese Foreign Office spokesman, had told them of his intention to visit Australia soon, and had indicated that Japan would welcome the establishment of an Australian embassy in Tokyo. The idea that the Japanese were raring to invade Australia was laughable. They were so attached to their homes and families that it was difficult to uproot them to go to Korea. On February 21st, at a welcome home meeting at the Blaxland Galleries, Adela fired the first of several blazing broadsides not only at Australians' ignorance of the Far East and of the balance of world power, but against that provincial smugness which had irked her in the last few years of the Women's Guild of Empire, that blank, tepid suburbanity that had moved D. H. Lawrence to denunciation, and drove Vere Gordon Childe, the great archaeologist, when he came back to Australia after an absence of nearly forty years, to tease a Melbourne audience by comparing its way of life with the far more vital culture of tenth-century Iceland.

Adela thanked her listeners for their loyalty and their realization that despite allegations to the contrary, she was acting in what she honestly believed to be the interests of Australia by calling attention to plain facts, however awkward. Progress, even survival, depended on flexibility of mind and acceptance of the certainty that 'lesser breeds' could become major powers. Gauls, Britons and Anglo-Saxons had all once appeared as 'lesser breeds' to Imperial Rome; Britain herself had seemed insignificant to the might of the Spanish Empire; and only a hundred and sixty years earlier Britain had regarded America as a puny and presumptuous colony. All these were white peoples. But now Japan had proved that it was the turn of non-whites to re-enter the struggle for power. It was, in her opinion, a sign of decadence as well as stupidity to refuse to come to terms with this development. She herself had never been afraid to adapt herself to different trends, to train her sights on changing foes, who were yet always the same foes — arrogance, complacence, laziness — in different shapes. As a suffragette she had been 'up against the spirit as expressed in the newspapers and in the mouths of politicians that however they fuddled and muddled and failed, they ought to get the prize, and the whole world ought to stand still because they were out of breath'. She had fought that attitude as a socialist and as a champion of industrial peace, and was fighting it now as an advocate of realism about Australia's position in the world and her proper relations with Japan and the New Order in Asia. The European Powers, in their reckless scramble for commercial gain, showed no concern whatever for the Chinese people, who 'seethed with misery, disease and disorder at the very gates of Hong Kong, Shanghai and other callously profiteering treaty ports'. They had destroyed whatever remained of Chinese national unity and self-respect. The question was: Who was going to restore it — communist Russia or Japan? Chinese weakness was a menace to Japan, but there was no intention of turning China into a Japanese colony, or treating Chinese as inferiors. Every attempt was being made to encourage loyalty to, and pride in, Chinese institutions, language and culture, while substituting orderly and efficient administration for a mess of corruption. Chinese living in Japan were not persecuted, but left free to continue their business: in fact they were going to Japan to work, and to study in the universities, in greater numbers than ever before.

The ruling classes in Japan had not waited until the nation, or sections of it, were in a state of desperate revolt before granting the vote (to men), or a proper system of education. Japanese industrialists, without legal compulsion, saw that their employees were properly housed, fed and cared for in sickness, and girl workers were given courses in domestic economy to fit them to be good wives and mothers. Employers of girl 'home workers' gave them a marriage portion and acted as relatives to the children after marriage. The necessity for co-operation in the interests of the community was emphasized in schools, and though strikes did some-times occur, they were treated as distressing failures, a breach of etiquette on both sides, and not as a move in a class war. There was no scope for financial jugglery. 'Such a phenomenon as capitalists rushing their money out of Japan in a national crisis would not be considered natural. If any-one did it and the Government did not call him to account, he might well', said Adela, with evident approval, 'be assassinated.' Japanese religion was a religion of works and patriotism, with little time for spiritual theories spun finely over shabby practice. 'If we could abolish slums, unemploy-ment, gambling, dishonesty, meanness and violence from Australia, our example might cause non-Christian countries to seek to know the secret of our virtues.'

The crude picture of Japan waiting to jump into Australia's 'open spaces' was fantastic, since Japan's resources were more than fully stretched in the struggle to hold Russia at bay and develop Manchukuo. Was Australia really willing to go to war to preserve the old order of European greed in Asia, an order which was being challenged not only by Japan, but everywhere throughout Asia. 'It seems to me', Adela reasoned, 'that a starving, shivering, unprogressive Asia is no good to us, and that an orderly, prosperous and advancing Asia would enable us to develop Australia and build a nation here. I feel not only impatient but unhappy when I read the press and hear the pundits talking of boycotting Japan and teaching her not to be cocky, talking big with nothing—not even common sense—to back it up. My advice to all is: Take a tour to the East. Compare what you can see in the Philippines and China with what you will see in Japan, and then ask yourselves where the source of progress is and whether you would like to push Japan down to the level of China, or help lift China up to the level of Japan—I know what the answer would be.'

A few months later Adela (who with a number of followers had formed the People's Guild to continue—on her own terms—the policy of the Women's Guild of Empire, and to keep alive some of the youth clubs which had been associated with it) returned to the charge in a long lecture to the Geography Teachers' Association of New South Wales. Again she deplored the 'levity of the press and public men about the stupendous forces being generated around them'. It was no surprise that, faced with the problem of providing for seventy-four million people in an area roughly the same as that of the British Isles, and of trying to cure the communist-breeding wretchedness that Europeans had created in China, Japan had an authoritarian Government. That did not necessarily mean that it was evil. In fact, in some ways it was much more genuinely democratic than the Australian brand of parliamentary democracy. There was a steady and uninterrupted application, through a network of local authorities with very wide powers, to problems of social concern, instead of a wild shower of vote-catching promises, a sudden discovery by party politicians of national 'issues', every three years or so when election time came round. Government in Japan had always been authoritarian, stemming directly from a divinely ordained Emperor, and it had a record of enlightened administration—something hard to conceive, admittedly, when one thought of trusting *party* politicians with absolute power—but nevertheless true. The frugality of life in Japan (where the notion did not exist that one worked to pay others to entertain one in a leisure of appalling vacuity and vulgar irresponsibility) meant that its people had 'a hard core which will be very difficult to break down'.

Tom Walsh kept up the brisk barrage of Pankhurst didacticism with a long, closely reasoned pamphlet entitled *The New Order in Asia*. Two centuries of almost unresisted European depredation in Asia, he wrote, had ended with the emergence of Japan as a world power, though even now there was a tendency to underestimate her strength and determination just as it was still taken for granted that 'even the mediocrities of the West are superior to the greatest men of Asia'. The West assumed too glibly that China thought of Japan as a tyrant invader, whereas it was much more likely that millions of Chinese looked to Japan for liberation from the West. 'What Asiatic, regarding the position of the Chinese in the port of

Hong Kong, would not feel a thrill of satisfaction in the knowledge that the domination of the whites, with their cool, contemptuous indifference to the poverty and degradation of the Chinese, ends at Yokohama, where Asia confronts Europe on equal terms?' The Great War, reckoned Walsh, had demonstrated the selfishness of Europeans, and 'their helplessness to control the economic forces of capitalism, their own creation'. The present was bound, one way or another, but most probably through the conquest and revitalization of China by Japan, to complete Asia's independence from Europe, and might well be the first stage in the political and economic ascendancy of Asia over Europe. Why should Australia not welcome and assist Japan in her fight against the two dragons of Chinese disintegration and communist imperialism?

Adela's lecture to the Geography Teachers' Association had been delivered in September 1940, when Japan, impressed by the Nazi occupation of Denmark, Norway and the Low Countries, concluded the Tripartite Axis Pact with Germany and Italy. Though moderate civilian opinion in Japan was in favour of neutrality, the powerful army clique was already arguing that only America stood between them and the final establishment of the New Order. Yet with great, almost foolhardy courage Adela chose this moment to campaign as a candidate for the Federal Senate. Her pro-Japanese sentiments might seem to her the height of enlightened nationalism, but to citizens whose sons had enlisted to fight in the European war which she dismissed as a ghastly error for Britain and the British Commonwealth (win or lose), whose newspapers had taught them to regard the Japanese militarist regime as a grotesque offshoot of Nazism, and whose fears for the integrity of White Australia were dangerously near the surface, Adela's arguments seemed treasonable. Sylvia, with her championship of Ethiopia, had swum against an official tide more sluggish than menacing: Adela set herself against an oceanic prejudice which included the main current of Australian patriotism, a current moreover, which she herself had for many years done her best to strengthen. Of all the Pankhurst causes, this was the most impossibly doomed.

The failure of her attempt to become a senator was a foregone conclusion; and the very fact that she had made it drove her deep into an unpleasant isolation where curious figures beckoned and few of her friends, however loyal, could follow her. The handful of people who welcomed her stand had in fact already anticipated it in a cruder form, and centred round a magazine called *The Publicist*. This had been launched in 1935, with a policy similar to that of Mosley—anti-communism, a tendency to regard 'Jewish-inspired' international finance as the cause of all ills, and an admiration for Hitler, Mussolini and the militarist group in Japan. *The Publicist* had a tiny circulation and no political influence, but by 1940 it was beginning to attract attention from the authorities by its anti-British, anti-American and pro-Axis opinions. 'The occasion of Japan's 2,600th anniversary', wrote Percy Stephensen, its editor, in February 1940, 'is one which cannot be allowed to pass without cordial felicitations ... full-hearted, we Australian nationalists join in the joyful shout—Banzai!' The war against Germany was seen as a trick of purblind, unpatriotic, parliamentary politicians. 'Wanted,' jeered Stephensen, 'five hundred thousand young Australians, sound in wind and limb, for use in Europe as soil fertilizers. Apply to 10 Downing Street, England.' The incitement of Australian hostility to Japan, said *The Publicist,* would benefit the British and the Americans, but the truth was that Australia had nothing to fear from the Japanese, who were the very people, 'more than any other enterprising and progressive, with whom Australians could advance through reciprocity'.

Some time in the autumn of 1941, when it seemed possible, even probable, that Japan would join Germany in striking at Russia, Adela (who still, clad in a flowing Japanese gown, presided merrily at youth club dances and other functions) and her former Guild of Empire aide, Mrs Vera Parkinson, contacted Stephensen and his group with the suggestion of forming an Australia First Movement. At a meeting held in October— only ten people were present, including Adela Walsh and Mrs Parkinson: the Australia First Movement never mustered more than sixty-five members—Stephensen was elected president and Adela one of two organizers. The name, and indeed the aims, of the movement were almost certainly influenced by America First, a group which included several United States senators and prominent businessmen, and whose star speaker was that dream prince of 1927, Colonel Charles Lindbergh, the flying fool turned political theorist. Lindbergh had since 1938 been a strong advocate of British, French and American neutrality in the event of a European war, and of allowing Germany to expand eastward into Russia. What, he argued, was the point of expending Americans in a war which was bound to devastate Europe and therefore facilitate the spread of communism? Was it a sin to be logical about this? As he put it in April 1941: 'A refugee who steps from the gangplank and advocates war is acclaimed as a defender of freedom. A native-born American who opposes war is called a fifth columnist.' Even after Pearl Harbour he was heard regretting that the white race was divided in the war, instead of being united against the 'Mongolian'.

Adela's eagerness to find a platform and to expand the opposition to conventional thinking about the war had led her into very strange company. Her fellow organizer, Leslie Cahill, was, like herself, an ex-communist: he urged the formation of a secret propaganda organization in the armed forces (with which Adela's son Richard was serving) to foment anti-British feeling and press for Australia's secession from the Commonwealth. Other associates included a clerk who considered Australians 'gutless swine of the highest order', had corresponded with leading Nazis, and had written in *The Publicist*: 'God damn our white-livered politicians and their service to the Bank of England and the International Jews.' If Adela attended (as did several undercover government agents) meetings of *The Publicist*'s Yabba Club in November 1941, she heard members applauding statements that England was 'buggered', that German bombing would soon bring submission, that Churchill was 'the greatest calamity that had ever befallen Britain', and that the British Empire had spread nothing but 'poverty, corrugated iron and dirt'. Realizing the danger as well as the futility of being associated with such random authoritarian cranks, she resigned from the Australia First Movement soon after the Japanese attack on Pearl Harbour, Hong Kong, Malaya, and Singapore in December 1941 (the sequel to a long economic blockade by Britain and America) had precipitated the Pacific war. She was, however, too late to escape the somewhat ponderous attentions of a Government now headed by John Curtin, who in the first world war, as a militant socialist, had fought with Adela in the anti-conscription campaign.

The scare of Japanese invasion brought panic plans for evacuating Australia north of the 'Brisbane Line'. Security police several times raided the Walshes' home at Wollstonecraft on the North Shore Line of Sydney, searching the house from top to bottom. No 'incriminating' evidence was found—the Walshes had been perfectly open in their controversy—but early in March 1942 daughter Ursula received a telephone call at work to say that her mother was being taken away for precautionary internment. About twelve other members of the Australia First Movement, and of the First Australia Movement, an organization of similar but even more farcical type in Western Australia, were also interned. In May Adela appealed to the Committee of the Supreme Court against detention without lawful justification. She was, she said, a loyal subject of the King. 'My mother', she continued, 'devoted her life to the welfare of the British nation and a statue to her memory was unveiled by Mr Baldwin. I am a sister of Dame Christabel Pankhurst, LL.B., who devoted her life to the welfare of the British nation. My sister's honour was conferred upon her by King George V, and I myself was honoured by His Majesty King George VI by the presentation of His Majesty's Coronation Medal.' She had, she claimed, devoted herself to the welfare of the Australian nation since she had arrived there in 1914. She had brought up seven children, all born in Australia, and her only son was serving with the army.

Her appeal was dismissed. Imprisonment was doubly distressing for her because Tom Walsh was, and had been for some time, gravely ill. Only the intervention of the family doctor prevented him from being moved, by government order, twenty miles inland. It was a sad end to a fighting partnership which had been a lively feature of Australian life for twenty-five years, a sad blow to their children, and a time of melancholy stock-taking for Adela herself. During her brief and fatal contact with Australia's caricature Fascist underworld, she must have glimpsed her own brand of imperialism and nationalism in a mirror at once distorting and chastening. She had time, too, to reflect on the dangers of political prophecy. Soviet Russia was now an ally of the Western Powers. America's isolationism had been torn to shreds by Japan's attempt to jackal Asia.

Certainly the core of Japanese resistance – until it was melted away by the atom bombs of August 1945 – proved, as Adela had said it would, extremely tough. Certainly Australia was forced to take Japan seriously even to the extent of refusing to send an army division to Burma at Churchill's urgent bidding. But in the months of her internment, which did not end until she hunger struck and the doctors at Concord Military Hospital refused to forcibly feed her, she must surely have absorbed the lesson which Sylvia had painfully learned: that the mania for finality, the excitement of theoretical confrontation, is a delusion whose seemingly brilliant light is reflected from all the autos-da-fé, the baleful, flickering, inquisitional will-o'-the-wisps of human history; that it is rooted deep in that *odium theologicum* which she had once so scornfully derided; that (in Christabel's terms) everyone, Conservative, Liberal, Socialist, Fascist, Nazi, Communist, or just plain Don't Know, is disabled by the subtle poison of original sin from coming anywhere near perfection; that it is better to light a small candle of justice in the dark than to seek to banish darkness by putting a torch to the all-consuming pyres of ideology. She may also have reflected that the Nazis had not abated their anti-Semitism (as she had rather coolly hoped that they might), and that the millions of Jews whom they were so busy exterminating were not all agents of amoral international finance or decency-sapping international communism. It must have struck her with sickening force that the holy war against Soviet Russia was (in the political philosophy which it had driven her to countenance) the one bad cause for which she – who had been jailed in Manchester, London and Melbourne – had been imprisoned. She – more than Sylvia, more even than Christabel, her mother's implacably zealous, though banished, daughter – must have suffered, and must have repented. For never again did she dabble in the politics of power.

CHAPTER TWO

COUNSEL FOR ETHIOPIA

While Adela was embarking on a conducted government tour of Japan, Sylvia was advising America to start a full-scale economic boycott of that country to free China from the Fascists of the Far East. Waiting for Mussolini, Humpty-Dumpty-like, to come off the fence and meet his appointed doom, she and Corio had to endure a further instalment of British appeasement of Italy, including a bribe offer of eight million tons of coal a year to offset the loss of supplies from Germany. Under government instructions, the British Council produced a pamphlet with a preface by Lord Halifax which, to say the least, bent over backwards to be fair to Mussolini.

> The Italian genius [wrote Lord Halifax] has developed a highly authoritarian regime which, however, threatens neither religious nor economic freedom, nor the security of other European nations. It is worthwhile to note that quite fundamental differences exist between the structure and principles of the Fascist state and those of the Nazi and Soviet states. The Italian system is founded on two rocks: first, the separation of Church and state, and the supremacy of the Church on matters not only of faith but of morals; second, the rights of labour. The political machinery of Fascism is, indeed, built up on trade unionism, while that of the German state is built up on the ruins of the German Labour movement ...

As if this was not enough, Churchill, as late as May 1940, wrote to Mussolini:

> I declare I have never been the enemy of Italian greatness nor even at heart the foe of the Italian lawgiver. Down the ages above all other calls comes the cry that the joint heirs of Latin and Christian civilization must not be ranged against each other in mortal strife. Hearken to it, I beseech you in all honour and respect, before the dread signal is given. It will never be given by us.

Sylvia, noting that neither Churchill nor Lord Halifax made mention of Italy's crimes against Ethiopia, fretted for the Duce to give the signal for mortal strife.

In the meantime, during the teasing reprieve of the phoney war, there were some skirmishes to be fought on the home front. First there was the Communist Peace Front to be exposed and demolished. In her all-embracing anti-Fascist enthusiasm she had been willing to tolerate a number of dubious fellow travellers. But when the London Federation of Peace Councils, of which she was vice-president, supported the Moscow line of an immediate truce with Hitler and acceptance of Nazi and Fascist conquests, and denounced the war as one of clashing and equally repre-hensible imperialisms, she resigned with a maximum of publicity. In a three-thousand-word letter, which went to Stalin as well as to Mrs Phoebe Pole, chairman of the London Federation, she reviewed the dismal record of appeasement, and concluded: 'Britain must go to war soon or late. Better let it come now, in defence of international justice, than finally for ourselves alone, with every pledge broken, every friend betrayed and vanquished.' She criticized *Plebs*, the journal of the National Council of Labour Colleges, for ridiculing the Allies' outmoded clinging to an economically chaotic small-nation sentimentality, and praising the Nazis for having built up a new economic system based on sound Marxist principles and offering a grand economic plan for Europe as a whole. The pacifism of superior persons of the saintly socialist type came under her frown in the person of Miss Muriel Lester, head of the Kingsley Hall Settlement in Bow, and a former disciple of Gandhi's attitude of non-resistance. In an open, almost playful, letter to President Roosevelt, Miss Lester had begged America *not* to join in the war. Instead, America should act (as indeed she had been wont to act since Versailles) as a purveyor of moral indignation and moral perspective.

> Appeal to us [twittered Miss Lester], one week for the sake of our old architecture; the next for the sake of our forests, fields and gardens; the next for the sake of youth and old age. Lecture us. Make fun of us. Pull our leg. Talk plainly to us in the name of God. Please show us British up – how very like Hitler we are in our race pride in India and our broken promises in Palestine. And show Hitler up – how like he is to us in his constantly assumed air of conscious recti-tude. Show us that it is not worse to covet Empire than to cleave to Empire.

If Britain learned humility and saved her soul, that would be clear spiritual gain, and she was almost certain to lose the war, since the Germans, in Miss Lester's view, were better soldiers and were led by 'a genius, however unpredictable'.

To Sylvia who, when she damned the first world war, had fought it, not lobbed pious platitudes at it, this was not Common Frontery but sheer, half-baked effrontery. It was, she rapped in *New Times,* 'humanitarianism gone blind and mad'. How could Miss Lester compare British institutions to Nazi slavery, or political blunders in Palestine with the mass murder of Jews? What about the almost complete independence of the Dominions, and the plan to give independence to India and other colonies after the war? And then, to call Hitler a genius! 'How appallingly Nazi propaganda has made its way, that the impression that such a monster is a genius should be produced in the mind of an English humanitarian! How strange that a woman whose life is dedicated to the education of the poor children of the East End slums can contemplate the victory of a power which would oppress these little ones, and force upon their young minds the cruel Nazi precepts of hatred and servility!' In an article written for the *Palestine Post* she denounced the Nazi view of women as breeders for the warrior state. 'We suffragettes who led the world struggle for women's citizenship', she urged, 'have a mission in the present crisis. We must aid our sisters in other lands to regain their lost freedom, and start by regaining our own!'

Her concern to prevent the victimization and exploitation of women in wartime led her to form, in October 1939, a Women's War Emergency Council to bring pressure on the Government to raise war separation allowances and old-age pensions and to insist that the price of butter, sugar, tea, cheese and other basic foods should be strictly controlled. At the beginning of November the Ministry of Food received a well-briefed deputation headed by Sylvia: but some of the wind was taken out of her sails when one of the two officials who received the deputation told her that he had read with interest her book *The Home Front* about civilian conditions in 1914-18, and asked her advice about opening a chain of government cost-price restaurants similar to those she had pioneered in Bow. In February 1940 friendly M.P.s, including Reginald Sorensen, arranged for her council to hold a meeting in a committee room of the House of Commons. M.P.s of all parties attended to hear her outline her programme of action. It was time, she insisted, to drop the old, cruel method of a means test for each family to assess the amount of separation allowances. This always bred bureaucracy, callousness and delay. A flat-rate system would avoid confusion and injustice and be much easier and cheaper to run. 'A considerable part of my adult life', she said, 'has been taken up with correspondence with government departments on behalf of poor folk who could not get the sums to which they were entitled.' By July, the *Star* reported that 'no small part of the pressure which led the Government to increase allowances for servicemen's wives and children has been due to Miss Pankhurst.'

In a New Year's editorial in *New Times,* she claimed that Ethiopia's continuing and unaided struggle against the dictator upon whom British politicians were still disgracefully fawning underlined an important point about the war. It should be one not only for international justice but for abolition of the colour bar: and Britain, with the largest coloured empire the world had ever seen, should give a clear lead. British colonial labour conditions and wages were often atrocious, and 'it would be well to consider giving outposts of Empire, whether Dominions or colonies, elected representatives at Westminster, as France's overseas possessions have in the French Parliament.' She predicted further Nazi aggression in Scandinavia and a German onslaught on Russia – especially after the apparent revelation of Soviet military weakness in Finland. But all this was a mere tuning of the engine of her zeal. On June 10th, 1940, Mussolini at last declared war, and Sylvia rapidly slipped into top anti-Fascist gear.

'Blackshirts of the Revolution,' Mussolini ranted from his balcony in the Piazza Venezia in Rome, 'men and women of the Empire and of the Kingdom of Albania, hearken! An hour marked by destiny is striking in the sky of our country ... Proletarian and Fascist Italy is on her feet, strong, proud and united as never before!' Churchill now produced his 'Jackal of Europe' phrase, and Corio, in *New Times,* issued a *Call to Italian Anti-Fascists.* 'At last! The long, agonizing vigil is over. The Fascist regime is an open and declared enemy. Mussolini is the traitor, not we! To his call to arms we answer: Yes, we shall fight, proud to do so at last – against you ... We shall free the Italian name from the shame you have cast upon it. Hitler and Mussolini are now one: united in crime and dis-honour they shall fall together.' *New Times* published the first of many protests against the internment of 'loyal' aliens – Italian, German and Polish – while known Fascists were left at liberty. The details were so minute and indisputable that the Home Secretary was forced to take appropriate action in some cases, and in August Sylvia received a type-written postcard signed 'Italian London Fascists' which read:

Madame Pankhurst: The invasion of England will take place in a few days. We shall punish you by order of our Leader as well you deserve for the article in your filthy paper. Your house in Woodford will be bombed and burned to the ground. Hitler knows your address. You will pay with your life if you publish any name in your paper. Do not dare to go out in the dark or you will be murdered.

This was encouragement indeed: and it was a novel experience for Sylvia to have the police guarding rather than arresting her. It braced her to try once more to bring Shaw to the point of public repentance. Corio, who in *New Times* wrote under the pen-names of 'Crastinus' or 'Luce', recalled how Shaw had rushed semi-facetiously to the defence of Mussolini in 1935, maintaining that the Duce differed from other politicians only in doing what they longed to do but dared not. Sylvia begged her old adversary to recant his praise of the corporate state and to back her campaign for the liberation of Ethiopia ('it has always seemed to me a terrible thing that a mind so acute as yours was unable to pierce the sham and cruelty of Fascism'). Shaw refused to be drawn and produced one of the red herrings of which he had so plentiful a supply. 'Dear Sylvia,' he replied, 'As you are now Counsel for Ethiopia, why do you not show how dearly we are paying for the wicked South African tyranny which forbids a black man to acquire a skilled trade? We now need a million or more skilled mechanics, and nothing but our own Hitlerism is preventing us from having two million Zulus making weapons for us faster than we could use them up. *There* is something for you to get on with.' Shaw had no more intention in 1940 than in 1910 of acting as the tame tomcat of any Pankhurst, even of Sylvia, his 'idiot-genius'.

The Emperor Haile Selassie had been flown by the Royal Air Force to the Sudan. There in the Pink Palace of Khartoum, as the symbol of Ethiopian resistance, he was treated with a deference which had been lacking during the five years of his exile in England. But despite their politeness, British officers in Khartoum showed marked reluctance to accept either the Emperor or the Ethiopian patriots in the field as allies. In their view the war had begun in 1939, not 1935, and Ethiopia was therefore to be classified as Occupied Enemy Territory. It was not until (on Wingate's advice) the Emperor telegraphed direct to Churchill that he was allowed to launch his own campaign. His tiny army of liberation (Gideon Force, named and led by Wingate) was composed of a thousand Ethiopian refugees and the same number of Sudanese troops. It joined with the guerrillas to rout a force twenty times larger, led by the Italian General Nasi, in the mountains of Gojjam. From the coast of the Red Sea, British and French troops under General Sir William Platt swept the Italians from the heights of Keren in Eritrea, then drove south to Addis Ababa.

Yet at first this success seemed improbable. It seemed more likely that in the absence of any firm plan for Ethiopia the Italian plan to advance from Eritrea and Ethiopia and join Rommel's troops in Egypt would be achieved. Sylvia redoubled her efforts to force the claims of Ethiopia on the public and the Government. To her it was a vital campaign, without which the moral symmetry of the Allied cause was incomplete. But in pressing its importance with the passionate tenacity that T. E. Lawrence had deployed to get 'justice' for his Arabs, she necessarily lacked the grand (and so ostensibly anti-Abyssinian) perspective of Churchill and the supremos of Allied strategy. It seemed to Sylvia that, apart from wanting to expend as few men and as little material as possible in a comparatively minor theatre of war, there was an air of reluctance and regret that Mussolini had been stupid enough to force intervention in Ethiopia, and so add a tiresome chore to a list of commitments already intolerably long. Why, she demanded (at a time of chronic shortage of war material),were not guns, ammunition, and even tanks, being supplied to the Abyssinian guerrillas, who had fought almost barehanded for five years? Why couldn't the Allies mount an intensive bombing of Italian troops in the outposts which they had been forced to garrison to control guerrilla raids? Why not arrange continuous morale-raising (and, for the Italians, morale-sapping) radio broadcasts from the Sudan, Kenya and British Somaliland? Why not make use of letters found on dead or captured Italian soldiers? Why was British propaganda so feeble, so deplorably un-anti-Italian? Apart from deluging officials of the Ministry of Information, from the minister (Brendan Bracken) downwards, with long, immensely urgent letters of criticism and advice, she paid several personal visits to the ministry, storming and weeping with such complete abandon that bewildered male officials sent for another ex-suffragette (Miss Elsie Bowerman, who had been Christabel's election agent at Smethwick in 1918, had edited the Women's Guild of Empire *Bulletin,* and was now briefing M.O.I. speakers) to try and cope with her. Yet one man from the ministry, sent unwillingly and rather tremblingly to placate Miss Pankhurst, found her very different from the termagant her letters had led him to expect. She received him, he remembers, in a study of almost incredible untidiness, books and papers piled everywhere—a magnificent working intellectual disarray. She was not, as he had feared, a cantankerous, knotty idealist, but 'a charming, slightly scatty, immensely overworked, rather bewildered old lady'.

In *New Times* and through her squad of sympathetic M.P.s, she agitated for a definite statement from Anthony Eden, the Foreign Secretary, that full Ethiopian independence was 'an essential British war aim', for the withdrawal of recognition of Italian rule, and for the inclusion of the Ethiopian national anthem (which, she suggested, was omitted in base deference to South African colour prejudice) among those of other Allies which were commonly broadcast by the B.B.C. In the Commons, R. A. Butler, then Under-Secretary of State for Foreign Affairs, admitted the logic of this last point, but claimed that the already large number of national anthems could not conveniently be added to. Winston Churchill was, to Sylvia, as suspect and supercilious in his attitude towards a seem-ingly unwanted ally as he had been towards the suffragettes. 'We British', he said in a broadcast made late in December 1940, 'doubted whether the Ethiopians had reached a stage in their development which warranted their inclusion in the League of Nations.' How dare he speak so slightingly of the people who even as he broadcast were helping to pin down Italian troops who might otherwise have turned the scales against the Allies in North Africa? Was it possible that British lukewarmness stemmed from clauses in the Anglo-Italian treaties of 1891 and 1894 which gave Italy a 'sphere of interest' in Ethiopia?

In February 1941 Haile Selassie left Khartoum to accompany Gideon Force into his own land, and on May 5th rode on a white charger into Addis Ababa, just as Marshal Badoglio had done six years before. At the same time, the *New Times* bookshop in Farringdon Street, London, was wrecked by an explosion—and Silvio Corio, from a B.B.C. studio, broadcast an appeal to the workers of Italy. 'Nobody in Italy', he said, 'desired war: still less this war, at the side of the barbarians of the North against whom our fathers conspired and fought in the streets and on the fields of battle. Why did Fascism send you to Libya and Ethiopia? To conquer colonies, when Italian land is left untilled for want of labour, implements and capital. Where are your trade unions, your co-operative societies?' War against England, he pointed out, was fratricidal in a special sense, since the British, more than any other people, had helped Italians to achieve national unity. Italy was the despised partner of Germany, to whose factories tens of thousands of Italians were being sent to forced labour and death. Italian workers should sabotage the Fascist regime in every possible way, and Italian soldiers should lay down their arms (they had already done so en masse in North Africa, where the Eighth Army talked of the surrender of 'about five acres of officers and two hundred acres of other ranks') and join 'the only war worth fighting, the war for freedom'.

But the war for freedom in Ethiopia, as Sylvia already suspected, was to involve a long and bitter conflict with the equivocal liberators from Britain. It was a conflict which she and Corio, unhampered by the diplomatic niceties which bound the Emperor (who, she complained, was held virtually a prisoner in his own capital), were peculiarly well-fitted, and rampantly keen, to wage. The most jealously watchful Ethiopian of all, Sylvia, with the experience of seven years as the Emperor's shadow Minister of Propaganda, prepared to attack a new front of official treachery, and in doing so reached a peak of strident, magnificently biased, but undoubtedly effective journalism and political lobbying remarkable even in her career. The flailing, all-action technique which she had developed in controversy with Asquith, Lloyd George, Lenin, the Communist Party of Great Britain, the laggards of Labour, Mrs Grundy, departments of government, George Bernard Shaw, and the elder Pankhursts, was now employed against all those (and there were many) who were content to leave Ethiopia as a British military protectorate, part of an East African bloc ruled from Nairobi, until the war was well over, and it was possible to see which way the Italian cat had finally jumped.

Sylvia was indignant that Miss Margery Perham, Reader in Colonial Administration at Oxford University (and even then accounted one of the world's leading authorities on Africa), was chosen to lecture officially on Ethiopia. This was no time, she thought, for a quibbling academic approach, lacking in personal knowledge and emotional involvement: and most certainly no time for Miss Perham, under the aegis of the Ministry of Information, to describe Italy as 'a wounded buffalo, poorly treated at the Versailles Peace Conference', to praise the money poured into the Italian colonies in Africa to build fine Roman roads, to imply that Ethiopians were so backward and disunited that they needed British supervision, and to plead for the return of Eritrea to Italy after the war. In the next few years Sylvia kept whacking away at the theory of Ethiopian incompetence and Italian efficiency wherever it raised its persistent head. Now it was a book by Christopher Hollis, arguing against the Ethiopian claim to Eritrea and sneering that, as a result of the Italian defeat, Ethiopia could return to 'the primal beastliness in which it has lived since the beginning of time'. Now it was *The Times,* also questioning the wisdom of adding Eritrea (many of whose inhabitants, it alleged, had willingly fought against Ethiopia) to Haile Selassie's 'Empire', and applauding news of good Italo-British relations — 'British troops, both officers and men, find many pleasant social contacts with the Italians', it reported. 'Several successful football matches and boxing contests have been arranged.' Fascists and their dupes, wrote Sylvia, 'voicing perverted doctrines of cruelty and oppression, red-handed with the blood of Ethiopian men, women and children, are no fit companions for the armies of liberation.' *The Times* complained of savage reprisals against Italians, but *New Times* quoted Sir Sidney Barton, British minister to Ethiopia until 1939, on the remarkable restraint shown by Ethiopians despite Italy's shocking atrocity record.

When the *News Review* and the *Irish Times* lauded the scientific efficiency of Italian administrators, and even hinted that a heavy hand had been necessary to bring any sort of order out of tribal chaos, Sylvia retorted: 'We are all enthusiasts for modern science, but if the price of it is enslavement to an alien power, the most primitive plough will always be preferred to the latest tractor.' Straight roads were no solace to widowed, childless mothers who had often been raped after being forced to watch their husbands and children beaten to death. 'There are higher and more vital things than roads and modern buildings. Take the canning factories of Norway — oh, no doubt the Nazi industrialists, with all their science, will have improved them, or their apologists will claim they did.' By the end of 1941 *World Review,* in its 'Cheers and Bouquets' column, was praising Lord Beaverbrook ('for doing in tank production what he had done in planes') and Miss Sylvia Pankhurst ('who has already started the battle against post-war appeasement of Italy'). In 1942 she intensified that battle. Why, she demanded, had the British military authorities in Ethiopia turned down an offer from highly qualified Jewish doctors in Palestine to help provide a badly needed health service in Ethiopia? Was this another example of anti-Semitism in that diehard army clique which had always admired the dictators and had choked with rage when, in the late 1930s, Leslie Hore-Belisha, the Jewish War Minister, had tried to modernize and democratize the officer corps? The Anglo-Ethiopian agreement, with its insulting decision to keep Ogaden province — which had been forcibly torn from Ethiopia by the Italians — under British military rule was, she stated, as harsh as if it had been aimed at a defeated foe: and indeed, for many months the British Government had habitually referred to Ethiopia as 'occupied enemy territory'.

It was high time that ordinary Britons knew something of the behaviour of their diplomatic and military representatives in and around Ethiopia during the Italian usurpation. The horrors and corruption of the Fascist regime, said *New Times* under the headline THE EMPEROR'S FIGHT WITH HIS LIBERATORS, had been suppressed not only in communiqués issued to the Italian press, but in the dispatches sent back to London by sympathetic British officials, whose social relations with Italian officials had not been disturbed by massacres, torture, the burning alive of entire families for possessing a portrait of their Emperor, religious persecution, the gallows in the market place of Addis Ababa always dangling their victims. Captain Erskine, British consul at Gore in Ethiopia, and Sir Stewart Syme, Governor of the Sudan, had sent back reports of the 'good show' the Italians were putting up, which would benefit trade with surrounding territories. The British authorities in the Sudan had even betrayed the activities of secret emissaries sent by Haile Selassie to make contact with resistance groups.

> These high authorities, great experts in colonial government and in the proper method of dealing with African peoples, persistently averred that the Duke of Aosta, who succeeded the butcher Graziani as viceroy, was far too friendly, far too true an Etonian, far too good a sportsman ever to permit a declaration of war on Great Britain. The Duce, too, despite his humble origin, was a fine fellow, the type of ruler under whom colonial government and expansion could flourish.

In 1943 she revealed that the B.B.C. had asked *New Times* to provide information about Ethiopia's progress, stipulating that it should contain 'nothing that would upset the Italians, as they are now' (the Allied invaders of Italy were being helped by ex-Fascist troops and partisans) 'our co-belligerents'. This, commented Sylvia, was 'a casual, though painful, indication of how some people regard the war and its vast issues', and added that she had been told that official sensitivity was such that articles in the *Eighth Army News* complaining of softness towards known Fascists —and of the profiteering of Italian shopkeepers—had been suppressed.

Her swashbuckling independence and hefty swipes at the iniquities of her own side did not shake the loyalty of her supporters, nor prevent her from securing big names for her periodic Ethiopian rallies in London. In

Sylvia Pankhurst photographed at 'West Dene' on the eve of her departure for Addis Ababa, June 1956

Above: September 28th, 1960: Sylvia Pankhurst's coffin is carried out of Holy Trinity Cathedral, Addis Ababa, after the funeral service

July 14th, 1964: suffragettes lay flowers of tribute at the foot of Mrs Pankhurst's statue, near the Houses of Parliament

March 1942, at a meeting held to celebrate the final breaking of Italian armed resistance in Ethiopia, she persuaded the United States ambassador, John G. Winant, Soviet Russia's ambassador, Ivan Maisky, the New Zealand high commissioner, and the counsellor of the Chinese embassy to speak under her chairmanship. The following month she was optimistic-ally inviting businessmen interested in trading with Ethiopia to contact *New Times,* and in August the Emperor's principal private secretary wrote informing her that a street in Addis Ababa had been named after her 'according to the instruction of His Imperial Majesty, in remembrance of your good work for Ethiopia'.

She now, like Lady Astor, possessed the diplomatic immunity of a national institution. But her well-informed needling did—as it was intended to—get right under the skin of some members of the Govern-ment. A *New Times* article of April 1944 attacked new plans to bar Ethiopia's access to the sea in Eritrea, alleged that there was talk of adding some of Ethiopia's territory to the British-controlled Sudan, and charged the British authorities with gross breach of faith in attempting to dis-member the country—and in their intention to fake a plebiscite supporting their aims. This article, like others, led to questions being asked in Parlia-ment. Instead of (as Eleanor Rathbone demanded) giving an assurance that no such plebiscite was being contemplated, Brendan Bracken, the Minister of Information, fumed that Miss Pankhurst's attack on England was 'worthy of Goebbels. It has insulted the British troops who rescued Ethiopia.' *New Times* was, in his opinion, 'a poisonous rag'. Into it, certainly, with Mrs Pankhurst dead and Christabel and Adela, for different reasons, *hors de combat,* Sylvia poured vials of wrath and scorn copious enough to have satisfied all three. For until Christabel produced *Present and Future,* any journal edited by a Pankhurst had lived a dangerous life.

New Times was prominent in the outcry when Sir Oswald and Lady Mosley, who had been allotted a four-room flat in Holloway prison and allowed to cook their own meals and to pay other detainees to perform domestic chores, were released in November 1943 on medical advice. Why release Mosley when many humble aliens, without money or influence, who were innocent of any connection with Nazism or Fascism and had lived in Britain for more than twenty years, were still interned? Now that Italy was in the process of being liberated and Mussolini (having been deposed and imprisoned by the Fascist Grand Council and flamboy-antly rescued from the Gran Sasso by helicopter) was president of a puppet German state, under virtual house arrest at Gargnano on Lake Garda

10

(where he continued to weave fetching personal myths in press interviews—'I am not a statesman,' he said. 'I am more like a mad poet'), Corio took up the question of which Italy the Allies should deal with. Had it really been necessary to parley with Badoglio, the man who had murdered his way to Addis Ababa with poison gas? If there were excuses for that, might they not be found for retaining the monarchy which had helped Mussolini to power, and for negotiating with the Papacy, which had done nothing to oppose Fascism and had congratulated Franco on a 'Christian victory'? The monarchy and all its ramifications must be rooted out. Italy must become a republic. And surely it was possible for the Allies to find honest men with whom to share the difficult period of transition, instead of accepting brand-new ex-Fascists on their own dubious terms?

Sylvia found the same willingness to use handy administrative tools, however morally tarnished, when, in November 1944, she made the long, thrilling journey to her Promised Land. She had been invited by the Emperor to come to Addis Ababa for the anniversary celebrations of his coronation, and to make a personal inspection of the site, and an assessment of the needs, of the Princess Tsahai Memorial Hospital. Launched by her in October 1942, soon after the death of Princess Tsahai, one of the Emperor's daughters, who had trained as a nurse in England, this project aimed not only to provide Ethiopia's first really modern hospital, but to establish a medical school to train Ethiopian doctors (as late as 1965 it was estimated that there were fewer than fifty of them). She saw the project, for which she had assembled an impressive council and a board of honorary medical advisers headed by Lord Horder, the royal physician, and for which she was tireless in raising funds, as an earnest of the good faith of ordinary British citizens (as opposed to the British Government and British military authorities) towards Ethiopia.

With official backing from the Ministry of Information (despite Brendan Bracken's attack on her in the Commons) she left Liverpool early in October in a sea convoy, arriving in Alexandria five weeks later. From Cairo she flew, in a plane full of naval and army officers, to Asmara in Eritrea. Now sixty-two, and never in robust health, she gasped for breath as the plane climbed to high altitude. But she gasped with indignation when she met the guests and heard the conversation during luncheon at M.O.I. headquarters in Asmara. There was 'an Ethiopian gentleman whom I afterwards learned is locally known as the Eritrean Quisling', and Dr Ullendorf, a young Palestinian Jew who was editing the *Eritrean Weekly News*. Dr Ullendorf told her that he opposed the return of Eritrea to Ethiopia and favoured a mandatory British Government in both countries. He also chided her and *New Times* for being insufficiently critical of Ethiopia, and his sentiments seemed to be approved by others present. Then there was the shock of having her passport and yellow fever certificate checked by Italians (because of a shortage of British personnel, she was told); and the opinions which she heard expressed at the British Institute and in the mess of the British Military Administrations (housed in a fine building with magnificent gardens, formerly occupied by the Duke of Aosta) were hardly more sympathetic than those with which Dr Ullendorf had shaken her. 'I could not help feeling it a mistake', she said in a dispatch to *New Times*, 'to confide so important a propaganda medium as the sole weekly newspaper in the language of the people (Tigrinya) to an editorship sharply opposed to Eritrean reunion with Ethiopia and even to Ethiopia's independence'.

It was a relief to find herself on solid, wholesome, idealistic ground when, seated on a chair outside her hotel, she received a deputation of Muslim and Christian Eritrean reunionists who presented her with an address of welcome which read: 'Sword of the Press! We have read your paper with which you fight for our country, Hamasien, and our Motherland, Ethiopia.' They gave her, too—tired, smiling and blinking back tears in the sunlight—a bouquet of roses tied with the red, green and yellow colours of Ethiopia, and each of them shook her hand. 'I never knew a more poignantly touching experience,' she wrote, 'I knew they were appealing through me to all in Britain and throughout the world who have aided the Ethiopian people this far, to keep true to the end, to heed and understand their heartfelt desire for reunion.' She insisted on visiting the native quarter, a hot huddle of dusty, overcrowded shacks meanly supplied with water—a violent contrast, she noted, with 'the bright and gay city of trees and gardens devoted entirely to strangers from overseas'.

On the flight from Asmara to Addis Ababa, though once again faint from lack of oxygen, she gazed down with avid excitement on the beauty below. 'The Red Sea a lovely peacock blue, the Arabian shore to the left of us; the African shore to the right, where the glorious blue sky faded to pale, misty green on the horizon ... everywhere sea and sand peppered, by the dried up water courses, with tiny tufts of brownish green. The blue, blue sea turns green at the edge, with a fringe of white beaches.' After refuelling at Aden and another sharp ascent, she had to lie down to rest, but got up to watch the scene as the plane flew over Ethiopia. 'A lake, rivers, then a wide stretch of vivid green broken by water came into view ... A flock of white birds far beneath us ... the plateau. I cannot describe the feeling it gave me. Neat, walled-in houses stood, often raised up on a knoll or nestling by a stream, with the round grey roofs of the tukuls' (mud huts with clay floors and grass roofs). 'Except for extensive woods capping the heights, every yard seemed cultivated ... a marvellous country, greatly favoured by nature, peopled by industrious cultivators.' Then the capital, Addis Ababa, hardly more than a shanty town save for the imperial palace, the churches, the great mausoleum of the Emperor Menelik and the buildings put up for Italian officials, but nevertheless the city of Sylvia's dreams.

At the airport she was greeted by Ato Tafara Worq, the Emperor's private secretary, who drove her to a pleasant guest house set in large grounds – one of several formerly occupied by members of the Italian legation. The rooms were filled with flowers, red and white carnations, scarlet and pink geraniums. A log fire burned in the hearth in the living-room. There was a study for her, complete with ample desk and writing materials; two menservants to look after her, an Ethiopian army major to act as her escort, and Imperial Guards patrolling the gardens with their masses of arum lilies and vivid red canna, wide avenues of graceful eucalyptus trees and sloping stretches of lawn. When she had taken it all in, Sylvia asked briskly: 'What is the programme?' Ato Tafara Worq replied: 'Complete rest for today – tomorrow you will see Their Majesties.' Later she was taken for a short drive. On returning she went straight to her desk to start the first of several enormous dispatches to *New Times*. 'I seem to be living in a dream,' she wrote, looking out over the grounds and patrolling guards and the clear, mild sunlight, seeing the silvery blue of the eucalyptus groves and the magnificent, lean lines of the hills surrounding the city. 'I was in Addis Ababa, strange yet familiar. The many photographs I had seen were now put together ... Ethiopian people in their traditional dress, with their donkeys and mules, their picturesque burdens – great black jars fastened by straps to the shoulders, baskets and basket tables, straw umbrellas, bundles of eucalyptus to burn under their ovens. A woman in a black cape riding a mule with an umbrella to shade her; a man, all in white, on a mule with a gaily embroidered scarlet saddle. I was enchanted and bewildered.'

Her painter's eye, long starved of light and loveliness, gloated on the exotic, eccentric surface texture of the land, which must have seemed like a magical fulfilment of the splendours of the childish imaginings of half a century ago in the sooty garden of the house in Russell Square. After a short, informal audience with the Emperor and Empress, she attended a banquet in the palace for the British delegation and members of the diplomatic corps in Addis Ababa. Unlike other correspondents, she found nothing absurd in the rich ceremonial, the tremendous flunkeydom, which surrounded the tiny figure of Haile Selassie.

> The servants who waited on us [she noted] wore the velvet uniform photographs of which I had seen in the American magazine *Life*. Terribly hot they must be in a tropical climate I thought, not realizing that all the year round Addis Ababa is neither hot nor cold. Nor did I realize how beautiful this uniform looks in the grey-walled palace – the coat of rich bottle green, the vest and trousers deep ruby crimson. They are straight, handsome men who wear it, and they served us with friendliness and grace. One great thing to learn in Ethiopia is this: the people are kind, from the highest to the most humble, they love to help you, but there is nothing servile about them.

Though still tiring easily in the high (8,000 feet) altitude, Sylvia's curiosity drove her to undertake, in the next few weeks, an energetic sightseeing tour – of schools, war orphanages, handicraft centres, a tobacco factory (managed by a Greek), a cotton factory at Dire Dawa (managed by a textile expert from Manchester), a cement factory and the government farm at Bishoftu. She watched abandoned Italian tractors and automobiles being ingeniously reconditioned, and was given a collection of Fascist atrocity photographs taken from dead or captured Italian soldiers – which she later put to frequent use. In a long broadcast from the radio station in Addis Ababa she spoke in glowing terms of what she had seen, and pledged herself to continue to work for Ethiopia and for reunion with Eritrea. She had been much impressed and angered by an interview with a Somali chieftain from the Ogaden, who, in traditional dress ('a sort of green cloth headgear, pink plaid skirt, with a string of amber beads on his wrist') came to spread his grievances before the sword of the press. Why, he asked, should not the people of the Ogaden be freed from military rule? British troops guarding the wells refused water to any Somalis who would not surrender their firearms – and some died of thirst rather than do this. Chiefs were under pressure to say that they wished to stay under British rule. Could she not make these facts known in her newspaper? Could she not! She also sent back a critical report of the new Anglo-Ethiopian agreement, signed while she was still in Addis Ababa, which not only set no time limit to British occupation of the Ogaden, but (in return for British control of railway, telegraph and other public services) made a miserly grant of three million pounds, spread over three years, for reconstruction – little enough for a country trying to recover from seven years of war, and almost insulting compared with the eighty-seven and a half million pounds granted to Italy by the United Nations. In a speech to the Ethiopia-Eritrean Association Sylvia gave full vent to her indignation. She recalled the leaflets, prepared in consultation with Haile Selassie and dropped by R.A.F. planes, promising reunion with Eritrea after the defeat of the Italians. Yet Italian judges and Italian Fascist law were being retained in Eritrea with the blessing of the British authorities; and she had heard reports that five Eritreans had been executed for the murder of one Italian ('for which I doubt not there was abundant provocation'), and a whole village machine-gunned for the murder of another. Italian judges must be removed and this hideous charge fully probed. Public meetings were forbidden in Eritrea, the Italian colour bar kept in force. 'What policy', she shouted, flaying her compatriots from her charmed circle of imperial privilege, 'lies behind this? Are we committing the dangerous folly of extending the hold of the Italians on the Horn of Africa? Can it be that Fascism, while being exterminated in Europe, is to be tolerated in Africa?'

The bitterness of her denunciations, the recklessness of some of her statements (even at dinner in the British embassy, she remarked of one official to whom she had taken a dislike that 'he was born half dead and now his age is telling against him') were at least intensified by the high emotion as well as the high altitude of Addis Ababa. She wept when she laid a wreath on the tomb of Princess Tsahai and on the monument to the victims of the Graziani massacre of 1937, and when, on Ethiopian Christmas morning (January 7th) she saw, among the three thousand school-children who assembled in the grounds of the palace to sing carols to the Emperor and to receive a gift from him, a whole class of crippled and wounded boys and girls – 'victims of Italian ferocity whose scars attest the wickedness of Fascism'. Her identification with the sufferings of Ethiopia was such that, in the early hours of Christmas morning she, normally anything but a churchgoer, attended a service in the Church of the Saviour of the World, and did not turn her wonderful battle map of a face aside when the resplendent Coptic priest, dipping his hands in holy water, touched her lightly on the cheek and lips. For her, it was a moving re-dedication to a fighting cause.

A life of catapult tensions had helped to propel her essentially un-scathed through the ambushes of a wearily obstructive world: ambushes which would have stopped anyone of less psychological momentum dead in her tracks. Yet it was a comfort to her in her sixties to know that in the remorseless activity which stretched ahead she would have a new helper by her side. Her son Richard, to whom she had dedicated *The Suffragette Movement* 'in the cherished hope that he may give his service to the collective work of humanity' was, though only seventeen, giving signs of tackling that mountainous assignment. Despite the unctuous gloom of newspaper predictions of 1928, his schooling had been uneventful; he had not withered in the glare of his mother's notoriety or suffered unduly from playground taunts. Already he showed a marked ability for historical research, and a keen desire to use it for the furtherance of his parents' crusade. In his mother's absence he had published a concise and useful Epitome of Ethiopian History in *New Times,* and an article on war criminals in which he pointed out that Italian offenders, because of their timely coat-turning, were likely to be treated with far greater leniency than their German and Japanese equivalents. 'Yet', he continued, on sound Sylvian lines, 'the Italian aggressions of 1896, 1912, 1935 and 1940 were not outshone in brutality by the Germans. The electrocution of the Senussis of Libya and the gassing and mutilation of Ethiopians were just as damnable as the Nazi burning and gassing of Poles and Jews.' Was there, he asked, a colour distinction even in the dark extremities of suffering? Was there to be an outcry about atrocities to Jews and gentiles, but silence about the agonies of Africans? When Sylvia returned to Woodford Green in the closing months of the war, she was full of a mother's pride as well as of the adventures of her great journey: a journey during which, with ungaggable integrity (or busybody insolence, accord-ing to one's interpretation), she had bitten the hand of the Government which had permitted her to go to Ethiopia, bitten it with a snarl so loud that it echoed about the troubled Horn of Africa for years to come.

PART SEVEN

THE PASSING OF
THE PANKHURSTS

CHAPTER ONE

ADELA AND CHRISTABEL

In 1943 two women—Dame Enid Lyons, widow of the former Prime Minister, and a Miss Tanguey—were elected to the Australian Federal Senate. But Adela, apart from the fatal bar of internment (however unjustly) as a bad security risk, had other preoccupations. Tom Walsh was mortally ill. Adela nursed him with all-absorbing devotion until his death in April 1943. After he died she was forced to sell their library and to work for her living: and during a war against which she had spoken, though for different reasons, almost as vehemently as against the war of 1914-18, it was hard for her to find a job. She got employment in the canteen of a munitions factory, but was dismissed. For a time she was nurse-companion to an old lady. She nursed her eldest, and favourite, daughter Sylvia through her last illness. Finally, she worked as a nurse in a centre for retarded children. She, who had begun her career at nineteen as a pupil-teacher in Manchester, whose winning ways with children had been noticed by other passengers on board the ship which had brought her to Melbourne in 1914, and who had brought up three step-children as well as four children of her own, found among these children set apart so inscrutably from conventional society (as she, through an excess of zeal, herself was), the best sphere for her dogged compassion, the best healer for her mental wounds.

As a socialist her editorship of *Dawn,* a magazine which aimed to root children in a soil of warm generosity, had been perhaps her most imaginative achievement; and her concern to give young people an outlet for their high spirits had been the best and most enduring part of her work for industrial peace. Like Mrs Pankhurst, she had recoiled from the specious but ultimately unspacious vistas of collectivism, and had ended by acting out in the most challenging form of personal involvement that faith in the family which she had so often proclaimed. Though she was not, like other members of the Australia First Movement, financially compensated for her internment by the government commission which, after sixty-nine sessions of evidence sifting, published its lengthy conclusions in 1946, she had already worked out her own necessary salvation. When her health failed and she had, reluctantly, to abandon her nursing, she lived with her children and spent much time with her grandchildren. She continued to read hungrily and widely, and just before her death in May 1961 at the Home of Peace Hospital in Wahroonga, Sydney, was received into the comprehensive Roman Catholic family. A friend of hers, she said — a Dominican nun — 'had made her feel important enough to join the Church'.

The Walshes' prophecy that unless the thrust of Asian discontent could be harnessed by Japan's New Order, it would be harnessed by communism was abundantly fulfilled. Adela saw the country for which she had spoken with such reckless acerbity crushed by atom bombs dropped from American planes. She saw America pouring out, in guilt, repentance and belated self-interest, money and propaganda to rebuild Japan as a bastion of anti-communism. She saw war in Korea, the proclamation of a communist republic in China, and America's obstinately continued backing of Chiang Kai Shek. She saw the wedge of communism split the Australian Labour Party into factions in the 1950s, the formation of an anti-communist Labour Party in 1955 and of the Democratic Labour Party in 1957. But she did not mount a platform in the Domain or get behind a typewriter to say 'I told you so'. She knew that her own salvation lay in the fact that she had been forced to turn her back on the scarecrow skeletons of ideology and to put her hand into the detailed, humbling wounds of flesh and blood as a final sacrifice to the Pankhurst daemon of service: and she knew that she could not make a campaign about that. She could only, in silence and faith, try to help some children.

Christabel, who had returned to California, this time to settle permanently, just before the war began, continued to view each successive tragedy of the nations as an omen of the Second Coming. Her adopted daughter Betty married an American, and Christabel pursued a pleasant social life as a high-level house guest, a role in which she did not forget a promise made at Chartwell to speak up for the justice of the Allied cause and the urgent need for America to join it. For about three months around the time of Pearl Harbour she was a guest in the palatial mansion of Mrs Francis de Lacy Hyde in Plainfield, New Jersey. Mrs Marjorie Greenbie, a fellow guest, remembers her vividly.

We usually [she writes] had breakfast with Christabel, and often long talks with her by the fire in the drawing-room in the evening.

I recall her as a rather gentle little lady with reddish hair. She never spoke of her suffrage activities, but she expounded at length a book on .the Second Coming which she was writing. What struck me was the clear logic of her remarks, which seemed irrefutable once one granted her premise, which we did not ... Another thing that struck me was that she, who had certainly thought the British Government something less than perfect in the days when suffrage was refused to women, now seemed to think it perfect in relation to India. In fact she was convinced that Britain was destined to carry the white man's burden for all coloured races, and was almost childishly amazed that lesser breeds without the law were not grateful for it. She used to look at us in surprise when we questioned the white man's right for ever to rule these lesser breeds and take the lion's share of their wealth. She was never shrill or difficult in argument, always gentle and courteous – but utterly impervious. Apart from what seemed to us her fixations, she was shrewd and apt in her comments. I remember one of her remarks about the American standard of living. 'The Americans', she said, 'are so wealthy because they have discovered the secret of insatiable desire.'

Though Christabel now seldom spoke of the fight for the vote, she was under pressure from old comrades to complete and publish her long-awaited account of it. In 1943 Annie Kenney (now Mrs Taylor) wrote her a long letter describing the tireless war work of women ('Is it not these women who are in very truth the servants of the Most High, keeping at bay the Evil One by incessant toil?'), and telling how she had opened her house at Letchworth at week-ends to friends in London, so that they could have two nights' sleep undisturbed by flying bombs. As a theosophist, she said, she was afraid that Christabel's religious approach was too narrow.

You know, Christabel, my dear, if what you are lecturing on is true, there are only a few millions who will be saved, the rest of us will still be here labouring in the vineyard to fulfil our mission to help in God's plan for the evolution and redemption of all mankind, North, South, East and West. I often think of our wonderful grandma, who used to say to us as children: 'Be careful how you use the sayings in the Bible, for Satan can quote the Bible to serve his own ends ... '

But most urgently of all, Annie wanted to know about the book. 'I do hope that you have written the real true history of our movement.'

Of the versions which had so far appeared, her own *Memories of a Militant*, she thought, came nearest to the truth.

> But what is *that* book compared to one written by *you*, the author and inspirer of the very movement itself? Who but you can ever give a true picture of your mother's schooldays, her romantic marriage, a wife, a young mother and a great leader? Who can speak as you can of her genuine *passion* for justice, her passionate indignation at *all* injustice? Is Sylvia's book to be the only one written by a Pankhurst to which film writers, historians etc. have to go for the history of your family and of the work that absolutely changed the position of women?

Could she not overcome her scruples about not publishing for fear of seeming to carp about episodes in Churchill's past in the midst of his heroic war leadership? A simple, gracious foreword would easily get over that difficulty. Annie revealed that she had recently been approached to advise about a film on the suffragettes. 'As sure as the sun shines, there will be young aspirants to film fame, sensing what they can do to make a name out of the Women's Movement.' Christabel must release her book. 'I feel in every fibre of my being that this is what your mother would have wished, and that it would give a wonderful finish to a great life ... Oh, Christabel, when we pass the border it is the records we leave behind that will mar or help the task that others have to perform ... '

But Dame Christabel, as American reporters called her, did not budge. Her typescript, though carefully edited, was not published until after her death. She was busy having her last major Second Adventist fling as one of the main speakers at a Christian Fellowship Bible Conference held in Los Angeles. Allied victory would come, she was sure, and despite the wreckage of war, material prosperity would increase. But sin, with all the humanly insoluble problems which it created, would remain. She hoped that after the war the churches of America, including those in Los Angeles ('that great stronghold of Christian witness') would 'play a great part in Christian evangelism, a sort of spiritual lend-lease, a consolation that will be more important even than gifts of food and clothing to the impoverished peoples of the world'. Journalist Alma Whitaker, interviewing Christabel for the *Los Angeles Times,* found her still wearing the kind of big black hat which she had begged her to throw away twelve years earlier. 'Christabel is with us again,' she wrote, under the headline PANKHURST TRADITION WHETS CHRISTABEL'S STEEL FOR SATAN, but now this remarkable Pankhurst is crusading against the Devil and all his works, instead of making life wretched for Britain's Parliament. She must have enjoyed that moment when King George VI made her a Dame Commander of the British Empire. For so many years during his reign she had been considered England's most preposterous brat! Her present crusade for 'the eradication of sin to follow in the wake of Allied victory' will be tougher. Aimée Semple Macpherson has not been able to achieve it in lo, these many years. But women owe a tremendous debt to Christabel. The least we can do is to further her crusade to the extent of our ability. If we exercise a tithe of the zeal that she shows, we can at least prove a dangerous subversive influence against His Satanic Majesty ...

By the end of the war, though, after more than twenty years of genteel if strenuous service to Second Adventism, Christabel eased off the speaker's circuit and settled down to become one of the pillars of the more stolid section of expatriate society in Hollywood. She was often to be seen walking the boulevards of Beverly Hills, a gently outlandish figure in her long flowing dress surmounted by a large picture hat, it might to be take tea with Dame May Whitty, the British actress and ex-suffragist, or to see Mary Pickford, who organized a feminist rally at which Dame Christabel spoke. She read omnivorously, enjoyed a local reputation as a shrewd observer of international politics, and several times appeared in this capacity, with other pundits, on television. She was a frequent attender at the Writers' Round Table, of which James Hilton, Richard Llewellyn, and that very conservative poet Alfred Noyes were prominent members. She retained her looks, and that air of faintly quizzical aloofness which had infuriated opponents and delighted supporters in the pre-1914 epoch. 'I think the term "lovely" particularly expresses Christabel,' writes Miss Jaime Palmer, who was an official of the Writers' Round Table. 'She had a flower-like quality, with clear white skin and a soft Madonna face. She was kind, but her eyes had an aloofness, as though she found it necessary constantly to guard against an invasion of her privacy. She always maintained this reserve, not inviting intimacy, and while listening with interest to the ideas of others, seldom spoke herself. Occasionally she acted as hostess for me, pouring tea, and was most gracious in that capacity.'

Useful legacies still, from time to time, fell her way: rather bizarrely in the case of Mrs Olivia Durand-Deacon, an elderly English widow whose corpse had been dissolved in a bath of acid by her murderer, John George Haigh, and who, in her will, bequeathed an annuity of two hundred and fifty pounds to Christabel. Among the earnest, affluent private debating societies which blossom and fade in the fertile self-importance of Hollywood residents, Dame Christabel flitted assiduously if rather ghostlily. There was the John O' London's Society of the British colony, and a 'world affairs' soirée at which she often closed the evening with a wide-ranging political commentary which usually ended on a Second Adventist note. She liked to attend summer concerts and winter recitals at the Hollywood Bowl, and for some five years lived as a paying guest with Mrs Shirley Jenney (an Englishwoman whose mother had worked for the W.S.P.U.) and her husband, a well-known physicist, in their English-style, half-timbered house. Mrs Jenney was a writer, but her main claim to local fame was as a clairaudient of the poet Shelley. The Jenney home, too, was a centre of that mildly intellectual, unmilitant sociologico-social life with which Christabel now filled the apparent vacuum of her retirement. It was as though that decade of ferocious precocity which began in 1905 had exhausted her capacity for major effort, and perhaps a quarter of a century of preaching the Second Coming justified a decade of harmless self-indulgence in a world which, as she had made so abundantly clear, could never be redeemed by human intervention. When she was seriously injured in an car accident in which the driver, a friend of hers, was killed, Christabel said, almost wistfully: 'You know, I am the one who should have died. I am not afraid of death. I believe in Heaven. But she *was* afraid.'

There was, in fact, a quality of dying fall about her last years. She seemed to be waiting to join Mother and the great company of the suffragette elect who had passed on to some ringing Valhalla of Higher Service. Though she seldom spoke of those days, though her typescript lay hidden in a trunk in the Jenney home, the piercing memories, the sharp animosities of the suffragette campaign, not the great blur of original sin and the far-off Divine Event, had the power to disturb her euphoric expatriate *persona*. She spoke with peculiar force and brilliance in February 1948 at a meeting commemorating the birthday of the American suffragist leader Susan B. Anthony, a character close to her own (less outspoken) convictions. Like Christabel, Susan Anthony, a bristlingly dedicated spinster, had achieved a kind of sublimated motherhood within the women's movement, and preached a 'new epoch of single women' who, unencumbered by husbands or maternal cares, would influence, even direct, the nation's affairs from their own homes. Hearing of Christabel's speech, Mary R. Beard, the historian, wrote from Connecticut to the Susan B. Anthony Memorial Committee in Los Angeles.

I wish I could have had a word with Christabel Pankhurst at the Susan B. celebration this time, for I knew her intimately in England during my almost three-year sojourn there at the beginning of this century. Mrs Pankhurst was so hospitable to my husband and me and we loved her so much at that time that I would have liked to hold Christabel's hand in mine and greet her again, however apart we may be now 'spiritually'.

In the last two years of her life, by which time she had moved to Ocean Avenue, Santa Monica, tentacles from the past reached out to tweak Christabel back into the arena of the Suffragette Fellowship, where hard knocks were still given and taken. By 1956 the Fellowship was buzzing with the news that Roger Fulford, the English historian, was writing a book about women's emancipation in Britain (published in 1957 under the title *Votes for Women*), and that there were signs that he would follow the Sylvia Pankhurst-George Dangerfield line and was taking much evidence from suffragists who considered that the last two years of Pankhurst militancy did more to postpone than hasten the granting of the vote. The buzz reached Santa Monica, and became louder after the publication of Fulford's book—which if anything exceeded the fears of the pro-Pankhursts. There were some sharp exchanges between Christabel and Mrs Teresa Billington-Greig, who in 1907, with Mrs Despard, had led the 'revolt' against Pankhurst 'despotism' which resulted in the formation of the Women's Freedom League; who had herself, in 1911, written a book highly critical of extremist militancy; and who was known to have supplied Fulford with ammunition. She wanted information about Christabel's later career in order to complete a lecture on the Pankhursts. Not only did Christabel refuse to give any information, but she questioned the value of harking back to the past. Men did not waste time, she said, on discussing how *they* got the vote. They concentrated on using it, and on persuading their womenfolk to use it, in such a way as virtually to monopolize the government of the nation. Why did not women who had fought to end such a state of affairs continue the struggle until it was really won, until women played their due part in the higher reaches of government, diplomacy, the law and the civil service?

Against her will, but bowing to the wishes of the Suffragette Fellowship,

Christabel agreed to record an interview for a B.B.C. television programme on the women's movement. The programme sparked off an old controversy when Lady Violet Bonham Carter (now Baroness Asquith of Yarnbury: the daughter of former Prime Minister Herbert Asquith) asserted that suffragettes had thrown red pepper at their political opponents. Exactly the opposite was the truth, said the Suffragette Fellowship: one militant had been nearly blinded by a fling of anti-suffragist red pepper. Angry letters were written to the B.B.C. and Christabel was distressed by the rumpus and confirmed in her view that the raking over of old ashes was a dangerous pastime. Yet before the end of 1957 she was caught up in a full-throttle controversy. Ever since 1934 she had smouldered with resentment about Dame Ethel Smyth's essay on Mrs Pankhurst, and regret that she had allowed her to publish it, even in a revision which, in her opinion, had not been nearly drastic enough. When she noticed a letter in the London *Sunday Times* from Herbert Van Thal appealing for material for a biography of Dame Ethel, she rushed into action, sending Mr Van Thal (who had been present at the memorable clash between the two women in Peter Davies's office) a long and minutely detailed analysis of what she considered objectionable or inaccurate in the essay, and strongly pleading that all mention of Dame Ethel's friendship with Mrs Pankhurst should be omitted from the memoir, and any account of her part in the suffragette movement kept to a minimum. When Christabel learned that Mr Van Thal had abandoned the project because he had discovered that Miss Christopher St John, herself an ex-suffragette, had nearly completed a biography, she immediately contacted her with a similar request to which (to the sad detriment of her book) Miss St John agreed.

On February 13th, 1958, only a few months after this act of strenuous piety to her mother's memory—an act which, as she told Mr Van Thal, had greatly eased her mind—Christabel (quite unexpectedly, for she had not been ill, had seldom, unlike Sylvia and Adela, known sickness) died. She was found by her landlady, bolt upright in a chair in her apartment in Santa Monica, facing the view of the Pacific which had been a particular delight of hers. ('Now deceased—Darling Christabel', wrote Mabel Tuke, in her late eighties, as she scored through yet another of the old, dear names in her address book.) She looked very much what, ever since 1918, she had in essence been—a handsome figurehead who never found a worthy prow after the suffragette ship, but lived on as a curious, well-preserved, much admired museum piece. The feeble spray of religious controversy had been a poor substitute, after all, for the blizzarding spume of a whole sea of enraged anti-feminists.

At the memorial service in the Church of St Martin-in-the-Fields, Trafalgar Square, she was firmly re-attached to her old vessel. Survivors of her pirate crew turned out in force with their campaign medals and ribbons (a woman who had lost hers had printed her prison sentences on a piece of paper and pinned it to her lapel). From the pulpit, eighty-six-year-old Lord Pethick-Lawrence spoke of Christabel as the most brilliant political tactician of her time, the Girl Who Slew the Dragon which guarded the Establishment against female intruders, one of the few people who 'changed the course of human history and changed it for the better'. No one found for her moving words of obituary such as Brailsford had conjured up for Mrs Pankhurst. The money raised for a permanent memorial was used not for a separate monument, but to add a plaque of the young Christabel to the existing statue of her mother. It was as the outrageously young, outrageously pretty and impertinent pirate chief defying the Government ('If it is necessary we shall not hesitate to burn a palace,' she had threatened in March 1912, just before her escape to Paris, 'we will terrorize the lot of you'), and not as the lively but pessimistic First Lady of Second Adventism, that she was remembered. The Son of God had caught her on the emotional rebound. But she had given her best to the burning love-hate affair of the pre-war women's movement.

CHAPTER TWO

GOD BLESS YOU, MADAM

While Adela, from the wreckage of her political career and of personal bereavement, slowly constructed a new and healingly obscure usefulness in social service and grandmotherhood, and Christabel drifted to her strange end in Santa Monica, Sylvia continued publicly to crackle and coruscate with a display of virtuoso Ethiopian fire works until the very moment of her death. On her return from Addis Ababa in 1945 she toiled tremendously to present Ethiopia's claims to repossession of the former Italian colonies of Eritrea and Somalia. Not only did she hold public meetings, lobby M.P.s, lead parades of women bearing posters horrific with pictures of Italian atrocities, agitate in *New Times,* and go to Paris to pester delegates to the peace conference, but she wrote a small library of books, booklets and pamphlets which were sent to delegates of the United Nations Organization.

In her view, as presented in her booklet *The Ethiopian People: Their Rights and Progress,* British and French Somaliland, as well as Eritrea and Somalia, should have been joined to Ethiopia to form a natural geographic and economic unit. During the sixty years of Italian colonial rule, she claimed, many people had emigrated from Eritrea and Somalia to Ethiopia, where they had been given full citizenship and even posts in the Government. Racial discrimination, economic stagnancy, and slavery (both open and in the form of forced labour) were the hallmarks of Italian 'civilization'. She quoted the evidence of European travellers and explorers, notably Henry Salt's *A Voyage to Ethiopia* (1809) as proof that in the early nineteenth century Eritrea was regarded as part of Ethiopia. She denied that the Somalis were 'natural enemies' of Ethiopia; that Ethiopia would be unable to prevent the outbreak of murderous civil war between pro- and anti-Ethiopian factions; that (as many experts maintained) Eritrea and Somalia would suffer economically under the rule of an Emperor hard put to it to finance basic developments in his own unexpanded dominion; and that British military administration of the Ogaden was necessary to prevent serious incidents on the border with Somalia.

She had hoped that the victory of the Labour Party in the general election of 1945 (her old friend and benefactor Frederick Pethick-Lawrence, soon to become Lord Pethick-Lawrence, was made Secretary of State for India) might bring greater sympathy for her point of view. But she was mistaken. The tactics of the Cold War meant that Britain — and even the United States, which had not recognized the Italian regime in Ethiopia — were ready, like Soviet Russia, to bid for influence in Italy by negotiating for a return of Eritrea or Somalia, or parts of both (the permutations varied bewilderingly in the next four years). Ethiopia was not represented at the conference which worked out the terms of peace with Italy, Marshal Graziani was only mildly punished (and not even tried for his terrorist atrocities in Ethiopia). Sylvia pumped a constant stream of protestant letters to a largely hostile or apathetic press, and encouraged reunionists in Eritrea and ex-Italian Somaliland to demonstrate with extra verve in order to bring pressure on U.N.O. By 1947 Italian newspapers were grumbling about her part in provoking serious riots in Mogadishu, which broke out again in 1948 and 1949 in defiance of a ban on demonstrations imposed by the British military authorities, and in which many lives were lost. In 1949 the *Giornale d'Italia* charged her with the 'principle moral responsibility' for bloodshed in a clash between police and enthusiasts of the Somali Youth League. Towards the end of that year, however, the issue was settled when the United Nations voted in favour of a ten-year Italian trusteeship in Somalia, with General Nasi (who had been Graziani's deputy in Ethiopia, and had been listed as a war criminal) as administrator.

U.N.O. IS DEAD, proclaimed Richard Pankhurst in *New Times,* and Sylvia led another poster parade from Fleet Street to the Houses of Parliament. She also blasted *The Times* for asserting that Ethiopia had no indigenous culture, no art, and no notated music ('Has some peevish spirit of colonialism contributed to this deplorable exhibition of insular lack of knowledge?'), and stated that there was an ever-growing stream of refugees to Ethiopia from the 'Italian terror' in Somalia. But flail as she might, her cause seemed in danger of total defeat. In the summer of 1950 a polyglot U.N. commission consisting of representatives of Norway, Burma, Pakistan, Guatemala and (this she considered a vile insult) South Africa, visited Eritrea to sound local opinion. Only Norway recommended the restoration of the country to Ethiopia. Other suggestions included the creation of an independent sovereign state of Eritrea. Not until December did there come a gleam of light — when the General Assembly of the

United Nations voted for federation of Eritrea with Ethiopia. This was a
compromise—she wanted a full merger: but at least years of suspense had
ended in a semblance of victory. Quickly she and her son—now, after a
period of study under Professor Harold Laski at the London School of
Economics, Dr Richard Pankhurst, B.SC., PH.D.—set to work on a history
of *The Last Phase of the Reunion Struggle,* to which Lady Pethick-Lawrence
contributed a foreword. In the disappointment of a distinctly modified
triumph, Sylvia took another swing at the British obstructionism which
she had fought tooth and nail ever since the Emperor Haile Selassie had
re-entered Addis Ababa in May 1941.

> The policy which General Wavell and the War Office had adopted
> for the territory was of course unknown to Eritrean leaders [she
> wrote]. They had no conception that Eritrea, Somaliland and even
> Ethiopia were to be officially regarded as occupied enemy territory
> and administered as such by officials appointed by General Wavell.
> These officials were mostly colonial civil servants imbued with the
> practice of white supremacy and African subordination. At their
> head was Sir Philip Mitchell, Governor of Uganda, Mr R. H. Hone,
> Attorney-General of Uganda, and the Hon. Francis Rodd, afterwards
> Lord Rennell of Rodd. A memorandum issued by Sir Philip Mitchell
> indicated the guiding principles on which Eritrea and former Italian
> Somaliland should be governed. Italian law and regulations should be
> maintained as far as possible, and if Italian judges and magistrates are
> willing to remain in office, they may be permitted to function, with
> such safeguards as may appear desirable.

Sylvia did not, in her avalanche of books, pamphlets, articles and
letters (by now she was employing one full-time and four part-time
secretaries, and if called to the phone was apt to bark 'Who is it? What do
you want? Please be brief. I am a busy woman') neglect her fund-raising
for the Princess Tsahai Memorial Hospital. In 1947 she organized an
exhibition of Ethiopian arts and crafts at Foyle's bookshop in London, and
appeared on television to talk about it. She made several radio appeals,
presided over garden parties, and persuaded Dame Sybil Thorndike,
Donald (now Sir Donald) Wolfit and other well-known stars to give
charity recitals or matinées. Lord Amulree (a Liberal peer and a distinguished physician), who was president of the council of the Memorial
Hospital, still shudders to recall Sylvia's cliff-hanging approach.

She was [he says] dumpy and untidy, rather the shape of a cottage loaf. But she had immense personal charm, and was quite ruthless in a naive way. She would overspend on equipment by thousands of pounds after the committee had agreed on a go-slow. She always said the money would come in, and it always did. But we had our anxious moments. It was a sign that she had done something drastic when she arrived particularly untidy, wisps of hair floating, papers awry, flustered – and then confessed.

At a bazaar held in 1949 actress Wendy Hiller stressed the urgency of raising the last £15,000 of the £100,000 target, not only for the sake of improving health services in Ethiopia, but 'to keep Miss Pankhurst from going to prison again'. The money did come in, and in October 1951 Sylvia and Richard left for a six-month visit to Ethiopia, to be present at the official opening of the hospital (with its Sylvia Pankhurst wing) in November, and to gather material for first-hand reports for *New Times* and for Sylvia's new project, a huge *Cultural History of Ethiopia*.

She saw schools, churches, farms, oil wells in the Ogaden (by this time largely restored to Ethiopian rule), factories, prisons, government offices, police stations and military, naval and air force stations, comprehensively assessing for herself the progress which had been made in the seven years which had passed since her wartime visit. In a broadcast from Addis Ababa she listed the Emperor, Her Majesty Queen Elizabeth II, General de Gaulle, trade unions, co-operative societies, women's organizations, miners, nurses, doctors, authors, artists, old-age pensioners – and Lord Wavell – among the donors to the Princess Tsahai Memorial Hospital. The West Indian islands of Trinidad and Tobago had sent a thousand pounds. It was pleasant to record such international generosity. But, at a reunion of patriots (resistance fighters) in Addis Ababa's National Theatre, she did not attempt to disguise her disgust at the post-war treatment of Ethiopia. The failure to reunite Ethiopia, Eritrea and Italian Somaliland at the end of the war was, she said, 'one of the great injustices of history', and added: 'My own country was largely responsible for the failure. We were only in part exonerated by what we did to assist the liberation of Ethiopia from the enemy yoke in 1941. In the former Italian Somaliland liberation will come also, and we must work for it.' The Emperor decorated her with Ethiopia's highest honours, the Order of Sheba and the Order of Patriots with five palms.

Her unrepentantly reunionist tirades were treated seriously by General

Nasi, who promptly banned her books and *New Times,* which was also (together with the *Daily Worker, Health and Efficiency, Camera Studies in the Nude,* and various communist and Pan-African publications) excluded from British Somaliland—whose administration she characterized as incompetent and obstructive. She also alleged that the British caretaker administration in Eritrea had failed to prevent much wanton destruction to the vital port of Massawa and other key points, just before federation with Ethiopia took place. Yet in Woodford Green she was now regarded with affectionate, protective pride.

> You would never have imagined [says a former neighbour of hers in Charteris Road] that she had done all those things. She was just a little, old-fashioned, mildly spoken, elderly lady in black to us—in appearance she reminded me so much of Queen Victoria in her later years. I took my daughter to tea with Miss Pankhurst once. She showed us round the house (which was in a terrible mess) as if it had been a palace. There were no saucers, but she handed us teacups with spoons in them. She had real dignity. My daughter, who was only ten, told her what she should do to tidy the garden up, and Miss Pankhurst listened very carefully and patiently.

Sylvia was the big, perhaps the only, local celebrity. Journalists and photographers were interested in her doings and sayings. She spoke on the radio and appeared on television. For this she could be forgiven a multitude of sins—even for speaking up, at a meeting in Trafalgar Square, for Seretse Khama, exiled from Bechuanaland because he had married an English typist; deploring the attitude of Kenya settlers to Mau Mau and Jomo Kenyatta; and, finally, backing her son in his conscientious objection to national military service. He would willingly have fought against Fascism and Nazism, he told his tribunal. He would be willing to help arrest the British Colonial Secretary, but he objected to the use of force against Kenyans.

This development brought a spate of press articles. Under the headline SUFFRAGETTE AND SON: AT 70 SYLVIA PANKHURST SPEAKS FOR THE MAN WHO MADE HEADLINES AS A BABY, an *Evening Standard* interviewer wrote: 'Sylvia still has a vaguely 1910 look: grey hair scooped back, an ancient black corded silk coat over a drab cardigan, no nonsense, no jewellery, not so much as a ring. And of course no make-up. Lipstick in particular she abhors. Not only does it spoil the shape of the mouth, she asserts, it reveals the "slave mentality".' She did not think Richard's tribunal had quite understood his claim. His case, she explained, was rather like that of John Bright in the Crimean War or Lloyd George in the Boer War. It was perfectly logical to object to particular wars and particular weapons, though some people objected to *any* wars and *any* weapons. She could not, honestly, imagine Richard killing anyone. He had always been a gentle boy, and had even refused to play with toy soldiers. What time was there for such fripperies? Her own fourteen-hour working day started with a rapid but conscientious reading of a mixed bag of correspondence (of the kind featured on the 'Have You Any Problems?' page of a woman's magazine) – letters from women whose husbands had left them, whose lovers had abandoned them, unmarried mothers seeking affiliation orders, widows with queries about their pension. How did she manage about the housework, the cooking? There was a daily help, she said, but if she did not turn up 'we all go into the kitchen and cook something when we feel like it. But food is not important to us.' Money? 'I manage. I've had two useful legacies from friends who were with me in the suffragette movement' (when she died in 1954 Lady Pethick-Lawrence left an annuity of fifty pounds to Sylvia, one hundred pounds to Richard). 'Then there are royalties from my books and money from articles.'

She was, she said, appalled by the apathy of English women. Married women still had precious few rights, whereas in Ethiopia, if a marriage broke up, the wife was entitled to half the combined property. Women should be fighting for peace, picketing the United Nations, lobbying Parliament, 'as we fought for the vote'. And there were plenty of other things to campaign about. The cinema, for instance, and T.V. 'Films are deplorable. Many crimes are directly influenced by American gangster violence. When Richard was smaller, I used to take him to the pictures sometimes, but we were always having to come out – all those insipid blondes and people being murdered.' She felt that the question of children's toys could do with some close attention. 'I was reading the other day about little children being sold real daggers. Why don't women *do* something about it?'

Corio never figured in these interviews, never appeared with Sylvia on public occasions. Right up to the time of his death, which was near, he stayed strictly in the background. His main concern was *New Times*: he supervised printing arrangements, took a personal interest in distribution, did much of the editing, and occasionally wrote articles, always under one of his pen-names, in which he formally referred to Sylvia as 'Miss Pankhurst'. The English climate did not suit him: he suffered latterly from asthma. Lord Amulree attended him, but in January 1954, after a long period of invalidism, he died, aged eighty. This most curious, elusive, effective, sniped at and tirelessly sniping militant partnership was ended.

> Today [said his obituary in *New Times* which still carefully avoided any hint of possessive intimacy] we sorrowfully announce the death of a great comrade who strove steadfastly for Ethiopia throughout the years of her struggle against the Italian aggressor ... To his own generation of Italians devoted to freedom and progress Corio was always the friendly guide, counsellor and interpreter on their visits to Britain. Malatesta, Mordigliani, Claudio Treves and Serrati were among the many who sought his aid in London ... When he came to England he helped Francis McCullagh with his book *Italy's War for the Desert*, a forthright exposure of the atrocities and corruptions attendant on the Italian conquest of Libya. At that time he was London correspondent for several newspapers, including the socialist *Avanti!* ... He enlisted the ready help of the future editor of *New Times and Ethiopia News*, and worked zealously with her in her efforts to warn the British and world public of the menace of the Fascist dictatorship ...

In private, Sylvia showed the fullness of her grief. She wept for days and for a time was gravely ill with coronary thrombosis. But in October 1954, when the Emperor Haile Selassie reached England for a state visit (one stop on an extensive world tour), she was bubbling over with her usual vitality. She attended a banquet in his honour at the Guildhall, two receptions at the Ethiopian embassy, and a meeting in the House of Commons. In 1955 *New Times* applauded Ethiopia's Imperial Charter for an Animals' Protection Society ('Whereas', ran the proclamation, 'it is Our desire to promote the mitigation of animal suffering and the advancement of the practice of humanity towards the inferior classes of animated beings ... ') and hailed the newly revised Ethiopian constitution, which ordered election by full adult suffrage of Members of Parliament. Yet Article Four of the constitution made clear the theocratic basis of government ('By virtue of His Imperial Blood, as well as by the authority He has received, the person of the Emperor is sacred, His dignity is inviolable, and His power indisputable'). *New Times,* however, indignantly denied a statement in *The Economist* that Haile Selassie was 'comparable in modern history only with the Tsar of Russia or the Sultan of Turkey', and pointed out that the alleged reluctance of educated Ethiopians to 'do jobs which entail putting on overalls' was one which was still very common in Britain. It complained of inaccuracies in a B.B.C. programme on the government of Ethiopia, which was also critical of the Emperor's brand of benevolent despotism. 'It often happens', wrote Sylvia, 'that when some rare creative humanitarian genius is devoting all the force of unusually abounding energies to the welfare of his creatures, the very magnitude of the resultant achievements attracts a multitude of destructive and bitter critics. Yet these critics usually offer no adverse comment on rulers whose lives are entirely devoted to personal pleasure ... '

In a letter to the *Manchester Guardian*, Sylvia attacked an article written by an American who, after nine years' teaching in Addis Ababa, criticized inadequate, insanitary premises and violent extremes of wealth and poverty, and asserted that the families of Ethiopian students overseas were held as hostages for their return. Of course, reasoned Sylvia, there was poverty in Ethiopia: that was why the country was receiving Point Four aid. But the talk about hostages was quite untrue, A large proportion of Ethiopians studying abroad were orphans whose parents had been killed by the Italians. And 'the one per cent of Ethiopians whom your correspondent considers live in luxury know nothing of such riches as are found in America. I would', she crushingly ended, 'inquire whether he recommends equalitarian communism for the U.S.A. as well as for Ethiopia?'

But her most massive job of rebuttal, requiring almost a whole issue of *New Times* in April 1956, was reserved for John Gunther's book *Inside Africa,* and especially for the chapters on Ethiopia and Haile Selassie, which, though conceding the need for autocracy, and paying tribute to the Emperor's ability and integrity, proceeded to take Ethiopia apart to see what made that extraordinary country tick. If Gunther had read Sylvia's books, he made only the slightest reference to them: but he praised Margery Perham's 'indispensable' *The Government of Ethiopia,* which, he said, though 'fair-minded, authoritative and not particularly critical', was not on sale in Addis Ababa (Miss Perham herself, he revealed, had for long been refused entry into Ethiopia). Press censorship was rigid, fear of criticism morbid, educational attainment often pathetically low. The university college in Addis Ababa had been left uncompleted because there were not sufficient students of suitable qualifications to make it necessary. Addis Ababa ('New Flower'), though a city of 350,000 people, 'looked as if it had been dropped piecemeal from an aeroplane carrying rubbish'. He saw lines of petitioners waiting with bribes to see venal

government officials. Sanitation was so primitive that only the antisepti-
cally high altitude prevented serious epidemics. The Christian clergy —
one in every five adult males was said to be a priest — was probably the
most numerous and illiterate in the world: yet half the population was in
fact pagan or Muslim. The Italian invasion, though cruel, had given the
country 'a badly needed jolt', and the money which the Italians had spent
on public services formed 'the bedrock of the country's physical progress'. Despite the vaunted new constitution Ethiopia was not a democracy.
No political opposition was allowed, the Emperor selected members of
the upper house of Parliament himself, and offending politicians were
banished to a kind of Ethiopian 'Siberia'. Not even the person of the
Emperor escaped Gunther's breezy irreverence. In his long khaki cape and
large pith sun-helmet he looked 'something like a mushroom'. He was so
small that a cushion had to be placed on the floor to prevent his feet
dangling when he sat on the throne.

Gunther's account was, wrote Sylvia in *New Times*, hasty and super-
ficial, and heavily influenced by the attitude of Miss Perham, who in 1941
had advocated British trusteeship for Ethiopia. But Sylvia's real answer to
Gunther's lèse majesté was contained in her huge *Ethiopia: A Cultural
History*, published at the end of 1955, and a labour of most devoted love.
To make its 735 pages and 169 illustrations available to the public at all
Sylvia not only relied on her customary loyal nucleus of subscribers, but
used the proceeds of a sale of the Red Cottage café and land. Richard
Pankhurst's research helped to make the book — as was recognized
by leading journals, including *The Times Educational Supplement* — a
monumental survey which ranged from the remote stirrings of Ethiopian
consciousness to an analysis of the modernization presided over by Haile
Selassie, to whom the book was dedicated ('Guardian of Education,
Pioneer of Progress, Leader and Defender of his People in Peace and
War'). Those who still maintained that Ethiopia had no native art or
culture were effectively demolished by ten chapters on the art, illuminated
manuscripts, music and educational achievements of the Coptic Church.
The Portuguese and early Protestant missions, the Egyptian and Turkish
invasions, and the Italian usurpation were chronicled in detail, and it was
even noted that the imperial palace in Addis Ababa had *not* been built by
the Italians, but completed in 1934 and furnished by the London firm of
Waring and Gillow. Alas, for all its wealth of information, for all its
favourable reviews, the book did not command a fraction of the circulation of Gunther's brash but lively coverage. All things Ethiopian, at least

in the concluding sections of the book, were limned in too glaringly Pankhurstian black and white for those who wanted unpartisan history. In her anxiety not to heap obstacles in the path of the infant democracy or the toiling Emperor, she heaped them in the path of the sophisticated reader's credulity.

She was, in fact, at least in her attitude to outsiders, the touchy, love-blinded Mother of her Adopted Nation, to which, at the Emperor's invitation, she prepared, in the spring of 1956, to emigrate with her son. The accumulation of twenty-five years was sorted over at West Dene. Two drawings of Keir Hardie were accepted by the National Portrait Gallery. It was announced that, after twenty years, publication of *New Times* (which still had an international circulation of more than ten thousand) would cease: but that in Addis Ababa Sylvia and her son would produce a monthly journal, the *Ethiopia Observer*. Tributes from many lands dropped through the letter box, none more touching than that from a reader in Nigeria. 'As I read the sadness of the closing down,' he wrote, 'tears welled from my eyes ... You marshalled facts against the aggressor when even your own Government was doing everything to please him. You were a factor that helped to make Ethiopia what she is today' (already African nationalists were beginning to see imperial Ethiopia as a symbol of anti-colonial inspiration: and certainly *New Times* had done much to foster this). 'We Africans will always revere your name. Where are the mighties of yesteryears—Mussolini, Graziani, Chamberlain, Hoare, Laval, the soldiers of Italy who cut off people's heads and gloried in it? Where are they? God bless you, madam, God bless you.'

One of her last acts before leaving England was to visit the Foreign Office to ask about rumours that Britain intended to put a case for resuming control of the Ogaden (the last Reserved Area of which had not been released to Ethiopia until 1955) from the British Somaliland Protectorate. She was told that—as Britain had feared originally—Ethiopian police were unable to control border banditry. She regarded this statement, she said, as a blatant attempt to extend the British protectorate, and demanded to know when *its* people were to get self-government? It was, she was informed, impossible to fix a date: the Foreign Office thought it had been a mistake to promise self-government by 1960 to the Somalis under Italian trusteeship. Surrounded as (to her) Ethiopia seemed to be by scheming Britons, General Nasi and his Italian 'Peace Corps', and Kikuyu-hunting British settlers in Kenya, Sylvia must have longed to get to her sentry post in Addis Ababa, just as in 1919 she had yearned over the plight of revolutionary Russia, her gigantic underdog of yore, encircled by yelping capitalist curs.

By the end of June she was ready for the great uprooting. Sitting on a chair in her study, wearing her black silk coat, black gloves, white blouse, black skirt and a close-fitting black velvet hat, this bulldog Briton, who strove as much for the honour of her own country as for the good of Ethiopia, raised her right hand — as the cameras clicked — in a gesture of almost pontifical benediction. A few weeks later the contents of West Dene were auctioned. Small dealers and local housewives (curious to see the flown old eagle's eyrie) bid for the books and the rather battered furniture. To this day, Woodford Green residents will show you 'Miss Pankhurst's books' or ask you to sit on 'Miss Pankhurst's chair'.

Sylvia, with her son and her white Persian cat (a great favourite with the Emperor's grandchildren) was back in her spacious grace-and-favour bungalow, among the eucalyptus trees and maskal daisies she loved so much. Within days she was hard at work gathering material for the *Ethiopia Observer,* for which, in the next four years, she wrote more than half a million words. 'The mission of the *Ethiopia Observer*', she briskly proclaimed in the first number, 'is to mirror each and every facet of Ethiopia's present renaissance. It will be the first periodical ever published simultaneously in England and Ethiopia, and will contain definitive articles on economics, politics, history, culture, education and the arts.' There followed a whole series of special issues, compiled with the help of Richard (who was appointed a lecturer in the university college) — on the rebuilding of Addis Ababa (under the supervision of Sir Patrick Abercrombie, the British town planner), on Ethiopian women, on education, health services, industrial progress, agriculture, transport and communications (the *Encyclopaedia Britannica* was taken to task for saying that there were no roads for wheeled traffic outside the capital), on Kenya, Eritrea, the Ethiopian patriots, the rock churches of Lalibela, the conference of independent African states in Addis Ababa in June 1960, and even on the Queen of Sheba in European art and on the Ethiopian ancestry of the Russian poet Alexander Pushkin.

Pencil and note pad at the ready, Sylvia travelled thousands of miles, sometimes by Land-Rover over bone-rattling tracks, not only to get copy, but to keep Ethiopia on its toes. Government officials grew to expect, and in some cases to dread, her peremptory phone calls. 'I am Miss Pankhurst,' she told the Governor of the Ogaden. 'I want to see the

Ogaden again. Tell me what there is new to see there.' Her wide-ranging, short-notice visits were almost as much a cause of mingled apprehension and pride as those of the Emperor himself. She was, in fact, a kind of honorary Empress of Ethiopia. She abhorred vagueness or indecision, and insisted on hard facts and practical details. When, for instance, she was told that odourless mats were needed on which coffee could be dried, she immediately arranged for bamboo mats to be made by the inmates of a rehabilitation centre in time for the next harvest. She took a close interest in the Princess Tsahai Memorial Hospital, conferring with its staff on the kind of equipment which she should ask the committee in London to buy. Once she stopped her car in the street to collect a small crippled boy she saw, and took him straight to the orthopaedic surgeon for treatment. She was ever resolving to learn Amharic, founded a social service centre, invited donations of land for a series of children's playgrounds in Addis Ababa, planned a maternity wing for her hospital, agitated for the establishment of a nation-wide blood donor service, drew up schemes for a chain of employment bureaux and a rehabilitation centre for mental patients, organized an official roster of visitors to prisons and hospitals, pressed for an orthopaedic centre to manufacture artificial limbs, and did much to promote the holding of an International Women's Seminar in Addis Ababa in 1960 and to brief Ethiopian women for their part in it.

It was as though the shamelessly meddlesome vitality of all four Pankhurst women churned relentlessly in her ageing body. Often she was at her desk until midnight and later, writing letters, articles, memoranda, wearing out dozens of fountain pens (her one extravagance), turning night into day (like Van Gogh painting with candles stuck in the brim of his hat in the streets of Arles: or like the art student she had been nearly fifty years before, trying to paint in the dusk on the balcony of her room in Venice) in a last furious blaze of creative humanitarian zeal. She was too busy, or too tactful, to complain about the presence of Italian hoteliers, restaurateurs and shopkeepers, and the influx of Nazis who, after 1945, fled to Addis Ababa to escape war trials. More distressing to her was the dwindling of British influence. British teachers, numerous before the war, were now few and far between. Even the British Council had closed its office in Addis Ababa for seven years. Was this part of a childish petulance at the Emperor's determination to manœuvre free of stifling British 'protection'? Often she went to the palace, exempt from the rigid bowing-while-walking-backwards etiquette which other foreigners had to observe, to discuss the progress of the renaissance with the Emperor. In the cosmopolitan group of advisers — Scandinavian, Czech, Greek, Indian, Israeli and American as well as British — with whom he, with deliberate catholicity, surrounded himself, she was pre-eminent in affection as well as estimation.

She seldom left her desk except on definite, usually journalistic, business, but occasionally she would allow herself to be driven about Addis Ababa, revelling in its numerous wooded hills, the deep courses of meandering streams, and above all the slender, lofty eucalyptus — 'in the season of great rains,' she wrote, 'a blending of blues, greens and greys, haunting in its wistful loveliness'. Sometimes she would be taken into the countryside and sit quite silently, alone, looking at the marvellous spread of valleys and mountains and lakes, communing intensely and recuperatively with the grandeurs of nature. 'I often feel I should like to paint again in this beautiful country,' she wrote to Mrs Elsa Fraenkel, who in 1959 organized an exhibition of Sylvia's paintings and drawings in London, 'but I am always busy and I feel that if I were to make a start I should be terribly disappointed with what I could produce after this interval of fifty years.' She sent back old, yellowing photographs of the huge designs she had done for the W.S.P.U. fête of 1909 — an achievement she still remembered with special pleasure.

She enjoyed the companionship of her son and of his wife, a Rumanian Jewish girl he had met in London. Their home was a meeting place for Ethiopian writers and artists whose work she had published in *New Times* (and continued to publish in the *Ethiopia Observer*: she was a keen patron of the arts, quick to appreciate and encourage new talent). She still wrote poetry herself, and, with all those millions of variegated words behind her, and flowing staunchlessly still from her, liked nothing better than to sit on the lawn and talk about books and writing. Now and again she attended official functions. In 1958 Sefton Delmer's report on Ethiopia for the *Daily Express* was headed SURPRISE! LOOK WHO'S HERE! MISS PANKHURST! The occasion was an exhibition of children's art in the Soviet Information office. 'Solemn Ethiopians', said Delmer, 'trot around admiring water colours and crayon sketches by six- to sixteen-year-olds from Ocholsk to Omsk. And who is this genial, blue-eyed English gentlewoman with the silvery hair hobnobbing with the comrades over vodka and zakusi? Why, it's that grand old suffragette Sylvia Pankhurst. Here in Addis Ababa, with energy undimmed, she is carrying on a campaign to liberate Africans from their European oppressors.' She rejoiced in the strange emergence of Addis Ababa as the capital, the Geneva, of the

New Africa, with Haile Selassie as the acknowledged elder statesman and father figure of such seasoned revolutionaries as Jomo Kenyatta, Kwame Nkrumah, Ben Bella and Sekou Touré. African nationalists who had spent their lives denouncing imperialism accepted imperial decorations from the Lion of Judah: and perhaps Nkrumah picked up a few mis-guided Messianic ideas from him. By 1960 Ethiopia was accepting aid from Soviet Russia and the People's Republic of Yugoslavia, and Haile Selassie was talking as to the manner born (perhaps with some help from Miss Pankhurst) about the duty of boycotting South Africa, and chiding the Great White Powers: 'Do not seek to perpetuate, in some different guise, the old forms of economic and political exploitation and oppression. Africa needs and desires and welcomes the help of others, but must nevertheless be left to develop herself, her people, her resources, as Africans determine. Leave to us, freely and without qualms, the choice between good and evil, between justice and injustice, between oppression and liberty. Our choice will be the right one, and history will judge us, and you, the better for it.' Brave words, and odd ones, coming from the ruler of a country which for centuries had considered itself as apart from Africa, and had looked down from the heights of its mountains and its Christian civilization on the benighted blacks of the burning plains.

One of Sylvia's last journalistic safaris was a long trip by Land-Rover to a prison farm at Robi. She slept in the prison hospital, tested the prisoners' diet, approved of the fact that they were not confined in cells and were learning a wholesome trade in magnificent surroundings. On the way back, the party stopped at 'a frugal mountain dwelling, reached by steps carved from the rock, a house all breadth and little depth, built on a narrow ledge. All the family were assembled to greet the prison director, their relative—the elderly parents and the younger generation, among them lovely girls in bright cardigans with flowered skirts of pretty muslin—and then the dogs lazily gnawing their bones ... ' She noted the dusky purple rain clouds of the highlands, which, when she arrived back in Addis Ababa, had 'vanished in the calm of a mellifluent golden sky'. Not long after this, on September 15th, 1960, she watched the hero's reception given to Abebe Bikila, the Ethiopian runner who had won the marathon event in the Olympic Games held in Rome. 'We are pleased', said the Emperor, as he made Bikila a Chevalier of the Order of the Star of Ethiopia, 'to witness today the first crowning event of the sports organization which we sponsored in our own lifetime.' A week later, Sylvia planned to go camping with Richard and her daughter-in-law. But

11

an attack of coronary thrombosis forced her to stay in her bedroom. There, with the election manifesto which her father had written as an I.L.P. parliamentary candidate in Manchester in 1895 hanging on the wall above her bed, she died on September 27th, aged seventy-eight. The drudging and drilling of the old citizen-soldier were over.

The funeral service at Holy Trinity Cathedral was attended by the Emperor and the Imperial Family, by the entire Ethiopian Cabinet, and by every member of the diplomatic corps in Addis Ababa. Thousands of people, who only a few days earlier — as was the universal custom — had waved to her as she drove through the streets, crammed the approaches to the cathedral to watch the Emperor lead the long procession of mourners and lay a wreath on Sylvia's grave. The coffin, covered with gleaming gold cloth, was carried by soldiers of the elite Imperial Guard. Over it, with a final irony, Coptic priests and acolytes, surrounding the silent remains of this dynamo of humanism in a ring of Christian piety, performed their ancient rites: which was fitting enough, for Sylvia, though never a convert, had allowed her aesthetic appreciation of the beautiful though cancerous incrustations of the Coptic faith to charm her iconoclastic puritanism.

Sylvia Pankhurst [said the Minister of the Interior, Ras Andargatchew Massai, in his funeral oration] is the great lady who, following in the steps of her mother, was throughout her life the advocate of all human beings who were refused their rights ... We must remember that she served Ethiopia in the country's darkest hour, not only with all her moral support but also by selling her property to obtain money with which to assist Ethiopian exiles, so that she became poor. Therefore Ethiopia's friend, the great Englishwoman Miss Sylvia Pankhurst, should be called a true Ethiopian patriot ... Sylvia Pankhurst, the Emperor and the Ethiopian people, whom you sincerely and honestly served, now stand weeping around you. Your history will live forever written in blood, with the history of the Ethiopian patriots. Since by His Imperial Majesty's wish you rest in peace in the soil of Ethiopia, we consider you an Ethiopian. May God, who has surely witnessed your noble deeds, keep you in a place of honour.

In the brilliant sunshine the coffin, shaded by the superbly embroidered parasols of the clergy, was lowered into a grave dug in the most sacred ground where many of the patriots had been buried. Sylvia not being one of the Christian names known to the Ethiopian Church, she had been given, in her absence, the tremendous name of WALATA KRISTOS— Daughter of Christ.

The news of her death brought a great, warm, cosmopolitan rain of tributes. Lord Pethick-Lawrence ('I send my deep sympathy, not untinged by a sense of triumph in a great and courageous life spent in the service of her fellow beings and now nobly brought to its ineluctable conclusion'); Norah Smyth; Edward Watson ('I am proud to say I was one of her bodyguards in the West End'); a Polish-Jewish refugee ('She was one of the very few people in England who were kind to me'); Mrs Clarissa Burgoyne, widow of Major Burgoyne, who had been killed while organizing Red Cross activities in Ethiopia in 1935 ('Accept my tribute to a lady who was above all an essentially English type'); Lynn Martin, an American poet who had for a time been a schoolteacher in Addis Ababa ('She was a very grand person in both the casual and exact sense of that word'); Senekula Mulumba, a Ugandan political leader ('We have lost the general of the most sincere and selfless fighters for freedom, justice and democracy'); Joseph Murumbi, a leader of the Kenya African Union ('We Africans will always regard her as being a great friend of our people'); Lij Endalkatchew Makonnen, Ethiopian ambassador in London ('Her whole life exemplified the liberal and humanitarian spirit which gives Britain her undisputed position of moral and spiritual leadership').

But the briefest tribute, and the one which she herself had most treasured, had been paid three years before her death, on a visit to the agricultural school at Jimma, where the pupils had presented her with a little clay tablet on which was inscribed the one word—OTHERS.

CHAPTER THREE

POST MORTEMS, OR
A POSSE OF PANKHURSTS

In July 1959, just before the Dame Christabel Pankhurst memorial was unveiled by the then Lord Chancellor, Viscount Kilmuir (who predictably congratulated the suffragettes on their 'courage, temerity, tenacity and high principle in forcing open the door of masculine privilege'), a group of ex-militants gathered in the Lincoln's Inn flat of Lord Pethick-Lawrence to talk over old times and listen to a recording made by Christabel immediately after her release from Holloway prison in 1908. 'The reasons why women should have the vote', said the clear, rather governessy voice, naggingly logical even through the crackle of the ancient disc, 'should be obvious to every fair-minded person. Taxation and representation should go together, therefore women taxpayers are entitled to the vote. Men got the vote not by persuading but by alarming the legislators. Similar measures must be adopted by women. The militant methods of women today are clearly thought out and vigorously pursued. We have waited too long for political justice. We refuse to wait any longer.'

Christabel's long-awaited account of the suffragette movement, salvaged by Grace Roe in California and edited by Lord Pethick-Lawrence, had appeared a few weeks earlier. Called *Unshackled,* and firmly subtitled *The Story of How We Won The Vote,* it was a carefully documented presentation of the suffragette case, told with a minimum of human interest and detail and a maximum of cold, if biased, courtroom reasoning. Reviewers – mainly women – tended to be as supercilious as the politicians against whom the Pankhursts and their cohorts had raged. 'A lively but tendentious period piece,' said *The Times.* 'My mother right or wrong seems to sum up Dame Christabel's simple creed.' One critic confessed that, despite the tragic implications of the events described, she had found herself rocking with laughter at the naiveté and pious hypocrisy (especially the 'loyal' glossing over of differences within the women's movement) of Christabel's writing, for all the world as though this kind of 'loyalty', in far more blatant form, does not pervade most male politicians' memoirs. Other pundits smiled at the 'smug' atmosphere of the Pankhurst ménage, that hot-house of purposeful culture and self-important high-mindedness, smirked at its quintessential Victorianism. Taking a cue perhaps from George Dangerfield, they made much play with the farcical element in the deadly female earnestness ('when around the smoking ruins of some house or church', Dangerfield had written in his *Strange Death of Liberal England*, 'there is discovered the dread evidence of a few hairpins or a feminine galosh'), and even dismissed the W.S.P.U. as 'one of the comic side-shows of history, like some of the Puritan sects'.

Yet if the clothes and fanatical sentiments of the Pankhursts and their followers, who after all risked life and limb (numbers of them subsequently died as a result of bruising mêlées with the police and with hooligans in the crowds which gathered to watch their clothes rip in the tragi-comedy of their maenadic onslaught on authority), are considered good for a giggle, what of their opponents? What of the massive pomposity and absurd conceit of Gladstone, Balfour, Lloyd George and Asquith? And what, if one is going to indulge in the easy, anachronistic horselaugh, of the ugly, lay-preacher ludicrousness of *their* clothes? This kind of criticism, if criticism it can legitimately be called, is as old as Aristophanes, or, to be more exact, as the humorists of the 1840s. George Cruikshank, the great cartoonist and illustrator, in his *Comic Almanack* of 1849, facetiously pictured the 'Frightful State of Things if Female Agitation is Allowed Only For a Minute'. There followed a catalogue of horrors based on the fact, then taken for granted, that a women's rebellion was a matter for vaudeville sketches rather than for serious concern.

Total abolition of latchkeys — All men proved to be brutes taken to business in the morning by the Nurse and fetched home at night by the Cook — The wretched criminals are carried away by the overpowering force of Women's Mission — Five thousand helpless husbands, whose only crime is their unfortunate sex, incarcerated in the Thames tunnel! Not a glass of grog or a newspaper or a cigar is allowed them!! Hundreds perish daily for the want of the common necessities of life!!! The Black Hole of Calcutta is beaten hollow!!!! etc.

In 1913, by which time the Pankhursts had forced the women's rebellion from the pages of the funnies into the streets, public halls, golf courses, letter boxes and newspaper columns of the land, Laurence Housman, a keen supporter of their campaign, in his pamphlet *The Bawling Brotherhood*, turned Cruikshank's representative Victorian thesis upside down in

order to ridicule the stock anti-suffragist arguments. In his country of
Happy Parallel women had governed from time immemorial, filling all
the great offices of state and directing the activities of men in field and
factory ('there was not a single industry that secured to its employees less
than a living wage from which the law excluded them') and in the armed
forces – for it was obvious that mere uneducated brawn was there simply
for the benefit of the homes of the nation, and must be controlled by the
women who ran them. Suddenly a section of men, known as the Bawling
Brotherhood (the suffragettes were popularly known as the Shrieking
Sisterhood) began to agitate against this logic, and to demand the vote.
This, argued the Female Establishment, was ridiculous. How could creatures
incapable of risking their lives in childbirth, without which the state would
not exist, claim a share in its regulation? They were 'the irresponsible sex'
and must expect to be treated as such. If indoor, sedentary careers were
opened to them, men would become soft and effeminate and would lose
that 'manly bloom and vigour from open-air life which gave them their
chief attraction for women'. The crudity of men's habits and language
clearly unfitted them for parliamentary duties. There was something
ridiculous in the very notion of such born underlings aspiring to any kind
of intellectual dignity. "Fancy a man in a pair of trousers, a cut-away coat
and mutton-chop whiskers sitting upon the Woolsack!" said the women.
And having fancied it to themselves, they laughed consumedly, and
considered that they had provided for their side an absolutely knock-
down argument.' As for admitting men, with their deliberately encouraged blood-sporting instincts, to the medical profession, why that too was
out of the question unless one wished to encourage vivisection and brutal
orgies of surgical experimentation.

Of course the women's movement was deeply rooted in Victorianism,
like the attitudes against which it strove. Of course the Pankhursts were
puritans, thrusting surface pleasures aside (Mrs Pankhurst wrote and spoke
scathingly of the Society men and women upon whom, increasingly, she
relied for W.S.P.U. funds) as they stripped for action. The women's
movement was, in fact, the last stage in the puritan bourgeois revolution,
with its many envious thrusts into the magic circle of the *status quo,* which
had started as far back as the sixteenth century. But it was the full-blooded,
Martin Marprelate fury of the militants, not the polite insinuations of the
constitutionalists, which forced Laurence Housman, Henry Nevinson,
H. N. Brailsford and other male intellectuals to take sides and spread the
contagion in the enemy camp. It was the Lysistrata-like extremism of

Emmeline and Christabel which, miraculously, tapped the steaming underground river of women's resentment and vengeful sexual frolic (of which Euripides, Aristophanes, Boccaccio, Chaucer, Rabelais, Shakespeare, Congreve, Flaubert and Dostoevsky had given scarifying glimpses) and harnessed it to the unlikely mills of political and social reform.

As these turbulent waters, strained through the Pankhurst purifier-compressor, rushed to their grand employ, they frothed and rainbowed and effervesced. There was a Dionysian abandon about the Pankhurst guerrillas. In their zany iconoclasm they really did, in the words of Ethel Smyth's *March of the Women*, 'laugh a defiance'. The suffragette movement was, Irishly enough, puritanism at its zestful, cavalier best, something to be celebrated (perhaps in a spectacular musical), not sniffed at — part, indeed, except for, the Irish revolt, almost the whole of the colourful folklore of a preternaturally drab century. One has only to listen to suffragettes (now in their seventies, eighties or even nineties) reminisce to get an exhilarating whiff of it. Lady Gollancz, widow of the well-known publisher, whose mother and three older sisters went to prison as militants, and whose father spent a lot of money providing bail for women under arrest, remembers how her mother, Mrs Lowy, joined the W.S.P.U. after hearing Mrs Pankhurst speak — because she 'obviously meant business'. Her example was followed by a friend who for years had been galled by her husband's practice, when taking the family on holiday, of relegating her and the children to an inferior boarding house while he, the breadwinner, lorded it in an expensive hotel, unbothered by the patter of tiny feet and tongues. Lady Gollancz, apart from taking part in a telegraph-wire-cutting exercise, was present at the 1914 'raid' on Buckingham Palace, when women threw egg-shells filled with coloured ink at policemen, knocked off their helmets (this always temporarily immobilized them), and made their horses sit down by striking their hindlegs hard near the joint. Mrs Lowy, who resembled Mrs Pankhurst, was often used as a decoy to foil detectives. Just before her death on Derby Day, Emily Wilding Davison asked Mrs Lowy to disguise her, and went away in borrowed finery with a switch of dark curly hair concealing her own reddish locks. The sharp impact of the Pankhursts released a gay fountain of conspiratorial excitement in the Lowy family.

Mary Leigh, the first suffragette to be forcibly fed, talks of the time when she arranged to meet Emily Davison (both were on the run) in a cemetery in a London suburb, by the grave of a man called Patrick Kennedy. 'I remember the grave had a sort of glass dome on it. But it was dark and foggy and I couldn't find it. Eventually I called out, "Where's Pat Kennedy?" A hand was clapped over my mouth and Emily said, "Shut up, I'm here." ' Theresa Garnett had a marvellous story of gate-crashing a grand Foreign Office reception attended by several cabinet ministers. An anonymous well-wisher had sent an invitation card, and Miss Garnett was supplied with a suitably impressive escort.

Inspector Jarvis [who knew most of the suffragettes by sight] and a group of detectives were at the bottom of the stairs. I got past by dint of furious play with an enormous fan. Then I 'lost' my escort, went to the far end of the room, and concealed myself on a window ledge behind banks of flowers. When the room was full, I vollied out my Votes for Women piece. Dead silence. Inspector Jarvis threaded through the crush of guests to take me away. There was a long walk to the exit. People fell back on either side to leave us a gangway. I felt like royalty, nodding right and left, repeating my message as I did so. The funniest part of the whole thing was a report in the newspapers next day. One headline I remember said SUFFRAGETTE DISGUISED AS LADY PENETRATES FOREIGN OFFICE RECEPTION.

But with the gay, Scarlet Pimpernel exploits went a furious sense of compassion for *all* the victims of male bungling, a blazing impatience with the cruel humbug. Mrs Pankhurst led her Salvation Army into a Dickensian underworld of callous squalor—dark slums, incest, child rape, drunkenness and violence. One upper-class Scottish suffragette talked of the incident that gave her the final push to unexpurgated militancy.

It was at a lunch-hour factory gate meeting near Hull. I saw a small, ragged boy hanging around, and asked him why he was there. Because he was hungry, he said, and was hoping to get some leftover scraps from the canteen. I thought then, If this is the best kind of society men's government can produce, it's high time women took a hand. I was choking with anger and humiliation, and begged Mrs Pankhurst to let me go to London and take part in one of the deputations to Parliament. That's how I went to prison the first time.

Prison itself, apart from providing yet another theatre of protest, provided also—and this, too, may well have been foreseen by the immensely shrewd Mrs Pankhurst—a crash course in seamy (and of course man-made) sociology for suffragettes, the first of whom to be arrested were piled in with common offenders: prostitutes, thieves, child murderers, whose plight could often be traced back to an episode of seduction and desertion. What more calculated to rouse militancy to fever pitch? Jessie Kenney, who was imprisoned in Holloway in 1907, says her worst memory is of a young girl under sentence of death for killing her illegitimate baby. In chapel, the 'murderess' was screened off behind a red curtain. Shocked and infuriated (why should *she* bear the full burden of guilt while her seducer went scot free?), Miss Kenney and other militants sent a message to W.S.P.U. headquarters, and, largely due to Pankhurst agitation, the girl's sentence was reduced, her crime listed as manslaughter instead of murder. Such prison reform as there was in Britain between the wars was achieved largely as a result of the revelations and persistent pressure of the suffragettes – and of that other group of high-minded, predominantly middle-class nonconformist jail-birds, the conscientious objectors of the first world war.

Mrs Pankhurst did not exaggerate when, in the first mass meetings of her anti-V.D. campaign in Canada in 1921, she stressed that it was her experience of the crookedness and blank male hypocrisy of local and national government, whatever its political label, which was the driving force of her militancy. For twenty years before she founded the W.S.P.U. her mind had been crammed to bursting point with the evidence of man's inhumanity to women. The cries of the damned, the flames of an earthly hell, crackled in her ears, creating a megalomaniac certainty of personal mission. Christabel's cool political strategy provided the outlet which alone, perhaps, prevented her mother's mind from giving way under the strain of impotence and frustration. Between them, these two women organized and led that greatest of historical rarities, a successful slave revolt – 'one of the finest fights against tyranny the world has ever seen!' Mary Leigh will tell you, in tones of bannered pride. Mrs Pankhurst and her daughter Sylvia, though in violent political disagreement, came close, in their talent for public martyrdom, to being a joint incarnation of the Female Christ predicted, or prayed for, by Florence Nightingale. They certainly answered Miss Nightingale's other great *cri de cœur* – 'Give us back our suffering. Suffering rather than indifferentism, for out of nothing comes nothing, but out of suffering may come the cure. Better have pain than paralysis.' They – and Christabel too, in her brilliantly sustained, though psychologically withering, role of *dea ex machina* – were true priestesses of the people: an achievement made in deliberate opposition to one of the prime satanic texts of the women's movement, the celebrated passage about prostitutes from Lecky's *History of Morals*. 'Herself the supreme type of vice,' he had written, with sublime smugness, 'she is ultimately the most efficient guardian of virtue. But for her, the unchallenged purity of countless homes would be polluted ... On that one degraded and ignoble form are heaped the passions that might have filled the world with shame. She remains the eternal priestess of humanity, blasted for the sins of the people.' These so-called priestesses, though Lecky omitted to mention this, might be barely, if at all, out of their teens. When girls of twelve and thirteen were found in a French brothel and brought into court to give evidence against their employers, the judge quickly intervened when they began to mention names of their clients: 'You must not', he thundered Mosaically, 'befoul the name of a respectable man!'

Against such preposterous humbug the Pankhursts fought, and continued to fight, with every fibre of their being. Their battle cries were not remarkable for psycho-sexual subtlety. Theirs was, perhaps had to be, an A.B.C., Victoria Cross, Tennysonian, Charge of the Light Brigade, Female Galahad morality. In the first world war this, in the case of Mrs Pankhurst and Christabel, merged easily into the routine pseudo-spirituality of jingo patriotism, a virulent denunciation of rotters, slackers, socialists, conscientious objectors, Huns and enemy aliens. Yet in 1940 the nation turned to Churchill, a monumental anachronism by the progressive standards of the 'twenties and 'thirties, for another dose of black-and-white Hun-hate and pre-Freudian psychology to nerve them for war. All the Pankhurst women attacked what seemed to them humbug (and evil humbug at that: for each enemy to them, who knew the power of righteous indignation to move mountains of indifference, was a supreme, satanic enemy), whether it was communism, Fabian socialism, milk-and-water Conservatism, false reticence about venereal diseases, belief in the possibility of German democracy, the sanctity of marriage (or the insidious foes of that sanctity), the iniquities of Fascism or – in Adela's view – the foolishness of refusing to see the anti-communist good as well as the anti-democratic bad in it.

When it came to the crunch – and in a world of mass media and universal involvement the crunch was never far away – things had to be seen in penny plain, tuppence coloured terms. There was little room for sophistication or the splitting of intellectual hairs. If one played the political game at all, one must play to win. If one preached at all, one must preach for a decision. It was better to be a bad loser than to prepare oneself, with defeatist humility, to lose with good grace. There was, alas, no moral equivalent of war, no substitute for courage. The turning of the composite League of Nations cheek to the insolent slaps of reaction might be easier, but was no less despicable, than national or personal cowardice. The refusal to fight in *any* war was a mere sheltering behind a parapet of principle. It was always, in the last analysis, a case of giving all or nothing at all.

Such, though in kaleidoscopic permutation, was the central gospel, the common ground, of the Pankhursts, as true in the 'twenties, 'thirties, 'forties and 'fifties, as it had been during the suffrage campaign. Life, in fact, was a battlefield. Not to take sides, not to be *able* to take sides, was the real tragedy and the ultimate sin. The Whole Truth was a mirage, an excuse for inaction, a satanic deceit. The only truth that mattered was what one knew to be right; and though it might be relative, its claims were absolute. Though each of these women fought for liberty as she conceived it, all were resolutely unlibertine: each liberty won was to be used as a foothold on the painful but obligatory ascent of the mountain of perfection. The Pankhursts, indeed, were the sort of people D. H. Lawrence had in mind when, in one of his moods of violent quietism, he wrote: 'They are simply eaten up with caring. They are so busy caring about Fascism, and the League of Nations, or whether France is right or Marriage is threatened, that they never know where they are. They inhabit abstract space, the desert void of politics, principle, right and wrong.' Why this endless search for the 'point' of things? 'There is no point, life and love are life and love, a bunch of violets is a bunch of violets, and to drag in the idea of a point is to ruin everything. Live and let live ... flower and fade, follow the natural curve which flows on, pointless ... '

The Pankhursts had their natural, pointful curve. They expected results from all their campaigns, not merely in their own lifetime, but, since life was short and there were so many matters to put right, within a decade at most. Christabel's Second Adventism, her hope that Christ would return to the earth before she died, was only another manifestation of the family impatience with tinkering reformism. These women looked for a clinching dénouement, they wanted to be *there* when the victory was won. 'On the whole,' wrote Sylvia to Teresa Billington-Greig in 1956, 'the victory of Ethiopia has been the most satisfactory achievement I have seen. Votes for Women was marred for me by its partial character and the fact that there was not a sufficiently intelligent, progressive and active movement to make it as effective as one would have desired.' She maintained that if the non-militants had only been militant, the Government, deprived of its favourite contrast between the 'reasonable' Mrs Fawcett and the 'hooligan' Mrs Pankhurst, would have been forced to capitulate before the first world war. Yet suffragist expectations had been excessive. 'Granted the vote has brought an all-round improvement in many directions, the improvement has been gradual rather than dramatic. The fall of Fascism and the defeat of the Italians in Ethiopia *was* complete and dramatic.' The 1955 Ethiopian constitution, she pointed out, had given the vote to all men and women over twenty-one. 'I drafted a Bill', she added, 'to achieve that throughout the British colonies and protectorates, but thus far no M.P. has had the courage to introduce it.'

She was at too fantastically full an Ethiopian, Pan-African stretch to pay any close attention to the snail's pace of social and economic justice for women. But in February 1943, the twenty-fifth anniversary of the first instalment of the vote ('the fancy franchise', as she called it in *New Times,* 'created to put women in an artificial minority') she noted that 'though women's heroism and devotion to duty is a commonplace of the day's news,' equal pay for equal work seemed as far off as ever, and men got larger compensation for loss by enemy action. Worse still, the Beveridge report, the blueprint for the post-war welfare state on which Harold Wilson was a principal researcher, still took the old line that a national wages policy must be based on the fact that men more often had a family or dependants to support than women. After the war, she talked and wrote about the need for women to 'do something', but clearly, like her mother, had little faith in the ability of gradualist women's organizations such as the hold-all National Council of Women (which included the remnants of suffragism as well as a plethora of professional groups) to do much more than pass resolutions and put their faith in Parliament. Much of the youthful idealism and militancy which did exist in both sexes was monopolized by the Campaign for Nuclear Disarmament, and in Sylvia's view this was as it should be. She was still capable of bursts of hot anger when she saw the kind of smooth committee-woman whom the Pank-hursts, being bad or at least eccentric organization women, had always loathed, being loaded with honours and influence. 'Dear Mrs Drake,' she wrote in 1954, 'Is it not possible to protest against the broadcasting, if not also the honouring by a seat on royal commissions, of that foul traitor— who, while the suffragettes were hunger striking, appeared on the Albert Hall platform, surrounded by reactionaries like Lord Cromer and Lord

Curzon, protesting against women having the vote? She has had her reward for her treachery to women. A protest to the B.B.C. should be made by every woman who values her citizenship.'

Christabel preserved a Dame-becoming silence on such matters. In any case she was always, as was Mrs Pankhurst, concerned to preserve the myth of a United Female Front, to prove that, despite their share of original sin, women could rise above the human frailty of internecine bickering. Unbound by the ladylikeness with which Mrs Pankhurst and Christabel had sought to clear the suffragettes from the accusation of bohemian nihilism, Sylvia had been able to give fuller play to a rich, intensely human personality. Yet on occasions even Christabel showed impatience with the failure of women to exploit the victories of the pioneers. Why didn't women use their votes to increase the number of women M.P.s (which had not, and has not, reached to more than a quarter of the Women's Freedom League's 1919 target of one hundred), and see to it that women were given control of the *major* ministries and got more than a token representation in the Cabinet? If Israel (this was in 1956) could have a woman Foreign Minister, why not Britain?

But she did not suggest *how* women voters were to be persuaded to take a feminist line, or to stop, in most cases, voting as their husbands did. In America, politicians referred to the female vote as a 'multiplication table', and in 1929 Alice Stone Blackwell, a former suffragist leader, wrote in bitter disappointment: 'Mrs Poyser's immortal saying' (a saying which the shrewd Mrs Fawcett had often quoted in the 1890s) 'about women being fools because God made them to match the men, is proving itself true.' What was the point, British newspapers grumbled in 1928 at the time of the flapper vote, of enfranchising five million young women who exposed their knees because they had no minds to reveal? Even the radically socialist Professor G. D. H. Cole was grudging in his welcome to this instalment of progress. Though women, he said, had to get equality of franchise as a matter of principle, it would probably mean a vast increase in the forces of reaction. This, of course, would not have worried Christabel. More distressing to her was the paucity of women politicians, reflecting both an unwillingness to adopt women parliamentary candidates unless they were absolutely outstanding (though male nonentities continue to clutter the Commons), and the competing pulls of public and family life. She may have dreamed of a mass penetration of Parliament by brilliant embattled spinsters of her own erstwhile calibre. But the resistance, not least of women, to such dedicated yet somehow inhuman creatures, is still all but insuperable. Far more to the militant point was Lady Astor's line. 'I come near to despising women in the mass for allowing this cheat to go on,' she said, referring to the delay in implementing government promises about equal pay. 'If all the women M.P.s had a sit-down strike, they would soon get equal pay.' Perhaps Christabel, so ingeniously and ruthlessly militant outside the walls of the Palace of Westminster, would have been overwhelmed with gratitude, storied stones and *noblesse oblige* if she had got inside. She would probably have made less headway than Lady Astor against the steady pressure of the fact that, as Sylvia realized only too well, all men are not only Tories, but rabid reactionaries, when it comes to the politics of sex. The existence of a huge female electorate may have forced them to conceal their prejudices, but they are still mighty prejudiced. All M.P.s, in any case, whatever their sex and however conscientious, are ignorant of the existence, let alone the details, of many of the real problems of their constituents. The individual member is terribly, and increasingly, impotent. Lady Astor was shocked to learn that only tremendous energy, unremitting application, and the luck of the parliamentary draw enabled a member to *introduce* a private bill, let alone get it on to the statute book. Hence the continued need for such organizations as the Six Point Group or the National Council of Women, in Britain, or the National Organization for Women, recently formed in America 'to take action to bring women into full participation in the mainstream of Society NOW'.

Certainly Britain's women's organizations (including trade unionists) have enough grievances to make their disbandment a remote prospect. *Discrimination Against Women,* a recent survey published by the National Council for Civic Liberties, concluded that the national economy is still based on what is in effect the sweated labour of the more than eight million women who go out to work. Not only does union demarcation of women's from men's work ensure that the average woman's industrial wage is little more than half that of a man, but only the feeblest attempt is made to provide facilities for looking after the children or elderly relatives of the four million married women in jobs. Even where, as in the civil service and the professions, equal pay has been established, selection procedures are so designed that few women reach positions of real influence, and so are made to feel freakish and to behave, often, somewhat freakishly. Girls' education is still academically inferior to boys', with a heavy emphasis on domestic science and mothercraft. This emphasis is powerfully abetted by newspapers and magazines—especially women's magazines, with their enormous circulations, which present man-pleasing (either before or within marriage) and home-building-and-beautifying as the real tasks of all balanced, or 'female', women. They certainly do little to draw attention to sex injustices. The fact, for instance, that semi-skilled or even skilled women engineers on machine work can be paid less than a man who sweeps the workshop floor; that admission to medical schools is decided on a sex ratio which ensures that less than twenty-five per cent of entrants are women; that in certain sections of the Foreign Service women must retire on marriage; that there are never more than three women (and usually less) on English juries; that the Anglican Church Assembly dismissed the possibility of female clergy on the ground that no woman was present at the first Pentecost; that a wife who is the 'guilty' party in divorce proceedings may be required to support her children, though she is not their legal guardian; that local authorities and building societies often ask single women seeking property mortgages for a male guarantor. The U.S. Government's Commission on the Status of Women, appointed by President Kennedy at the instigation of Mrs Roosevelt, covered much the same ground and arrived at similar con-clusions.

This was the kind of grudge inventory (far from exhaustive) which Sylvia Pankhurst and other ex-militants such as Charlotte Despard and Teresa Billington-Greig had in mind when they talked of the need for a revival of suffragette tactics. But they must have known, in their hearts of hearts, that this was an impossibility. Where to start? What, in such a conflict of priorities, should be selected as the compelling issue? Equal pay? But that, unlike votes for women, would soon be submerged in a flood of experts and royal commissions, time-and-motion studies and hair-splitting definitions. It would be hard to generate a guerrilla panache in such an atmosphere. Furthermore, the forcibly leisured upper- and middle-class women who formed the suffragette spearhead, now, in a changed society, *have* (whether they like it or not) to get out and earn a living. Not even Mrs Pankhurst could summon the recruits or the funds for a para-military task force of women. If she did, the relentless triviality of feature writers and T.V. camera teams would soon turn them into a temporary branch of the entertainment industry. If there is a place for female militancy in the corporate welfare state, in which almost everyone, man or woman, is forced into step, and bureaucracy paws at, rather than battles, bureaucracy, it might be along the lines of the Pankhurst-Drum-mond industrial campaigns—a counter-chaos of housewives going on strike to teach their husbands not to go on strike. Yet such an action would (as women perhaps realize) be a mean one; helping to stifle a protest which is as much a gesture of hatred for that tyranny of machines against which William Morris, Edward Carpenter and Sylvia Pankhurst raged, as a political or mercenary move, more a slave revolt than a crypto-communist conspiracy.

The miraculous transformation of society in the expectation of which the suffragettes had striven and suffered had not happened, though according to some their masterful rage had had some curious side effects. Male inversion, wrote Wyndham Lewis in *The Art of Being Ruled* (1926), was 'an integral part of feminism ... the "homo" is the legitimate child of the suffragette.' In *The Apes of God* (1930) he examined in harsh but hilarious detail the gruff or twittery lesbians and the 'militant anti-he-man perverts' who, he considered, had emerged the victors from the battle-fields of feminism, aestheticism (à la Oscar Wilde) and 'poetic' nationalism (à la Rupert Brooke). Twenty years later, in *Rude Assignment,* he sardonically prophesied that the continuation of the sex war and the inexorable demands of the factories of the machine age would cause the emergence of a third, neuter, sex. Man, as man, would become an anachronism. Many of the specifically 'masculine' attributes would disappear. The 'dethroning' of the paterfamilias in his squalid little domestic 'castle' would be a main feature of the demasculinizing process. Sterile, desexed drones were needed for the Brave New World with its huge, drab regiment of androgynous wage-earners. And perhaps after all this development might bring a real emancipation for both men and women. The 'little man' of the twentieth century would surely be 'far happier in a monastery; happier still in a men's communal dwelling, collective farm, barracks, bunk-house, club: anywhere liberated from the crushing responsibilities of sex, of fatherhood, and upkeep of a dirty little castle. As to the woman, is there any question that *she* would be far better off as a member of the "third sex" — with her pin-up boy over her spinster's cot, no children dragging at her like a rag doll, with some such healthy work as a bus conductress or (a little grander) a confidential secretary?'

The old, wide roads of glory down which the pioneers marched, have turned into a series of dreary blind alleys, blocked by a hand-wringing government department, in turn blocked by a balance of payments crisis. Pankhurstian militancy could only thrive, it seems, in an age of private enterprise, the twilight of which it so brilliantly enlivened. The main area of the sex war is now, as Dr Stopes thought it should be, in the home, and particularly in bed. This in-fighting has little time or use for abstract slogans or votes or the wrongs of women in industry, but concentrates—at least in the pages of such truculent neo-feminist writers as Penelope Mortimer, Iris Murdoch, Edna O'Brien and Doris Lessing—on the struggle not for equality but for complete ascendancy. 'Englishmen', remarks Mrs Mortimer in *The Pumpkin Eater*, 'will recognize everything about their women except their identities as people. They really believe men are people and women are women.' Militant heroines of this fictional war forcefully instruct their lovers how to give them maximum satisfaction, and have power fantasies in which legions of drone-like men make love to them simultaneously.

Sylvia would have joined Christabel in denouncing such distorted militancy ('This was not the kind of liberty which Mother and I fought for'). She had challenged Mrs Grundy in the same spirit of nineteenth-century rationalism which had led Charles Bradlaugh to refuse to swear on the Bible when he took his seat in the House of Commons, not to create a climate in which the private act of sex was bandied about as a chatter subject and ORGASMS FOR WOMEN became the slogan of advancing feminism, before whose deadly message epicene males turned pale and tried to flee (perhaps to the therapeutically undidactic arms of one of Lecky's eternal priestesses). The Pankhursts, uninhibited as they were by the devastating insights of twentieth-century psycho-analysis, never advocated the humiliation of men, but aimed rather to shame them into a keener humanity, a nobler manliness. Strange, even snigger-making sentiments, perhaps, yet based on a psychological truth which Virginia Woolf enunciated (only half jestingly?) in *A Room of One's Own*.

> Women [she wrote] have served all these centuries as looking-glasses possessing the magic and delicious power of reflecting the figure of man at twice its natural size. Without that power probably the earth would still be swamp and jungle ... If she begins to tell the truth, the figure in the looking-glass shrinks; his fitness for life is diminished ... How is he to go on giving judgment, civilizing natives, making laws, writing books, dressing up and speechifying at banquets? The looking-glass vision is of supreme importance. Take it away and man may die, like the drug fiend deprived of his cocaine.

True comradeliness, mutual magnification—which Sylvia and Corio, Adela and Tom Walsh, the anarchist lovers Emma Goldman and Alexander Berkman, perhaps achieved—is no doubt the best, but infinitesimally rare, answer. Sylvia, despite her own eminence (flats in Bethnal Green as well as streets in Addis Ababa and Asmara are named after her) was willing to act as a magnifying glass to Haile Selassie as well as to the Ethiopian people, accepting the priority of overcoming human inertia at all rather than quarrelling about the sex of the overcomer.

For all their extravagances, struck out in the heat of warfare, the Pankhursts were not inverted and essentially defensive feminists, but inspired human beings who happened to be women. This was the secret of their strength, a strength which Mrs Pankhurst, Adela, and, pre-eminently, Sylvia, continued to deploy long after the W.S.P.U. had faded into the past. They ransacked the political creeds of their time, and found them lacking in sincerity, not only about the injustices of women, but about almost every injustice except electoral defeat. So they fashioned their own engines of concern, hewed out their own channels for *caring*. For, apart from a psychological and financial need to stay in harness, it *was* a quite apocalyptic concern that sustained Mrs Pankhurst, physically ailing as she was, in the campaigns of her last decade. It was a burning generosity of spirit, a hatred of meanness, which took Sylvia and Adela on their great sweeps of political exploration and vivid self-identification. They were heirs of the great Victorian upthrust of socialist concern, whose finest flowering in Europe was in Rosa Luxemburg, the Polish-Jewish revolutionary murdered in Berlin in January 1919. Sylvia (and to a lesser extent Adela) were, in their tearaway communist phase, the nearest British equivalents to Rosa Luxemburg. Like her, they called upon the masses to rise, but shrank from the necessity for a dictatorship to stimulate and discipline their destiny. They wanted a hot, spontaneous, joyous response, and could not settle for less. 'To be human is the main thing,' wrote Rosa Luxemburg, Sylvia's heroine, 'and that means to be strong and clear and *of good cheer* in spite of and because of everything. To be human means throwing one's life on to the scales of destiny if need be, to be joyful for every fine day and for every beautiful cloud.' This was exactly Sylvia's poetic, almost mystic brand of Marxism. And in all their threshing impatience to embody their visions, in their recurrent anguish at the sad uninflammability of the masses, neither Sylvia, Adela nor Mrs Pankhurst ever lost sight of that radical humanitarianism which, as interpreted by Dr Pankhurst, had driven them into public life. Their duty was their pleasure.

'The spirit of the new days, of our days,' wrote William Morris in *News from Nowhere,* 'was to be delight in the life of the world: intense and overweening love of the very skin and surface of the earth on which man dwells, such as a lover has in the fair flesh of the woman he loves.' This was the spirit in which the Pankhursts went out to slay their dragons of apathy. It was a spirit which did not exclude, indeed heightened, a sense of exacting patriotism. They believed in the duty, the ability of Britain to lead the world in moral regeneration.

But in Christabel, the Pankhurst passion for total victory, for a final, irreversible adjustment of the scales, could not survive the shock of disillusion. Her clairvoyance of human frailty forced her to seek a refuge of recoil in the fixities of a faith which, if it could not be proved, could not be disproved. As with T. E. Lawrence, that one short, whirlwind, guerrilla campaign, the energizing of the seemingly unenergizable (decadent Arabs, knuckle-under women), the god-like disposing of other people's lives, had drained the virtue, the ability to soldier routinely on, out of her. The lingering contacts with top people, the long-lingering physical youthfulness, the continued articulacy, seemed to hint at inner fires still capable of flaring in renewed public action. But the will to break back, to tinker with the old dirty engine of the world, had gone. The illusion of another, cleaner dispensation which no vile human bungling could tarnish was as psychologically vital to Christabel as was the dusty heat of the old arena to her mother and two sisters — that indefatigable posse of Pankhursts for ever circling the great, recalcitrant herd with their little lassoes of hope and conviction: those undisillusionable apostles of human perfectibility.

They had their moments of exhaustion, their bouts of depression, their inklings of futility. As early as 1918 Sylvia had stepped aside to survey the turbulent flood beneath which she believed the shoots of an earthly paradise of social justice were sprouting. By the waters of her communist millennium she lamented: 'It is the open, progressive mind, the tender heart, the fearless comradely spirit which are needed and are so difficult, so infinitely difficult, for poor faulty human beings to attain.' It was the tenacious struggle to attain and diffuse that spirit which made her (even above the mother whom, despite their estrangement, she so fiercely loved and defended) perhaps the greatest Englishwoman of her time, and certainly one of its most moving and heartening public figures.

I salute you, Christabel, as an honourable casualty. ('It is charged against the militants,' you wrote in that famous, splendid editorial in *The Suffragette* of May 3rd 1913, 'that they bring strife and violence into the world ... Violence has a place in the scheme of things ... The Creator has not disdained to use it. New lives come to birth in pain and struggle. Great storms break and leave a fresh and shining world behind them ... When militancy has done its work, then will come sweetness and cleanness, respect and trust, perfect equality and justice into the partnership between men and women ... '). I salute you, Emmeline, Sylvia and Adela, for being such wonderful, crazy, intolerant and sometimes intolerable busybodies; for daring to appoint yourself Honorary, Perpetual Ombuds-women of the Human Race as long as there was health, or merely breath, in your bodies; for scorning the well-documented defeatism of the experts. Your tourneys bring, paradoxically, to mind, those fighting words of Henry Miller in *Tropic of Cancer*.

> More obscene than anything is inertia. More blasphemous than the bloodiest oath is paralysis. If there is only a gaping wound left then it must gush forth, though it produce nothing but toads and bats and homunculi ... I'm here as a plenipotentiary from the realm of free spirits. I'm here to create a fever and a ferment. 'In some ways', says the eminent astronomer, 'the material universe appears to be passing away like a tale that is told, dissolving into nothingness like a vision.' That seems to be the general feeling underlying the empty bread-basket of learning. Myself, I don't believe it. I don't believe a f——g thing these bastards try to shove down our throats.

Neither, in their own less lurid language, did the Pankhursts.

SELECT BIBLIOGRAPHY

BALDWIN, Rt Hon. Stanley, *On England and Other Addresses* (Hodder, 1926)

BEAUVOIR, Simone de, *The Second Sex* (Cape, 1949)

BLYTHE, Ronald, *The Age of Illusion: England in the Twenties and Thirties* (Hamish Hamilton, 1963)

BROAD, Lewis, *Winston Churchill* (Hutchinson, 1943)

CARELESS, J. M. S., *Canada: A Story of Challenge* (Cambridge, 1953)

CARPENTER, Edward, *Towards Democracy (1883-1905)* (Allen & Unwin, 1905)

CHILDE, Vere Gordon, *How Labour Governs* (Labour Publishing Co., 1923)

CLARK, Manning, *A Short History of Australia* (Heinemann, 1963)

COLE, G. D. H., and POSTGATE, R., *A History of the Common People 1746-1946* (Methuen, 1946)

COLLIS, Maurice, *Nancy Astor: an informal biography* (Faber, 1960)

CREIGHTON, Donald, *Dominion of the North* (Macmillan, 1958)

CROSS, Colin, *The Fascists in Britain* (Barrie & Rockliff and Pall Mall, 1961)

CRUIKSHANK, George, *Comic Almanack* (David Bogue, 1849)

DANGERFIELD, George, *The Strange Death of Liberal England* (Constable, 1936)

DATA RESEARCH LTD, *Discrimination Against Women: a study prepared for the National Council for Civic Liberties* (1964)

DUNNE, J. W., *An Experiment With Time* (Faber, 1927)

FRY, E. C., *Tom Barker and the I.W.W.* (Australian Society for the Study of Labour History, 1965)

FULFORD, Roger, *Votes for Women* (Faber, 1957)

GALBRAITH, J. K., *The Great Crash, 1929* (Hamish Hamilton, 1955)

GALLACHER, William, *Revolt on the Clyde* (Lawrence & Wishart, 1936)

GOLDMAN, Emma, *Living My Life* (Duckworth, 1932)

GOLDRING, Douglas, *The Nineteen Twenties* (Nicholson & Watson, 1945)

GOLLANCZ, Victor (editor), *The Making of Women: Oxford Essays in Feminism* (Allen & Unwin, 1917)

GRAVES, Robert, *Goodbye To All That* (Cape, 1929)

GRAVES, Robert, and HODGE, Alan, *The Long Week-End* (Faber, 1940)

GUNTHER, John, *Inside Africa* (Hamish Hamilton, 1955)

HIBBERT, Christopher, *Benito Mussolini: The Rise and Fall of Il Duce* (Longmans, 1962)

HOUSMAN, Laurence, 'The Bawling Brotherhood'—a pamphlet reproduced in Volume II of *British Pamphleteers,* edited by Reginald Reynolds (Wingate, 1951)

HUXLEY, Aldous, *Crome Yellow* (Chatto and Windus, 1921)

KAMM, Josephine, *Rapiers and Battleaxes* (Allen & Unwin, 1966)

KENNEY, Annie, *Memories of a Militant* (E. Arnold, 1924)

KLUGMANN, James, article on the foundation of the Communist Party of Great Britain in *Marxism Today,* January 1960

KOESTLER, Arthur, *Darkness at Noon* (Cape, 1940)

LANG, J. T., *I Remember* (Invincible, Sydney, 1956)

LANSBURY, George, *My Life* (Constable, 1928)

LARDNER, John, chapter on the Lindbergh Legends in *The Aspirin Age,* edited by Isabel Leighton (J. Lane, 1950)

LENIN, V., *Lenin on Britain* (Lawrence & Wishart, 1934), for Lenin's correspondence and conversation with Sylvia Pankhurst and William Gallacher

LEWIS, Percy Wyndham, *The Art of Being Ruled* (Chatto & Windus, 1926); *The Apes of God* (The Arthur Press, 1930); *The Old Gang and the New Gang* (Desmond Harmsworth, 1933); *Rude Assignment* (Hutchinson, 1950)

MACKENZIE, Norman, *Women in Australia* (F. W. Cheshire, Melbourne, 1962)

MARWICK, Arthur, *The Deluge: A Study of British Society in the First World War* (Bodley Head, 1965); *The Explosion of British Society 1914-1962* (Pan, 1963)

MITCHELL, David, *Women on the Warpath: The Story of the Women of the First World War* (Cape, 1966)

MITFORD, Jessica, *Hons and Rebels* (Gollancz, 1960)

MONTEFIORE, Dora, *From a Victorian to a Modern* (E. Archer, 1927)

MORRIS, William, *News from Nowhere* (Nelson, 1890); *Selected Writings,* edited by Asa Briggs (Penguin, 1962)

MUGGERIDGE, Malcolm, *The Thirties* (Hamish Hamilton, 1940)

NIGHTINGALE, Florence, 'Cassandra', appendix to *The Cause* by R. Strachey, (G. Bell, 1928)

NETTL, J. P., *Rosa Luxemburg* (Oxford University Press, 1966)

PANKHURST, Dame Christabel, *The Lord Cometh!* (Marshall, Morgan & Scott, 1923); *Pressing Problems of the Closing Age* (Marshall, Morgan & Scott, 1924): *The World's Unrest, or Visions of the Dawn* (Morgan & Scott, 1926); *Unshackled, or How We Won the Vote* (Hutchinson, 1959)

PANKHURST, Mrs Emmeline, *My Own Story* (Eveleigh Nash, 1914)

PANKHURST, E. Sylvia, *Soviet Russia As I Saw It* (Worker's Dreadnought Publishers, 1921); *India and the Earthly Paradise* (Sunshine Publishing House, Bombay, 1926); *Delphos, or the Future of International Language* (Kegan Paul, 1928); *Save the Mothers* (Allen & Unwin, 1930); Translation of the poems of Mihail Eminescu (Kegan Paul, Trench, Trubner & Co., 1930); *The Suffragette Movement* (Longmans, Green & Co., 1931); *The Home Front* (Hutchinson, 1932); *The Life of Emmeline Pankhurst* (Laurie, 1935); essay in *Myself When Young*, a symposium edited by Margot Asquith (Frederick Muller, 1938); *The Ethiopian People: Their Rights and Progress* (published privately, 1946); *Ethiopia and Eritrea: The Last Phase of the Reunion Struggle* (written in collaboration with Dr R. K. P. Pankhurst) (Lalibela House, 1952; *Ethiopia: A Cultural History* (Lalibela House, 1955)

PETHICK-LAWRENCE, Mrs Emmeline, *My Part in a Changing World* (Gollancz, 1938)

PETHICK-LAWRENCE, Frederick, *Fate Has Been Kind* (Hutchinson, 1943)

POLLITT, Harry, 'The Dockers Said No!', a chapter in *We Did Not Fight: Experiences of War Resisters 1914-18*, edited by Julian Bell (Cobden-Sanderson, 1935)

POSTGATE, R., WILKINSON, Ellen, and HORRABIN, J. F., *A Workers' History of the General Strike* (N.C.L.C. Publishing Society, 1927)

Report of the Commission of Inquiry into Matters Relating to the Detention of Certain Members of the Australia First Movement (Sydney, March 1946)

SELTMAN, Charles, *Women in Antiquity* (Thames and Hudson, 1956)

SINCLAIR, Andrew, *The Better Half: The Emancipation of the American Woman* (Cape, 1966)

SMYTH, Dame Ethel, *Female Pipings in Eden* (Peter Davies, 1934)

STOPES, Dr Marie Carmichael, *Married Love: A New Contribution to the Solution of Sex Difficulties* (A. C. Fifield, 1918)

STORRY, Richard, *A History of Modern Japan* (Cassell, 1956)

STRACHEY, Ray, *The Cause* (G. Bell, 1928)

SWANWICK, Helena, *I Have Been Young* (Gollancz, 1938)

SYMONS, Julian, *The General Strike* (Cresset, 1957); *The Thirties; A Dream Revolved* (Cresset, 1960)

TAYLOR, A. J. P., *The Origins of the Second World War* (Hamish Hamilton, 1961)

TURNER, Ian, *Industrial Labour and Politics: The Dynamics of the Labour Movement in Eastern Australia 1900-1921* (Australian National University and Cambridge University Press, 1965)

War Cabinet Committee *Report on Women In Industry* (1919)

WALSH, Adela Pankhurst, and WALSH, Thomas, *Japan As Viewed by Foreigners* (Robert Dey Son & Co., Sydney, 1940)

WALSH, Adela Pankhurst, *Conditions in Japan* (Robert Dey Son & Co., 1940); *What We Should Know About the Orient* (Robert Dey Son & Co., 1940)

WALSH, Thomas, *The New Order in Asia* (Robert Dey Son & Co., 1940)

WEIR, L. MacNeill, M.P., *The Tragedy of Ramsay MacDonald* (Secker & Warburg, 1938)

WEST, Rebecca, essay on Mrs Pankhurst in *The Post-Victorians,* a symposium (Ivor Nicholson & Watson, 1933)

WOOD, Neal, *Communism and British Intellectuals* (Gollancz, 1959)

YOUNG, G. M., *Stanley Baldwin* (Rupert Hart-Davis, 1952)

Apart from the newspaper and magazine sources indicated in the text, I would like to mention that I have made use of articles about Mrs Pankhurst which appeared in the *Victoria Daily Times* and the *Victoria Daily Colonist,* and have found the following feature articles of particular interest: 'Aunt Emmeline', an interview with Mrs Pankhurst's niece, Miss Enid Goulden Bach (*The Times,* July 7th, 1958); 'Women In The House', a survey of women M.P.s by Godfrey Smith (*Sunday Times* magazine, 1964); 'Women Talking About Themselves', an article by Mary Stott (Guardian, October 4th, 1965); 'Those Literary Furies', by Ruth Inglis (*Nova* magazine, October 1965). As a guide to Sylvia Pankhurst's career as suffragette, artist, journalist, author, poet, and Ethiopian publicist, and on her last years in Ethiopia, the memorial issue of the *Ethiopia Observer* (Vol. 5 No. 1) edited and partly written by her son, Dr Richard Pankhurst, is invaluable. The coverages in the *Weekend Telegraph,* the *Sunday Times* magazine, and the *Observer* magazine which appeared in January 1965, on the occasion of H.M. Queen Elizabeth's state visit to Ethiopia, provide useful background information.

INDEX

Mortimer, Penelope, 337
Moscow, 51, 89–92, 95
Mosley, Sir Oswald, 181–2, 247, 254, 257, 259, 289
Mulumba, Senekula, 323
Municipal Corporations Bill (1869), 20
Murdoch, Iris, 337
Murmansk, 92
Murumbi, Joseph, 323
Mussolini, Benito, 108, 147, 183, 185–6, 225–6, 234, 247, 250–53, 257, 259, 262, 267, 275, 279, 282–4, 289–90

NASI, GENERAL, 284, 309, 311–12, 317
National Council for Combating Venereal Diseases (Canada), 137, 139–42, 145, 149
National Council of Women, 332, 334
National Government (Great Britain), 225
National Organization for Women (U.S.A.), 334
National Progressive Party (Canada), 136
National Union of Societies for Equal Citizenship, 65
National Union of Women's Suffrage Societies, 65
National Women's Party (U.S.A.), 207
Navigation Act (Australia), 119
Nevinson, Henry, 204, 209, 326
Newbold, Walton, 104
News Chronicle, 253
News of the World, 186
News Review, 287
New Times and Ethiopia News, 255–6, 259, 261–3, 281–3, 285, 287–91, 295, 309, 311–316
Newton, Sir Alfred, 96–7
New York, 78, 130–31, 139, 153, 229
New York Times, 133, 203, 208, 229–30
Nightingale, Florence, 126, 235, 329
Nkrumah, Kwame, 321
Noel-Baker, Philip, 255
Normanton, Helena, 204
Northcliffe, Lord, 51, 77, 79, 126, 128
Northumberland, Duke of, 163
Noyes, Alfred, 303

O'BRIEN, EDNA, 337
Observer, the, 251
Organization for the Maintenance of Supplies (O.M.S.), 170
Orwell, George, 257
Ottawa, 145, 148
Oxford and Asquith, Margot Countess of, 260

Palestine Post, 281
Palmer, Jaime, 303
Pankhurst, Adela: birth, 22; childhood and schooldays, 24–5, 27; family tensions, 40, 47; sails for Australia, 47; emergence as leader of socialist feminist movement, 55–6; on World War I, 56; Put Up the Sword, 57; meets Tom Walsh, 58; Betrayed, 59; editor of Dawn, 59; marriage, 59; imprisonments, 60, 276–7; 'on verge of communism', 73; family life, 111, 220; moves to Sydney, 114; 'The Party and the Crisis' letter, 115; and formation of Australian Communist Party, 115; 'Communism and Social Purity', 115; incites unemployed to violence, 117; affection for Tom Walsh, 119; influence of, 119–120; true successor to her mother, 210; leaves Communism for Socialism, 213 ff; launches Guild of Empire, 221; gives vitality to middle-class feminism, 221; editor of Empire Gazette, 221; attacks Communist-inspired peace movements, 224; attitude to dictators, 225–6, 267; visit to Japan, 226, 267–70; Japan as Viewed by Foreigners, 269; pro-Japanese activities, 270–77, 300; family illnesses and deaths, 299; forced to work for living, 299; as nurse for retarded children, 299–300; becomes Roman Catholic, 300; death, 300; achievements and strength of, 338; salute to, 340
Pankhurst, Betty, 129, 142, 155, 300
Pankhurst, Christabel, 19; birth, 22; childhood and schooldays, 24–5, 27–8; and her mother, 28, 39, 74, 124, 134, 154, 194, 195, 197, 198, 236–7; early suffragette activity, 29 ff; arrests and imprisonments, 30; escapes to France, 33–4; steps up sex war, 37–9; The Dangers of Marriage, 38; family tensions, 40, 45; refuses subsidy for East Enders, 45; in World War I, 50 ff; stands as Parliamentary candidate, 53–4; damns League of Nations, 61; on Ireland, 66; and revolution in sexual standards, 66–7; damns pacifists, 72; anxious to restore order, 74; announces intention to stand for Westminster, 74–5; and Versailles, 75–7; testimonial fund for, 77, 125; advertises for non-political work, 123; Sylvia Pankhurst's portrait of, 123–5; writes for Weekly Dispatch, 126–128; defends her celibacy, 126; in Canada, 128–9, 141–2, 146, 229; in America, 142,